Enterprise JavaBeans™

THE JAVA™ SERIES

Enterprise JavaBeans™

Second Edition

Richard Monson-Haefel

O'REILLY®

Beijing · Cambridge · Farnham · Köln · Paris · Sebastopol · Taipei · Tokyo

SHROFF PUBLISHERS & ~~DISTRIBUTORS~~ **PVT. LTD.**
Mumbai   *Calcutta*

Enterprise JavaBeans™, Second Edition
by Richard Monson-Haefel

Copyright © 1999, 2000 O'Reilly & Associates, Inc. All rights reserved. ISBN: 1-56592-869-5
Cover photo Copyright © 1994 Digital Media.

Originally published by O'Reilly & Associates, Inc., 101 Morris Street, Sebastopol, CA 95472, USA

Editor: Mike Loukides

Production Editor: Melanie Wang

Cover Designer: Hanna Dyer

Printing History:

June 1999:	First Edition.
March 2000:	Second Edition.

First Indian Reprint: March 2000
ISBN: 81-7366-270-3

Published by **Shroff Publishers and Distributors Pvt. Ltd.**, Room No. 8/9, Patel Building, First Floor, 8/16, M.K. Amin Marg, Fort, Mumbai 400 001, Tel: (91 22) 263 1572, 264 1488, Fax: (91 22) 262 3551, e-mail: spd@vsnl.com. Printed at Rose Fine Arts, Kurla, Mumbai

For my wife and best friend,
Hollie

Table of Contents

Preface

What Is Enterprise JavaBeans?

When Java™ was first introduced, most of the IT industry focused on its graphical user interface characteristics and the competitive advantage it offered in terms of distribution and platform independence. Today, the focus has broadened considerably: Java has been recognized as an excellent platform for creating enterprise solutions, specifically for developing distributed server-side applications. This shift has much to do with Java's emerging role as a universal language for producing implementation-independent abstractions for common enterprise technologies. The JDBC™ API is the first and most familiar example. JDBC provides a vendor-independent Java interface for accessing SQL relational databases. This abstraction has been so successful that it's difficult to find a relational database vendor that doesn't support JDBC. Java abstractions for enterprise technologies have expanded considerably to include JNDI (Java Naming and Directory Interface™) for abstracting directory services, JMX (Java Management Extensions) for abstracting access to computer devices on a network, JMS™ (Java Messaging Service) for abstracting access to different message-oriented middleware products, and so on.

Enterprise JavaBeans™ is the latest technology abstraction in the Java family, and perhaps the most ambitious. Enterprise JavaBeans (EJB) provides an abstraction for component transaction monitors (CTMs). Component transaction monitors represent the convergence of two technologies: traditional transaction processing monitors, such as CICS, TUXEDO, and Encina, and distributed object services, such as CORBA (Common Object Request Broker Architecture), DCOM, and native Java RMI. Combining the best of both technologies, component transaction monitors provide a robust, component-based environment that simplifies distributed development while automatically managing the most complex aspects of enterprise computing, such as object brokering, transaction management, security, persistence, and concurrency.

Enterprise JavaBeans defines a server-side component model that allows business objects to be developed and moved from one brand of CTM to another. A component (a bean) presents a simple programming model that allows the developer to focus on its business purpose. An EJB server (a CTM that conforms to the Enterprise JavaBeans specification) is responsible for making the component a distributed object and for managing services such as transactions, persistence, concurrency, and security. In addition to defining the bean's business logic, the developer defines the bean's runtime attributes in a way that is similar to choosing the display properties of visual widgets. The transactional, persistence, and security behaviors of a component can be defined by choosing from a list of properties. The end result is that Enterprise JavaBeans makes developing distributed component systems that are managed in a robust transactional environment much easier. For developers and corporate IT shops that have struggled with the complexities of delivering mission-critical, high-performance distributed systems using CORBA, DCOM, or Java RMI, Enterprise JavaBeans provides a far simpler and more productive platform on which to base development efforts.

Enterprise JavaBeans has quickly become a de facto industry standard. Many vendors announced their support even before the specification was finalized. CTM products that conform to the EJB standard have come from every sector of the IT industry, including the TP monitor, CORBA ORB, application server, relational database, object database, and web server industries. Some of these products are based on proprietary models that have been adapted to EJB; many more wouldn't even exist without EJB.

In short, Enterprise JavaBeans provides a standard distributed component model that greatly simplifies the development process and allows beans that are developed and deployed on one vendor's EJB server to be easily deployed on a different vendor's EJB server. This book will provide you with the foundation you need to develop vendor-independent EJB solutions.

Who Should Read This Book?

This book explains and demonstrates the fundamentals of the Enterprise JavaBeans architecture. Although EJB makes distributed computing much simpler, it is still a complex technology that requires a great deal of time to master. This book provides a straightforward, no-nonsense explanation of the underlying technology, Java classes and interfaces, component model, and runtime behavior of Enterprise JavaBeans.

Although this book focuses on the fundamentals, it's no "dummy's" book. Enterprise JavaBeans embodies an extremely complex and ambitious enterprise technology. While using EJB may be fairly simple, the amount of work required to truly understand and master EJB is significant. Before reading this book, you should be fluent with the Java language and have some practical experience developing business solutions. Experience with distributed object systems is not a must, but you will need some experience with JDBC (or at least an understanding of the basics) to follow the examples in this book. If you are unfamiliar with the Java language, I recommend that you pick up a copy of *Learning Java*™ by Patrick Neimeyer and Jonathan Knudsen, formerly *Exploring Java*™, (O'Reilly). If you are unfamiliar with JDBC, I recommend *Database Programming with JDBC*™ *and Java*™ by George Reese (O'Reilly). If you need a stronger background in distributed computing, I recommend *Java*™ *Distributed Computing* by Jim Farley (O'Reilly).

Organization

Here's how the book is structured. The first three chapters are largely background material, placing Enterprise JavaBeans in the context of related technologies, and explaining at the most abstract level how the EJB technology works and what makes up an enterprise bean. Chapters 4 through 7 go into detail about developing enterprise beans of various types. Chapters 8 and 9 could be considered "advanced topics," except that transactions (Chapter 8) are essential to everything that happens in enterprise computing, and design strategies (Chapter 9) help you deal with a number of real-world issues that influence bean design. Chapter 10 describes in detail the XML deployment descriptors used in EJB 1.1. Finally, Chapter 11 is an overview of the Java™ 2, Enterprise Edition (J2EE) with regard to EJB 1.1.

Chapter 1, Introduction
> This chapter defines component transaction monitors and explains how they form the underlying technology of the Enterprise JavaBeans component model.

Chapter 2, Architectural Overview
> This chapter defines the architecture of the Enterprise JavaBeans component model and examines the difference between the two basic types of enterprise beans: entity beans and session beans.

Chapter 3, Resource Management and the Primary Services
> This chapter explains how the EJB-compliant server manages an enterprise bean at runtime.

Chapter 4, Developing Your First Enterprise Beans
This chapter walks the reader through the development of some simple enterprise beans.

Chapter 5, The Client View
This chapter explains in detail how enterprise beans are accessed and used by a remote client application.

Chapter 6, Entity Beans
This chapter provides an in-depth explanation of how to develop container-managed and bean-managed entity beans and describes their runtime behavior.

Chapter 7, Session Beans
This chapter provides an in-depth explanation of how to develop stateless and stateful session beans and describes their runtime behavior. .

Chapter 8, Transactions
This chapter provides an in-depth explanation of transactions and describes the transactional model defined by Enterprise JavaBeans.

Chapter 9, Design Strategies
This chapter provides some basic design strategies that can simplify your EJB development efforts and make your EJB system more efficient.

Chapter 10, XML Deployment Descriptors
This chapter provides an in-depth explanation of the XML deployment descriptors used in EJB 1.1.

Chapter 11, Java 2, Enterprise Edition
This chapter provides an overview of the Java 2, Enterprise Edition and explains how EJB 1.1 fits into this new platform.

Appendix A, The Enterprise JavaBeans API
This appendix provides a quick reference to the classes and interfaces defined in the EJB packages (javax.ejb and javax.ejb.deployment).

Appendix B, State and Sequence Diagrams .
This appendix provides diagrams that clarify the life cycle of enterprise beans at runtime.

Appendix C, EJB Vendors
This appendix provides information about the vendors of EJB servers.

Appendix D, New Features in EJB 1.1
This appendix provides a summary of the changes from EJB 1.0 to EJB 1.1.

Software and Versions

This book covers Enterprise JavaBeans Version 1.1 and Version 1.0, including all optional features. It uses Java language features from the Java 1.1 platform and JDBC. Because the focus of this book is to develop vendor-independent Enterprise JavaBeans components and solutions, I have stayed away from proprietary extensions and vendor-dependent idioms. Any EJB-compliant server can be used with this book; you should be familiar with that server's specific installation, deployment, and runtime management procedures to work with the examples. To find out the details of deploying, running, and accessing beans within any specific server, consult your EJB vendor's documentation; these details aren't covered by the EJB specification.

This book covers both EJB 1.1 and EJB 1.0. These two versions have a lot in common, but when they differ, text specific to each version is clearly marked. Feel free to skip version-specific sections that do not concern you. Unless indicated, the source code in this book has been written for EJB 1.1. Changes for EJB 1.0 are indicated in comments.

Examples developed in this book are available from *ftp://ftp.oreilly.com/pub/examples/java/ejb*. The examples are organized by chapter.

Conventions

Italic is used for:

- Filenames and pathnames
- Hostnames, domain names, URLs, and email addresses
- New terms where they are defined

Constant width is used for:

- Code examples and fragments
- Class, variable, and method names, and Java keywords used within the text
- SQL commands, table names, and column names
- XML elements and tags

Constant width bold is used for emphasis in some code examples.

Constant width italic is used to indicate text that is replaceable. For example, in *BeanNamePK*, you would replace *BeanName* with a specific bean name.

An Enterprise JavaBean consists of many parts; it's not a single object, but a collection of objects and interfaces. To refer to an Enterprise JavaBean as a whole, we use the name of its remote interface in Roman type. For example, we will refer to the BaggageHandler bean when we want to talk about the bean in general. If we put the name in a constant width font, we are referring explicitly to the bean's remote interface. So `BaggageHandler` is the remote interface that defines the business methods of the BaggageHandler bean.

Comments and Questions

Please address comments and questions concerning this book to the publisher:

O'Reilly & Associates, Inc.
101 Morris Street
Sebastopol, CA 95472
(800) 998-9938 (in the U.S. or Canada)
(707) 829-0515 (international or local)
(707) 829-0104 (fax)

You can also send us messages electronically. To be put on our mailing list or to request a catalog, send email to:

info@oreilly.com

To ask technical questions or comment on the book, send email to:

bookquestions@oreilly.com

We have a web site for the book, where we'll list errata and any plans for future editions. You can access this page at:

http://www.oreilly.com/catalog/entjbeans2/

For more information about this book and others, see the O'Reilly web site at:

http://www.oreilly.com/

The author maintains a web site for the discussion of EJB and related distributed computing technologies (*http://www.ejbnow.com*). EJBNow.com provides news about this book as well as code tips, articles, and an extensive list of links to EJB resources.

Acknowledgments

While there is only one name on the cover of this book, the credit for its development and delivery is shared by many individuals. Michael Loukides, my editor, was pivotal to the success of this book. Without his experience, craft, and guidance, this book would not have been possible.

Many expert technical reviewers helped ensure that the material was technically accurate and true to the spirit of Enterprise JavaBeans. At the top of the list is Tim

Rohaly of jGuru.com, whose contributions as a technical reviewer were critical to the success of the second edition. Of special note are Sriram Srinivasan of BEA, Anne Thomas of the Patricia Seybold Group, and Ian McCallion of IBM Hursley. They contributed greatly to my understanding of component transaction monitors and EJB design philosophies. Special thanks also go to Jim Farley, author of ·*Java*™ *Distributed Computing* (O'Reilly, 1998), James D. Frentress of ITM Corp., Andrzej Jan Taramina of Accredo Systems, Marc Loy, co-author of *Java*™ *Swing* (O'Reilly, 1998), Don Weiss of Step 1, Mike Slinn of The Dialog Corporation, and Kevin Dick of Kevin Dick & Associates. The contributions of these technical experts were critical to the technical and conceptual accuracy of this book. They brought a combination of industry and real-world experience to bear, and helped to make this the best book on Enterprise JavaBeans published today.

Several other individuals have made contributions that helped to make this book worthy of an O'Reilly publication. Maggie Mezquita, Greg Hartzel, and Jon Jamsa of BORN Information Services, and John Klug of Gelco all contributed to the first edition of this book. They helped me to refine the content so that it was more focused and understandable.

Thanks also to Vlad Matena of Sun Microsystems, the primary architect of Enterprise JavaBeans, who answered several of my most complex questions. Thanks to all the participants in the EJB-INTEREST mailing list hosted by Sun Microsystems for their interesting and sometimes controversial, but always informative, postings.

Finally, the most sincere gratitude must be extended to my wife, Hollie, for supporting and assisting me through two years of painstaking research and writing which were required to produce two editions of this book. Without her unfailing support and love, this book would not have been completed.

1

Introduction

This book is about Enterprise JavaBeans (Versions 1.1 and 1.0), Java's new component model for enterprise applications. Just as the Java platform has revolutionized the way we think about software development, Enterprise JavaBeans promises to revolutionize the way we think about developing mission-critical enterprise software. It combines server-side components with distributed object technologies such as CORBA and Java RMI to greatly simplify the task of application development. It automatically takes into account many of the requirements of business systems: security, resource pooling, persistence, concurrency, and transactional integrity.

This book shows you how to use Enterprise JavaBeans to develop scalable, portable business systems. But before we can start talking about EJB itself, we'll need a brief introduction to the technologies addressed by EJB, such as component models, distributed objects, and component transaction monitors (CTMs). It's particularly important to have a basic understanding of component transaction monitors, the technology that lies beneath EJB. In Chapters 2 and 3, we'll start looking at EJB itself and see how enterprise beans are put together. The rest of this book is devoted to developing enterprise beans for an imaginary business and discussing advanced issues.

It is assumed that you're already familiar with Java; if you're not, *Exploring Java™* by Patrick Niemeyer and Josh Peck is an excellent introduction. This book also assumes that you're conversant in the JDBC API, or at least SQL. If you're not familiar with JDBC, see *Database Programming with JDBC™ and Java™*, by George Reese.

One of Java's most important features is platform independence. Since it was first released, Java has been marketed as "write once, run anywhere." While the hype has gotten a little heavy-handed at times, code written with Sun's Java programming language is remarkably platform independent. Enterprise JavaBeans isn't just platform independent—it's also implementation independent. If you've worked with JDBC, you know a little about what this means. Not only can the JDBC API run on a Windows machine or on a Unix machine, it can also access any vendor's relational database that has a JDBC driver. You don't have to code to a particular database implementation; just change drivers and you change databases. It's the same with Enterprise JavaBeans. Ideally, an Enterprise JavaBeans component, an enterprise bean, can run in any application server that implements the Enterprise JavaBeans (EJB) specification.* This means that you can develop and deploy your EJB business system in one server, such as IBM's WebSphere, and later move it to a different EJB server, such as BEA's WebLogic or Gemstone/J. Implementation independence means that your business components are not dependent on the brand of server, which means there are more options before you begin development, during development, and after deployment.

Setting the Stage

Before defining Enterprise JavaBeans more precisely, let's set the stage by discussing a number of important concepts: distributed objects, business objects, and component transaction monitors.

Distributed Objects

Distributed computing allows a business system to be more accessible. Distributed systems allow parts of the system to be located on separate computers, possibly in many different locations, where they make the most sense. In other words, distributed computing allows business logic and data to be reached from remote locations. Customers, business partners, and other remote parties can use a business system at any time from almost anywhere. The most recent development in distributed computing is *distributed objects*. Distributed object technologies such as Java RMI, CORBA, and Microsoft's DCOM allow objects running on one machine to be used by client applications on different computers.

Distributed objects evolved from a legacy form of three-tier architecture, which is used in TP monitor systems such as IBM's CICS or BEA's TUXEDO. These systems separate the presentation, business logic, and database into three distinct tiers (or layers). In the past, these legacy systems were usually composed of a

---

* Provided that the bean components and EJB servers comply with the specification and no proprietary functionality is used in development.

"green screen" or dumb terminals for the presentation tier (first tier), COBOL or PL/1 applications on the middle tier (second tier), and some sort of database, such as DB2, as the backend (third tier). The introduction of distributed objects in recent years has given rise to a new form of three-tier architecture. Distributed object technologies make it possible to replace the procedural COBOL and PL/1 applications on the middle tier with business objects. A three-tier distributed business object architecture might have a sophisticated graphical user interface (GUI), business objects on the middle tier, and a relational or some other database on the backend. More complex architectures are often used in which there are many tiers: different objects reside on different servers and interact to get the job done. Creating these n-tier architectures with Enterprise JavaBeans is particularly easy.

Server-Side Components

Object-oriented languages, such as Java, C++, and Smalltalk, are used to write software that is flexible, extensible, and reusable—the three axioms of object-oriented development. In business systems, object-oriented languages are used to improve development of GUIs, to simplify access to data, and to encapsulate the business logic. The encapsulation of business logic into *business objects* has become the most recent focus in the information technology industry. Business is fluid, which means that a business's products, processes, and objectives evolve over time. If the software that models the business can be encapsulated into business objects, it can become flexible, extensible, and reusable, and therefore evolve as the business evolves.

A server-side component model defines an architecture for developing *distributed business objects*. They combine the accessibility of distributed object systems with the fluidity of objectified business logic. Server-side component models are used on the middle-tier application servers, which manage the components at runtime and make them available to remote clients. They provide a baseline of functionality that makes it easy to develop distributed business objects and assemble them into business solutions.

Server-side components, like other components, can be bought and sold as independent pieces of executable software. They conform to a standard component model and can be executed without direct modification in a server that supports that component model. Server-side component models often support attribute-based programming, which allows the runtime behavior of the component to be modified when it is deployed, without having to change the programming code in the component. Depending on the component model, the server administrator can declare a server-side component's transactional, security, and even persistence behavior by setting these attributes to specific values.

As new products are developed and operating procedures change, server-side components can be reassembled, changed, and extended so that the business system reflects those changes. Imagine a business system as a collection of server-side components that model concepts like customers, products, reservations, and warehouses. Each component is like a Lego block that can be combined with other components to build a business solution. Products can be stored in the warehouse or delivered to a customer; a customer can make a reservation or purchase a product. You can assemble components, take them apart, use them in different combinations, and change their definitions. A business system based on *server-side components* is fluid because it is objectified, and it is accessible because the components can be distributed.

Component Transaction Monitors

A new breed of software called *application servers* has recently evolved to manage the complexities associated with developing business systems in today's Internet world. An application server is often made up of some combination of several different technologies, including web servers, ORBs, MOM (message-oriented middleware), databases, and so forth. An application server can also focus on one technology, such as distributed objects. The type of application server this book is concerned with is based on a distributed object technology such as CORBA, Java RMI, or DCOM. Application servers that are based on distributed objects vary in sophistication. The simplest facilitate connectivity between the client applications and the distributed objects and are called object request brokers (ORBs). ORBs allow client applications to locate and use distributed objects easily. ORBs, however, have frequently proven to be inadequate in high-volume transactional environments. ORBs provide a communication backbone for distributed objects, but they fail to provide the kind of robust infrastructure that is needed to handle larger user populations and mission-critical work. In addition, ORBs provide a fairly crude server-side component model that places the burden of handling transactions, concurrency, persistence, and other system-level considerations on the shoulders of the application developer. These services are not automatically supported in an ORB. Application developers must explicitly access these services (if they are available) or, in some cases, develop them from scratch.

Early in 1999, Anne Thomas of the Patricia Seybold Group coined the term *component transaction monitor* (CTM) to describe the most sophisticated distributed object application servers. CTMs evolved as a hybrid of traditional TP monitors and ORB technologies. They implement robust server-side component models that make it easier for developers to create, use, and deploy business systems. CTMs provide an infrastructure that can automatically manage transactions, object distribution, concurrency, security, persistence, and resource management. They are capable of handling huge user populations and mission-critical work, but also provide value to smaller systems because they are easy to use. CTMs are the ulti-mate application server. Other terms for this kind of technology include object transaction monitor (OTM), component transaction server, distributed compo-nent server, COMware, and so forth. This book uses the term "component transaction monitor" because it embraces the three key characteristics of this technology: the use of a component model, the focus on transactional management, and the resource and service management typically associated with monitors.

Enterprise JavaBeans: Defined

Sun Microsystems' definition of Enterprise JavaBeans is:

> The Enterprise JavaBeans architecture is a component architecture for the devel-opment and deployment of component-based distributed business applications. Applications written using the Enterprise JavaBeans architecture are scalable, transactional, and multi-user secure. These applications may be written once, and then deployed on any server platform that supports the Enterprise JavaBeans spec-ification.[*]

Wow! Now that's a mouthful and not atypical of how Sun defines many of its Java technologies—have you ever read the definition of the Java language itself? It's about twice as long. This book offers a shorter definition:

> Enterprise JavaBeans is a standard server-side component model for component transaction monitors.

We have already set the stage for this definition by briefly defining the terms dis-tributed objects, server-side components, and component transaction monitors. To provide you with a complete and solid foundation for learning about Enter-prise JavaBeans, this chapter will now expand on these definitions.

Distributed Object Architectures

EJB is a component model for component transaction monitors, which are based on distributed object technologies. Therefore, to understand EJB you need to understand how distributed objects work. Distributed object systems are the foun-dation for modern three-tier architectures. In a three-tier architecture, as shown in Figure 1-1, the presentation logic resides on the client (first tier), the business logic on the middle tier (second tier), and other resources, such as the database, reside on the backend (third tier).

All distributed object protocols are built on the same basic architecture, which is designed to make an object on one computer look like it's residing on a different

---

[*] Sun Microsystems' *Enterprise JavaBeans™ Specification, v1.1,* Copyright 1999 by Sun Microsystems, Inc.

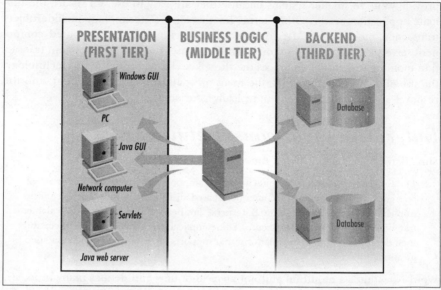

Figure 1-1. Three-tier architecture

computer. Distributed object architectures are based on a network communication layer that is really very simple. Essentially, there are three parts to this architecture: the object server, the skeleton, and the stub.

The *object server* is the business object that resides on the middle tier. The term "server" can be a little confusing, but for our purposes the object on the middle tier can be called the "object server" to distinguish it from its counterparts, the stub and skeleton. The object server is an instance of an object with its own unique state. Every object server class has matching stub and skeleton classes built specifically for that type of object server. So, for example, a distributed business object called Person would have matching Person_Stub and Person_Skeleton classes. As shown in Figure 1-2, the object server and skeleton reside on the middle tier, and the stub resides on the client.

The *stub* and the *skeleton* are responsible for making the object server, which lives on the middle tier, look as if it is running locally on the client machine. This is accomplished through some kind of *remote method invocation* (RMI) protocol. An RMI protocol is used to communicate method invocations over a network. CORBA, Java RMI, and Microsoft DCOM all use their own RMI protocol.* Every

---

* The acronym RMI isn't specific to Java RMI; it was in use long before Java came along. This section uses RMI to describe distributed object protocols in general. Java RMI is the Java language version of a distributed object protocol.

instance of the object server on the middle tier is wrapped by an instance of its matching skeleton class. The skeleton is set up on a port and IP address and listens for requests from the stub. The stub resides on the client machine and is connected via the network to the skeleton. The stub acts as the object server's surrogate on the client and is responsible for communicating requests from the client to the object server through the skeleton. Figure 1-2 illustrates the process of communicating a method invocation from the client to the server object and back. The stub and the skeleton hide the communication specifics of the RMI protocol from the client and the implementation class, respectively.

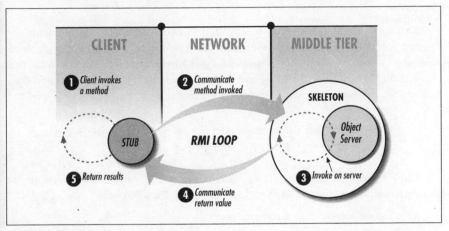

Figure 1-2. RMI loop

The stub implements an interface with the same business methods as the object itself, but the stub's methods do not contain business logic. Instead, the business methods on the stub implement whatever networking operations are required to forward the request to the object server and receive the results. When a client invokes a business method on the stub, the request is communicated over the network by streaming the name of the method invoked, and the values passed in as parameters, to the skeleton. When the skeleton receives the incoming stream, it parses the stream to discover which method is requested, and then invokes the corresponding business method on the object server. Any value that is returned from the method invoked on the object server is streamed back to the stub by the skeleton. The stub then returns the value to the client application as if it had processed the business logic locally.

Rolling Your Own Distributed Object

The best way to illustrate how distributed objects work is to show how you can implement a distributed object yourself, with your own distributed object protocol. This will give you some appreciation for what a true distributed object protocol like CORBA does. Actual distributed object systems such as DCOM, CORBA, and Java RMI are, however, much more complex and robust than the simple example we will develop here. The distributed object system we develop in this chapter is only illustrative; it is not a real technology, nor is it part of Enterprise JavaBeans. The purpose is to provide you with some understanding of how a more sophisticated distributed object system works.

Here's a very simple distributed object called `PersonServer` that implements the `Person` interface. The `Person` interface captures the concept of a person business object. It has two business methods: `getAge()` and `getName()`. In a real application, we would probably define many more behaviors for the `Person` business object, but two methods are enough for this example:

```
public interface Person {
    public int getAge() throws Throwable;
    public String getName() throws Throwable;
}
```

The implementation of this interface, `PersonServer`, doesn't contain anything at all surprising. It defines the business logic and state for a `Person`:

```
public class PersonServer implements Person {
    int age;
    String name;

    public PersonServer(String name, int age){
        this.age = age;
        this.name = name;
    }
    public int getAge(){
        return age;
    }
    public String getName(){
        return name;
    }
}
```

Now we need some way to make the `PersonServer` available to a remote client. That's the job of the `Person_Skeleton` and `Person_Stub`. The `Person` interface describes the concept of a person independent of implementation. Both the `PersonServer` and the `Person_Stub` implement the `Person` interface because they are both expected to support the concept of a person. The `PersonServer` implements the interface to provide the actual business logic and state; the

Person_Stub implements the interface so that it can look like a Person business object on the client and relay requests back to the skeleton, which in turn sends them to the object itself. Here's what the stub looks like:

```java
import java.io.ObjectOutputStream;
import java.io.ObjectInputStream;
import java.net.Socket;

public class Person_Stub implements Person {
    Socket socket;

    public Person_Stub() throws Throwable {
        // Create a network connection to the skeleton.
        // Replace "myhost" with your own IP Address of your computer.
        socket = new Socket("myhost",9000);
    }
    public int getAge() throws Throwable {
        // When this method is invoked, stream the method name to the
        // skeleton.
        ObjectOutputStream outStream =
            new ObjectOutputStream(socket.getOutputStream());
        outStream.writeObject("age");
        outStream.flush();
        ObjectInputStream inStream =
            new ObjectInputStream(socket.getInputStream());
        return inStream.readInt();
    }
    public String getName() throws Throwable {
        // When this method is invoked, stream the method name to the
        // skeleton.
        ObjectOutputStream outStream =
            new ObjectOutputStream(socket.getOutputStream());
        outStream.writeObject("name");
        outStream.flush();
        ObjectInputStream inStream =
            new ObjectInputStream(socket.getInputStream());
        return (String)inStream.readObject();
    }
}
```

When a method is invoked on the Person_Stub, a String token is created and streamed to the skeleton. The token identifies the method that was invoked on the stub. The skeleton parses the method-identifying token, invokes the corresponding method on the object server, and streams back the result. When the stub reads the reply from the skeleton, it parses the value and returns it to the client. From the client's perspective, the stub processed the request locally. Now let's look at the skeleton:

```java
import java.io.ObjectOutputStream;
```

```java
import java.net.Socket;
import java.net.ServerSocket;

public class Person_Skeleton extends Thread {
    PersonServer myServer;

    public Person_Skeleton(PersonServer server){
        // Get a reference to the object server that this skeleton wraps.
        this.myServer = server;
    }
    public void run(){
        try {
            // Create a server socket on port 9000.
            ServerSocket serverSocket = new ServerSocket(9000);
            // Wait for and obtain a socket connection from stub.
            Socket socket = serverSocket.accept();
            while (socket != null){
                // Create an input stream to receive requests from stub.
                ObjectInputStream inStream =
                    new ObjectInputStream(socket.getInputStream());
                // Read next method request from stub. Block until request is
                // sent.
                String method = (String)inStream.readObject();
                // Evaluate the type of method requested.
                if (method.equals("age")){
                    // Invoke business method on server object.
                    int age = myServer.getAge();
                    // Create an output stream to send return values back to
                    // stub.
                    ObjectOutputStream outStream =
                        new ObjectOutputStream(socket.getOutputStream());
                    // Send results back to stub.
                    outStream.writeInt(age);
                    outStream.flush();
                } else if(method.equals("name")){
                    // Invoke business method on server object.
                    String name = myServer.getName();
                    // Create an output stream to send return values back to
                    // the stub.
                    ObjectOutputStream outStream =
                        new ObjectOutputStream(socket.getOutputStream());
                    // Send results back to stub.
                    outStream.writeObject(name);
                    outStream.flush();
                }
            }
        } catch(Throwable t) {t.printStackTrace();System.exit(0); }
    }
```

```
        public static void main(String args [] ){
            // Obtain a unique instance Person.
            PersonServer person = new PersonServer("Richard", 34);
            Person_Skeleton skel = new Person_Skeleton(person);
            skel.start();
        }
    }
```

The Person_Skeleton routes requests received from the stub to the object server, PersonServer. Essentially, the Person_Skeleton spends all its time waiting for the stub to stream it a request. Once a request is received, it is parsed and delegated to the corresponding method on the PersonServer. The return value from the object server is then streamed back to the stub, which returns it as if it was processed locally.

Now that we've created all the machinery, let's look at a simple client that makes use of the Person:

```
    public class PersonClient {
        public static void main(String [] args){
            try {
                Person person = new Person_Stub();
                int age = person.getAge();
                String name = person.getName();
                System.out.println(name+" is "+age+" years old");
            } catch(Throwable t) {t.printStackTrace();}
        }
    }
```

This client application shows how the stub is used on the client. Except for the instantiation of the Person_Stub at the beginning, the client is unaware that the Person business object is actually a network proxy to the real business object on the middle tier. In Figure 1-3, the RMI loop diagram is changed to represent the RMI process as applied to our code.

As you examine Figure 1-3, notice how the RMI loop was implemented by our distributed Person object. RMI is the basis of distributed object systems and is responsible for making distributed objects *location transparent*. Location transparency means that a server object's actual location—usually on the middle tier—is unknown and unimportant to the client using it. In this example, the client could be located on the same machine or on a different machine very far away, but the client's interaction with the business object is the same. One of the biggest benefits of distributed object systems is location transparency. Although transparency is beneficial, you cannot treat distributed objects as local objects in your design because of the performance differences. This book will provide you with good distributed object design strategies that take advantage of transparency while maximizing the distributed system's performance.

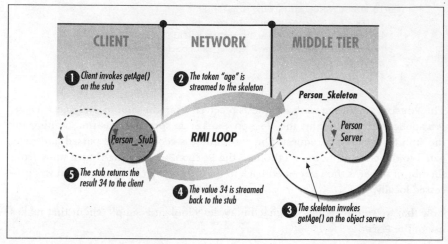

Figure 1-3. RMI Loop with Person business object

When this book talks about the stub on the client, we will often refer to it as a *remote reference* to the object server. This allows us to talk more directly about the object server and its representation on the client.

Distributed object protocols such as CORBA, DCOM, and Java RMI provide a lot more infrastructure for distributed objects than the Person example. Most implementations of distributed object protocols provide utilities that automatically generate the appropriate stubs and skeletons for object servers. This eliminates custom development of these constructs and allows a lot more functionality to be included in the stub and skeleton.

Even with automatic generation of stubs and skeletons, the Person example hardly scratches the surface of a sophisticated distributed object protocol. Real world protocols like Java RMI and CORBA IIOP provide error and exception handling, parameter passing, and other services like the passing of transaction and security context. In addition, distributed object protocols support much more sophisticated mechanisms for connecting the stub to the skeleton; the direct stub-to-skeleton connection in the Person example is fairly primitive.

Real distributed object protocols, like CORBA, also provide an Object Request Broker (ORB), which allows clients to locate and communicate with distributed objects across the network. ORBs are the communication backbone, the switchboard, for distributed objects. In addition to handling communications, ORBs generally use a naming system for locating objects and many other features such as reference passing, distributed garbage collection, and resource management. However, ORBs are limited to facilitating communication between clients and distributed object servers. While they may support services like transaction management and security, use of these services is not automatic. With ORBs, most of the responsibility for creating system-level functionality or incorporating services falls on the shoulders of the application developer.

Component Models

The term "component model" has many different interpretations. Enterprise Java-Beans specifies a *server-side* component model. Using a set of classes and interfaces from the javax.ejb packages, developers can create, assemble, and deploy components that conform to the EJB specification.

The original JavaBeans™, the java.beans package in the core Java API, is also a component model, but it's not a server-side component model like EJB. In fact, other than sharing the name "JavaBeans," these two component models are completely unrelated. A lot of the literature has referred to EJB as an extension of the original JavaBeans, but this is a misrepresentation. Other than the shared name, and the fact that they are both Java component models, the two APIs serve very different purposes. EJB does not extend or use the original JavaBeans component model.

The original JavaBeans (the java.beans package) is intended to be used for *intra*process purposes, while EJB (the javax.ejb package) is designed to be used for *inter*process components. In other words, the original JavaBeans was not intended for distributed components. JavaBeans can be used to solve a variety of problems, but is primarily used to build clients by assembling visual (GUI) and nonvisual widgets. It's an excellent component model, possibly the best component model for intraprocess development ever devised, but it's not a server-side component model. EJB is designed to address issues involved with managing distributed business objects in a three-tier architecture.

Given that JavaBeans and Enterprise JavaBeans are completely different, why are they both called component models? In this context, a component model defines a set of interfaces and classes in the form of Java packages that must be used in a particular way to isolate and encapsulate a set of functionality. Once a component is defined, it becomes an independent piece of software that can be distributed and used in other applications. A component is developed for a specific purpose but not a specific application. In the original JavaBeans, a component might be a push button or spreadsheet that can be used in any GUI application according to the rules specified in the original JavaBeans component model. In EJB, a component might be a customer business object that can be deployed in any EJB server and used to develop any business application that needs a customer business object.

Component Transaction Monitors

The CTM industry grew out of both the ORB and the transaction processing monitor (TP monitor) industries. The CTM is really a hybrid of these two technologies that provides a powerful, robust distributed object platform. To better understand what a CTM is, we will examine the strengths and weakness of TP monitors and ORBs.

TP Monitors

Transaction processing monitors have been evolving for about 30 years (CICS was introduced in 1968) and have become powerful, high-speed server platforms for mission-critical applications. Some TP products like CICS and TUXEDO may be familiar to you. TP monitors are operating systems for business systems whose applications are written in languages like COBOL. It may seem strange to call a TP monitor an "operating system," but because they control an application's entire environment, it's a fitting description. TP monitor systems automatically manage the entire environment that a business system runs in, including transactions, resource management, and fault tolerance. The business logic in TP monitors is made up of procedural applications that are often accessed through network messaging or remote procedure calls (RPC), which are ancestors of RMI. Messaging allows a client to send a message directly to a TP monitor requesting that some application be run with certain parameters. It's similar in concept to the Java event model. Messaging can be synchronous or asynchronous, meaning that the sender may or may not be required to wait for a response. RPC is a distributed mechanism that allows clients to invoke procedures on applications in a TP monitor as if the procedure was executed locally. The primary difference between RPC and RMI is that RPC is used for *procedure*-based applications and RMI is used for distributed *object* systems. With RMI, methods can be invoked on a specific object identity, a specific business entity. In RPC, a client can call procedures on a specific type of application, but there is no concept of object identity. RMI is object oriented; RPC is procedural.

TP monitors have been around for a long time, so the technology behind them is as solid as a rock; that is why they are used in many mission-critical systems today. But TP monitors are not object oriented. Instead, they work with procedural code that can perform complex tasks but has no sense of identity. Accessing a TP monitor through RPC is like executing static methods; there's no such thing as a unique object. In addition, because TP monitors are based on procedural applications, and not objects, the business logic in a TP monitor is not as flexible, extensible, or reusable as business objects in a distributed object system.

Object Request Brokers

Distributed objects allow unique objects that have state and identity to be distributed across a network so that they can be accessed by other systems. Distributed object technologies like CORBA and Java RMI grew out of RPC with one significant difference: when you invoke a distributed object method, it's on an object instance, not an application procedure. Distributed objects are usually deployed on some kind of ORB, which is responsible for helping client applications find distributed objects easily.

ORBs, however, do not define an "operating system" for distributed objects. They are simply communications backbones that are used to access and interact with unique remote objects. When you develop a distributed object application using an ORB, all the responsibility for concurrency, transactions, resource management, and fault tolerance falls on your shoulders. These services may be available and implemented in an ORB, but the application developer is responsible for incorporating them into the business objects. In an ORB, there is no concept of an "operating system," where system-level functionality is handled automatically. The lack of implicit system-level infrastructure places an enormous burden on the application developer. Developing the infrastructure required to handle concurrency, transactions, security, persistence, and everything else needed to support large user populations is a Herculean task that few corporate development teams are equipped to accomplish.

CTMs: The Hybrid of ORBs and TP Monitors

As the advantages of distributed objects became apparent, the number of systems deployed using ORBs increased very quickly. ORBs support distributed objects by employing a somewhat crude server-side component model that allows distributed objects to be connected to a communication backbone, but don't implicitly support transactions, security, persistence, and resource management. These services must be explicitly accessed through APIs by the distributed object, resulting in more complexity and, frequently, more development problems. In addition, resource management strategies such as instance swapping, resource pooling, and activation may not be supported at all. These types of strategies make it possible for a distributed object system to scale, improving performance and throughput and reducing latency. Without automatic support for resource management, application developers must implement homegrown resource management solutions, which requires a very sophisticated understanding of distributed object systems. ORBs fail to address the complexities of managing a component in a high-volume, mission-critical environment, an area where TP monitors have always excelled.

With three decades of TP monitor experience, it wasn't long before companies like IBM and BEA began developing a hybrid of ORBs and TP monitor systems, which we refer to as component transaction monitors. These types of application servers combine the fluidity and accessibility of distributed object systems based on ORBs with the robust "operating system" of a TP monitor. CTMs provide a comprehensive environment for server-side components by managing concurrency, transactions, object distribution, load balancing, security, and resource management automatically. While application developers still need to be aware of these facilities, they don't have to explicitly implement them when using a CTM.

The basic features of a CTM are distributed objects, an infrastructure that includes transaction management and other services, and a server-side component model. CTMs support these features in varying degrees; choosing the most robust and feature-rich CTM is not always as critical as choosing one that best meets your needs. Very large and robust CTMs can be enormously expensive and may be overkill for smaller projects. CTMs have come out of several different industries, including the relational database industry, the application server industry, the web server industry, the CORBA ORB industry, and the TP monitor industry. Each vendor offers products that reflect their particular area of expertise. However, when you're getting started, choosing a CTM that supports the Enterprise JavaBeans component model may be much more important than any particular feature set. Because Enterprise JavaBeans is implementation independent, choosing an EJB CTM provides the business system with the flexibility to scale to larger CTMs as needed. We will discuss the importance of EJB as a standard component model for CTMs later in this chapter.

Analogies to Relational Databases

This chapter spent a lot of time talking about CTMs because they are essential to the definition of EJB. The discussion of CTMs is not over, but to make things as clear as possible before proceeding, we will use relational databases as an analogy for CTMs.

Relational databases provide a simple development environment for application developers, in combination with a robust infrastructure for data. As an application developer using a relational database, you might design the table layouts, decide which columns are primary keys, and define indexes and stored procedures, but you don't develop the indexing algorithm, the SQL parser, or the cursor management system. These types of system-level functionality are left to the database vendor; you simply choose the product that best fits your needs. Application developers are concerned with how business data is organized, not how the database engine works. It would be waste of resources for an application developer to write a relational database from scratch when vendors like Microsoft, Oracle, and others already provide them.

Distributed business objects, if they are to be effective, require the same system-level management from CTMs as business data requires from relational databases. System-level functionality like concurrency, transaction management, and resource management is necessary if the business system is going to be used for large user populations or mission-critical work. It is unrealistic and wasteful to expect application developers to reinvent this system-level functionality when commercial solutions already exist.

CTMs are to business objects what relational databases are to data. CTMs handle all the system-level functionality, allowing the application developer to focus on the business problems. With a CTM, application developers can focus on the design and development of the business objects without having to waste thousands of hours developing the infrastructure that the business objects operate in.

CTMs and Server-Side Component Models

CTMs require that business objects adhere to the server-side component model implemented by the vendor. A good component model is critical to the success of a development project because it defines how easily an application developer can write business objects for the CTM. The component model is a contract that defines the responsibilities of the CTM and the business objects. With a good component model, a developer knows what to expect from the CTM and the CTM understands how to manage the business object. Server-side component models are great at describing the responsibilities of the application developer and CTM vendor.

Server-side component models are based on a specification. As long as the component adheres to the specification, it can be used by the CTM. The relationship between the server-side component and the CTM is like the relationship between a CD-ROM and a CD player. As long as the component (CD-ROM) adheres to the player's specifications, you can play it.

A CTM's relationship with its component model is also similar to the relationship the railway system has with trains. The railway system manages the train's environment, providing alternate routes for load balancing, multiple tracks for concurrency, and a traffic control system for managing resources. The railway provides the infrastructure that trains run on. Similarly, a CTM provides server-side components with the entire infrastructure needed to support concurrency, transactions, load balancing, etc.

Trains on the railway are like server-side components: they all perform different tasks but they do so using the same basic design. The train, like a server-side component, focuses on performing a task, such as moving cars, not managing the environment. For the engineer, the person driving the train, the interface for controlling the train is fairly simple: a brake and throttle. For the application developer, the interface to the server-side component is similarly limited.

Different CTMs may implement different component models, just as different railways have different kinds of trains. The differences between the component models vary, like railway systems having different track widths and different controls, but the fundamental operations of CTMs are the same. They all ensure that business objects are managed so that they can support large populations of users in mission-critical situations. This means that resources, concurrency, transactions, security, persistence, load balancing, and distribution of objects can be handled automatically, limiting the application developer to a simple interface. This allows the application developer to focus on the business logic instead of the enterprise infrastructure.

MTS

Microsoft was one of the first vendors to ship a CTM, the Microsoft Transaction Server (MTS). MTS uses a server-side component model and a distributed component service based on DCOM. When MTS was introduced in 1996, it was exciting because it provided a very comprehensive environment for business objects. With MTS, application developers can write COM (Common Object Model) components without worrying about system-level concerns. Once a business object is designed to conform to the COM model, MTS will take care of everything else, including transaction management, concurrency, resource management—everything! MTS makes it simple for application developers. If they want to influence how a business object interacts with system-level services, they use property sheets. It's like setting properties of a GUI widget in Visual Basic: just bring up the property sheet and choose the transactional context, the security attributes, the name binding, and other properties from a list box or from some other GUI widget. Once the business objects are deployed in MTS, their remote interfaces can be assembled like building blocks into business solutions.

Although the features provided by MTS are great and its application developer API is very simple, as an open standard, MTS falls short. MTS is Microsoft's proprietary CTM, which means that using it binds you to the Microsoft platform. This may not be so bad, because MTS and DCOM work well, and the Microsoft platform is pervasive. If, however, your company is expected to deploy on a non-Microsoft platform or to non-Microsoft clients, MTS is not a viable solution. In addition, MTS only supports stateless components; it doesn't support persistent objects. Although stateless components can offer higher performance, business systems need the kind of flexibility offered by CTMs that include stateful and persistent components.

EJB and CORBA CTMs

Until the fall of 1997, non-Microsoft CTMs were pretty much nonexistent. Promising products from IBM, BEA, and Hitachi were on the drawing board, while MTS was already on the market. Although the non-MTS designs were only designs, they all had one thing in common: they all used CORBA as a distributed object service.

Most non-Microsoft CTMs were focused on the more open standard of CORBA so that they could be deployed on non-Microsoft platforms and support non-Microsoft clients. CORBA is both language and platform independent, so CORBA CTM vendors could provide their customers with more implementation options. The problem with CORBA CTM designs was that they all had different server-side component models. In other words, if you developed a component for one vendor's CTM, you couldn't turn around and use that same component in another vendor's CTM. The component models were too different.

With Microsoft's MTS far in the lead (it had already been around a year), CORBA-based CTM vendors needed a competitive advantage. One problem CTMs faced was a fragmented CORBA market where each vendor's product was different from the next. A fragmented market wouldn't benefit anyone, so the CORBA CTM vendors needed a standard to rally around. Besides the CORBA protocol, the most obvious standard needed was a component model, which would allow clients and third-party vendors to develop their business objects to one specification that would work in any CORBA CTM. Microsoft was, of course, pushing their component model as a standard—which was attractive because MTS was an actual working product—but Microsoft didn't support CORBA. The OMG (Object Management Group), the same people who developed the CORBA standard, were defining a server-side component model. This held promise because it was sure to be tailored to CORBA, but the OMG was slow in developing a standard—at least too slow for the evolving CTM market.

In 1997, Sun Microsystems was developing the most promising standard for server-side components called Enterprise JavaBeans. Sun offered some key advantages. First, Sun was respected and was known for working with vendors to define the best solutions possible. Sun had a habit of adopting the best ideas in the industry and then making the Java implementation an open standard—usually successfully. The Java database connectivity API, called JDBC, was a perfect example. Based largely on Microsoft's own ODBC, JDBC offered vendors a more flexible model for plugging in their own database access drivers. In addition, developers found the JDBC API much easier to work with. Sun was doing the same thing in its newer technologies like the JavaMail™ API and the Java Naming and Directory Interface (JNDI). These technologies were still being defined, but the collaboration among vendors was encouraging and the openness of the APIs was attractive. Although CORBA offered an open standard, it attempted to standardize very low-level facilities like security and transactions. Vendors could not justify rewriting existing products such as TUXEDO and CICS to the CORBA standards. EJB got around that problem by saying it doesn't matter how you implement the low-level services; all that matters is all the facilities be applied to the components according to the specification—a much more palatable solution for existing and prospective CTM vendors. In addition, the Java language offered some pretty enticing advantages, not all of them purely technical. First, Java was a hot and sexy technology and simply making your product Java-compatible seemed to boost your exposure in the market. Java also offered some very attractive technical benefits. Java was more or less platform independent. A component model defined in the Java language would have definite marketing and technical benefits.

As it turned out, Sun had not been idle after it announced Enterprise JavaBeans. Sun's engineers had been working with several leading vendors to define a flexible and open standard to which vendors could easily adapt their existing products. This was a tall order because vendors had different kinds of servers including web servers, database servers, relational database servers, application servers, and early CTMs. It's likely that no one wanted to sacrifice their architecture for the common good, but eventually the vendors agreed on a model that was flexible enough to accommodate different implementations yet solid enough to support real mission-critical development. In December of 1997, Sun Microsystems released the first draft specification of Enterprise JavaBeans and vendors have been flocking to the server-side component model ever since.

Benefits of a Standard Server-Side Component Model

So what does it mean to be a standard server-side component model? Quite simply, it means that you can develop business objects using the Enterprise JavaBeans (EJB) component model and expect them to work in any CTM that supports the complete EJB specification. This is a pretty powerful statement because it largely eliminates the biggest problem faced by potential customers of CORBA-based CTM products: fear of vendor "lock-in." With a standard server-side component model, customers can commit to using an EJB-compliant CTM with the knowledge that they can migrate to a better CTM if one becomes available. Obviously, care must be taken when using proprietary extensions developed by vendors, but this is nothing new. Even in relational database industry—which has been using the SQL standard for a couple of decades—optional proprietary extensions abound.

Having a standard server-side component model has benefits beyond implementation independence. A standard component model provides a vehicle for growth in the third-party products. If numerous vendors support EJB, then creating add-on products and component libraries is more attractive to software vendors. The IT industry has seen this type of cottage industry grow up around other standards like SQL, where hundreds of add-on products can be purchased to enhance business systems whose data is stored in SQL-compliant relational databases. Report generating tools and data warehouse products are typical examples. .The GUI component industry has seen the growth of its own third-party products. A healthy market for component libraries already exists for GUI component models like Microsoft's ActiveX and Sun's original JavaBeans component models.*

Similarly, Enterprise JavaBeans will benefit from third-party products. It is likely that ERP systems and business object frameworks based on EJB will thrive. As an example, IBM's San Francisco business object framework is migrating to the EJB component model. We will also see cottage industries grow up around EJB. Add-on products that provide services to EJB-compliant systems like credit card processing, legacy database access, and other business services will be introduced. These types of products will make development of EJB systems simpler and faster than the alternatives, making the EJB component model attractive to corporate IS and server vendors alike. It is also likely that a small market for prepackaged EJB components will also develop.

Titan Cruises: An Imaginary Business

To make things a little easier, and more fun, we will attempt to discuss all the concepts in this book in the context of one imaginary business, a cruise line called Titan. A cruise line makes a particularly interesting example because it incorporates several different businesses: a cruise has cabins that are similar to hotel rooms, serves meals like a restaurant, offers various recreational opportunities, and needs to interact with other travel businesses.

This type of business is a good candidate for a distributed object system because many of the system's users are geographically dispersed. Commercial travel agents, for example, who need to book passage on Titan ships will need to access the reservation system. Supporting many—possibly hundreds—of travel agents requires a robust transactional system to ensure that agents have access and reservations are completed properly.

Throughout this book we will build a fairly simple slice of Titan's EJB system that focuses on the process of making a reservation for a cruise. This will give us an opportunity to develop enterprise beans like Ship, Cabin, TravelAgent, ProcessPayment, and so forth. In the process, you will need to create relational database tables for persisting data used in the example. It is assumed that you are familiar with relational database management systems and that you can create tables according to the SQL statements provided. EJB can be used with any kind of database or legacy application, but relational databases seem to be the most commonly understood database so we have chosen this as the persistence layer.

What's Next?

In order to develop business objects using EJB, you have to understand the life cycle and architecture of EJB components. This means understanding conceptually how EJB's components are managed and made available as distributed objects. Developing an understanding of the EJB architecture is the focus of the next two chapters.

2

Architectural Overview

As you learned in Chapter 1, Enterprise JavaBeans is a component model for component transaction monitors, the most advanced type of business application server available today. To effectively use Enterprise JavaBeans, you need to understand the EJB architecture, so this book includes two chapters on the subject. This chapter explores the core of EJB: how enterprise beans are distributed as business objects. Chapter 3 explores the services and resource management techniques supported by EJB.

To be truly versatile, the EJB component design had to be smart. For application developers, assembling enterprise beans is simple, requiring little or no expertise in the complex system-level issues that often plague three-tier development efforts. While EJB makes it easy for application developers, it also provides system developers (the people who write EJB servers) with a great deal of flexibility in how they support the EJB specification.

The similarities among different component transaction monitors (CTMs) allow the EJB abstraction to be a standard component model for all of them. Each vendor's CTM is implemented differently, but they all support the same primary services and similar resource management techniques. The primary services and resource management techniques are covered in more detail in Chapter 3, but some of the infrastructure for supporting them is addressed in this chapter.

The Enterprise Bean Component

Enterprise JavaBeans server-side components come in two fundamentally different types: *entity beans* and *session beans*. A good rule of thumb is that entity beans model business concepts that can be expressed as nouns. For example, an entity bean might represent a customer, a piece of equipment, an item in inventory, or

23

even a place. In other words, entity beans model real-world objects; these objects are usually persistent records in some kind of database. Our hypothetical cruise line will need entity beans that represent cabins, customers, ships, etc.

Session beans are an extension of the client application and are responsible for managing processes or tasks. A Ship bean provides methods for doing things directly to a ship but doesn't say anything about the context under which those actions are taken. Booking passengers on the ship requires that we use a Ship bean, but also requires a lot of things that have nothing to do with the Ship itself: we'll need to know about passengers, ticket rates, schedules, and so on. A session bean is responsible for this kind of coordination. Session beans tend to manage particular kinds of activities, for example, the act of making a reservation. They have a lot to do with the relationships between different enterprise beans. A Travel-Agent session bean, for example, might make use of a Cruise, a Cabin, and a Customer—all entity beans—to make a reservation.

The activity that a session bean represents is fundamentally transient: you start making a reservation, you do a bunch of work, and then it's finished. A session bean doesn't represent something in a database. Obviously, session beans have lots of side effects on the database: in the process of making a reservation, you might create a new Reservation by assigning a Customer to a particular Cabin on a particular Ship. All of these changes would be reflected in the database by actions on the respective entity beans. Session beans like TravelAgent, which is responsible for making a reservation on a cruise, can even access a database directly and perform reads, updates, and deletes to data. But there's no TravelAgent record in the database—once the reservation is made, it's done.

What makes this distinction difficult is that it's extremely flexible. The relevant distinction for Enterprise JavaBeans is that an entity bean has persistent state; a session bean models interactions but doesn't have persistent state.

Classes and Interfaces

A good way to understand the design of enterprise beans is to look at how you'd go about implementing one. To implement an enterprise bean, you need to define two interfaces and one or two classes:

Remote interface

The remote interface for an enterprise bean defines the bean's business methods: the methods a bean presents to the outside world to do its work. The remote interface extends `javax.ejb.EJBObject`, which in turn extends `java.rmi.Remote`. (We'll call the rather shadowy entity that actually implements this interface the *EJB object*.)

Home interface

The home interface defines the bean's life cycle methods: methods for creating new beans, removing beans, and finding beans. The home interface extends `javax.ejb.EJBHome`, which in turn extends `java.rmi.Remote`. (We'll call the object that implements the home interface the *EJB home*.)

Bean class

The bean class actually implements the bean's business methods. Note, however, that the bean class usually does not implement the bean's home or remote interfaces. However, it must have methods matching the signatures of the methods defined in the remote interface and must have methods corresponding to some of the methods in the home interface. If this sounds perfectly confusing, it is. We'll try to clarify this as we go along. An entity bean must implement `javax.ejb.EntityBean`; a session bean must implement `javax.ejb.SessionBean`. Both `EntityBean` and `SessionBean` extend `javax.ejb.EnterpriseBean`.

Primary key

The primary key is a very simple class that provides a pointer into the database. Only entity beans need a primary key; the only requirement for this class is that it implements `java.io.Serializable`.

The complexity—particularly all the confusion about classes implementing the methods of an interface but not implementing the interface itself—comes about because enterprise beans exist in the middle between some kind of client software and some kind of database. The client never interacts with a bean class directly; it always uses the methods of the bean's home and remote interfaces to do its work, interacting with stubs that are generated automatically. (For that matter, a bean that needs the services of another bean is just another client: it uses the same stubs, rather than interacting with the bean class directly.)

There are also lots of interactions between a bean and its server. These interactions are managed by a "container," which is responsible for presenting a uniform interface between the bean and the server. (Although it's incorrect, many people use the terms "container" and "server" interchangeably. We won't promise consistency ourselves. But it's helpful to understand the difference.) The container is responsible for creating new instances of beans, making sure that they are stored properly by the server, and so on. Tools provided by the container's vendor do a tremendous amount of work behind the scenes. At least one tool will take care of creating the mapping between entity beans and records in your database. Other tools generate a lot of code based on the home interface, the remote interface, and the bean class itself. The code generated does things like create the bean, store it in the database, and so on. This code (in addition to the stubs) is what actually implements the two interfaces, and is the reason your bean class doesn't have to.

Before going on let's first establish some conventions. When we speak about an enterprise bean as a whole, its remote interface, home interface, bean class, and so forth, we will call it by its remote-interface name, followed by the word "bean." For example, an enterprise bean that is developed to model a cabin on a ship will be called the "Cabin bean." Notice that we didn't use a constant width font for "Cabin." We do this because we are referring to all the parts of the bean (remote interface, home interface, bean class, etc.) as a whole, not just one particular part like the remote interface or bean class. When we are talking about the remote interface of the Cabin bean we will use constant width. For example, the remote interface for the Cabin bean is called the Cabin remote interface. Likewise, we use constant width for the names of the classes that make up the other parts of the bean. The bean class itself would be called CabinBean, the home interface CabinHome, and the primary key would be called CabinPK.

The remote interface

Having introduced the machinery, let's look at how to build a bean. In this section, we will examine the Cabin bean, an entity bean that models a cabin on a cruise ship. Let's start with its remote interface.

We'll define the remote interface for a Cabin bean using the interface called Cabin, which defines business methods for working with cabins. All remote-interface types extend the javax.ejb.EJBObject interface.

```
import java.rmi.RemoteException;

public interface Cabin extends javax.ejb.EJBObject {
    public String getName() throws RemoteException;
    public void setName(String str) throws RemoteException;
    public int getDeckLevel() throws RemoteException;
    public void setDeckLevel(int level) throws RemoteException;
}
```

These are methods for naming the cabin and methods for setting the cabin's deck level; you can probably imagine lots of other methods that you'd need, but this is enough to get started. All of these methods declare that they throw Remote-Exception, which is required of any method that can be invoked through RMI. EJB requires the use of Java RMI-IIOP conventions, although the underlying protocol can be CORBA IIOP, Java Remote Method Protocol (JRMP), or some other protocol. Java RMI-IIOP will be discussed in more detail in the next chapter.

The home interface

The home interface defines life-cycle methods and methods for looking up beans. The home interface extends javax.ejb.EJBHome. We'll call the home interface for the Cabin bean CabinHome and define it like this:

```
import java.rmi.RemoteException;
import javax.ejb.CreateException;
import javax.ejb.FinderException;

public interface CabinHome extends javax.ejb.EJBHome {
    public Cabin create(int id)
        throws CreateException, RemoteException;
    public Cabin findByPrimaryKey(CabinPK pk)
        throws FinderException, RemoteException;
}
```

The create() method will be responsible for initializing an instance of our bean. If your application needs it, you can provide other create() methods, with different arguments.

In addition to the findByPrimaryKey(), you are free to define other methods that provide convenient ways to look up Cabin beans—for example, you might want to define a method called findByShip() that returns all the cabins on a particular ship. Find methods like these are only used in EntityBean types and are not used in SessionBean types.

The bean class

Now let's look at an actual bean. Here's the code for the CabinBean; it's a sparse implementation, but it will show you how the pieces fit together:

```
import javax.ejb.EntityContext;

public class CabinBean implements javax.ejb.EntityBean {

    public int id;
    public String name;
    public int deckLevel;

    // EJB 1.0: return void
    public CabinPK ejbCreate(int id){
        this.id = id;
        // EJB 1.0 no return statement
        return null;
    }
    public void ejbPostCreate(int id){
        // do nothing
    }
```

```java
    public String getName(){
        return name;
    }
    public void setName(String str){
        name = str;
    }
    public int getDeckLevel(){
        return deckLevel;
    }
    public void setDeckLevel(int level){
        deckLevel = level;
    }

    public void setEntityContext(EntityContext ctx){
        // not implemented
    }
    public void unsetEntityContext(){
        // not implemented
    }
    public void ejbActivate(){
        // not implemented
    }
    public void ejbPassivate(){
        // not implemented
    }
    public void ejbLoad(){
        // not implemented
    }
    public void ejbStore(){
        // not implemented
    }
    public void ejbRemove(){
        // not implemented
    }
}
```

NOTE   The // EJB 1.0 comments indicate how to modify the code to work
           with an EJB 1.0 server. As written, this code (and the other exam-
           ples in this book) assume EJB 1.1, unless otherwise noted.

The set and get methods for the cabin's name and deck level are the business
methods of the CabinBean; they match the business methods defined by the
bean's remote interface, Cabin. The CabinBean class has state and business
behavior that models the concept of a cabin. The business methods are the only
methods that are visible to the client application; the other methods are visible
only to the EJB container. The other methods are required by the EJB component
model and are not really part of the bean class's public business definition.

The ejbCreate() and ejbPostCreate() methods initialize the instance of the bean class when a new cabin record is to be added to the database. The last seven methods in the CabinBean are defined in the javax.ejb.EntityBean interface. These methods are state management callback methods. The EJB server invokes these callback methods on the bean class when important state management events occur. The ejbRemove() method, for example, notifies an entity bean that its data is about to be deleted from the database. The ejbLoad() and ejbStore() methods notify the bean instance that its state is being read or written to the database. The ejbActivate() and ejbPassivate() methods notify the bean instance that it is about to be activated or deactivated, a process that conserves memory and other resources. setEntityContext() provides the bean with an interface to the EJB server that allows the bean class to get information about itself and its surroundings. unsetEntityContext() is called by the EJB server to notify the bean instance that it is about to be dereferenced for garbage collection.

All these callback methods provide the bean class with *notifications* of when an action is about to be taken, or was just taken, on the bean class's behalf by the EJB server. These notifications simply inform the bean of an event, the bean doesn't have to do anything about it. The callback notifications tell the bean where it is during its life cycle, when it is about to be loaded, removed, deactivated, and so on. Most of the callback methods pertain to persistence, which can be done automatically for the bean class by the EJB server. Because the callback methods are defined in the javax.ejb.EntityBean interface, the bean class must implement them, but it isn't required to do anything meaningful with the methods if it doesn't need to. Our bean, the CabinBean, won't need to do anything when these callback methods are invoked, so these methods are empty implementations. Details about these callback methods, when they are called and how a bean should react, are covered in Chapter 6.

The primary key

Certain public fields of an entity bean are stored in a database. These fields are called *persistent fields*. Determining how the data in the database relates to the persistent fields of the bean class is called *data mapping*. When a bean is deployed into an EJB server, its persistent fields must be mapped to the database. The data used to populate persistent fields in the bean instance is obtained using a primary key. The primary key is a pointer that helps locate data that describes a unique record or entity in the database; it is used in the findByPrimaryKey() method of the home interface to locate a specific entity. Primary keys are defined by the bean developer and must be some type of serializable object. Here's the primary key for the Cabin bean:

```
public class CabinPK implements java.io.Serializable{
    public int id;
```

```
    public int hashCode(){
        return id;
    }
    public boolean equals(Object obj){
        if (obj instanceof CabinPK){
            if (((CabinPK)obj).id == id)
                return true;
        }
        return false;
    }
}
```

Most EJB container vendors provide some kind of tool, available at deployment time, that helps to map the primary key and the bean's persistent fields to the database. These kinds of tools may present the persistent fields of the bean as well as the structure of the database in a graphical presentation. The person deploying the bean simply ties the bean's fields to its representation in the database, which could be relational database columns, an objectified version of the database, or a more direct mapping to an object database.

What about session beans?

CabinBean is an entity bean, but a session bean wouldn't be all that different. It would extend SessionBean instead of EntityBean; it would have an ejbCreate() method that would initialize the bean's state, but no ejbPostCreate(). Session beans don't have an ejbLoad() or ejbStore() because session beans are not persistent. While session beans have a setSessionContext() method, they don't have an unsetSessionContext() method. Finally, a session bean would provide an ejbRemove() method, which would be called to notify the bean that the client no longer needs it. However, this method wouldn't tell the bean that its data was about to be removed from the database, because a session bean doesn't represent data in the database.

Session beans don't have a primary key. That's because session beans are not persistent themselves, so there is no need for key that maps to the database.

Deployment Descriptors and JAR Files

Much of the information about how beans are managed at runtime is not addressed in the interfaces and classes discussed previously. You may have noticed, for example, that we didn't talk about how beans interact with security, transactions, naming, and other services common to distributed object systems. As you know from prior discussions, these types of primary services are handled automatically by the EJB CTM server, but the EJB server still needs to know how to apply the primary services to each bean class at runtime. To do this, we use *deployment descriptors.*

Deployment descriptors serve a function very similar to property files. They allow us to customize behavior of software (enterprise beans) at runtime without having to change the software itself. Property files are often used with applications, but deployment descriptors are specific to a class of enterprise bean. Deployment descriptors are also similar in purpose to property sheets used in Visual Basic and PowerBuilder. Where property sheets allow us to describe the runtime attributes of visual widgets (background color, font size, etc.), deployment descriptors allow us to describe runtime attributes of server-side components (security, transactional context, etc.). Deployment descriptors allow certain runtime behaviors of beans to be customized, without altering the bean class or its interfaces.

When a bean class and its interfaces have been defined, a deployment descriptor for the bean is created and populated with data about the bean. Frequently, IDEs (integrated development environments) that support development of Enterprise JavaBeans will allow developers to graphically set up the deployment descriptors using visual utilities like property sheets. After the developer has set all the properties for a bean, the deployment descriptor is saved to a file. Once the deployment descriptor is complete and saved to a file, the bean can be packaged in a JAR file for deployment.

JAR (*Java ar*chive) files are ZIP files that are used specifically for packaging Java classes (and other resources such as images) that are ready to be used in some type of application. JARs are used for packaging applets, Java applications, JavaBeans, and Enterprise JavaBeans. A JAR file containing one or more enterprise beans includes the bean classes, remote interfaces, home interfaces, and primary keys (EntityBean types only), for each bean. It also contains one deployment descriptor, which is used for all the beans in the JAR files. When a bean is deployed, the JAR's path is given to the container's deployment tools, which read the JAR file. The container uses the deployment descriptor to learn about the beans contained in the JAR file.

NOTE   EJB 1.0 also requires information in the JAR manifest (a kind of table of contents for the JAR), to denote which entry points to the deployment descriptor. When a bean is deployed, the JAR's path is given to the container's deployment tools, which read the JAR file. The first thing read out of the JAR file after the manifest is the deployment descriptor.

EJB 1.1 doesn't use the JAR's manifest; the first thing read in the JAR is the deployment descriptor.

When the JAR file is read at deployment time, the container tools read the deployment descriptor to learn about the bean and how it should be managed at runtime. The deployment descriptor tells the deployment tools what kind of beans are in the JAR file (SessionBean or EntityBean), how they should be managed in transactions, who has access to the beans at runtime, and other runtime attributes of the beans. The person who is deploying the bean can alter some of these settings, like transactional and security access attributes, to customize the bean for a particular application. Many container tools provide property sheets for graphically reading and altering the deployment descriptor when the bean is deployed. These graphical property sheets are similar to those used by bean developers.

The deployment descriptors help the deployment tools to add beans to the EJB container. Once the bean is deployed, the properties described in the deployment descriptors will continue to be used to tell the EJB container how to manage the bean at runtime.

EJB 1.0: Deployment descriptors

Enterprise JavaBeans Version 1.0 uses a set of serializable classes to set and store the deployment descriptor information. Instances of these classes are created and populated with deployment information when the bean is developed, then serialized to a file. The container deploying the bean deserializes the deployment descriptor objects and reads their properties to obtain the deployment information.

Here are some of the property methods defined in the main descriptor class, DeploymentDescriptor. The method bodies have been omitted; what's important at this stage is to get a feel for what methods are defined by a descriptor.

```
public abstract Class javax.ejb.deployment.DeploymentDescriptor
    extends Object implements Serializable {

// The release version of the bean
protected int versionNumber;

// Get the AccessControlEntry objects for the enterprise bean.
public AccessControlEntry[] getAccessControlEntries() {}
// Get the control descriptor at the specified index.
public ControlDescriptor getControlDescriptors(int index) {}
// Get the enterprise bean's full class name.
public String getEnterpriseBeanClassName(){}
// Get enterprise bean's environment properties.
public Properties getEnvironmentProperties() {}
// Get the full name of the enterprise bean's home interface.
public String getHomeInterfaceClassName() {}
// Get the full name of the enterprise bean's remote interface.
public String getRemoteInterfaceClassName() {}
```

```
    // Set the AccessControlEntry objects for the enterprise bean.
    public void setAccessControlEntries(AccessControlEntry values []){}
    // Set the control descriptor at the specified index.
    public void setControlDescriptors(int index, ControlDescriptor value) {}
    // Set the enterprise bean's full class name.
    public void setEnterpriseBeanClassName(String value) {}
    // Set enterprise bean's environment properties.
    public void setEnvironmentProperties(Properties value) {}
    // Set the full name of the enterprise bean's home interface.
    public void setHomeInterfaceClassName(String value) {}
    // Specify that the enterprise bean is reentrant.
    public void setReentrant(boolean value) {}
    // Set the full name of the enterprise bean's remote interface.
    public void setRemoteInterfaceClassName(String value) {}

    // ... Other set and get methods for properties follow.
}
```

The classes used to provide deployment information are found in the `javax.ejb.deployment` package, which has five deployment descriptor classes:

DeploymentDescriptor

The DeploymentDescriptor class is the abstract superclass for both Entity-Descriptor and SessionDescriptor. It provides the accessor methods for reading properties that describe the bean's version number, and the names of the classes for the bean's remote interface, home interface, and bean class. In addition, the deployment descriptor provides access to the Control-Descriptors and AccessControlEntrys.

ControlDescriptor

The ControlDescriptor class provides accessor methods for defining the security and transactional attributes of a bean at runtime. Control-Descriptors can be applied to the bean as a whole, or to specific methods of the bean. Any method that doesn't have a ControlDescriptor uses the default properties defined by the ControlDescriptor for the bean itself. Security properties in the ControlDescriptor indicate how Access-ControlEntrys are applied at runtime. Transactional properties indicate how the bean or specific method will be involved in transactions at runtime.

AccessControlEntry

Each AccessControlEntry identifies a person, group, or role that can access the bean or one of its methods. Like ControlDescriptor, AccessControl-Entry can be applied to the bean as a whole or to a specific method. An AccessControlEntry that is specific to a method overrides the default AccessControlEntrys set for the bean. The AccessControlEntrys are used in combination with the security properties in the ControlDescriptor to provide more control over runtime access to the bean and its methods.

`EntityDescriptor`

The `EntityDescriptor` class extends `DeploymentDescriptor` to provide properties specific to an `EntityBean` object. Entity bean properties include the name of the primary key class and what instance variables are managed automatically by the container.

`SessionDescriptor`

The `SessionDescriptor` class extends `DeploymentDescriptor` to provide properties specific to a `SessionBean` object. Session bean properties include a timeout setting (how long a session can go unused before it's automatically removed) and a stateless session property. The stateless session property indicates whether the session is a stateless session bean or a stateful session bean. (More about stateless and stateful session beans later.)

Several of the properties described by the deployment descriptors, such as transactional and security attributes, have not yet been discussed. Later we will discuss these topics in more detail, but for now it's important that you understand that the deployment descriptors in EJB 1.0 are serialized class instances that describe the bean and some of its runtime behavior to the container.

EJB 1.1: Deployment descriptors

Enterprise JavaBeans 1.1 dropped the serializable deployment descriptor classes used in EJB 1.0 in favor of a more flexible file format based on XML (Extensible Markup Language). The new XML deployment descriptors are text files structured according to a standard EJB DTD (Document Type Definition) that can be extended so the type of deployment information stored can evolve as the specification evolves. Chapter 10 provides a a detailed description of EJB 1.1 deployment descriptors. This section provides a brief overview of XML deployment descriptors.

The following deployment descriptor might be used to describe the Cabin bean:

```
<?xml version="1.0"?>

<!DOCTYPE ejb-jar PUBLIC "-//Sun Microsystems, Inc.//DTD Enterprise
JavaBeans 1.2//EN" "http://java.sun.com/j2ee/dtds/ejb-jar_1_1.dtd">


<ejb-jar>
    <enterprise-beans>
        <entity>
            <ejb-name>CabinEJB</ejb-name>
            <home>com.titan.cabin.CabinHome</home>
            <remote>com.titan.cabin.Cabin</remote>
            <ejb-class>com.titan.cabin.CabinBean</ejb-class>
            <prim-key-class>com.titan.cabin.CabinPK</prim-key-class>
            <persistence-type>Container</persistence-type>
            <reentrant>False</reentrant>
```

```
        </entity>
      </enterprise-beans>
    </ejb-jar>
```

The deployment descriptor for a real bean would have a lot more information; this example simply illustrates the type of information that you'll find in an XML deployment descriptor.

The second element in any XML document is !DOCTYPE. This element describes the organization that defined the DTD for the XML document, the DTD's version, and a URL location of the DTD. The DTD describes how a particular XML document is structured.

All the other elements in the XML document are specific to EJB 1.1. They do not represent all the elements used in deployment descriptors, but they illustrate the types of elements that are used. Here's what the elements mean:

ejb-jar

The root of the XML deployment descriptor. All other elements must be nested below this one. It must contain one enterprise-beans element as well as other optional elements.

enterprise-beans

Contains declarations for all the beans described by this XML document. It may contain entity and session elements, which describe entity beans and session beans respectively.

entity

Describes an entity bean and its deployment information. There must be one of these elements for every entity bean described by the XML deployment descriptor. (The session element is used in the same way to describe a session bean.)

ejb-name

The descriptive name of the bean. It's the name we use for the bean in conversation, when talking about the bean component as a whole.

home

The fully qualified class name of the home interface. This is the interface that defines the life-cycle behaviors (create, find, remove) of the bean.

remote

The fully qualified class name of the remote interface. This is the interface that defines the bean's business methods.

ejb-class

The fully qualified class name of the bean class. This is the class that implements the business methods of the bean.

`prim-key-class`
> The fully qualified class name of the bean's primary key. The primary key is used to find the bean data in the database.

The last two elements in the deployment descriptor, the persistence-type and reentrant elements, express the persistence strategy and concurrency policies of the entity bean. These elements are explained in more detail later in the book.

As you progress through this book, you will be introduced to the elements that describe concepts we have not covered yet, so don't worry about knowing all of the things you might find in a deployment descriptor.

The Unseen Pieces

We've done a lot of hand waving about the strange relationships between an enterprise bean and its interfaces. Now it's time to talk a little more precisely about what's going on. Unfortunately, we can't talk as precisely as we'd like. There are a number of ways for an EJB container to implement these relationships; we'll show some of the possibilities.

The two missing pieces are the EJB object itself and the EJB home. You will probably never see the EJB home and EJB object classes because their class definitions are proprietary to the vendor's EJB implementation and are generally not made public. This is good because it represents a separation of responsibilities along areas of expertise. As an application developer, you are intimately familiar with how your business environment works and needs to be modeled, so you will focus on creating the applications and beans that describe your business. System-level developers, the people who write EJB servers, don't understand your business, but they do understand how to develop CTMs and support distributed objects. It makes sense for system-level developers to apply their skills to mechanics of managing distributed objects but leave the business logic to you, the application developer. Let's talk briefly about the EJB object and the EJB home so you understand the missing pieces in the big picture.

The EJB object

This chapter has said a lot about a bean's remote interface, which extends the `EJBObject` interface. Who implements that interface? Clearly, the client stub: we understand that much. But what about the server side?

On the server side, an EJB object is a distributed object that implements the remote interface of the bean. It wraps the bean instance—that is, the enterprise bean class you've created (in our example, the `CabinBean`)—on the server and expands its functionality to include `javax.ejb.EJBObject` behavior. The EJB object is generated by the utilities provided by the vendor of your EJB container and is based on the bean classes and the information provided by the deployment descriptor. The EJB object wraps the bean instance and works with the container to apply transactions, security, and other system-level operations to the bean at runtime. Chapter 3 talks more about the EJB object's role with regard to system-level operations.

There are a number of strategies that a vendor can use to implement the EJB object; Figure 2-1 illustrates three possibilities.

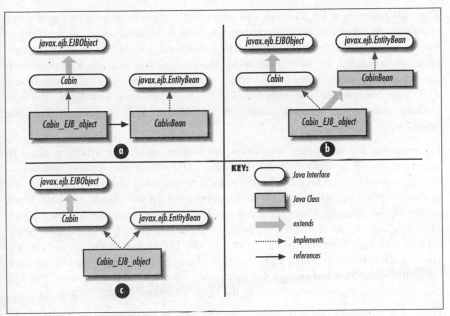

Figure 2-1. Three ways to implement the EJB object

In Figure 2-1(a) you see that the EJB object is a classic wrapper because it holds a reference to the bean class and delegates the requests to the bean. Figure 2-1(b) shows that the EJB object class actually extends the bean class, adding functionality specific to the EJB container. In Figure 2-1(c), you see that the bean class is no longer included in the model. In this case, the EJB object has both a proprietary implementation required by the EJB container and bean class method implementations that were copied from the bean class's definition.

The EJB object design that is shown in Figure 2-1(a) is perhaps the most common. Throughout this book, particularly in the next chapter, we will explain how EJB works with the assumption that the EJB object wraps the bean class instance as depicted in Figure 2-1(a). But the other implementations are used; it shouldn't make a difference which one your vendor has chosen. The bottom line is that you never really know much about the EJB object: its implementation is up to the vendor. Knowing that it exists and knowing that its existence answers a lot of questions about how enterprise beans are structured, should be sufficient. Everything that any client (including other enterprise beans) really needs to know about any bean is described by the remote and home interfaces.

The EJB home

The EJB home is a lot like the EJB object. It's another class that's generated automatically when you install an enterprise bean in a container. It implements all the methods defined by the home interface and is responsible for helping the container in managing the bean's life cycle. Working closely with the EJB container, the EJB home is responsible for locating, creating, and removing enterprise beans. This may involve working with the EJB server's resource managers, instance pooling, and persistence mechanisms, the details of which are hidden from the developer.

For example, when a create method is invoked on the home interface, the EJB home creates an instance of the EJB object which references a bean instance of the appropriate type. Once the bean instance is associated with the EJB object, the instance's matching ejbCreate() method is called. In the case of an entity bean, a new record is inserted into the database. With session beans the instance is simply initialized. Once the ejbCreate() method has completed, the EJB home returns a remote reference (i.e., a stub) for the EJB object to the client. The client can then begin to work with the EJB object by invoking business methods using the stub. The stub relays the methods to the EJB object; in turn, the EJB object delegates those method calls to the bean instance.

Figure 2-2 illustrates the architecture of EJB with the EJB home and EJB object implementing the home interface and remote interface respectively. The bean class is also shown as being wrapped by the EJB object.

Deploying a bean

The EJB object and EJB home are generated during the deployment process. After the files that define the bean (the home interface, the remote interface, and the bean classes) have been packaged into a JAR file, the bean is ready to be deployed: that is, added to an EJB container so that it can be accessed as a distributed component. During the deployment process, tools provided by the EJB container vendor generate the EJB object and EJB home classes by examining the deployment descriptor and the other interfaces and classes in the JAR file.

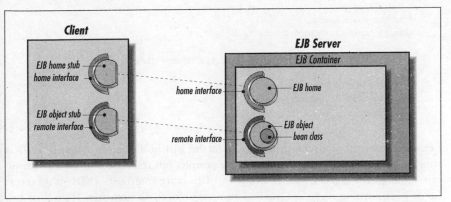

Figure 2-2. EJB architecture

Using Enterprise Beans

Now that you actually have a bean to work with, let's look at how a client would work with a bean to do something useful. We'll start with the Cabin bean that was defined earlier. A cabin is a thing or place whose description is stored in a database. To make the example a little bit more real, imagine that there are other entity beans, including a Ship, Cruise, Ticket, Passenger, Employee, and so on.

Getting Information from an Entity Bean

Imagine that a GUI client needs to display information about a particular cruise, including the cruise name, the ship name, and a list of cabins. Using the cruise ID obtained from a text field, we can use some of our beans to populate the GUI with data about the requested cruise. Here's what the code would look like:

```
CruiseHome cruiseHome = ... getCruiseHome();
// Get the cruise id from a text field.
String cruiseID = textFields1.getText();
// Create an EJB primary key from the cruise id.
CruisePrimaryKey pk = new CruisePrimaryKey(cruiseID);
// Use the primary key to find the cruise.
Cruise cruise = cruiseHome.findByPrimaryKey(pk);
// Set text field 2 to show the cruise name.
textField2.setText(cruise.getName());
// Get a remote reference to the ship that will be used
// for the cruise from the cruise bean.
Ship ship = cruise.getShip();
// Set text field 3 to show the ship's name.
textField3.setText(ship.getName());
```

```
// Get a list of all the cabins on the ship as remote references
// to the cabin beans.
Cabin [] cabins = ship.getCabins();

// Iterate through the enumeration, adding the name of each cabin
// to a list box.
for (int i = 0; i < cabins.length; i++){
    Cabin cabin = cabins[i];
    listBox1.addItem(cabin.getName());
}
```

Let's start by getting a remote reference to the EJB home for an entity bean that represents a cruise. It's not shown in the example, but references to the EJB home are obtained using JNDI. Java Naming and Directory Interface (JNDI) is a powerful API for locating resources, such as remote objects, on networks. It's a little too complicated to talk about here, but rest assured that it will be covered in subsequent chapters.

We read a cruise ID from a text field, use it to create a primary key, and use that primary key together with the EJB home to get a Cruise, the object that implements the business methods of our bean. Once we have the appropriate cruise, we can ask the cruise to give us the Ship that will be used for the cruise. We can then get a list of Cabins from the Ship and display the names of the Cabins in the client.

Entity beans model data and behavior. They provide a system with a reusable and consistent interface to data in the database. The behavior used in entity beans is usually focused on applying business rules that pertain directly to changing data. In addition, entity beans can model relationships with other entities. A ship, for example, has many cabins. We can get a list of cabins owned by the ship by invoking the ship.getCabins() method.

Entity beans are shared by many clients. An example is the Ship bean. The behavior and data associated with a Ship bean will be used concurrently by many clients on the system. There are only three ships in Titan's fleet, so it's easy to imagine that several clients will need to access these entities at the same time. Entity beans are designed to service multiple clients, providing fast, reliable access to data and behavior while protecting the integrity of data changes. Because entity beans are shared, we can rest assured that everyone is using the same entity and seeing the same data as it changes. In other words, we don't have duplicate entities with different representations of the same data.*

---

* This is dependent on the isolation level set on the bean's data, which is discussed in more detail in Chapter 8.

Modeling Workflow with Session Beans

Entity beans are useful for objectifying data and describing business concepts that can be expressed as nouns, but they're not very good at representing a process or a task. A Ship bean provides methods and behavior for doing things directly to a ship, but it does not define the context under which these actions are taken. The previous example retrieved data about cruises and ships; we could also have modified this data. And if we had gone to enough effort, we could have figured out how to book a passenger—perhaps by adding a Customer bean to a Cruise bean or adding a customer to a list of passengers maintained by the ship. We could try to shove methods for accepting payment and other tasks related to booking into our client application, or even into the Ship or Cabin beans, but that's a contrived and inappropriate solution. We don't want business logic in the client application—that's why we went to a multitier architecture in the first place. Similarly, we don't want this kind of logic in our entity beans that represent ships and cabins. Booking passengers on a ship or scheduling a ship for a cruise are the types of activities or functions of the business, not the Ship or the Cabin bean, and are therefore expressed in terms of a process or task.

Session beans act as agents for the client managing business processes or tasks; they're the appropriate place for business logic. A session bean is not persistent like an entity bean; nothing in a session bean maps directly into a database or is stored between sessions. Session beans work with entity beans, data, and other resources to control *workflow*. Workflow is the essence of any business system because it expresses how entities interact to model the actual business. Session beans control tasks and resources but do not themselves represent data.

The following code demonstrates how a session bean, designed to make cruise line reservations, might control the workflow of other entity and session beans to accomplish this task. Imagine that a piece of client software, in this case a user interface, obtains a remote reference to a TravelAgent session bean. Using the information entered into text fields by the user, the client application books a passenger on a cruise:

```
// Get the credit card number from the text field.
String creditCard = textField1.getText();
int cabinID = Integer.parseInt(textField2.getText());
int cruiseID = Integer.parseInt(textField3.getText());

// Create a new Reservation session passing in a reference to a
// customer entity bean.
TravelAgent travelAgent = TravelAgentHome.create(customer);

// Set cabin and cruise IDs.
travelAgent.setCabinID(cabinID);
travelAgent.setCruiseID(cruiseID);
```

```
// Using the card number and price, book passage.
// This method returns a Ticket object.
Ticket ticket = travelAgent.bookPassage(creditCard, price);
```

This is a fairly *coarse-grained* abstraction of the process of booking a passenger on a cruise. Coarse-grained means that most of the details of the booking process are hidden from the client. Hiding the *fine-grained* details of workflow is important because it provides us with more flexibility in how the system evolves and how clients are allowed to interact with the EJB system.

The following listing shows some of the code included in the `TravelAgentBean`. The `bookPassage()` method actually works with three entity beans, the Customer, Cabin, and Cruise beans, and another session bean, the ProcessPayment bean. The ProcessPayment bean provides several different methods for making a payment including check, cash, and credit card. In this case, we are using the ProcessPayment session to make a credit card purchase of a cruise ticket. Once payment has been made, a serializable `Ticket` object is created and returned to the client application.

```java
public class TravelAgentBean implements javax.ejb.SessionBean {

    public Customer customer;
    public Cruise cruise;
    public Cabin cabin;

    public void ejbCreate(Customer cust) {
        customer = cust;
    }
    public Ticket bookPassage(CreditCard card, double price)
        throws IncompleteConversationalState {
        // EJB 1.0: also throws RemoteException

        if (customer == null || cruise == null || cabin == null) {
            throw new IncompleteConversationalState();
        }
        try {
            ReservationHome resHome = (ReservationHome)
                getHome("ReservationHome",ReservationHome.class);
            Reservation reservation =
            resHome.create(customer, cruise, cabin,price);
            ProcessPaymentHome ppHome = (ProcessPaymentHome)
                getHome("ProcessPaymentHome",ProcessPaymentHome.class);
            ProcessPayment process = ppHome.create();
            process.byCredit(customer, card, price);

            Ticket ticket = new Ticket(customer,cruise,cabin,price);
            return ticket;
        } catch(Exception e){
```

```
        // EJB 1.0: throw new RemoteException("",e);
        throw new EJBException(e);
    }
}

// More business methods and EJB state management methods follow.
}
```

This example leaves out some details, but it demonstrates the difference in purpose between a session bean and an entity bean. Entity beans represent the behavior and data of a business object, while session beans model the workflow of beans. The client application uses the TravelAgent bean to perform a task using other beans. For example, the TravelAgent bean uses a ProcessPayment bean and a Reservation bean in the process of booking a passage. The ProcessPayment bean processes a credit card and the Reservation bean records the actual reservation in the system. Session beans can also be used to read, update, and delete data that can't be adequately captured in an entity bean. Session beans don't represent records or data in the database like entity beans but can access data in the database.

All the work performed by TravelAgent session bean could have been coded in the client application. Having the client interact directly with entity beans is a common but troublesome design approach because it ties the client directly to the details of the business tasks. This is troublesome for two reasons: any change in the entity beans and their interaction require changes to the client, and it's very difficult to reuse the code that models the workflow.

Session beans are coarse-grained components that allow clients to perform tasks without being concerned with the details that make up the task. This allows developers to update the session bean, possibly changing the workflow, without impacting the client code. In addition, if the session bean is properly defined, other clients that perform the same tasks can reuse it. The ProcessPayment session bean, for example, can be reused in many other areas besides reservations, including retail and wholesale sales. For example, the ship's gift shop could use the ProcessPayment bean to process purchases. As a client of the ProcessPayment bean, the TravelAgent bean doesn't care how ProcessPayment works; it's only interested in the ProcessPayment bean's coarse-grained interface, which validates and records charges.

Moving workflow logic into a session bean also helps to thin down the client applications and reduce network traffic and connections. Excessive network traffic is actually one of the biggest problems in distributed object systems. Excessive traffic can overwhelm the server and clog the network, hurting response times and performance. Session beans, if used properly, can substantially reduce network traffic by limiting the number of requests needed to perform a task. In distributed objects, every method invocation produces network traffic. Distributed objects communicate requests using an RMI loop. This requires that data be streamed between the stub and skeleton with every method invocation. With session beans, the interaction of beans in a workflow is kept on the server. One method invocation on the client application results in many method invocations on the server, but the network only sees the traffic produced by one method call on the session bean. In the TravelAgent bean, the client invokes bookPassage(), but on the server, the bookPassage() method produces several method invocations on the home interface and remote interface of other beans. For the network cost of one method invocation, the client gets several method invocations.

In addition, session beans reduce the number of network connections needed by the client. The cost of maintaining many network connections can be very high, so reducing the number of connections that each client needs is important in improving the performance of the system as a whole. When session beans are used to manage workflow, the number of connections that each client has to the server is substantially reduced, which improves the EJB server's performance. Figure 2-3 compares the network traffic and connections used by a client that only uses entity beans to that used by a client that uses session beans.

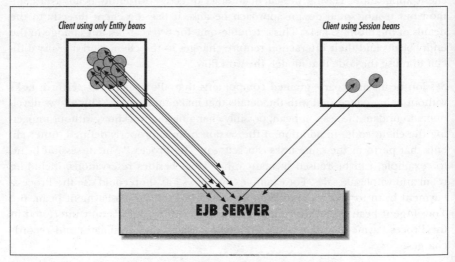

Figure 2-3. Session beans reduce network traffic and thin down clients

Session beans also limit the number of stubs used on the client, which saves the client memory and processing cycles. This may not seem like a big deal, but without the use of session beans, a client might be expected to manage hundreds or even thousands of remote references at one time. In the TravelAgent bean, for example, the bookPassage() method works with several remote references, but the client is only exposed to the remote reference of the TravelAgent bean.

Stateless and stateful session beans

Session beans can be either stateful or stateless. Stateful session beans maintain *conversational state* when used by a client. Conversational state is not written to a database; it's state that is kept in memory while a client uses a session. Maintaining conversational state allows a client to carry on a conversation with a bean. As each method on the bean is invoked, the state of the session bean may change, and that change can affect subsequent method calls. The TravelAgent session bean, for example, may have many more methods than the bookPassage() method. The methods that set the cabin and cruise IDs are examples. These set methods are responsible for modifying conversational state. They convert the IDs into remote references to Cabin and Cruise beans that are later used in the bookPassage() method. Conversational state is only kept for as long as the client application is actively using the bean. Once the client shuts down or releases the TravelAgent bean, the conversational state is lost forever. Stateful session beans are not shared among clients; they are dedicated to the same client for the life of the bean.

Stateless session beans do not maintain any conversational state. Each method is completely independent and uses only data passed in its parameters. The Process-Payment bean is a perfect example of a stateless session bean. The ProcessPayment bean doesn't need to maintain any conversational state from one method invocation to the next. All the information needed to make a payment is passed into the byCreditCard() method. Stateless session beans provide the highest performance in terms of throughput and resource consumption of all the bean types because few stateless session bean instances are needed to serve hundreds, possibly thousands of clients. Chapter 7 talks more about the use of stateless session beans.

The Bean-Container Contract

The environment that surrounds the beans on the EJB server is often referred to as the *container*. The container is more a concept than a physical construct. Conceptually, the container acts as an intermediary between the bean class and the EJB server. The container manages the EJB objects and EJB homes for a particular type of bean and helps these constructs to manage bean resources and apply primary services like transactions, security, concurrency, naming, and so forth, to the bean instances at runtime. Conceptually, an EJB server may have many containers, each of which may contain one or more types of enterprise beans. As you will discover a little later, the container and the server are not clearly different constructs, but the EJB specification defines the component model in terms of the container responsibilities, so we will follow that convention here.

Enterprise bean components interface with the EJB server through a well-defined component model. The EntityBean and SessionBean interfaces are the bases of this component model. As we learned earlier, these interfaces provide callback methods that notify the bean class of state management events in its life cycle. At runtime, the container invokes the callback methods on the bean instance when appropriate state management events occur. When the container is about to write an entity bean instance's state to the database, for example, it first calls the bean instance's ejbStore() method. This provides the bean instance with an opportunity to do some clean up on its state just before it's written to the database. The ejbLoad() method is called just after the bean's state is populated from the database, providing the bean developer with an opportunity to manage the bean's state before the first business method is called.* Other callback methods can be used by the bean class in a similar fashion. EJB defines when these various callback methods are invoked and what can be done within their context. This provides the bean developer with a predictable runtime component model.

While all the callback methods are declared in bean interfaces, a meaningful implementation of the methods is not mandatory. In other words, the method body of any or all of the callback methods can be left empty in the bean class. Beans that implement one or more callback methods are usually more sophisticated and access resources that are not managed by the EJB system. Enterprise beans that wrap legacy systems often fall into this category.

javax.ejb.EJBContext is an interface that is implemented by the container and is also a part of the bean-container contract. Entity type beans use a subclass of javax.ejb.EJBContext called javax.ejb.EntityContext. Session beans use a subclass called the javax.ejb.SessionContext. These EJBContext types provide the bean class with information about its container, the client using the bean, and the bean itself. They also provide other functionality that is described in more detail in Chapters 6 and 7. The important thing about the EJBContext types is that they provide the bean with information about the world around it, which the bean can use while processing requests from both clients and callback methods from the container.

NOTE   EJB 1.1 has expanded the bean's interface with the container to include a JNDI name space, called the environment context, which provides the bean with a more flexible and extensible bean-container interface. The JNDI environment context is discussed in detail later in this book.

---

* The ejbLoad() and ejbStore() behavior illustrated here is for container-managed persistence. With bean-managed persistence the behavior is slightly different. This is examined in detail in Chapter 6.

The Container-Server Contract

The container-server contract is not defined by the Enterprise JavaBeans specification. This was done to facilitate maximum flexibility for vendors defining their EJB server technologies. Other than isolating the beans from the server, the container's responsibility in the EJB system is a little vague. The EJB specification only defines a bean-container contract and does not define the container-server contract. It is difficult to determine, for example, exactly where the container ends and the server begins when it comes to resource management and other services.

In the first generation of EJB servers this ambiguity was not a problem because most EJB server vendors also provide EJB containers. Since the vendor provides both the container and the server, the interface between the two can remain proprietary. In future generations of the EJB specification, however, some work may be done to define the container-server interface and delimit the responsibilities of the container.

One advantage of defining a container-server interface is that it allows third-party vendors to produce containers that can plug into any EJB server. If the responsibilities of the container and server are clearly defined, then vendors who specialize in the technologies that support these different responsibilities can focus on developing the container or server as best matches their core competency. The disadvantage of a clearly defined container-server interface is that the plug-and-play approach could impact performance. The high level of abstraction that would be required to clearly separate the container interface from the server, would naturally lead to looser binding between these large components, which always results in lower performance. The following rule of thumb best describes the advantages and disadvantages associated with a container-server interface: the tighter the integration, the better the performance; the higher the abstraction, the greater the flexibility. The biggest deterrent to defining a container-server interface is that it would require the definition of low-level facilities, which was one of the problems that established CTM vendors had with CORBA. Allowing vendors to implement low-level facilities like transactions and security as they see fit is one of EJB's biggest attractions for vendors.

Many EJB-compliant servers actually support several different kinds of middleware technologies. It's quite common, for example, for an EJB server to support the vendor's proprietary CTM model as well as EJB, servlets, web server functionality, and other server technologies. Defining an EJB container concept is useful for clearly distinguishing what part of the server supports EJB from all the other services it provides.

This said, we could define the responsibilities of containers and servers based on current implementations of the EJB specification. In other words, we could examine how current vendors are defining the container in their servers and use this as a guide. Unfortunately, the responsibilities of the container in each EJB server largely depend on the core competency of the vendor in question. Database vendors, for example, implement containers differently from TP monitor vendors. The strategies for assigning responsibilities to the container and server are so varied that it would provide little value in understanding the overall architecture to discuss the container and server separately. Instead, this book addresses the architecture of the EJB system as if the container and server were one component.

The remainder of this book treats the EJB server and the container as the same thing and refers to them collectively as the EJB server, container, system, or environment.

Summary

This chapter covered a lot of ground describing the basic architecture of an EJB system. At this point you should understand that beans are business object components. The home interface defines life-cycle methods for creating, finding, and destroying beans and the remote interface defines the public business methods of the bean. The bean class is where the state and behavior of the bean are implemented.

There are two basic kinds of beans: session and entity. Entity beans are persistent and represent a person, place, or thing. Session beans are extensions of the client and embody a process or a workflow that defines how other beans interact. Session beans are not persistent, receiving their state from the client, and they live only as long as the client needs them.

The EJB object and EJB home are conceptual constructs that delegate method invocations to the bean class from the client and help the container to manage the bean class. The client does not interact with the bean directly. Instead, the client software interacts with EJBObject and EJBHome stubs, which are connected to the EJB object and EJB homes respectively. The EJB object implements the remote interface and expands the bean class's functionality. The EJB home implements the home interface and works closely with the container to create, locate, and remove beans.

Beans interact with their container through the well-defined bean-container contract. This contract provides callback methods, the EJBContext, and the JNDI environment context (EJB 1.1 only). The callback methods notify the bean class that it is involved in state management event. The EJBContext and JNDI environment context provides the bean instance with information about its environment. The container-server contract is not well defined and remains proprietary at this time. Future versions of EJB may specify the container-server contract.

3

Resource
Management and the
Primary Services

Chapter 2 discussed the basic architecture of Enterprise JavaBeans (EJB), including the relationship between the bean class, remote interfaces, the EJB object and EJB home, and the EJB server. These architectural components define a common model for distributed server-side components in component transaction monitors (CTMs).

One of the reasons CTMs are such great distributed object platforms is that they do more than just distribute objects: they manage the resources used by distributed objects. CTMs are designed to manage thousands, even millions, of distributed objects simultaneously. To be this robust, CTMs must be very smart resource managers, managing how distributed objects use memory and processing power. EJB recognizes that some of the resource management techniques employed by CTMs are very common, and it defines interfaces that help developers create beans that can take advantage of these common practices.

EJB CTMs are also great distributed object brokers. Not only do they help clients locate the distributed objects they need, they also provide many services that make it much easier for a client to use the objects correctly. CTMs commonly support six primary services: concurrency, transaction management, persistence, object distribution, naming, and security. These services provide the kind of infrastructure that is necessary for a successful three-tier system.

This chapter discusses both the resource management facilities and the primary services that are available to Enterprise JavaBeans.

Resource Management

One of the fundamental benefits of using EJB servers is that they are able to handle heavy workloads while maintaining a high level of performance. A large business system with many users can easily require thousands of objects—even millions of objects—to be in use simultaneously. As the number of interactions among these objects increase, concurrency and transactional concerns can degrade the system's response time and frustrate users. EJB servers increase performance by synchronizing object interactions and sharing resources.

There is a relationship between the number of clients connected and the number of distributed objects that are required to service them. As client populations increase, the number of distributed objects and resources required increases. At some point, the increase in the number of clients will impact performance and diminish throughput. EJB explicitly supports two mechanisms that make it easier to manage large numbers of beans at runtime: instance pooling and activation.

Instance Pooling

The concept of pooling resources is nothing new. A commonly used technique is to pool database connections so that the business objects in the system can share database access. This trick reduces the number of connections needed, which reduces resource consumption and increases throughput. Pooling and reusing database connections is less expensive than creating and destroying connections as needed. Some CTMs also apply resource pooling to server-side components; this technique is called *instance pooling*. Instance pooling reduces the number of component instances, and therefore resources, needed to service client requests. In addition, it is less expensive to reuse pooled instances than to frequently create and destroy instances.

As you already know, EJB clients interact with the remote interfaces that are implemented by EJB objects. Client applications never have direct access to the actual bean. Instead, they interact with EJB objects, which wrap bean instances. Instance pooling leverages indirect access to beans to provide better performance. In other words, since clients never access beans directly, there's no fundamental reason to keep a separate copy of each bean for each client. The server can keep a much smaller number of beans around to do the work, copying data into or out of them as needed. Although this sounds like a resource drain, when done correctly, it greatly reduces the resources actually required at any one time.

The entity bean life cycle

To understand how instance pooling works, let's examine the life cycle of an entity bean. EJB defines the life cycle of an entity bean in terms of its relationship to the instance pool. An entity bean exists in one of three states:

No state

When a bean instance is in this state, it has not been instantiated yet. We identify this state to provide a beginning and an end for the life cycle of a bean instance.

Pooled state

When an instance is in the pooled state, it has been instantiated by the container but has not yet been associated with an EJB object.

Ready State

A bean instance in this state has been associated with an EJB object and is ready to respond to business method invocations.

Overview of state transitions

Each EJB vendor implements instance pooling for entity beans differently, but all instance pooling strategies attempt to manage collections of bean instances so that they are quickly accessible at runtime. To create an instance pool, the EJB container creates several instances of a bean class and then holds onto them until they are needed. As clients make business method requests, bean instances from the pool are assigned to the EJB objects associated with the clients. When the EJB object doesn't need the instance any more, it's returned to the instance pool. An EJB server maintains instance pools for every type of bean deployed. Every instance in an instance pool is *equivalent*; they are all treated equally. Instances are selected arbitrarily from the instance pool and assigned to EJB objects as needed.

Soon after the bean instance is instantiated and placed in the pool, it's given a reference to a javax.ejb.EJBContext provided by the container. The EJBContext provides an interface that the bean can use to communicate with the EJB environment. This EJBContext becomes more useful when the bean instance moves to the Ready State.

NOTE   EJB 1.1 has extended the bean's interface with its environment to include a JNDI context called the environment context. The function of the environment context in EJB 1.1 is not critical to this discussion and will be addressed in more detail later in the chapter.

When a client uses an EJB home to obtain a remote interface to a bean, the container responds by creating an EJB object. Once created, the EJB object is assigned a bean instance from the instance pool. When a bean instance is assigned to an EJB object, it officially enters the Ready State. From the Ready State, a bean instance can receive requests from the client and callbacks from the container. Figure 3-1 shows the sequence of events that result in an EJB object wrapping a bean instance and servicing a client.

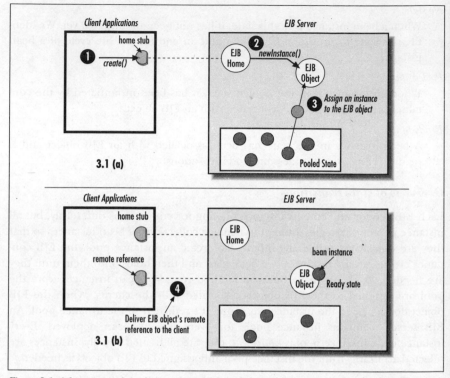

Figure 3-1. A bean moves from the instance pool to the Ready State

When a bean instance moves into the Ready State, the EntityContext takes on new meaning. The EntityContext provides information about the client that is using the bean. It also provides the instance with access to its own EJB home and EJB object, which is useful when the bean needs to pass references to itself to other instances, or when it needs to create, locate, or remove beans of its own class. So the EntityContext is not a static class; it is an interface to the container and its state changes as the instance is assigned to different EJB objects.

When the client is finished with a bean's remote reference, either the remote reference passes out of scope or one of the bean's remove methods is called.* Once a bean has been removed or is no longer in scope, the bean instance is disassociated from the EJB object and returned to the instance pool. Bean instances can also be returned to the instance pool during lulls between client requests. If a client request is received and no bean instance is associated with the EJB object, an

---

* Both the EJBHome and the EJBObject interfaces define methods that can be used to remove a bean.

instance is retrieved from the pool and assigned to the EJB object. This is called *instance swapping.*

After the bean instance returns to the instance pool, it is again available to service a new client request. Figure 3-2 illustrates the complete life cycle of a bean instance.

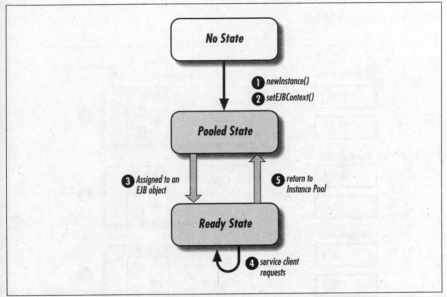

Figure 3-2. Life cycle of a bean instance

The number of instances in the pool fluctuates as instances are assigned to EJB objects and returned to the pool. The container can also manage the number of instances in the pool, increasing the count when client activity increases and lowering the count during less active periods.

Instance swapping

Stateless session beans offer a particularly powerful opportunity to leverage instance pooling. A stateless session bean does not maintain any state between method invocations. Every method invocation on a stateless session bean operates independently, performing its task without relying on instance variables. This means that any stateless session instance can service requests for any EJB object of the proper type, allowing the container to swap bean instances in and out between method invocations made by the client.

Figure 3-3 illustrates this type of instance swapping between method invocations. In Figure 3-3(a), instance A is servicing a business method invocation delegated by EJB object 1. Once instance A has serviced the request, it moves back to the instance pool (Figure 3-3(b)). When a business method invocation on EJB object 2 is received, instance A is associated with that EJB object for the duration of the operation (Figure 3-3(c)). While instance A is servicing EJB object 2, another method invocation is received by EJB object 1 from the client, which is serviced by instance B (Figure 3-3(d)).

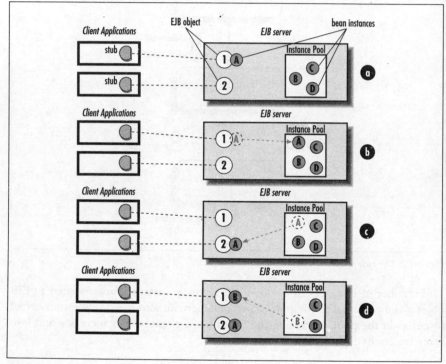

Figure 3-3. Stateless session beans in a swapping strategy

Using this swapping strategy allows a few stateless session bean instances to serve hundreds of clients. This is possible because the amount of time it takes to perform most method invocations is substantially shorter than the pauses between method invocations. The periods in a bean instance's life when it is not actively servicing the EJB object are unproductive; instance pooling minimizes these inactive periods. When a bean instance is finished servicing a request for an EJB object, it is immediately made available to any other EJB object that needs it. This allows fewer stateless session instances to service more requests, which decreases resource consumption and improves performance.

Stateless session beans are declared stateless in the deployment descriptor. Nothing in the class definition of a session bean is specific to being stateless. Once a bean class is deployed as stateless, the container assumes that no conversational state is maintained between method invocations. So a stateless bean can have instance variables, but because bean instances can be servicing several different EJB objects, they should not be used to maintain conversational state.

Implementations of instance pooling vary, depending on the vendor. One way that instance pooling implementations often differ is in how instances are selected from the pool. Two of the common strategies are FIFO and LIFO. The FIFO (first in, first out) strategy places instances in a queue, where they wait in line to service EJB objects. The LIFO (last in, first out) uses more of stack strategy, where the last bean that was added to the stack is the first bean assigned to the next EJB object. Figure 3-3 uses a LIFO strategy.

The Activation Mechanism

Unlike stateless session beans, stateful session beans maintain state between method invocations. This is called *conversational state* because it represents the continuing conversation with the stateful session bean's client. The integrity of this conversational state needs to be maintained for the life of the bean's service to the client. Stateful session beans do not participate in instance pooling like stateless session beans and entity beans. Instead, activation is used with stateful session beans to conserve resources. When an EJB server needs to conserve resources, it can evict stateful session beans from memory. This reduces the number of instances maintained by the system. To passivate the bean and preserve its conversational state, the bean's state is serialized to a secondary storage and maintained relative to its EJB object. When a client invokes a method on the EJB object, a new stateful instance is instantiated and populated from the passivated secondary storage.

Passivation is the act of disassociating a stateful bean instance from its EJB object and saving its state. Passivation requires that the bean instance's state be held relative to its EJB object. After the bean has been passivated, it is safe to remove the bean instance from the EJB object and evict it from memory. Clients are completely unaware of the deactivation process. Remember that the client uses the bean's remote interface, which is implemented by an EJB object, and therefore does not directly communicate with the bean instance. As a result, the client's connection to the EJB object can be maintained while the bean is passivated.

Activating a bean is the act of restoring a stateful bean instance's state relative to its EJB object. When a method on the passivated EJB object is invoked, the container automatically instantiates a new instance and sets its fields equal to the data stored during passivation. The EJB object can then delegate the method invocation to the bean as normal. Figure 3-4 shows activation and passivation of a stateful bean. In Figure 3-4(a), the bean is being passivated. The state of instance B is read and held relative to the EJB object it was serving. In Figure 3-4(b), the bean has been passivated and its state preserved. Here, the EJB object is not associated with a bean instance. In Figure 3-4(c), the bean is being activated. A new instance, instance C, has been instantiated and associated with the EJB object, and is in the process of having its state populated. The instance C is populated with the state held relative to the EJB object.

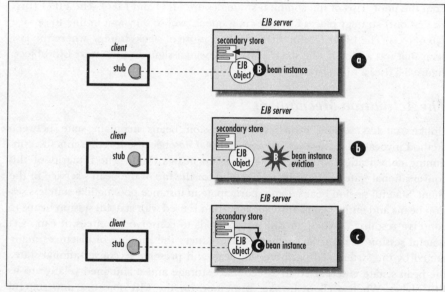

Figure 3-4. The activation process

The exact mechanism for activating and passivating stateful beans is up to the vendor, but all stateful beans are serializable and thus provide at least one way of temporarily preserving their state. While some vendors take advantage of the Java serialization mechanism, the exact mechanism for preserving the conversational state is not specified. As long as the mechanism employed follows the same rules as Java serialization with regard to transitive closure of serializable objects, any mechanism is legal. Because Enterprise JavaBeans also supports other ways of saving a bean's state, the transient property is not treated the same when activating a passivated bean as it is in Java serialization. In Java serialization, transient fields are always set back to the initial value for that field type when the object is deserialized. Integers are set to zero, Booleans to `false`, object references to `null`, etc. In EJB, transient fields are not necessarily set back to their initial values but can maintain their original values, or any arbitrary value, after being activated. Care should be taken when using transient fields, since their state following activation is implementation specific.

The activation process is supported by the state-management callback methods discussed in Chapter 2. Specifically, the `ejbActivate()` and `ejbPassivate()` methods notify the stateful bean instance that it is about to be activated or passivated, respectively. The `ejbActivate()` method is called immediately following the successful activation of a bean instance and can be used to reset transient fields to an initial value if necessary. The `ejbPassivate()` method is called immediately prior to passivation of the bean instance. These two methods are especially helpful if the bean instance maintains connections to resources that need to be manipulated or freed prior to passivation and reobtained following activation. Because the stateful bean instance is evicted from memory, open connections to resources are not maintained. The exceptions are remote references to other beans and the `SessionContext`, which must be maintained with the serialized state of the bean and reconstructed when the bean is activated.

NOTE   EJB 1.1 also requires that the references to the JNDI environment context, home interfaces, and the UserTransaction be maintained through passivation.

Entity beans do not have conversational state that needs to be serialized like stateful beans; instead, the state of entity bean instances is persisted directly to the database. Entity beans do, however, leverage the activation callback methods (`ejbActivate()` and `ejbPassivate()`) to notify the instance when it's about to be swapped in or out of the instance pool. The `ejbActivate()` method is invoked immediately after the bean instance is swapped into the EJB object, and the `ejbPassivate()` method is invoked just before the instance is swapped out.

Primary Services

There are many value-added services available for distributed applications. The OMG (the CORBA governing body), for example, has defined 13 of these services for use in CORBA-compliant ORBs. This book looks at six value-added services that are called the *primary services*, because they are required to create an effective CTM. The primary services include concurrency, transactions, persistence, distributed objects, naming, and security.

The six primary services are not new concepts; the OMG defined interfaces for a most of them in CORBA some time ago. In most traditional CORBA ORBs, services are add-on subsystems that are explicitly utilized by the application code. This means that the server-side component developer has to write code to use primary service APIs right alongside their business logic. The use of primary services becomes complicated when they are used in combination with resource management techniques because the primary services are themselves complex. Using them in combination only compounds the problem.

As more complex component interactions are discovered, coordinating these services becomes a difficult task, requiring system-level expertise unrelated to the task of writing the application's business logic. Application developers can become so mired in the system-level concerns of coordinating various primary services and resource management mechanisms that their main responsibility, modeling the business, is all but forgotten.

EJB servers automatically manage all the primary services. This relieves the application developers from the task of mastering these complicated services. Instead, developers can focus on defining the business logic that describes the system, and leave the system-level concerns to the CTM. The following sections describe each of the primary services and explain how they are supported by EJB.

Concurrency

Session beans do not support concurrent access. This makes sense if you consider the nature of both stateful and stateless session beans. A stateful bean is an extension of one client and only serves that client. It doesn't make sense to make stateful beans concurrent if they are only used by the client that created them. Stateless session beans don't need to be concurrent because they don't maintain state that needs to be shared. The scope of the operations performed by a stateless bean is limited to the scope of each method invocation. No conversational state is maintained.

Entity beans represent data in the database that is shared and needs to be accessed concurrently. Entity beans are shared components. In Titan's EJB system, for example, there are only three ships: *Paradise*, *Utopia*, and *Valhalla*. At any given moment the Ship entity bean that represents the *Utopia* might be accessed by hundreds of clients. To make concurrent access to entity beans possible, EJB needs to protect the data represented by the shared bean, while allowing many clients to access the bean simultaneously.

In a distributed object system, problems arise when you attempt to share distributed objects among clients. If two clients are both using the same EJB object, how do you keep one client from writing over the changes of the other? If, for example, one client reads the state of an instance just before a different client makes a change to the same instance, the data that the first client read becomes invalid. Figure 3-5 shows two clients sharing the same EJB object.

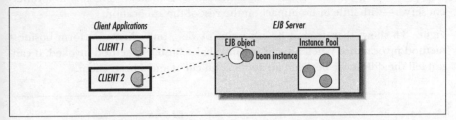

Figure 3-5. Clients sharing access to an EJB object

EJB has addressed the dangers associated with concurrency by implementing a simple solution: EJB, by default, prohibits concurrent access to bean instances. In other words, several clients can be connected to one EJB object, but only one client thread can access the bean instance at a time. If, for example, one of the clients invokes a method on the EJB object, no other client can access that bean instance until the method invocation is complete. In fact, if the method is part of a larger transaction, then the bean instance cannot be accessed at all, except within the same transactional context, until the entire transaction is complete.

Since EJB servers handle concurrency automatically, a bean's methods do not have to be made thread-safe. In fact, the EJB specification prohibits use of the synchronized keyword. Prohibiting the use of the thread synchronization primitives prevents developers from thinking that they control synchronization and enhances the performance of bean instances at runtime. In addition, EJB explicitly prohibits beans from creating their own threads. In other words, as a bean developer you cannot create a thread within a bean. The EJB container has to maintain complete control over the bean to properly manage concurrency, transactions, and persistence. Allowing the bean developer to create arbitrary threads would compromise the container's ability to track what the bean is doing, and thus would make it impossible for the container to manage the primary services.

Reentrance

When talking about concurrency, we need to discuss the related concept of reentrance. Reentrance is when a thread of control attempts to reenter a bean instance. In EJB, bean instances are nonreentrant by default, which means that loopbacks are not allowed. Before I explain what a loopback is, it is important that you understand a very fundamental concept in EJB: enterprise beans interact using each other's remote references and do not interact directly. In other words, when bean A operates on bean B, it does so the same way an application client would, by using B's remote interface as implemented by an EJB object. This rule enforces complete location transparency. Because interactions with beans always take place using remote references, beans can be relocated—possibly to a different server—with little or no impact on the rest of the application.

Figure 3-6 shows that, from a bean's point of view, only clients perform business method invocations. When a bean instance has a business method invoked, it cannot tell the difference between an application client and a bean client.

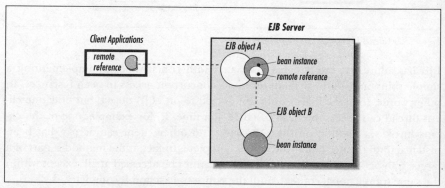

Figure 3-6. Beans access each other through EJB objects

A loopback occurs when bean A invokes a method on bean B that then attempts to make a call back to bean A. Figure 3-7 shows this type of interaction. In Figure 3-7, client 1 invokes a method on bean A. In response to the method invocation, bean A invokes a method on bean B. At this point, there is no problem because client 1 controls access to bean A and bean A is the client of bean B. If, however, bean B attempts to call a method on bean A, it would be blocked because the thread has already entered bean A. By calling its caller, bean B is performing a loopback. This is illegal by default because EJB doesn't allow a thread of control to reenter a bean instance. To say that beans are nonreentrant by default is to say that loopbacks are not allowed.

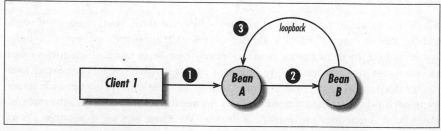

Figure 3-7. A loopback scenario

The nonreentrance policy is applied differently to session beans and entity beans. Session beans can never be reentrant, and they throw a `RemoteException` if a loopback is attempted. The same is true of a nonreentrant entity bean. Entity beans can be configured in the deployment descriptor to allow reentrance at deployment time. Making an entity bean reentrant, however, is discouraged by the specification.

As discussed previously, client access to a bean is synchronized so that only one client can access any given bean at one time. Reentrance addresses a thread of control—initiated by a client request—that attempts to reaccess a bean instance. The problem with reentrant code is that the EJB object—which intercepts and delegates method invocations on the bean instance—cannot differentiate between reentrant code and multithreaded access from the same client with the same transactional context. (More about transactional context in Chapter 8.) If you permit reentrance, you also permit multithreaded access to the bean instance. Multithreaded access to a bean instance can result in corrupted data because threads impact each other's work trying to accomplish their separate tasks.

It's important to remember that reentrant code is different from a bean instance that simply invokes its own methods at an instance level. In other words, method `foo()` on a bean instance can invoke its own public, protected, default, or private methods directly as much as it wants. Here is an example of intra-instance method invocation that is perfectly legal:

```
public HypotheticalBean extends EntityBean {
    public int x;

    public double foo() {
        int i = this.getX();
        return this.boo(i);
    }
    public int getX() {
        return x;
    }
    private double boo(int i) {
        double value = i * Math.PI;
        return value;
    }
}
```

In the previous code fragment, the business method, `foo()`, invokes another business method, `getX()`, and then a private method, `boo()`. The method invocations made within the body of `foo()` are intra-instance invocations and are not considered reentrant.

Transactions

Component transaction monitors (CTMs) were developed to bring the robust,
scalable transactional integrity of traditional TP monitors to the dynamic world of
distributed objects. Enterprise JavaBeans, as a server-side component model for
CTMs, provides robust support for transactions.

A transaction is a unit-of-work or a set of tasks that are executed together. Transactions are atomic; in other words, *all* the tasks in a transaction must be completed
together to consider the transaction a success. In the previous chapter we used the
TravelAgent bean to describe how a session bean controls the interactions of other
beans. Here is a code snippet showing the bookPassage() method described in
Chapter 2:

```
public Ticket bookPassage(CreditCard card, double price)
throws IncompleteConversationalState { // EJB 1.0: also throws RemoteException

    if (customer == null || cruise == null || cabin == null) {
        throw new IncompleteConversationalState();
    }
    try {
        ReservationHome resHome = (ReservationHome)
            getHome("ReservationHome",ReservationHome.class);
        Reservation reservation =
        resHome.create(customer, cruise, cabin, price);
        ProcessPaymentHome ppHome = (ProcessPaymentHome)
            getHome("ProcessPaymentHome",ProcessPaymentHome.class);
        ProcessPayment process = ppHome.create();
        process.byCredit(customer, card, price);

        Ticket ticket = new Ticket(customer, cruise, cabin, price);
        return ticket;
    } catch(Exception e) {
        // EJB 1.0: throw new RemoteException("",e);
        throw new EJBException(e);
    }
}
```

The bookPassage() method consists of two tasks that must be completed
together: the creation of a new Reservation bean and processing of the payment.
When the TravelAgent bean is used to book a passenger, the charges to the passenger's credit card and the creation of the reservation must both be successful. It
would be inappropriate for the ProcessPayment bean to charge the customer's
credit card if the creation of a new Reservation bean fails. Likewise, you can't
make a reservation if the customer credit card is not charged. An EJB server monitors the transaction to ensure that all the tasks are completed successfully.

Transactions are managed automatically, so as a bean developer you don't need to use any APIs to explicitly manage a bean's involvement in a transaction. Simply declaring the transactional attribute at deployment time tells the EJB server how to manage the bean at runtime. EJB does provide a mechanism that allows beans to manage transactions explicitly, if necessary. Setting the transactional attributes during deployment is discussed in Chapter 8, as is explicit management of transactions and other transactional topics.

Persistence

Entity beans represent the behavior and data associated with real-world people, places, or things. Unlike session type beans, entity beans are persistent. That means that the state of an entity is stored permanently in a database. This allows entities to be durable so that both their behavior and data can be accessed at any time without concern that the information will be lost because of a system failure.

When a bean's state is automatically managed by a persistence service, the container is responsible for synchronizing an entity bean's instance fields with the data in the database. This automatic persistence is called *container-managed* persistence. When beans are designed to manage their own state, as is often the case when dealing with legacy systems, it is called *bean-managed* persistence.

Each vendor gets to choose the exact mechanism for implementing container-managed persistence, but the vendor's implementation must support the EJB callback methods and transactions. The most common mechanisms used in persistence by EJB vendors are *object-to-relational persistence* and *object database persistence*.

Object-to-relational persistence

Object-to-relational persistence is perhaps the most common persistence mechanism used in distributed object systems today. Object-to-relational persistence involves mapping entity bean fields to relational database tables and columns. An entity bean's fields represent its state. In Titan's system, for example, the CabinBean models the business concept of a ship's cabin. The following code shows an abbreviated definition of the CabinBean:

```
public class CabinBean implements javax.ejb.EntityBean {
    public int id;
    public String name;
    public int deckLevel;

    // Business and component-level methods follow.
}
```

With object-to-relational database mapping, the variable fields of an entity bean correspond to columns in a relational database. The Cabin's name, for example, maps to the column labeled NAME in a table called CABIN in Titan's relational database. Figure 3-8 shows a graphical depiction of this type of mapping.

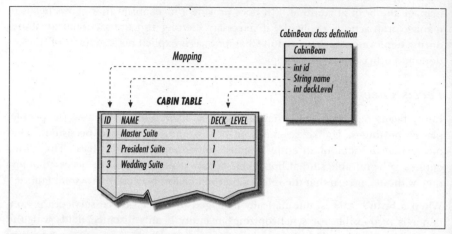

Figure 3-8. Object-to-relational mapping of entity beans

Really good EJB systems provide wizards or administrative interfaces for mapping relational database tables to the fields of entity bean classes. Using these wizards, mapping entities to tables is a fairly straightforward process and is usually performed at deployment time. Figure 3-9 shows WebLogic's object-to-relational mapping wizard.

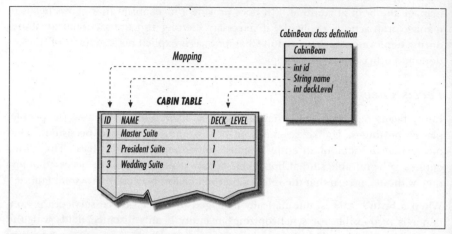

Figure 3-9. Object-to-relational mapping wizard

Once a bean's fields are mapped to the relational database, the container takes over the responsibility of keeping the state of an entity bean instance consistent with the corresponding tables in the database. This process is called *synchronizing* the state of the bean instance. In the case of CabinBean, bean instances at run-time will map one-to-one to rows in the CABIN table of the relational database. When a change is made to a Cabin bean, it is written to the appropriate row in the database. Frequently, bean types will map to more than one table. These are more complicated mappings, often requiring an SQL join. Good EJB deployment tools should provide wizards that make multitable mappings fairly easy.

In addition to synchronizing the state of an entity, EJB provides mechanisms for creating and removing entities. Calls to the EJB home to create and remove enti-ties will result in a corresponding insertion or deletion of records in the database. Because entities store their state in database tables, new records (and therefore bean identities) can be added to tables from outside the EJB system. In other words, inserting a record into the CABIN table—whether done by EJB or by direct access to the database—creates a new Cabin entity. It's not created in the sense of instantiating a Java object, but in the sense that the data that describes a Cabin entity has been added to the system.

Object-to-relational persistence can become very complex because objects don't always map cleanly to a relational database. Although you can specify any Java seri-alizable type as a container-managed field, Java objects don't always map seam-lessly to a relational database. You frequently need to convert Java types to some nonobject type just prior to synchronization so that the data can be stored in a relational database. Techniques for handling these types of problems are described in more detail in Chapter 9.

NOTE   EJB 1.1 allows the container-managed fields to include remote refer-
            ences to EJB objects (remote interface types) and EJB homes (home
            interface types). EJB 1.0 allows only Java primitives and serializable
            types as container-managed fields. While the ability to store an EJB
            reference in a container-managed field makes it much easier to
            model relationships between entity beans, it has made persistence
            more complicated for vendors. In EJB 1.1, the container must con-
            vert any container-managed field that holds a remote or home inter-
            face reference into a serializable primary key or handle. We'll learn
            more about container-managed fields in Chapter 6.

There are many other impedance mismatches when mapping object-to-relational databases, and some EJB vendor implementations deal with them better than oth-ers. Relational databases, however, are still a very good persistence store because they are stable and well-understood. There is no shortage of developers who understand them or products that support them. In addition, the large number c SQL-standard relational databases makes it fairly easy to migrate from one dat: base to another.

Object database persistence

Object-oriented databases are designed to preserve object types and object graph and therefore are a much better match for components written in an objec oriented language like Java. They offer a cleaner mapping between entity bean and the database than a traditional relational database. Serializable objects can b preserved without the mismatch associated with object-to-relational persistenc because the object's definition and state are simply saved *as is* to the database. Nc only are the object's definition and state saved to the database, complex relatior ships such as circular references can also be maintained. Because object database store the objects *as objects*, object databases are viewed by many developers as superior database technology for object persistence.

While object databases perform well when it comes to very complex object graph: they are still fairly new to business systems and are not as widely accepted as rela tional databases. As a result, they are not as standardized as relational database: making it more difficult to migrate from one database to another. In additior fewer third-party products exist that support object databases, like products fc reporting and data warehousing.

Several relational databases support extended features for native object persi tence. These databases allow some objects to be preserved in relational databas tables like other data types and offer some advantages over other databases.

Legacy persistence

EJB is often used to put an object wrapper on legacy systems, systems that ar based on mainframe applications or nonrelational databases. Container-manage persistence in such an environment requires a special EJB container designed sp cifically for legacy data access. Vendors might, for example, provide mapping too that allow beans to be mapped to IMS, CICS, b-trieve, or some other legacy appl cation.

Regardless of the type of legacy system used, container-managed persistence preferable to bean-managed persistence. With container-managed persistence, th bean's state is managed automatically, which is more efficient at runtime an more productive during bean development. Many projects, however, require tha beans obtain their state from legacy systems that are not supported by mappin tools. In these cases, developers must use bean-managed persistence, which mear that the developer doesn't use the automatic persistence service of the EJB serve

Chapter 6 describes both container-managed and bean-managed persistence in detail.

Distributed Objects

Three main distributed object services are available today: CORBA, Java RMI, and DCOM. Each of these services uses a different RMI network protocol, but they all accomplish basically the same thing: location transparency. DCOM is primarily used in the Microsoft Windows environment and is not well supported by other operating systems. Its tight integration with Microsoft products makes it a good choice for Microsoft-only systems. CORBA is neither operating-system specific nor language specific and is therefore the most open distributed object service of the three. It's an ideal choice when integrating systems developed in multiple programming languages. Java RMI is a Java language abstraction or programming model for any kind of distributed object protocol. In the same way that the JDBC API can be used to access any SQL relational database, Java RMI is intended to be used with almost any distributed object protocol. In practice, Java RMI has traditionally been limited to the Java Remote Method Protocol (JRMP)—known as Java RMI over JRMP—which can only be used between Java applications. Recently an implementation of Java RMI over IIOP (Java RMI-IIOP), the CORBA protocol, has been developed. Java RMI-IIOP is a CORBA-compliant version of Java RMI, which allows developers to leverage the simplicity of the Java RMI programming model, while taking advantage of the platform- and language-independent CORBA protocol, IIOP.*

When we discuss the remote interface, home interface, and other EJB interfaces and classes used on the client, we are talking about the client's view of the EJB system. The *EJB client view* doesn't include the EJB objects, container, instance swapping, or any of the other implementation specifics. As far as the client is concerned, a bean is defined by its remote interface and home interface. Everything else is invisible. As long as the EJB server supports the EJB client view, any distributed object protocol can be used.

Regardless of the protocol used, the server must support Java clients using the Java EJB client API, which means that the protocol must map to the Java RMI for EJB 1.0 or Java RMI-IIOP for EJB 1.1. Using Java RMI over DCOM seems a little far-fetched, but it is possible. Figure 3-10 illustrates the Java language EJB API supported by different distributed object protocols.

---

* Java RMI-IIOP is interoperable with CORBA ORBs that support the CORBA 2.3 specification. ORBs that support an older specification cannot be used with Java RMI-IIOP because they do not implement the Object by Value portion of the 2.3 specification.

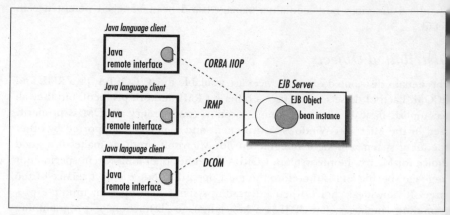

Figure 3-10. Java EJB client view supported by various protocols

EJB also allows servers to support access to beans by clients written in languages other than Java. An example of this is the EJB-to-CORBA mapping defined by Sun.* This document describes the CORBA IDL (Interface Definition Language) that can be used to access enterprise beans from CORBA clients. A CORBA client can be written in any language, including C++, Smalltalk, Ada, and even COBOL. The mapping also includes details about supporting the Java EJB client view as well as details on mapping the CORBA naming system to EJB servers and distributed transactions across CORBA objects and beans. Eventually, a EJB-to-DCOM mapping may be defined that will allow DCOM client applications written in languages like Visual Basic, Delphi, PowerBuilder, and others to access beans. Figure 3-11 illustrates the possibilities for accessing an EJB server from different distributed object clients.

As a platform-independent and language-independent distributed object protocol, CORBA is often thought of as the superior of the three protocols discussed here. For all its advantages, however, CORBA suffers from some limitations. Pass-by-value, a feature easily supported by Java RMI-IIOP, was only recently introduced in the CORBA 2.3 specification and is not well supported. Another limitation of CORBA is with casting remote proxies. In Java RMI-JRMP, you can cast or widen a proxy's remote interface to a subtype or supertype of the interface, just like any other object. This is a powerful feature that allows remote objects to be polymorphic. In Java RMI-IIOP, you have to call a special narrowing method to change the interface of a proxy to a subtype, which is cumbersome.

---

* Sun Microsystems' *Enterprise JavaBeans™ to CORBA Mapping, Version 1.1*, by Sanjeev Krishnan, Copyright 1999 by Sun Microsystems.

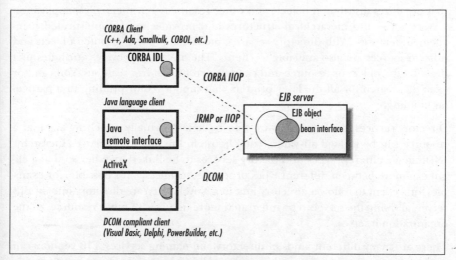

Figure 3-11. EJB accessed from different distributed clients

However, JRMP is has its own limitations. While JRMP may be a more natural fit for Java-to-Java distributed object systems, it lacks inherent support for both security and transactional services—support that is a part of the CORBA IIOP specification. This limits the effectiveness of JRMP in heterogeneous environments where security and transactional contexts must be passed between systems.

Naming

All distributed object services use a naming service of some kind. Java RMI-JRMP and CORBA use their own naming services. All naming services do essentially the same thing regardless of how they are implemented: they provide clients with a mechanism for locating distributed objects.

To accomplish this, a naming service must provide two things: object binding and a lookup API. *Object binding* is the association of a distributed object with a natural language name or identifier. The CabinHome object, for example, might be bound to the name "cabin.Home" or "room." A binding is really a pointer or an index to a specific distributed object, which is necessary in an environment that manages hundreds of different distributed objects. A *lookup API* provides the client with an interface to the naming system. Simply put, lookup APIs allow clients to connect to a distributed service and request a remote reference to a specific object.

Enterprise JavaBeans mandates the use of the Java Naming and Directory Interface (JNDI) as a lookup API on Java clients. JNDI supports just about any kind of naming and directory service. A directory service is a very advanced naming service that organizes distributed objects and other resources—printers, files, application servers, etc.—into hierarchical structures and provides more sophisticated management features. With directory services, metadata about distributed objects and other resources are also available to clients. The metadata provides attributes that describe the object or resource and can be used to perform searches. You can, for example, search for all the laser printers that support color printing in a particular building.

Directory services also allow resources to be linked virtually, which means that a resource can be located anywhere you choose in the directory services hierarchy. JNDI allows different types of directory services to be linked together so that a client can move between different types of services seamlessly. It's possible, for example, for a client to follow a directory link in a Novell NetWare directory into an EJB server, allowing the server to be integrated more tightly with other resources of the organization it serves.

There are many different kinds of directory and naming services; EJB vendors can choose the one that best meets their needs. All EJB servers, however, must provide JNDI access to their particular directory or naming service. EJB servers that support access to beans using non-Java clients must also support a naming system specific to the distributed object protocol used. The EJB-to-CORBA mapping, for example, specifies how EJB homes should be organized for CORBA Naming Service.

A Java client application would use JNDI to initiate a connection to an EJB server and to locate a specific EJB home. The following code shows how the JNDI API might be used to locate and obtain a reference to the EJB home CabinHome:

```
javax.naming.Context jndiContext =
    new javax.naming.InitialContext(properties);
Object ref = jndiContext.lookup("cabin.Home");
// EJB 1.0: Use Java native cast instead of narrow()
CabinHome cabinHome = (CabinHome)
    PortableRemoteObject.narrow(ref, CabinHome.class);

Cabin cabin = cabinHome.create(382, "Cabin 333",3);
cabin.setName("Cabin 444");
cabin.setDeckLevel(4);
```

The properties passed into the constructor of InitialContext tell the JNDI API where to find the EJB server and what JNDI service provider (driver) to load. The Context.lookup() method tells the JNDI service provider the name of the object to return from the EJB server. In this case, we are looking for the home interface to the Cabin bean. Once we have the Cabin bean's home interface, we can use it to create new cabins and access existing cabins.

Security

Enterprise JavaBeans servers might support as many as three kinds of security: authentication, access control, and secure communication. Only access control is specifically addressed in the EJB 1.0 and EJB 1.1 specifications.

Authentication

Simply put, authentication validates the identity of the user. The most common kind of authentication is a simple login screen that requires a username and a password. Once users have successfully passed through the authentication system, they are free to use the system. Authentication can also be based on secure ID cards, swipe cards, security certificates, and other forms of identification. While authentication is the primary safeguard against unauthorized access to a system, it is fairly crude because it doesn't police an authorized user's access to resources within the system.

Access control

Access control (a.k.a. authorization) applies security policies that regulate what a specific user can and cannot do within a system. Access control ensures that users only access resources for which they have been given permission. Access control can police a user's access to subsystems, data, and business objects, or it can monitor more general behavior. Certain users, for example, may be allowed to update information while others are only allowed to view the data.

Secure communication

Communication channels between a client and a server are frequently the focus of security concerns. A channel of communication can be secured by physical isolation (like a dedicated network connection) or by encrypting the communication between the client and the server. Physically securing communication is expensive, limiting, and pretty much impossible on the Internet, so we will focus on encryption. When communication is secured by encryption, the messages passed are encoded so that they cannot be read or manipulated by unauthorized individuals. This normally involves the exchange of cryptographic keys between the client and the server. The keys allow the receiver of the message to decode the message and read it.

Most EJB servers support secure communications—usually through SSL (secure socket layer)—and some mechanism for authentication, but EJB 1.0 and 1.1 only specify access control in their server-side component models. Authentication may be specified in subsequent versions, but secure communications will probably never be specified. Secure communications is really independent of the EJB specification and the distributed object protocol.

Although authentication is not specified in EJB, it is often accomplished using the JNDI API. In other words, a client using JNDI can provide authenticating information using the JNDI API to access a server or resources in the server. This information is frequently passed when the client attempts to initiate a JNDI connection to the EJB server. The following code shows how the client's password and username are added to the connection properties used to obtain a JNDI connection to the EJB server:

```
properties.put(Context.SECURITY_PRINCIPAL, userName );
properties.put(Context.SECURITY_CREDENTIALS, userPassword);

javax.naming.Context jndiContext =
    new javax.naming.InitialContext(properties);
Object ref= jndiContext.lookup("titan.CabinHome");
// EJB 1.0: Use Java native cast instead of narrow()
CabinHome cabinHome = (CabinHome)
    PortableRemoteObject.narrow(ref, CabinHome.class);
```

Enterprise JavaBeans 1.0 and 1.1 use slightly different models to control client access to beans and their methods. While EJB 1.0 access control is based on Identity objects with a method driven organization, EJB 1.1 changed authorization to be based on Principal types rather than Identity types and to be role-driven rather than method-driven.

EJB specifies that every client application accessing an EJB system must be associated with a security identity. The security identity represents the client as either a user or a role. A user might be a person, security credential, computer, or even a smart card. Normally, the user will be a person whose identity is assigned when he or she logs in. A role represents a grouping of identities and might be something like "manager," which is a group of user identities that are considered managers at a company.

When a client logs on to the EJB system, it is associated with a security identity for the duration of that session. The identity is found in a database or directory specific to the platform or EJB server. This database or directory is responsible for storing individual security identities and their memberships to groups.

Once a client application has been associated with an security identity, it is ready to use beans to accomplish some task. The EJB server keeps track of each client and its identity. When a client invokes a method on a home interface or a remote interface, the EJB server implicitly passes the client's identity with the method invocation. When the EJB object or EJB home receives the method invocation, it checks the identity to ensure that the client is allowed to invoke that method.

EJB 1.1: Role-driven access control

In EJB 1.1, the security identity is represented by a java.security.Principle object. As a security identity, the Principle acts as a representative for users, groups, organizations, smart cards, etc., to the EJB access control architecture. Deployment descriptors include tags that declare which logical roles are allowed to access which bean methods at runtime. The security roles are considered logical roles because they do not *directly* reflect users, groups, or any other security identities in a specific operational environment. Instead, security roles are mapped to real-world user groups and users when the bean is deployed. This allows a bean to be portable; every time the bean is deployed in a new system the roles can be mapped to the users and groups specific to that operational environment. Here is a portion of the Cabin bean's deployment descriptor that defines two security roles, ReadOnly and Administrator:

```
<security-role>
    <description>
        This role is allowed to execute any method on the bean.
        They are allowed to read and change any cabin bean data.
    </description>
    <role-name>
        Administrator
    </role-name>
</security-role>

<security-role>
    <description>
        This role is allowed to locate and read cabin info.
        This role is not allowed to change cabin bean data.
    </description>
    <role-name>
        ReadOnly
    </role-name>
</security-role>
```

The role names in this descriptor are not reserved or special names, with some sort of predefined meaning; they are simply logical names chosen by the bean assembler. In other words, the role names can be anything you want as long as they are descriptive.*

---

* For a complete understanding of XML, including specific rules for tag names and data, see *XML Pocket Reference*, by Robert Eckstein (O'Reilly).

How are roles mapped into actions that are allowed or forbidden? Once the security-role tags are declared, they can be associated with methods in the bean using method-permission tags. Each method-permission tag contains one or more method tags, which identify the bean methods associated with one or more logical roles identified by the role-name tags. The role-name tags must match the names defined by the security-role tags shown earlier.

```
<method-permission>
    <role-name>Administrator</role-name>
    <method>
        <ejb-name>CabinEJB</ejb-name>
        <method-name>*</method-name>
    </method>
</method-permission>
</method-permission>
    <role-name>ReadOnly</role-name>
    <method>
        <ejb-name>CabinEJB</ejb-name>
        <method-name>getName</method-name>
    </method>
    <method>
        <ejb-name>CabinEJB</ejb-name>
        <method-name>getDeckLevel</method-name>
    </method>
    <method>
        <ejb-name>CabinEJB</ejb-name>
        <method-name>findByPrimaryKey</method-name>
    </method>
</method-permission>
```

In the first method-permission, the Administrator role is associated with all methods on the Cabin bean, which is denoted by specifying the wildcard character (*) in the method-name of the method tag. In the second method-permission the ReadOnly role is limited to accessing only three methods: getName(), getDeckLevel(), and findByPrimaryKey(). Any attempt by a ReadOnly role to access a method that is not listed in the method-permission will result in an exception. This kind of access control makes for a fairly fine-grained authorization system.

Since an XML deployment descriptor can be used to describe more than one enterprise bean, the tags used to declare method permissions and security roles are defined in a special section of the deployment descriptor, so that several beans can share the same security roles. The exact location of these tags and their relationship to other sections of the XML deployment descriptor will be covered in more detail in Chapter 10.

When the bean is deployed, the person deploying the bean will examine the
security-role information and map each logical role to a corresponding user
group in the operational environment. The deployer need not be concerned with
what roles go to which methods; he can rely on the descriptions given in the
security-role tags to determine matches based on the description of the logical role. This unburdens the deployer, who may not be a developer, from having
to understand how the bean works in order to deploy it.

Figure 3-12 shows the same bean deployed in two different environments (labeled
X and Z). In each environment, the user groups in the operational environment
are mapped to their logical equivalent roles in the XML deployment descriptor so
that specific user groups have access privileges to specific methods on specific
beans.

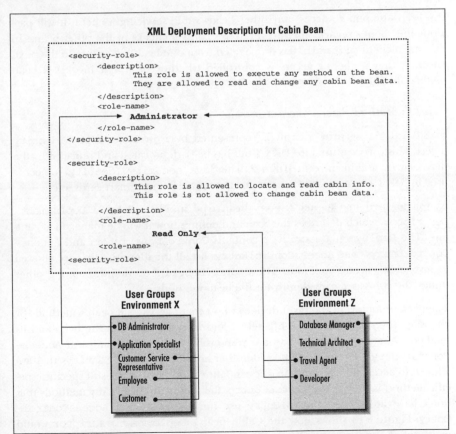

Figure 3-12. Mapping roles in the operational environment to logical roles in the deployment descriptor

As you can see from the figure, the ReadOnly role is mapped to those groups that should be limited to the get accessor methods and the find method. The Administrator role is mapped to those user groups that should have privileges to invoke any method on the Cabin bean.

The access control described here is implicit; once the bean is deployed the container takes care of checking that users only access methods for which they have permission. This is accomplished by propagating the security identity, the Principle, with each method invocation from the client to the bean. When a client invokes a method on a bean, the client's Principle is checked to see if it is a member of a role mapped to that method. If it's not, an exception is thrown and the client is denied permission to invoke the method. If the client is a member of a privileged role, the invocation is allowed to go forward and the method is invoked.

If a bean attempts to access any other beans while servicing a client, it will pass along the client's security identity for access control checks by the other beans. In this way, a client's Principle is propagated from one bean invocation to the next, ensuring that a client's access is controlled whether or not it invokes a bean method directly.

EJB 1.0: Method-driven access control

In EJB 1.0, the security identity is represented by a java.security.Identity object. This class was used in JDK 1.1 but has been deprecated and replaced by the new security architecture in JDK 1.2. The java.security.Identity object is used in JDK 1.1 to represent people, groups, organizations, smart cards, etc.

As you learned in Chapter 2, every bean type in EJB 1.0 has a Deployment-Descriptor, which describes the bean and defines how it will be managed at runtime. The DeploymentDescriptor contains ControlDescriptors and Access-ControlEntrys. The AccessControlEntrys list all the identities that are allowed to invoke the bean's methods. The ControlDescriptor defines, among other things, the runAs security identity for the bean methods.

The person deploying the bean decides who gets to access the bean's methods by choosing Identitys from the EJB server and mapping them to the bean and its methods. AccessControlEntrys are responsible for the mapping. An Access-ControlEntry contains a method identifier and a list of the Identitys that are allowed to access the method. An AccessControlEntry that doesn't specify a specific method is the default AccessControlEntry for the bean. Any methods that don't have an AccessControlEntry use the bean's default AccessControl-Entry. Figure 3-13 shows how the Cabin bean's DeploymentDescriptor would map a set of AccessControlEntrys defined for the CabinBean's methods.

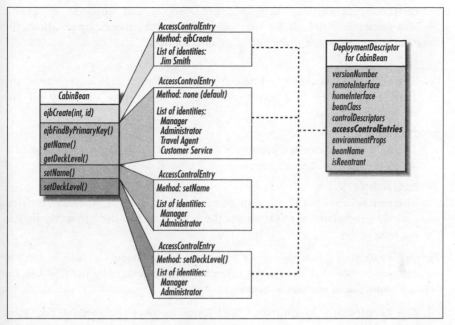

Figure 3-13. AccessControlEntrys for CabinBean

In addition to specifying the Identitys that have access to a bean's methods, the deployer also specifies the runAs Identity for the bean's methods. The runAs Identity was abandoned in EJB 1.1, but it's an important part of the EJB 1.0 access control architecture. While the AccessControlEntrys specify which Identitys have access to the bean's methods, the ControlDescriptors specify under which Identity the method will run. In other words, the runAs Identity is used as the bean's identity when it tries to invoke methods on other beans—this identity isn't necessarily the same as the identity that's currently accessing the bean. For example, it is possible to specify that the ejbCreate() method can only be accessed by Jim Smith but that it runs under Administrator's Identity. This is useful when beans or resources accessed in the body of the method require an Identity different from the one used to gain access to the method. The ejbCreate() method might call a method in bean X that requires the Administrator's Identity. If we want to use bean X in the ejbCreate() method, but we only want Jim Smith to create new cabins, we would use the ControlDescriptor and AccessControlEntry together to give us this kind of flexibility: the Access-ControlEntry for ejbCreate() would specify that only Jim Smith can invoke the method, and the ControlDescriptor would specify that the bean's runAs Identity is Administrator.

ControlDescriptors, like AccessControlEntrys, can apply to a specific method or act as a default for the bean. The ControlDescriptor allows the deployer to specify one of three possible runAs modes:

CLIENT_IDENTITY

The method runs under the calling client's Identity. In other words, the Identity used to gain access will also be the runAs Identity for the method.

SPECIFIED_IDENTITY

The method runs under a previously chosen Identity. The Identity used is set on the ControlDescriptor when the bean is deployed.

SYSTEM_IDENTITY

The method runs under a system Identity. The SYSTEM_IDENTITY is determined by the platform but is usually the Identity that the EJB server itself is running under.

Figure 3-14 illustrates how the runAs Identity can change in a chain of method invocations. Notice that the runAs Identity is the Identity used to test for access in subsequent method invocations.

1. The client who is identified as "Bill Jones" invokes the method foo() on bean A.

2. Before servicing the method, bean A checks to see if "Bill Jones" is in the AccessControlEntry for foo().

3. Once validated, foo() executes under the runAs Identity of the calling client.

4. While foo() is executing, it invokes method bar() on bean B.

5. Bean B checks method foo()'s runAs Identity ("Bill Jones") against the AccessControlEntry for method bar(). "Bill Jones" is in the AccessControlEntry's list of Identitys, so the method bar() is allowed to execute.

6. The method bar(), however, is executed under the Identity of "Administrator" as specified by bar()'s ControlDescriptor.

7. While bar() is executing, bean B invokes the method boo() on bean C.

8. Bean C checks and finds that bar()'s runAs Identity ("Administrator") is in the AccessControlEntry.

9. The ControlDescriptor for the method boo() requires that it be executed under the runAs Identity of the system.

This protocol applies equally to entity and stateless session beans. All the methods in a stateful session bean, however, have a single runAs Identity, which is the

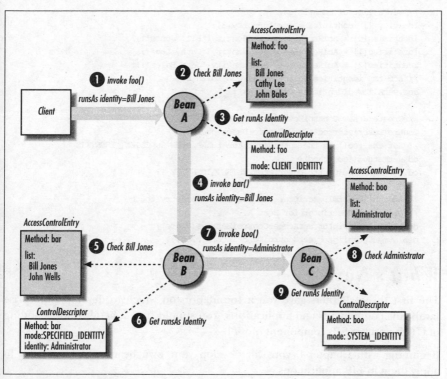

Figure 3-14. runAs Identity

Identity used to create the session—the identity used when ejbCreate() is invoked. In other words, subsequent methods invoked on a stateful bean instance must not specify a conflicting runAs identity.

Here is a code fragment that shows how the access control setting can be made programmatically in a DeploymentDescriptor. In this example, we are setting the access control attributes for bean A. The AclRepository type is an imaginary interface into a proprietary database or directory.

```
// Create a new AccessControlEntry.
AccessControlEntry ace = new AccessControlEntry();

// Get a reference to the method foo() using reflection.
Class beanClass = ABean.class;
Class parameters [] = new Class[0];
Method fooMethod = beanClass.getDeclaredMethod("foo", parameters);
// Add the method reference to the AccessControlEntry.
ace.setMethod(fooMethod);
```

```
// Get a list of identities.
Identity [] identities = new Identity[3];
identities[0] = AclRepository.getIdentity("Bill Jones");
identities[1] = AclRepository.getIdentity("Cathy Lee");
identities[2] = AclRepository.getIdentity("John Bales");
// Add the identities to the AccessControlEntry.
ace.setAllowedIdentities(identities);

// Create a new ControlDescriptor.
ControlDescriptor cd = new ControlDescriptor();
// Set the foo() as the method and the runAs mode as CLIENT_IDENTITY.
cd.setMethod(fooMethod);
cd.setRunAsMode(ControlDescriptor.CLIENT_IDENTITY );

// Add the ControlDescriptor and AccessControlEntry to the
// DeploymentDescriptor for Bean A.
deploymentDescriptor.setAccessControlEntries(0,ace);
deploymentDescriptor.setControlDescriptors(0,cd);
```

What's Next?

The first three chapters gave you a foundation on which to develop Enterprise JavaBeans components and applications. You should have a better understanding of CTMs and the EJB component model.

Beginning with Chapter 4, you will develop your own beans and learn how to apply them in EJB applications.

In this chapter:
• *Choosing and Setting Up an EJB Server*
• *Developing an Entity Bean*
• *Developing a Session Bean*

4

Developing Your First Enterprise Beans

Choosing and Setting Up an EJB Server

One of the most important features of EJB is that beans should work with containers from different vendors. That doesn't mean that selecting a server and installing your beans on that server are trivial processes. We'll start this chapter with a general discussion of how you select and set up a server.

The EJB server you choose should be compliant with the EJB 1.0 or EJB 1.1 specification. However, in the EJB 1.0 version of the specification, support for entity beans and container-managed persistence is optional. In EJB 1.1, support for entity beans is required. The first example in this chapter—and most of the examples in this book—assume that your EJB server supports entity beans and container-managed persistence.* The EJB server you choose should also provide a utility for deploying an enterprise bean. It doesn't matter whether the utility is command-line oriented or graphical, as long as it does the job. The deployment utility should allow you to work with prepackaged enterprise beans, i.e., beans that have already been developed and archived in a JAR file. Finally, the EJB server should support an SQL-standard relational database that is accessible using JDBC. For the database, you should have privileges sufficient for creating and modifying a few simple tables in addition to normal read, update, and delete capabilities. If you have chosen an EJB server that does not support an SQL standard relational database, you may need to modify the examples to work with the product you are using.

---

* Chapter 9 discusses how to work with servers that don't support entity beans. Chapter 6 includes a discussion of bean-managed persistence, which you can use if your server doesn't support container-managed persistence.

Setting Up Your Java IDE

To get the most from this chapter, it helps to have an IDE that has a debugger and allows you to add Java files to its environment. Several Java IDEs, like Symantec's Visual Cafe, IBM's VisualAge, Inprise's JBuilder, and Sun's Forte, fulfill this simple requirement. The debugger is especially important because it allows you to walk slowly through your client code and observe how the EJB client API is used.

Once you have an IDE set up, you need to include the Enterprise JavaBeans packages. These packages include javax.ejb and for EJB 1.0 javax.ejb.deployment. You also need the JNDI packages, including javax.naming, javax.naming.directory, and javax.naming.spi. In addition, you will need the javax.rmi package for EJB 1.1. All these packages can be downloaded from Sun's Java site (*http://www.javasoft.com*) in the form of ZIP or JAR files. They may also be accessible in the subdirectories of your EJB server, normally under the *lib* directory.

Developing an Entity Bean

There seems to be no better place to start than the Cabin bean, which we have been examining throughout the previous chapters. The Cabin bean is an entity bean that encapsulates the data and behavior associated with a real-world cruise ship cabin in Titan's business domain.

Cabin: The Remote Interface

When developing an entity bean, we first want to define the bean's remote interface. The remote interface defines the bean's business purpose; the methods of this interface must capture the concept of the entity. We defined the remote interface for the Cabin bean in Chapter 2; here, we add two new methods for setting and getting the ship ID and the bed count. The ship ID identifies the ship that the cabin belongs to, and the bed count tells how many people the cabin can accommodate.

```
package com.titan.cabin;

import java.rmi.RemoteException;

public interface Cabin extends javax.ejb.EJBObject {
    public String getName() throws RemoteException;
    public void setName(String str) throws RemoteException;
    public int getDeckLevel() throws RemoteException;
    public void setDeckLevel(int level) throws RemoteException;
    public int getShip() throws RemoteException;
    public void setShip(int sp) throws RemoteException;
```

```
    public int getBedCount() throws RemoteException;
    public void setBedCount(int bc) throws RemoteException;
}
```

The Cabin interface defines four properties: the name, deckLevel, ship, and bedCount. *Properties* are attributes of a bean that can be accessed by public set and get methods. The methods that access these properties are not explicitly defined in the Cabin interface, but the interface clearly specifies that these attributes are readable and changeable by a client.

Notice that we have made the Cabin interface a part of a new package named com.titan.cabin. In this book, we place all the classes and interfaces associated with each type of bean in a package specific to the bean. Because our beans are for the use of the Titan cruise line, we place these packages in the com.titan package hierarchy. We also create directory structures that match package structures. If you are using an IDE that works directly with Java files, create a new directory somewhere called *dev* (for development) and create the directory structure shown in Figure 4-1. Copy the Cabin interface into your IDE and save its definition to the *cabin* directory. Compile the Cabin interface to ensure that its definition is correct. The *Cabin.class* file, generated by the IDE's compiler, should be written to the *cabin* directory, the same directory as the *Cabin.java* file.

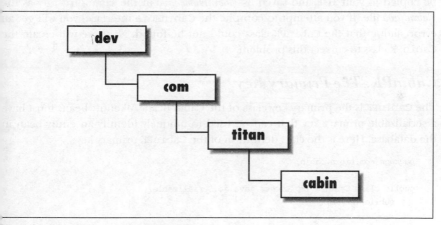

Figure 4-1. Directory structure for the Cabin bean

CabinHome: The Home Interface

Once we have defined the remote interface of the Cabin bean, we have defined the world's view of this simple entity bean. Next, we need to define the Cabin bean's home interface, which specifies how the bean can be created, located, and destroyed; in other words, the Cabin bean's life-cycle behavior. Here is a complete definition of the CabinHome home interface:

```
package com.titan.cabin;

import java.rmi.RemoteException;
import javax.ejb.CreateException;
import javax.ejb.FinderException;

public interface CabinHome extends javax.ejb.EJBHome {

    public Cabin create(int id)
        throws CreateException, RemoteException;

    public Cabin findByPrimaryKey(CabinPK pk)
        throws FinderException, RemoteException;
}
```

The CabinHome interface extends the javax.ejb.EJBHome and defines two life-cycle methods: create() and findByPrimaryKey(). These methods create and locate Cabin beans. Remove methods (for deleting beans) are defined in the javax.ejb.EJBHome interface, so the CabinHome interface inherits them. This interface is packaged in com.titan.cabin, just like the Cabin interface. It should be copied to your IDE and saved as *CabinHome.java* in the same directory as the *Cabin.java* file. If you attempt to compile the CabinHome interface, you will get an error stating that the CabinPK class could not be found. Next, we will create the CabinPK class to correct this problem.

CabinPK: The Primary Key

The CabinPK is the primary key class of the Cabin bean. All entity beans must have a serializable primary key that can be used to uniquely identify an entity bean in the database. Here is the class definition of the CabinPK primary key:

```
package com.titan.cabin;

public class CabinPK implements java.io.Serializable {
    public int id;

    public int hashCode() {
        return id;
    }
    public boolean equals(Object obj) {
        if (obj instanceof CabinPK) {
            return (id == ((CabinPK)obj).id);
        }
        return false;
    }
}
```

The primary key belongs to the com.titan.cabin package and implements the java.io.Serializable interface. The CabinPK defines one public attribute, id. This id field is used to locate specific Cabin entities or records in the database at runtime. EJB 1.1 requires that we override the Object.hashCode() and Object.equals() methods; EJB 1.0 doesn't require this, but it's a good practice regardless of the version of EJB you are using. These methods ensure that the primary key evaluates properly when used with hash tables and in other situations.* Later, we will learn that the primary key must encapsulate attributes that match one or more container-managed fields in the bean class. In this case, the id field will have to match a field in the CabinBean class. Copy the CabinPK definition into your IDE, and save it to the cabin directory as *CabinPK.java* file. Compile it. Now that CabinPK has been compiled, you should be able to compile CabinHome without errors.

CabinBean: The Bean Class

You have now defined the complete client-side API for creating, locating, removing, and using the Cabin bean. Now we need to define CabinBean, the class that provides the implementation on the server for the Cabin bean. The CabinBean class is an entity bean that uses container-managed persistence, so its definition will be fairly simple. In addition to the callback methods discussed in Chapters 2 and 3, we must also define EJB implementations for most of the methods defined in the Cabin and CabinHome interfaces. Here is the complete definition of the CabinBean class in EJB 1.1:

```
// EJB 1.1 CabinBean
package com.titan.cabin;

import javax.ejb.EntityContext;

public class CabinBean implements javax.ejb.EntityBean {

    public int id;
    public String name;
    public int deckLevel;
    public int ship;
    public int bedCount;

    public CabinPK ejbCreate(int id) {
        this.id = id;
        return null;
    }
}
```

---

* In Chapters 6 and 9, we discuss implementing the hashCode() and equals() methods in more detail.

```java
    public void ejbPostCreate(int id) {
        // Do nothing. Required.
    }
    public String getName() {
        return name;
    }
    public void setName(String str) {
        name = str;
    }
    public int getShip() {
        return ship;
    }
    public void setShip(int sp) {
        ship = sp;
    }
    public int getBedCount() {
        return bedCount;
    }
    public void setBedCount(int bc) {
        bedCount = bc;
    }
    public int getDeckLevel() {
        return deckLevel;
    }
    public void setDeckLevel(int level ) {
        deckLevel = level;
    }

    public void setEntityContext(EntityContext ctx) {
        // Not implemented.
    }
    public void unsetEntityContext() {
        // Not implemented.
    }
    public void ejbActivate() {
        // Not implemented.
    }
    public void ejbPassivate() {
        // Not implemented.
    }
    public void ejbLoad() {
        // Not implemented.
    }
    public void ejbStore() {
        // Not implemented.
    }
    public void ejbRemove() {
        // Not implemented.
    }
}
```

And here's the CabinBean class for EJB 1.0. It differs only in the return value of
ejbCreate():

```java
// EJB 1.0 CabinBean
import javax.ejb.EntityContext;

public class CabinBean implements javax.ejb.EntityBean {

    public int id;
    public String name;
    public int deckLevel;
    public int ship;
    public int bedCount;

    public void ejbCreate(int id) {
        this.id = id;
    }
    public void ejbPostCreate(int id) {
        // Do nothing. Required.
    }
    public String getName() {
        return name;
    }
    public void setName(String str) {
        name = str;
    }
    public int getShip() {
        return ship;
    }
    public void setShip(int sp) {
        ship = sp;
    }
    public int getBedCount() {
        return bedCount;
    }
    public void setBedCount(int bc) {
        bedCount = bc;
    }
    public int getDeckLevel() {
        return deckLevel;
    }
    public void setDeckLevel(int level ) {
        deckLevel = level;
    }

    public void setEntityContext(EntityContext ctx) {
        // Not implemented.
    }
```

```
public void unsetEntityContext() {
    // Not implemented.
}
public void ejbActivate() {
    // Not implemented.
}
public void ejbPassivate() {
    // Not implemented.
}
public void ejbLoad() {
    // Not implemented.
}
public void ejbStore() {
    // Not implemented.
}
public void ejbRemove() {
    // Not implemented.
}
}
```

The CabinBean class belongs to the com.titan.cabin package, just like the interfaces and primary key class. The CabinBean class can be divided into four sections for discussion: declarations for the container-managed fields, the ejbCreate() methods, the callback methods, and the remote interface implementations.

Declared fields in a bean class can be persistent fields and property fields. These categories are not mutually exclusive. The persistent field declarations describe the fields that will be mapped to the database. A persistent field is often a property (in the JavaBeans sense): any attribute that is available using public set and get methods. Of course, a bean can have any fields that it needs; they need not all be persistent, or properties. Fields that aren't persistent won't be saved in the database. In CabinBean, all the fields are persistent.

The id field is persistent, but it is not a property. In other words, id is mapped to the database but cannot be accessed through the remote interface. The primary key, CabinPK, also contains an integer field called id, just like the CabinBean. This means that the primary key for the CabinBean is its id field because the signatures match.

The name, deckLevel, ship, and bedCount fields are persistent fields. They will be mapped to the database at deployment time. These fields are also properties because they are publicly available through the remote interface.

In the case of the Cabin bean, there was only one create() method, so there is only one corresponding ejbCreate() method and one ejbPostCreate() method, which is shown in both the EJB 1.1 and EJB 1.0 listings. When a client invokes a method on the home interface, it is delegated to a matching ejb-Create() method on the bean instance. The ejbCreate() method initializes the fields; in the case of the CabinBean, it sets the id field to equal the passed integer.

In the case of EJB 1.0, the ejbCreate() method returns void for container-managed persistence; this method returns the bean's primary key in bean-managed persistence. In EJB 1.1, the ejbCreate() method always returns the primary key type; with container-managed persistence, this method returns the null value. It's the container's responsibility to create the primary key. Why the change? Simply put, the change makes it easier for a bean-managed bean to extend a container-managed bean. In EJB 1.0, this is not possible because Java won't allow you to overload methods with different return values. Container-managed and bean-managed persistence was touched on in Chapter 3 and is discussed in detail in Chapter 6.

Once the ejbCreate() method has executed, the ejbPostCreate() method is called to perform any follow-up operations. The ejbCreate() and ejbPostCreate() methods must have signatures that match the parameters and (optionally) the exceptions of the home interface's create() method. However, ejb-Create() and ejbPostCreate() aren't required to throw the RemoteException or CreateException. The EJB container throws these exceptions automatically at runtime if there is a problem with communications or some other system-level problem.

The findByPrimaryKey() method is not defined in container-managed bean classes. With container-managed beans you do not explicitly declare find methods in the bean class. Instead, find methods are generated at deployment and implemented by the container. With bean-managed beans (beans that explicitly manage their own persistence), find methods must be defined in the bean class. Our Cabin bean is a container-managed bean, so we will not need to define its find method. In Chapter 6, when you develop bean-managed entity beans, you will define the find methods in the bean classes you develop.

The business methods in the CabinBean match the signatures of the business methods defined in the remote interface. These include getName(), setName(), getDeckLevel(), setDeckLevel(), getShip(), setShip(), getBedCount(), and setBedCount(). When a client invokes one of these methods on the remote interface, the method is delegated to the matching method on the bean class. Again, the business methods do not throw the RemoteException like the matching methods in the remote interface. In both the ejbCreate() and remote interface methods, it is possible to define application or custom exceptions. If a custom exception is defined, both the interface method and its matching method in the bean class must throw it. We will learn more about custom exceptions in Chapter 6.

The entity context methods are responsible for setting and unsetting the EntityContext. The EntityContext is an interface implemented by the EJB container that provides the bean with information about the container, the identity of the client, transactional control, and other environmental information if the bean needs it. Because the Cabin bean is a very simple container-managed bean, this example does not use the EntityContext. Subsequent examples in Chapter 6 will make good use of the EntityContext.

The CabinBean class implements javax.ejb.EntityBean, which defines five callback methods: ejbActivate(), ejbPassivate(), ejbLoad(), ejbStore(), and ejbRemove(). The container uses these callback methods to notify the CabinBean of certain events in its life cycle. Although the callback methods are implemented, the implementations are empty. The CabinBean is simple enough that it doesn't need to do any special processing during its life cycle. When we study entity beans in more detail in Chapter 6, we will take advantage of these callback methods.

That's enough talk about the CabinBean definition. Now that you are familiar with it, copy it to your IDE, save it to the cabin directory as *CabinBean.java*, and compile it.

You are now ready to create a deployment descriptor for the Cabin bean. The deployment descriptor performs a function similar to a properties file. It describes which classes make up a bean and how the bean should be managed at runtime. During deployment, the deployment descriptor is read and its properties are displayed for editing. The deployer can then modify and add settings as appropriate for the application's operational environment. Once the deployer is satisfied with the deployment information, he or she uses it to generate the entire supporting infrastructure needed to deploy the bean in the EJB server. This may include adding the bean to the naming system and generating the bean's EJB object and EJB home, persistence infrastructure, transactional support, resolving bean references, and so forth.

Although most EJB server products provide a wizard for creating and editing deployment descriptors, we will create ours directly so that the bean is defined in a vendor-independent manner. This requires some manual labor, but it gives you a much better understanding of how deployment descriptors are created. Once the deployment descriptor is finished, the bean can be placed in a JAR file and deployed on any EJB-compliant server of the appropriate version.

EJB 1.1: The Deployment Descriptor

An XML deployment descriptor for every example in this book has already been created and is available from the download site. If you haven't downloaded the examples, do so now. The examples are packaged in a ZIP file and organized by chapter and bean, so you will need to put the *ejb-jar.xml* file from the directory *chapter4/EJB11/com/titan/cabin* in the ZIP file. When you create the JAR file to deploy the Cabin bean, this *ejb-jar.xml* file *must* be in the JAR as *META-INF/ejb-jar.xml* in order for it to be found. If it has any other name or any other location, this deployment descriptor will not be used.

Here's a quick peek at the deployment descriptor for the Cabin bean, so you can get a feel for how an XML deployment descriptor is structured and the type of information it contains:

```xml
<?xml version="1.0"?>

<!DOCTYPE ejb-jar PUBLIC "-//Sun Microsystems, Inc.//DTD Enterprise
JavaBeans 1.1//EN" "http://java.sun.com/j2ee/dtds/ejb-jar_1_1.dtd">

<ejb-jar>
 <enterprise-beans>
   <entity>
      <description>
           This Cabin enterprise bean entity represents a cabin on
           a cruise ship.
      </description>
      <ejb-name>CabinBean</ejb-name>
      <home>com.titan.cabin.CabinHome</home>
      <remote>com.titan.cabin.Cabin</remote>
      <ejb-class>com.titan.cabin.CabinBean</ejb-class>
      <persistence-type>Container</persistence-type>
      <prim-key-class>com.titan.cabin.CabinPK</prim-key-class>
      <reentrant>False</reentrant>

      <cmp-field><field-name>id</field-name></cmp-field>
      <cmp-field><field-name>name</field-name></cmp-field>
      <cmp-field><field-name>deckLevel</field-name></cmp-field>
      <cmp-field><field-name>ship</field-name></cmp-field>
      <cmp-field><field-name>bedCount</field-name></cmp-field>
   </entity>
 </enterprise-beans>

 <assembly-descriptor>
  <security-role>
     <description>
          This role represents everyone who is allowed full access
          to the cabin bean.
     </description>
     <role-name>everyone</role-name>
  </security-role>
```

```
<method-permission>
  <role-name>everyone</role-name>
  <method>
      <ejb-name>CabinBean</ejb-name>
      <method-name>*</method-name>
  </method>
</method-permission>

<container-transaction>
  <method>
      <ejb-name>CabinBean</ejb-name>
      <method-name>*</method-name>
  </method>
  <trans-attribute>Required</trans-attribute>
</container-transaction>
</assembly-descriptor>
</ejb-jar>
```

The `<!DOCTYPE>` element describes the purpose of the XML file, its root element, and the location of its DTD. The DTD is used to verify that the document is structured correctly. This element is discussed in detail in Chapter 10 and is not important to understanding this example.

The rest of the elements are nested one within the other and are delimited by a beginning tag and ending tag. The structure is really not very complicated. If you have done any HTML coding you should already understand the format. An element always starts with *<name of tag>* tag and ends with *</name of tag>* tag. Everything in between—even other elements—is part of the enclosing element.

The first major element is the `<ejb-jar>` element, which is the root of the document. All the other elements must lie within this element. Next is the `<enterprise-beans>` element. Every bean declared in an XML file must be included in this section. This file only describes the Cabin bean, but we could define several beans in one deployment descriptor.

The `<entity>` element shows that the beans defined within this tag are entity beans. Similarly, a `<session>` element describes session beans; since the Cabin bean is an entity bean, we don't need a `<session>` element. In addition to a description, the `<entity>` element provides the fully qualified class names of the remote interface, home interface, bean class, and primary key. The `<cmp-field>` elements list all the container-managed fields in the entity bean class. These are the fields that will be persisted in the database and are managed by the container at runtime. The `<entity>` element also includes a `<reentrant>` element that can be set as True or False depending on whether the bean allows reentrant loopbacks or not.

The next section of the XML file, after the <enterprise-bean> element, is enclosed by the <assembly-descriptor> element, which describes the security roles and transactional attributes of the bean. It may seem odd to separate this information from the <enterprise-beans> element, since it clearly applies to the Cabin bean, but in the scheme of things it's perfectly natural. An XML deployment descriptor can describe several beans, which might all rely on the same security roles and transactional attributes. To make it easier to deploy several beans together, all this common information is separated into the <assembly-descriptor> element.

There is another reason (perhaps a more important reason) for separating information about the bean itself from the security roles and transactional attributes. The EJB 1.1 specification clearly defines the responsibilities of different participants in the development and deployment of beans. We don't address these development roles in this book because they are not critical to learning the fundamentals of EJB. For now, it's enough to know that the person who develops the bean and the person who assembles the beans into an application have separate responsibilities and therefore separate parts of the XML deployment descriptor. The bean developer is responsible for everything within the <enterprise-beans> element; the bean assembler is responsible for everything within the <assembly-descriptor>. In our example, we're playing both roles, developing the beans and assembling them. But in real life, you might buy a set of beans developed by a third-party vendor, who would have no idea how you intend to use the beans, what your security requirements are, etc.

The <assembly-descriptor> contains the <security-role> elements and their corresponding <method-permission> elements, which were described in Chapter 3 under "Security." In this example there is one security role, everyone, which is mapped to all the methods in the Cabin bean using the <method-permission> element. (The * in the <method-name> element means "all methods").

The container-transaction element declares that all the methods of the Cabin bean have a Required transactional attribute. Transactional attributes are explained in more detail in Chapter 8, but for now it means that all the methods must be executed within a transaction. The deployment descriptor ends with the enclosing tab of the <ejb-jar> element.

Copy the Cabin bean's deployment descriptor into the same directory as the class files for the Cabin bean files (*Cabin.class, CabinHome.class, CabinBean.class,* and *CabinPK.class*) and save it as *ejb-jar.xml.* You have now created all the files you need to package your EJB 1.1 Cabin bean. Figure 4-2 shows all the files that should be in the *cabin* directory.

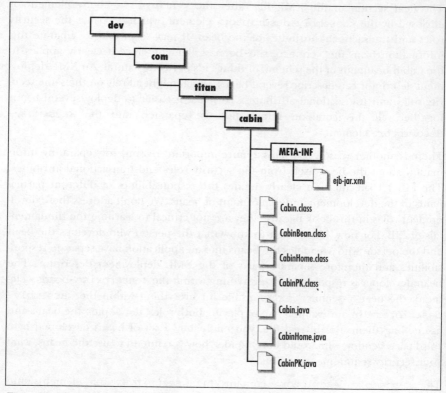

Figure 4-2. The Cabin bean files (EJB 1.1)

EJB 1.0: The Deployment Descriptor

Here is a Java application that instantiates, populates, and serializes a DeploymentDescriptor for the EJB 1.0 Cabin bean:

```
package com.titan.cabin;

import javax.ejb.deployment.EntityDescriptor;
import javax.ejb.deployment.ControlDescriptor;
import javax.naming.CompoundName;
import com.titan.cabin.CabinBean;
import java.util.Properties;
import java.io.FileOutputStream;
import java.io.ObjectOutputStream;
import java.lang.reflect.Field;

public class MakeDD {
```

```
public static void main(String [] args) {
  try {
    if (args.length <1){
      System.out.println("must specify target directory");
      return;
    }

    EntityDescriptor cabinDD = new EntityDescriptor();

    cabinDD.setEnterpriseBeanClassName("com.titan.cabin.CabinBean");
    cabinDD.setHomeInterfaceClassName("com.titan.cabin.CabinHome");
    cabinDD.setRemoteInterfaceClassName("com.titan.cabin.Cabin");
    cabinDD.setPrimaryKeyClassName("com.titan.cabin.CabinPK");

    Class beanClass = CabinBean.class;
    Field [] persistentFields = new Field[5];
    persistentFields[0] = beanClass.getDeclaredField("id");
    persistentFields[1] = beanClass.getDeclaredField("name");
    persistentFields[2] = beanClass.getDeclaredField("deckLevel");
    persistentFields[3] = beanClass.getDeclaredField("ship");
    persistentFields[4] = beanClass.getDeclaredField("bedCount");

    cabinDD.setContainerManagedFields(persistentFields);

    cabinDD.setReentrant(false);

    CompoundName jndiName = new CompoundName("CabinHome",
                                             new Properties());
    cabinDD.setBeanHomeName(jndiName);

    ControlDescriptor cd = new ControlDescriptor();

    cd.setIsolationLevel(ControlDescriptor.TRANSACTION_READ_COMMITTED);
    cd.setTransactionAttribute(ControlDescriptor.TX_REQUIRED);

    cd.setRunAsMode(ControlDescriptor.CLIENT_IDENTITY);

    cd.setMethod(null);
    ControlDescriptor [] cdArray = {cd};
    cabinDD.setControlDescriptors(cdArray);

    String fileSeparator =
        System.getProperties().getProperty("file.separator");
    if (! args[0].endsWith(fileSeparator))
        args[0] += fileSeparator;

    FileOutputStream fos = new FileOutputStream(args[0]+"CabinDD.ser");
    ObjectOutputStream oos = new ObjectOutputStream(fos);
    oos.writeObject(cabinDD);
    oos.flush();
```

```
        oos.close();
        fos.close();

        } catch (Throwable t) { t.printStackTrace();}
    }
}
```

Copy this definition into your IDE, save it in the *cabin* directory, and compile it. When you run the application, MakeDD, use the path to the *cabin* directory, where all the other Cabin bean files are stored, as a command-line parameter:

```
\dev % java com.titan.cabin.MakeDD com/titan/cabin

F:\..\dev>java com.titan.cabin.MakeDD com\titan\cabin
```

If you run this application, you should end up with a file called *CabinDD.ser* in the *com/titan/cabin* directory. This is your serialized DeploymentDescriptor for the Cabin bean. Now that you know that the application works properly, let's look at it in more detail. We begin with the creation of the EntityDescriptor:

```
EntityDescriptor cabinDD = new EntityDescriptor();
```

An entity descriptor is a DeploymentDescriptor that has been extended to support entity beans. If we were creating a DeploymentDescriptor for a session bean, we would use the SessionDescriptor subclass. Notice that we are not extending EntityDescriptor to create a special cabin DeploymentDescriptor. We are using the EntityDescriptor class provided by the EJB package javax.ejb.deployment.

The EntityDescriptor describes the classes and interfaces used by the Cabin bean. The next section of code sets the names of the bean class, the home interface, the remote interface, and the primary key. All of these set methods are defined in the EntityDescriptor's superclass, DeploymentDescriptor, except for setPrimaryKeyClassName(); this method is defined in the EntityDescriptor class.

```
cabinDD.setEnterpriseBeanClassName("com.titan.cabin.CabinBean");
cabinDD.setHomeInterfaceClassName("com.titan.cabin.CabinHome");
cabinDD.setRemoteInterfaceClassName("com.titan.cabin.Cabin");
cabinDD.setPrimaryKeyClassName("com.titan.cabin.CabinPK");
```

When the bean is deployed, the deployment tools will read these properties so that the tools can locate the bean interfaces and primary key class and generate all the supporting code, such as the EJB object and EJB home.

The next section is a little more complicated. Our Cabin bean is going to be a container-managed entity bean, which means that the container will automatically handle persistence. To handle persistence, the container must know which of the CabinBean's fields it is responsible for. Earlier, it was decided that the id, name, deckLevel, ship, and bedCount fields were all persistent fields in the

CabinBean. The following code tells the EntityDescriptor that these fields are container managed by using the Reflection API to pass an array of Field objects to setContainerManagedFields():

```
Class beanClass = CabinBean.class;
Field [] persistentFields = new Field[5];
persistentFields[0] = beanClass.getDeclaredField("id");
persistentFields[1] = beanClass.getDeclaredField("name");
persistentFields[2] = beanClass.getDeclaredField("deckLevel");
persistentFields[3] = beanClass.getDeclaredField("ship");
persistentFields[4] = beanClass.getDeclaredField("bedCount");

cabinDD.setContainerManagedFields(persistentFields);
```

Although the code tells the EntityDescriptor which fields are container-managed, it doesn't describe how these fields will map to the database. The actual mapping of the fields to the database depends on the type of database and on the EJB server used. The mapping is vendor- and database-dependent, so we won't worry about it just now. When the bean is actually deployed in some EJB server, the deployer will map the container-managed fields to whatever database is used.

The next line tells the EntityDescriptor that the Cabin bean is nonreentrant. We discussed the problems associated with reentrant beans in Chapter 3. Entity beans are not reentrant by default, but it never hurts to make this explicit.

```
cabinDD.setReentrant(false);
```

The following code uses the JNDI API to set the lookup name of the bean in the EJB server's directory structure. In Chapter 3, we saw that Enterprise JavaBeans requires servers to support the use of JNDI for organizing beans in a directory structure. Later, when we create a client application, the name we assign to the Cabin bean will be used to locate and obtain a remote reference to the bean's EJB home.

```
CompoundName jndiName = new CompoundName("CabinHome", new Properties());
cabinDD.setBeanHomeName(jndiName);
```

We have created a directory entry that places the bean under the name *Cabin-Home*. Although it makes sense to assign names that reflect the organization of your beans, you can give the EJB home any lookup name you like. We could have used other names assigned to the Cabin bean, like *HomeCabin* or just *cabin*.

Next, we create a ControlDescriptor to set the bean's transactional and security attributes:

```
ControlDescriptor cd = new ControlDescriptor();

cd.setIsolationLevel(ControlDescriptor.TRANSACTION_READ_COMMITTED);
cd.setTransactionAttribute(ControlDescriptor.TX_REQUIRED);
```

```
cd.setRunAsMode(ControlDescriptor.CLIENT_IDENTITY);

cd.setMethod(null);
ControlDescriptor [] cdArray = {cd};
cabinDD.setControlDescriptors(cdArray);
```

After creating the `ControlDescriptor`, we set its transactional attributes. This includes setting the transactional context and isolation level. Transactions are fairly complicated and are discussed in detail in Chapter 8. Essentially, we are saying that the bean must be executed in a transaction and that the bean is not accessible by any other client while executing a transaction. Next, we set the runAs mode of the bean. The runAs mode determines how the bean's methods will execute at runtime. In this case, the methods will be executed under the identity that invoked the bean. This means that any other beans or resources accessed by the method will be validated based on the client's identity. Then we set the methods that the `ControlDescriptor` represents and add the `ControlDescriptor` to the `EntityDescriptor`. Here we set the method to `null`, which means that the `ControlDescriptor` is the default for all methods of the Cabin bean. Any method that doesn't have its own `ControlDescriptor` uses the default `ControlDescriptor` for the bean. In this case, we only specify a default descriptor. Once all the properties on the `ControlDescriptor` have been set, it is added to the `EntityDescriptor`.

Finally, we serialize the `EntityDescriptor` with all its Cabin bean properties to a file called *CabinDD.ser*. This serialized `EntityDescriptor` should be saved to the same directory that holds all the other files for the Cabin bean, the *dev/com/titan/ cabin* directory.

```
String fileSeparator = System.getProperties().getProperty("file.separator");
if (! args[0].endsWith(fileSeparator))
    args[0] += fileSeparator;

FileOutputStream fos = new FileOutputStream(args[0]+"CabinDD.ser");
ObjectOutputStream oos = new ObjectOutputStream(fos);
oos.writeObject(cabinDD);
oos.flush();
oos.close();
fos.close();
```

The first part of the serialization section simply determines whether the path ends with a file separator for that operating system. If it doesn't, the code adds one. The second part serializes the deployment descriptor to a file called *CabinDD.ser* in the directory passed in at the command line.

You have now created everything you need to package your EJB 1.0 Cabin bean for deployment. Figure 4-3 shows all the files that should be in the *cabin* directory.

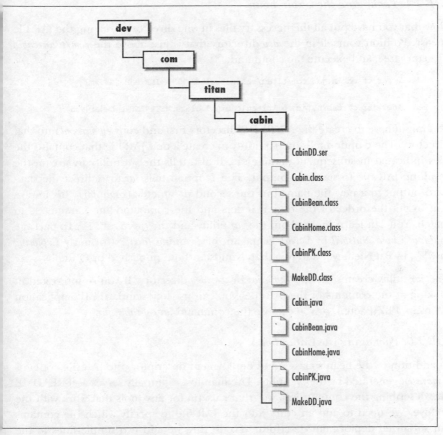

Figure 4-3. The Cabin bean files (EJB 1.0)

cabin.jar: The JAR File

The JAR file is a platform-independent file format for compressing, packaging, and delivering several files together. Based on ZIP file format and the ZLIB compression standards, the JAR (Java archive) packages and tool were originally developed to make downloads of Java applets more efficient. As a packaging mechanism, however, the JAR file format is a very convenient way to "shrink-wrap" components and other software for delivery to third parties. The original Java-Beans component architecture depends on JAR files for packaging, as does Enterprise JavaBeans. The goal in using the JAR file format in EJB is to package all the classes and interfaces associated with a bean, including the deployment descriptor into one file. The process of creating an EJB JAR file is slightly different between EJB 1.1 and EJB 1.0.

EJB 1.1: Packaging the Cabin bean

Now that you have put all the necessary files in one directory, creating the JAR file is easy. Position yourself in the *dev* directory that is just above the *com/titan/cabin* directory tree, and execute the command:

```
\dev % jar cf cabin.jar com/titan/cabin/*.class META-INF/ejb-jar.xml

F:\..\dev>jar cf cabin.jar com\titan\cabin\*.class META-INF\ejb-jar.xml
```

You might have to create the *META-INF* directory first and copy *ejb-jar.xml* into that directory. The c option tells the *jar* utility to create a new JAR file that contains the files indicated in subsequent parameters. It also tells the *jar* utility to stream the resulting JAR file to standard output. The f option tells *jar* to redirect the standard output to a new file named in the second parameter (*cabin.jar*). It's important to get the order of the option letters and the command-line parameters to match. You can learn more about the *jar* utility and the java.util.zip package in *Java™ in a Nutshell* by David Flanagan, or *Learning Java™* (formerly *Exploring Java™*), by Pat Niemeyer and Jonathan Knudsen (both published by O'Reilly).

The *jar* utility creates the file *cabin.jar* in the *dev* directory. If you're interested in looking at the contents of the JAR file, you can use any standard ZIP application (WinZip, PKZIP, etc.), or you can use the command *jar tvf cabin.jar.*

EJB 1.0: Packaging the Cabin bean

In addition to the bean's classes and deployment descriptor, the JAR file contains a *manifest* generated by the *jar* utility. The manifest essentially serves as a README file, describing the contents in a way that's useful for any tools that work with the archive. We need to add an entry into the JAR file to specify which file contains our serialized deployment descriptor. To do this, we add two simple lines to the manifest by creating an ASCII text file named *manifest*:

```
Name: com/titan/cabin/CabinDD.ser
Enterprise-Bean: True
```

That's it! When we run the *jar* utility, we will tell it to use our manifest information when it build the JAR. The manifest for this bean is now complete. A manifest is always organized as a set of name-value pairs that describe the files in the JAR file. In this case, we need to point to the location of the serialized deployment descriptor and define the JAR as an EJB JAR. The first line points to the serialized EntityDescriptor, *CabinDD.ser*, for the Cabin bean. Notice that forward slashes ("/") must be used as path separators; this could be confusing if you are used to the Windows environment. The next line of the manifest identifies the JAR as an EJB JAR. Most EJB server deployment tools check for this name-value pair before trying to read the JAR file's contents. Save the manifest in the *cabin* directory where all the other Cabin bean files are located. It should be saved as the file name *manifest* with no extension.

Now that you have put all the necessary files in one directory, creating the JAR file is easy. Position yourself in the *dev* directory that is just above the *com/titan/cabin* directory tree, and execute the following command:

```
\dev % jar cmf com/titan/cabin/manifest cabin.jar com/titan/cabin/*.class \
com/titan/cabin/*.ser

F:\..\dev>jar cmf com\titan\cabin\manifest cabin.jar com\titan\cabin\*.class
com\titan\cabin\*.ser
```

If you want, you may remove the *MakeDD.class* file from the JAR archive, since it's not a standard EJB class and the EJB deployment tools do not use it. Leaving it there will not impact deployment of the Cabin bean.

Creating a CABIN Table in the Database

One of the primary jobs of a deployment tool is mapping entity beans to databases. In the case of the Cabin bean, we must map its id, name, deckLevel, ship, and bedCount (the bean's container-managed fields) to some data source. Before proceeding with deployment, you need to set up a database and create a CABIN table. You can use the following standard SQL statement to create a CABIN table that will be consistent with the examples provided in this chapter:

```
create table CABIN
(
    ID int primary key,
    SHIP_ID int,
    BED_COUNT int,
    NAME char(30),
    DECK_LEVEL int
)
```

This statement creates a CABIN table that has five columns corresponding to the container-managed fields in the CabinBean class. Once the table is created and connectivity to the database is confirmed, you can proceed with the deployment process.

Deploying the Cabin Bean

Deployment is the process of reading the bean's JAR file, changing or adding properties to the deployment descriptor, mapping the bean to the database, defining access control in the security domain, and generating vendor-specific classes needed to support the bean in the EJB environment. Every EJB server product has its own deployment tools, which may provide a graphical user interface, a set of command-line programs, or both. Graphical deployment "wizards" are the easiest deployment tools to work with.

EJB 1.1 deployment tools

A deployment tool reads the JAR file and looks for the *ejb-jar.xml* file. In a graphical deployment wizard, the deployment descriptor elements will be presented in a set of property sheets similar to those used to customize visual components in environments like Visual Basic, PowerBuilder, JBuilder, and Symantec Café. Figure 4-4 shows the deployment wizard used in the J2EE Reference Implementation.

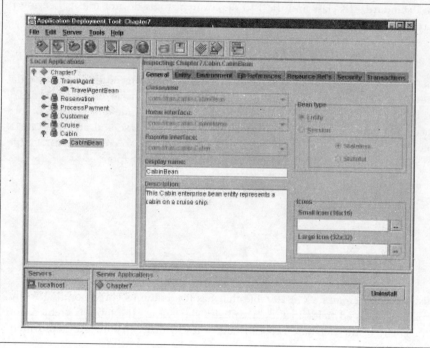

Figure 4-4. J2EE Reference Implementation's deployment wizard

The J2EE Reference Implementation's deployment wizard has fields and panels that match the XML deployment descriptor. You can map security roles to users groups, set the JNDI look up name, map the container-managed fields to the database, etc.

EJB 1.0 deployment tools

A deployment tool reads the JAR file and uses the manifest to locate the bean's serialized deployment descriptor. Once the deployment descriptor file has been located, it is deserialized into an object and its properties are read by invoking its get methods. In a graphical deployment wizard, these properties will be presented to the deployer in a set of property sheets, similar to those used to customize visual components in environments like Visual Basic, PowerBuilder, JBuilder, and Symantec Cafe. Figure 4-5 shows the deployment wizard used in BEA's WebLogic EJB server.

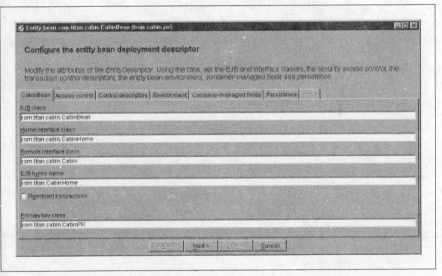

Figure 4-5. WebLogic deployment wizard

The WebLogic deployment wizard has fields and panels that match properties and deployment classes specified in the javax.ejb.deployment package. The "CabinBean" tab, for example, contains text fields for each of the interfaces and classes that we described in the Cabin bean's EntityDescriptor, the *CabinDD.ser*. There is also an "Access control" tab that corresponds to the Access-ControlEntry class, and a "Control descriptors" tab that corresponds to the ControlDescriptor class. In addition, there is a "Container-managed fields" tab that shows the container-managed fields we defined when creating the *CabinDD.ser*. Graphical deployment wizards provided by other EJB products will look different but provide the same kinds of features.

At this point, you can choose to change deployment information, such as the transactional isolation level, to change the Cabin bean's JNDI name, or to

deselect one of the container-managed fields. You can also add properties to the
deployment descriptor, for example, by setting the AccessControlEntrys for the
methods and adding environment properties. The *CabinDD.ser* that we created
should have specified the minimum information that most EJB servers need to
deploy the bean without changes. It is likely that all you will need to do is specify
the persistence mapping from the container-managed fields to the CABIN table in
the relational database.

Different EJB deployment tools will provide varying degrees of support for mapping container-managed fields to a data source. Some provide very robust and
sophisticated graphical user interfaces, while others are simpler and less flexible.
Fortunately, mapping the CabinBean's container-managed fields to the CABIN
table is a fairly straightforward process. Read the documentation for the deployment tool provided by your EJB vendor to determine how to do this mapping.
Once you have finished the mapping, you can complete the deployment of the
bean and prepare to access it from the EJB server.

Creating a Client Application

Now that the Cabin bean has been deployed in the EJB server, we want to access it
from a remote client. When we say remote, we are not necessarily talking about a
client application that is located on a different computer, just one that is not part
of the EJB server. In this section, we will create a remote client that will connect to
the EJB server, locate the EJB home for the Cabin bean, and create and interact
with several Cabin beans. The following code shows a Java application that is
designed to create a new Cabin bean, set its name, deckLevel, ship, and
bedCount properties, and then locate it again using its primary key:

```
package com.titan.cabin;

import com.titan.cabin.CabinHome;
import com.titan.cabin.Cabin;
import com.titan.cabin.CabinPK;

import javax.naming.InitialContext;
import javax.naming.Context;
import javax.naming.NamingException;
import java.rmi.RemoteException;
import java.util.Properties;

public class Client_1 {
    public static void main(String [] args) {
        try {
            Context jndiContext = getInitialContext();
            Object ref =
                jndiContext.lookup("CabinHome");
```

```
            CabinHome home = (CabinHome)
            // EJB 1.0:Use Java cast instead of narrow( )
               PortableRemoteObject.narrow(ref,CabinHome.class);
            Cabin cabin_1 = home.create(1);
            cabin_1.setName("Master Suite");
            cabin_1.setDeckLevel(1);
            cabin_1.setShip(1);
            cabin_1.setBedCount(3);

            CabinPK pk = new CabinPK();
            pk.id = 1;

            Cabin cabin_2 = home.findByPrimaryKey(pk);
            System.out.println(cabin_2.getName());
            System.out.println(cabin_2.getDeckLevel());
            System.out.println(cabin_2.getShip());
            System.out.println(cabin_2.getBedCount());

        } catch (java.rmi.RemoteException re){re.printStackTrace();}
          catch (javax.naming.NamingException ne){ne.printStackTrace();}
          catch (javax.ejb.CreateException ce){ce.printStackTrace();}
          catch (javax.ejb.FinderException fe){fe.printStackTrace();}
    }

    public static Context getInitialContext()
        throws javax.naming.NamingException {

        Properties p = new Properties();
        // ... Specify the JNDI properties specific to the vendor.
        return new javax.naming.InitialContext(p);
    }
}
```

To access an enterprise bean, a client starts by using the JNDI package to obtain a directory connection to a bean's container. JNDI is an implementation-independent API for directory and naming systems. Every EJB vendor must provide directory services that are JNDI-compliant. This means that they must provide a JNDI service provider, which is a piece of software analogous to a driver in JDBC. Different service providers connect to different directory services—not unlike JDBC, where different drivers connect to different relational databases. The method getInitialContext() contains logic that uses JNDI to obtain a network connection to the EJB server.

The code used to obtain the JNDI Context will be different depending on which EJB vendor you are using. You will need to research your EJB vendor's requirements for obtaining a JNDI Context appropriate to that product.

The code used to obtain a JNDI Context in Gemstone/J, for example, might look something like the following:

```
public static Context getInitialContext() throws javax.naming.NamingException {
    Properties p = new Properties();
    p.put(com.gemstone.naming.Defaults.NAME_SERVICE_HOST,"localhost");
    String port = System.getProperty("com.gemstone.naming.NameServicePort",
                            "10200");
    p.put(com.gemstone.naming.Defaults.NAME_SERVICE_PORT, port);
    p.put(Context.INITIAL_CONTEXT_FACTORY,"com.gemstone.naming.GsCtxFactory");
    return new InitialContext(p);
}
```

The same method developed for BEA's WebLogic Server would be different:

```
public static Context getInitialContext()
    throws javax.naming.NamingException {
    Properties p = new Properties();
    p.put(Context.INITIAL_CONTEXT_FACTORY,
            "weblogic.jndi.TengahInitialContextFactory");
    p.put(Context.PROVIDER_URL, "t3://localhost:7001");
    return new javax.naming.InitialContext(p);
}
```

Once a JNDI connection is established and a context is obtained from the getIntialContext() method, the context can be used to look up the EJB home of the Cabin bean:

EJB 1.1: Obtaining a remote reference to the home interface

The previous example uses the PortableRemoteObject.narrow() method as prescribed in EJB 1.1:

```
Object ref = jndiContext.lookup("CabinHome");
CabinHome home = (CabinHome)
// EJB 1.0: Use Java cast instead of narrow()
    PortableRemoteObject.narrow(ref,CabinHome.class);
```

The PortableRemoteObject.narrow() method is new to EJB 1.1. It is needed to support the requirements of RMI over IIOP. Because CORBA supports many different languages, casting is not native to CORBA (some languages don't have casting). Therefore, to get a remote reference to CabinHome, we must explicitly narrow the object returned from lookup(). This has the same effect as casting and is explained in more detail in Chapter 5.

The name used to find the Cabin bean's EJB home is set by the deployer using a deployment wizard like the one pictured earlier. The JNDI name is entirely up to the person deploying the bean; it can be the same as the bean name set in the XML deployment descriptor or something completely different.

EJB 1.0: Obtaining a remote reference to the home interface

In EJB 1.0, you do not need to use the `PortableRemoteObject.narrow()` method to cast objects to the correct type. EJB 1.0 allows the use of Java native casting to narrow the type returned by the JNDI API to the home interface type. When you see the `PortableRemoteObject` being used, replace it with Java native casting as follows:

```
CabinHome home = (CabinHome)jndiContext.lookup("CabinHome");
```

To locate the EJB home, we specify the name that we set using the `Deployment-Descriptor.setBeanHomeName(String name)` method in the `MakeDD` application earlier. If this lookup succeeds, the `home` variable will contain a remote reference to the Cabin bean's EJB home.

Creating a new Cabin bean

Once we have a remote reference to the EJB home, we can use it to create a new Cabin entity:

```
Cabin cabin_1 = home.create(1);
```

We create a new `Cabin` entity using the `create(int id)` method defined in the home interface of the Cabin bean. When this method is invoked, the EJB home works with the EJB server to create a Cabin bean, adding its data to the database. The EJB server then creates an EJB object to wrap the Cabin bean instance and returns a remote reference to the EJB object to the client. The `cabin_1` variable then contains a remote reference to the Cabin bean we just created.

NOTE   In EJB 1.1, we don't need to use the `PortableRemoteObject.narrow()` method to get the EJB object from the home reference, because it was declared as returning the Cabin type; no casting was required. We don't need to explicitly narrow remote references returned by `findByPrimaryKey()` for the same reason.

With the remote reference to the EJB object, we can update the `name`, `deckLevel`, `ship`, and `bedCount` of the Cabin entity:

```
Cabin cabin_1 = home.create(1);
cabin_1.setName("Master Suite");
cabin_1.setDeckLevel(1);
cabin_1.setShip(1);
cabin_1.setBedCount(3);
```

Figure 4-6 shows how the relational database table that we created should look after executing this code. It should contain one record.

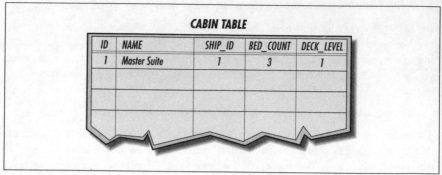

Figure 4-6. CABIN table with one cabin record

After an entity bean has been created, a client can locate it using the findByPrimaryKey() method in the home interface. First, we create a primary key of the correct type, in this case CabinPK, and set its field id to equal the id of the cabin we want. (So far, we only have one cabin available to us.) When we invoke this method on the home interface, we get back a remote reference to the EJB object. We can now interrogate the remote reference returned by findByPrimaryKey() to get the Cabin entity's name, deckLevel, ship, and bedCount:

```
CabinPK pk = new CabinPK();
pk.id = 1;

Cabin cabin_2 = home.findByPrimaryKey(pk);
System.out.println(cabin_2.getName());
System.out.println(cabin_2.getDeckLevel());
System.out.println(cabin_2.getShip());
System.out.println(cabin_2.getBedCount());
```

Copy and save the Client_1 application to any directory, and compile it. If you haven't started your EJB server and deployed the Cabin bean, do so now. When you're finished, you're ready to run the Client_1 in your IDE's debugger so that you can watch each step of the program. Your output should look something like the following:

```
Master Suite
1
1
3
```

You just created and used your first entity bean! Of course, the client application doesn't do much. Before going on to create session beans, create another client that adds some test data to the database. Here we'll create Client_2 as a modification of Client_1 that populates the database with a large number of cabins for three different ships:

```
package com.titan.cabin;

import com.titan.cabin.CabinHome;
import com.titan.cabin.Cabin;
import com.titan.cabin.CabinPK;

import javax.naming.InitialContext;
import javax.naming.Context;
import javax.naming.NamingException;
import javax.ejb.CreateException;
import java.rmi.RemoteException;
import java.util.Properties;

public class Client_2 {

    public static void main(String [] args) {
        try {
            Context jndiContext = getInitialContext();

            Object ref =
                jndiContext.lookup("CabinHome");
            CabinHome home = (CabinHome)
            // EJB 1.0: Use Java native cast
                PortableRemoteObject.narrow(ref,CabinHome.class);
            // Add 9 cabins to deck 1 of ship 1.
            makeCabins(home, 2, 10, 1, 1);
            // Add 10 cabins to deck 2 of ship 1.
            makeCabins(home, 11, 20, 2, 1);
            // Add 10 cabins to deck 3 of ship 1.
            makeCabins(home, 21, 30, 3, 1);

            // Add 10 cabins to deck 1 of ship 2.
            makeCabins(home, 31, 40, 1, 2);
            // Add 10 cabins to deck 2 of ship 2.
            makeCabins(home, 41, 50, 2, 2);
            // Add 10 cabins to deck 3 of ship 2.
            makeCabins(home, 51, 60, 3, 2);

            // Add 10 cabins to deck 1 of ship 3.
            makeCabins(home, 61, 70, 1, 3);
            // Add 10 cabins to deck 2 of ship 3.
            makeCabins(home, 71, 80, 2, 3);
            // Add 10 cabins to deck 3 of ship 3.
            makeCabins(home, 81, 90, 3, 3);
            // Add 10 cabins to deck 4 of ship 3.
            makeCabins(home, 91, 100, 4, 3);
```

```
            for (int i = 1; i <= 100; i++){
                CabinPK pk = new CabinPK();
                pk.id = i;
                Cabin cabin = home.findByPrimaryKey(pk);
                System.out.println("PK = "+i+", Ship = "+cabin.getShip()
                    + ", Deck = "+cabin.getDeckLevel()
                    + ", BedCount = "+cabin.getBedCount()
                    + ", Name = "+cabin.getName());
            }

        } catch (java.rmi.RemoteException re) {re.printStackTrace();}
          catch (javax.naming.NamingException ne) {ne.printStackTrace();}
          catch (javax.ejb.CreateException ce) {ce.printStackTrace();}
          catch (javax.ejb.FinderException fe) {fe.printStackTrace();}
    }

    public static javax.naming.Context getInitialContext()
        throws javax.naming.NamingException{
      Properties p = new Properties();
      // ... Specify the JNDI properties specific to the vendor.
      return new javax.naming.InitialContext(p);
    }

    public static void makeCabins(CabinHome home, int fromId, int toId,
                                  int deckLevel, int shipNumber)
      throws RemoteException, CreateException {

      int bc = 3;
      for (int i = fromId; i <= toId; i++) {
          Cabin cabin = home.create(i);
          int suiteNumber = deckLevel*100+(i-fromId);
          cabin.setName("Suite "+suiteNumber);
          cabin.setDeckLevel(deckLevel);
          bc = (bc==3)?2:3;
          cabin.setBedCount(bc);
          cabin.setShip(shipNumber);
      }
    }
}
```

Copy this code into your IDE, save, and recompile the Client_2 application. When it compiles successfully, run it. There's lots of output—here are the first few lines:

```
PK = 1, Ship = 1, Deck = 1, BedCount = 3, Name = Master Suite
PK = 2, Ship = 1, Deck = 1, BedCount = 2, Name = Suite 100
PK = 3, Ship = 1, Deck = 1, BedCount = 3, Name = Suite 101
PK = 4, Ship = 1, Deck = 1, BedCount = 2, Name = Suite 102
PK = 5, Ship = 1, Deck = 1, BedCount = 3, Name = Suite 103
```

```
PK = 6, Ship = 1, Deck = 1, BedCount = 2, Name = Suite 104
PK = 7, Ship = 1, Deck = 1, BedCount = 3, Name = Suite 105
...
```

You now have 100 cabin records in your CABIN table, representing 100 cabin entities in your EJB system. This provides a good set of test data for the session bean we will create in the next section, and for subsequent examples throughout the book.

Developing a Session Bean

Session beans act as agents to the client, controlling workflow (the business process) and filling the gaps between the representation of data by entity beans and the business logic that interacts with that data. Session beans are often used to manage interactions between entity beans and can perform complex manipulations of beans to accomplish some task. Since we have only defined one entity bean so far, we will focus on a complex manipulation of the Cabin bean rather than the interactions of the Cabin bean with other entity beans. In Chapter 7, after we have had the opportunity to develop other entity beans, interactions of entity beans within session beans will be explored in greater detail.

Client applications and other beans use the Cabin bean in a variety of ways. Some of these uses were predictable when the Cabin bean was defined, but most were not. After all, an entity bean represents data—in this case, data describing a cabin. The uses to which we put that data will change over time—hence the importance of separating the data itself from the workflow. In Titan's business system, for example, we will need to list and report on cabins in ways that were not predictable when the Cabin bean was defined. Rather than change the Cabin bean every time we need to look at it differently, we will obtain the information we need using a session bean. Changing the definition of an entity bean should only be done within the context of a larger process—for example, a major redesign of the business system.

In Chapters 1 and 2, we talked hypothetically about a TravelAgent bean that was responsible for the workflow of booking a passage on a cruise. This session bean will be used in client applications accessed by travel agents throughout the world. In addition to booking tickets, the TravelAgent bean also provides information about which cabins are available on the cruise. In this chapter, we will develop the first implementation of this listing behavior in the TravelAgent bean. The listing method we develop in this example is admittedly very crude and far from optimal. However, this example is useful for demonstrating how to develop a very simple stateless session bean and how these session beans can manage other beans. In Chapter 7, we will rewrite the listing method. This "list cabins" behavior is used by travel agents to provide customers with a list of cabins that can accommodate the customer's needs. The Cabin bean does not directly support the kind of list, nor should it. The list we need is specific to the TravelAgent bean, so it's the Travel-Agent bean's responsibility to query the Cabin beans and produce the list.

Before we get started, we will need to create a development directory for the TravelAgent bean, as we did for the Cabin bean. We name this directory *travel-agent* and nest it below the *com/titan* directory, which also contains the *cabin* directory (see Figure 4-7).

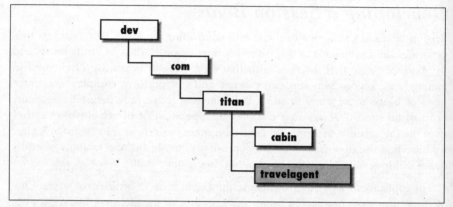

Figure 4-7. Directory structure for the TravelAgent bean

TravelAgent: The Remote Interface

As before, we start by defining the remote interface so that our focus is on the business purpose of the bean, rather than its implementation. Starting small, we know that the TravelAgent will need to provide a method for listing all the cabins available with a specified bed count for a specific ship. We'll call that method listCabins(). Since we only need a list of cabin names and deck levels, we'll define listCabins() to return an array of Strings. Here's the remote interface for TravelAgent:

```
package com.titan.travelagent;

import java.rmi.RemoteException;
import javax.ejb.FinderException;

public interface TravelAgent extends javax.ejb.EJBObject {

    // String elements follow the format "id, name, deck level"
    public String [] listCabins(int shipID, int bedCount)
        throws RemoteException;
```

Copy the `TravelAgent` interface definition into your IDE, and save it to the *travelagent* directory. Compile the class to ensure that it is correct.

TravelAgentHome: The Home Interface

The second step in the development of any bean is to create the home interface. The home interface for a session bean defines the create methods that initialize a new session bean for use by a client.

Find methods are not used in session beans; they are used with entity beans to locate persistent entities for use on a client. Unlike entity beans, session beans are not persistent and do not represent data in the database, so a find method would not be meaningful; there is no specific session to locate. A session bean is dedicated to a client for the life of that client (or less). For the same reason, we don't need to worry about primary keys; since session beans don't represent persistent data, we don't need a key to access that data.

```
package com.titan.travelagent;

import java.rmi.RemoteException;
import javax.ejb.CreateException;

public interface TravelAgentHome extends javax.ejb.EJBHome {
    public TravelAgent create()
        throws RemoteException, CreateException;
}
```

In the case of the TravelAgent bean, we only need a simple `create()` method to get a reference to the bean. Invoking this `create()` method returns a Travel-Agent remote reference that the client can use for the reservation process. Copy the `TravelAgentHome` definition into your IDE and save it to the *travelagent* directory. Compile the class to ensure that it is correct.

TravelAgentBean: The Bean Class

Using the remote interface as a guide, we can define the `TravelAgentBean` class that implements the `listCabins()` method. The following code contains the complete definition of `TravelAgentBean` for this example. Copy the Travel-AgentBean definition into your IDE and save it to the *travelagent* directory. Compile the class to ensure that it is correct. EJB 1.1 and EJB 1.0 differ significantly in how one bean locates another, so I have provided separate TravelAgentBean listings for each version.

EJB 1.1: *TravelAgentBean*

Here's the code for the EJB 1.1 version of the `TravelAgentBean`:

```
package com.titan.travelagent;

import com.titan.cabin.Cabin;
import com.titan.cabin.CabinHome;
import com.titan.cabin.CabinPK;
import java.rmi.RemoteException;
import javax.naming.InitialContext;
import javax.naming.Context;
import java.util.Properties;
import java.util.Vector;

public class TravelAgentBean implements javax.ejb.SessionBean {

    public void ejbCreate() {
    // Do nothing.
    }
    public String [] listCabins(int shipID, int bedCount) {

        try {
            javax.naming.Context jndiContext = new InitialContext();
            Object obj = jndiContext.lookup("java:comp/env/ejb/CabinHome");

            CabinHome home = (CabinHome)
                javax.rmi.PortableRemoteObject.narrow(obj, CabinHome.class);

            Vector vect = new Vector();
            CabinPK pk = new CabinPK();
            Cabin cabin;
            for (int i = 1; ; i++) {
                pk.id = i;
                try {
                    cabin = home.findByPrimaryKey(pk);
                } catch(javax.ejb.FinderException fe) {
                    break;
                }
                // Check to see if the bed count and ship ID match.
                if (cabin.getShip() == shipID &&
                    cabin.getBedCount() == bedCount) {
                    String details =
                        i+","+cabin.getName()+","+cabin.getDeckLevel();
                    vect.addElement(details);
                }
            }

            String [] list = new String[vect.size()];
            vect.copyInto(list);
            return list;
```

```
            } catch(Exception e) {throw new EJBException(e);}
    }

    private javax.naming.Context getInitialContext()
    throws javax.naming.NamingException {
        Properties p = new Properties();
        // ... Specify the JNDI properties specific to the vendor.
        return new javax.naming.InitialContext(p);
    }

    public void ejbRemove(){}
    public void ejbActivate(){}
    public void ejbPassivate(){}
    public void setSessionContext(javax.ejb.SessionContext cntx){}
}
```

Examining the listCabins() method in detail, we can address the implementation in pieces, starting with the use of JNDI to locate the CabinHome:

```
javax.naming.Context jndiContext = new InitialContext();

Object obj = jndiContext.lookup("java:comp/env/ejb/CabinHome");

CabinHome home = (CabinHome)
    javax.rmi.PortableRemoteObject.narrow(obj, CabinHome.class);
```

Beans are clients to other beans, just like client applications. This means that they
must interact with other beans in the same way that client applications interact
with beans. In order for one bean to locate and use another bean, it must first
locate and obtain a reference to the bean's EJB home. This is accomplished using
JNDI, in exactly the same way we used JNDI to obtain a reference to the
CabinHome in the client application we developed earlier. In EJB 1.1, all beans
have a default JNDI context called the environment context, which was discussed a
little in Chapter 3. The default context exists in the name space (directory) called
"java:comp/env" and its subdirectories. When the bean is deployed, any beans it
uses are mapped into the subdirectory "java:comp/env/ejb", so that bean references can be obtained at runtime through a simple and consistent use of the JNDI
default context. We'll come back to this when we take a look at the deployment
descriptor for the TravelAgent bean below.

Once the EJB home of the Cabin bean is obtained, we can use it to produce a list
of cabins that match the parameters passed. The following code loops through all
the Cabin beans and produces a list that includes only those cabins with the ship
and bed count specified:

```
Vector vect = new Vector();
CabinPK pk = new CabinPK();
Cabin cabin;
```

```
for (int i = 1; ; i++) {
  pk.id = i;
  try {
      cabin = home.findByPrimaryKey(pk);
  } catch(javax.ejb.FinderException fe){
      break;
  }
  // Check to see if the bed count and ship ID match.
  if (cabin.getShip() == shipID && cabin.getBedCount() == bedCount) {
      String details = i+","+cabin.getName()+","+cabin.getDeckLevel();
      vect.addElement(details);
  }
}
```

This method simply iterates through all the primary keys, obtaining a remote reference to each Cabin bean in the system and checking whether its ship and bedCount match the parameters passed in. The for loop continues until a FinderException is thrown, which would probably occur when a primary key is used that isn't associated with a bean. (This isn't the most robust code possible, but it will do for now.) Following this block of code, we simply copy the Vector's contents into an array and return it to the client.

While this is a very crude approach to locating the right Cabin beans—we will define a better method in Chapter 7—it is adequate for our current purposes. The purpose of this example is to illustrate that the workflow associated with this listing behavior is not included in the Cabin bean nor is it embedded in a client application. Workflow logic, whether it's a process like booking a reservation or obtaining a list, is placed in a session bean.

EJB 1.0: TravelAgentBean

Here's the code for the EJB 1.0 version of the TravelAgentBean:

```
package com.titan.travelagent;

import com.titan.cabin.Cabin;
import com.titan.cabin.CabinHome;
import com.titan.cabin.CabinPK;
import java.rmi.RemoteException;
import javax.naming.InitialContext;
import javax.naming.Context;
import java.util.Properties;
import java.util.Vector;

public class TravelAgentBean implements javax.ejb.SessionBean {

  public void ejbCreate() {
    // Do nothing.
  }
```

```java
    public String [] listCabins(int shipID, int bedCount)
      throws RemoteException {
        try {
            Context jndiContext = getInitialContext();
            CabinHome home = (CabinHome)jndiContext.lookup("CabinHome");

            Vector vect = new Vector();
            CabinPK pk = new CabinPK();
            Cabin cabin;
            for (int i = 1; ; i++) {
               pk.id = i;
               try {
                    cabin = home.findByPrimaryKey(pk);
               } catch(javax.ejb.FinderException fe) {
                    break;
               }
               // Check to see if the bed count and ship ID match.
               if (cabin.getShip() == shipID &&
                   cabin.getBedCount() == bedCount) {
                 String details =
                    i+","+cabin.getName()+","+cabin.getDeckLevel();
                 vect.addElement(details);
               }
            }

            String [] list = new String[vect.size()];
            vect.copyInto(list);
            return list;

        } catch (javax.naming.NamingException ne) {
            throw new RemoteException("Unable to locate CabinHome",ne);
        }
    }

    private javax.naming.Context getInitialContext()
    throws javax.naming.NamingException {
        Properties p = new Properties();
        // ... Specify the JNDI properties specific to the vendor.
        return new javax.naming.InitialContext(p);
    }

    public void ejbRemove(){}
    public void ejbActivate(){}
    public void ejbPassivate(){}
    public void setSessionContext(javax.ejb.SessionContext cntx){}

}
```

The most significant difference between this code and the EJB 1.1 code is the use of JNDI to locate the CabinHome:

```
Context jndiContext = getInitialContext();
CabinHome cabinHome = (CabinHome)jndiContext.lookup("CabinHome");
```

Beans interact with other beans in the same way that clients interact with beans. In order for one bean to locate and use another bean, it must first locate and obtain a reference to the bean's EJB home. This is accomplished using JNDI, in exactly the same way we used JNDI to obtain a reference to the CabinHome in the client application we developed earlier. If you take a close look at the method getInitialContext(), you will discover that it is exactly the same as the getInitialContext() method in the client classes defined earlier. The only difference is that the method is not static. You will need to change this code to match the correct settings for your EJB server. Once the EJB home of the Cabin bean is obtained, we can use it to produce our list of cabins that match the parameters passed.

The logic for finding beans with cabins that match the desired parameters is the same in EJB 1.1 and EJB 1.0. Again, it's a crude approach: we will define a better method in Chapter 7. Our purpose here is to demonstrate that the workflow associated with this listing behavior is not included in the Cabin bean nor is it embedded in a client application. Workflow logic, whether it's a process like booking a reservation or obtaining a list, is placed in a session bean.

EJB 1.1: TravelAgent Bean's Deployment Descriptor

The TravelAgent bean uses an XML deployment descriptor similar to the one used for the Cabin entity bean. Here is the *ejb-jar.xml* file used to deploy the TravelAgent. In Chapter 10, you will learn how to deploy several beans in one deployment descriptor, but for now the TravelAgent and Cabin beans are deployed separately.

```
<?xml version="1.0"?>

<!DOCTYPE ejb-jar PUBLIC "-//Sun Microsystems, Inc.//DTD Enterprise
JavaBeans 1.1//EN" "http://java.sun.com/j2ee/dtds/ejb-jar_1_1.dtd">
<ejb-jar>
  <enterprise-beans>
   <session>
     <ejb-name>TravelAgentBean</ejb-name>
     <home>com.titan.travelagent.TravelAgentHome</home>
     <remote>com.titan.travelagent.TravelAgent</remote>
     <ejb-class>com.titan.travelagent.TravelAgentBean</ejb-class>
     <session-type>Stateless</session-type>
     <transaction-type>Container</transaction-type>
```

```
    <ejb-ref>
      <ejb-ref-name>ejb/CabinHome</ejb-ref-name>
      <ejb-ref-type>Entity</ejb-ref-type>
      <home>com.titan.cabin.CabinHome</home>
      <remote>com.titan.cabin.Cabin</remote>
    </ejb-ref>
  </session>
</enterprise-beans>

<assembly-descriptor>
  <security-role>
    <description>
       This role represents everyone who is allowed full access
       to the cabin bean.
    </description>
    <role-name>everyone</role-name>
  </security-role>

  <method-permission>
    <role-name>everyone</role-name>
    <method>
        <ejb-name>TravelAgentBean</ejb-name>
        <method-name>*</method-name>
    </method>
  </method-permission>

  <container-transaction>
    <method>
        <ejb-name>TravelAgentBean</ejb-name>
        <method-name>*</method-name>
    </method>
    <trans-attribute>Required</trans-attribute>
  </container-transaction>
 </assembly-descriptor>
</ejb-jar>
```

Other than the <session-type> and <ejb-ref> elements, this XML deployment descriptor should make sense since it uses many of the same elements as the Cabin bean's. The <session-type> element can be Stateful or Stateless to indicate which type of session bean is used.

The <ejb-ref> element is used at deployment time to map the bean references used within the TravelAgent bean. In this case, the <ejb-ref> element describes the Cabin bean, which we already deployed. The <ejb-ref-name> element specifies the name that must be used by the TravelAgent bean to obtain a reference to the Cabin bean's home. The <ejb-ref-type> tells the container what kind of bean it is, Entity or Session. The <home> and <remote> elements specify the fully qualified interface names of the Cabin's home and remote bean interfaces.

When the bean is deployed, the <ejb-ref> will be mapped to the Cabin bean in the EJB server. This is a vendor-specific process, but the outcome should always be the same. When the TravelAgent does a JNDI lookup using the context name "java:comp/env/ejb/CabinHome" it will obtain a remote reference to the Cabin bean's home. The purpose of the <ejb-ref> element is to eliminate network specific and implementation specific use of JNDI to obtain bean references. This makes a bean more portable because the network location and JNDI service provider can change without impacting the bean code or even the XML deployment descriptor.

EJB 1.0: The TravelAgent Beans' Deployment Descriptor

Deploying the TravelAgent bean is essentially the same as deploying the Cabin bean, except we use a SessionDescriptor instead of an EntityDescriptor. Here is the definition of the MakeDD for creating and serializing a Session-Descriptor for the TravelAgentBean:

```
package com.titan.travelagent;

import javax.ejb.deployment.*;
import javax.naming.CompoundName;
import java.util.*;
import java.io.*;

public class MakeDD {

    public static void main(String [] args) {
        try {

            if (args.length <1) {
                System.out.println("must specify target directory");
                return;
            }

            SessionDescriptor sd = new SessionDescriptor();

            sd.setEnterpriseBeanClassName(
                "com.titan.travelagent.TravelAgentBean");
            sd.setHomeInterfaceClassName(
                "com.titan.travelagent.TravelAgentHome");
            sd.setRemoteInterfaceClassName(
                "com.titan.travelagent.TravelAgent");

            sd.setSessionTimeout(300);
            sd.setStateManagementType(SessionDescriptor.STATELESS_SESSION);
```

```
                ControlDescriptor cd = new ControlDescriptor();
                cd.setIsolationLevel(ControlDescriptor.TRANSACTION_READ_COMMITTED);
                cd.setMethod(null);
                cd.setRunAsMode(ControlDescriptor.CLIENT_IDENTITY);
                cd.setTransactionAttribute(ControlDescriptor.TX_REQUIRED);
                ControlDescriptor [] cdArray = {cd};
                sd.setControlDescriptors(cdArray);

                CompoundName jndiName =
                    new CompoundName("TravelAgentHome", new Properties());
                sd.setBeanHomeName(jndiName);

                String fileSeparator =
                    System.getProperties().getProperty("file.separator");
                if(! args[0].endsWith(fileSeparator))
                    args[0] += fileSeparator;

                FileOutputStream fis =
                    new FileOutputStream(args[0]+"TravelAgentDD.ser");
                ObjectOutputStream oos = new ObjectOutputStream(fis);
                oos.writeObject(sd);
                oos.flush();
                oos.close();
                fis.close();
            } catch(Throwable t) { t.printStackTrace(); }
        }
    }
```

The MakeDD definition for the TravelAgent bean is essentially the same as the one for the Cabin bean. The difference is that we are using a SessionDescriptor instead of an EntityDescriptor and the bean class names and JNDI name are different. We do not specify any container-managed fields because session beans are not persistent.

After instantiating the javax.ejb.SessionDescriptor, the MakeDD application sets the remote interface and bean class names:

```
    sd.setEnterpriseBeanClassName("com.titan.travelagent.TravelAgentBean");
    sd.setHomeInterfaceClassName("com.titan.travelagent.TravelAgentHome");
    sd.setRemoteInterfaceClassName("com.titan.travelagent.TravelAgent");
```

Next, we set two properties that control session timeouts (what happens if the bean is idle) and state management:

```
    sd.setSessionTimeout(300);
    sd.setStateManagementType(SessionDescriptor.STATELESS_SESSION);
```

setSessionTimeout() specifies how many seconds the session should remain alive if it is not being used. In MakeDD we specify 300 seconds. This means that if no method is invoked on the session for over five minutes, it will be removed and will no longer be available for use.* If a method is invoked on a bean that has timed out, a `javax.ejb.ObjectNotFoundException` will be thrown. Once a stateful session bean has timed out, all of its accumulated state is lost. When a session bean times out, the client must create a new TravelAgent bean by invoking the `TravelAgentHome.create()` method. The `setStateManagement()` method determines whether the bean is stateful or stateless. At this point in it its development, the `TravelAgentBean` doesn't have any conversational state that needs to be maintained from one method to the next, so we make it a stateless session bean, which is more efficient. Both of these methods are unique to session descriptors; there are no corresponding methods in the `EntityDescriptor` class.

The next section specifies the default `ControlDescriptor` for the `TravelAgent-Bean`. These settings are the same as those used in the Cabin bean. The isolation level determines the visibility of the data being accessed. Chapter 8 explores isolation levels in more detail. The transactional attribute, `TX_REQUIRED`, tells the EJB server that this bean must be included in the transactional scope of the client invoking it; if the client is not in a transaction, a new transaction must be created for the method invocation, as follows:

```
ControlDescriptor cd = new ControlDescriptor();
cd.setIsolationLevel(ControlDescriptor.TRANSACTION_READ_COMMITTED);
cd.setMethod(null);
cd.setRunAsMode(ControlDescriptor.CLIENT_IDENTITY);
cd.setTransactionAttribute(ControlDescriptor.TX_REQUIRED);
ControlDescriptor [] cdArray = {cd};
sd.setControlDescriptors(cdArray);
```

The next section creates a JNDI name for `TravelAgent`'s EJB home. When we use JNDI to look up the `TravelAgentHome`, this will be the name we specify:

```
CompoundName jndiName = new CompoundName("TravelAgentHome",new Properties());
```

Finally, the `MakeDD` serializes the `SessionDescriptor` to a file named *Travel-AgentDD.ser* and saves it to the *travelagent* directory.

You will need to compile and run the `MakeDD` class before continuing:

```
\dev % java com.titan.travelagent.MakeDD com/titan/travelagent

F:\..\dev>java com.titan.travelagent.MakeDD com\titan\travelagent
```

---

* Whether a session timeout is measured from creation time (the time the session bean is created) or from the time of last activity (when the last business method is invoked) is not clearly described in EJB 1.0. As a result, some vendors set the timeout relative to one of these two events (creation or last activity). Consult your vendor's documentation to determine your EJB server's timeout policy.

EJB 1.1: The JAR File

To place the TravelAgent bean in a JAR file, we use the same process we used for the Cabin bean. We shrink-wrap the TravelAgent bean class and its deployment descriptor into a JAR file and save to the *com/titan/travelagent* directory:

```
\dev % jar cf cabin.jar com/titan/travelagent/*.class META-INF/ejb-jar.xml

F:\..\dev>jar cf cabin.jar com\titan\travelagent\*.class META-INF\ejb-jar.xml
```

You might have to create the *META-INF* directory first, and copy *ejb-jar.xml* into that directory. The TravelAgent bean is now complete and ready to be deployed.

EJB 1.0: The JAR File

To place the TravelAgent bean in a JAR file, we use the same process we used for the Cabin bean. First, we have to create a manifest file, which we save in the *com/titan/travelagent* directory:

```
Name: com/titan/travelagent/TravelAgentDD.ser
Enterprise-Bean: True
```

Now that the manifest is ready, we can shrink-wrap the TravelAgent bean so that it's ready for deployment:

```
\dev % jar cmf com/titan/travelagent/manifest \
TravelAgent.jar com/titan/travelagent/*.class com/titan/travelagent/*.ser

F:\..\dev>jar cmf com\titan\travelagent\manifest TravelAgent.jar
com\titan\travelagent\*.class com\titan\travelagent\*.ser
```

The TravelAgent bean is now complete and ready to be deployed.

Deploying the TravelAgent Bean

To make your TravelAgent bean available to a client application, you need to use the deployment utility or wizard of your EJB server. The deployment utility reads the JAR file to add the TravelAgent bean to the EJB server environment. Unless your EJB server has special requirements, it is unlikely that you will need to change or add any new attributes to the bean. You will not need to create a database table for this example, since the TravelAgent bean is using only the Cabin bean and is not itself persistent. Deploy the TravelAgent bean and proceed to the next section.

Creating a Client Application

To show that our session bean works, we'll create a simple client application that uses it. This client simply produces a list of cabins assigned to ship 1 with a bed count of 3. Its logic is similar to the client we created earlier to test the Cabin bean: it creates a context for looking up `TravelAgentHome`, creates a Travel-Agent bean, and invokes `listCabins()` to generate a list of the cabins available. Here's the code:

```
package com.titan.travelagent;

import com.titan.cabin.CabinHome;
import com.titan.cabin.Cabin;
import com.titan.cabin.CabinPK;

import javax.naming.InitialContext;
import javax.naming.Context;
import javax.naming.NamingException;
import javax.ejb.CreateException;
import java.rmi.RemoteException;
import java.util.Properties;

public class Client_1 {
    public static int SHIP_ID = 1;
    public static int BED_COUNT = 3;

    public static void main(String [] args) {
        try {
            Context jndiContext = getInitialContext();

            Object ref = (TravelAgentHome)
                jndiContext.lookup("TravelAgentHome");
            TravelAgentHome home = (TravelAgentHome)
                // EJB 1.0: Use Java cast instead of narrow()
                PortableRemoteObject.narrow(ref,TravelAgentHome.class);

            TravelAgent reserve = home.create();

            // Get a list of all cabins on ship 1 with a bed count of 3.
            String list [] = reserve.listCabins(SHIP_ID,BED_COUNT);

            for(int i = 0; i < list.length; i++){
                System.out.println(list[i]);
            }

        } catch(java.rmi.RemoteException re){re.printStackTrace();}
        catch(Throwable t){t.printStackTrace();}
    }
    static public Context getInitialContext() throws Exception {
        Properties p = new Properties();
        // ... Specify the JNDI properties specific to the vendor.
        return new InitialContext(p);
    }
```

The output should look like this:

```
1,Master Suite              ,1
3,Suite 101                 ,1
5,Suite 103                 ,1
7,Suite 105                 ,1
9,Suite 107                 ,1
12,Suite 201                ,2
14,Suite 203                ,2
16,Suite 205                ,2
18,Suite 207                ,2
20,Suite 209                ,2
22,Suite 301                ,3
24,Suite 303                ,3
26,Suite 305                ,3
28,Suite 307                ,3
30,Suite 309                ,3
```

You have now successfully created the first piece of the TravelAgent session bean: a method that obtains a list of cabins by manipulating the Cabin bean entity.

5

The Client View

Developing the Cabin bean and the TravelAgent bean should have raised your confidence, but it should also have raised a lot of questions. So far, we have glossed over most of the details involved in developing, deploying, and accessing these beans. In this chapter and the ones that follow, we will slowly peel away the layers of the Enterprise JavaBeans onion to expose the details of EJB application development.

This chapter focuses specifically on the client's view of an EJB system. The client, whether it is an application or another bean, doesn't work directly with the beans in the EJB system. Instead, clients interact with a set of interfaces that provide access to beans and their business logic. These interfaces consist of the JNDI API and an EJB client-side API. JNDI allows us to find and access beans regardless of their location on the network; the EJB client-side API is the set of interfaces and classes that a developer uses on the client to interact with beans.

The best approach to this chapter is to read about a feature of the client view and then try to use that feature in the Cabin bean and TravelAgent bean client applications you worked with in Chapter 4. This will provide you with hands-on experience and a much clearer understanding of the concepts. Have fun, experiment, and you'll be sure to understand the fundamentals.

Locating Beans with JNDI

In Chapter 4, the client application started by creating an InitialContext, which it then used to get a remote reference to the homes of the Cabin and TravelAgent beans. The InitialContext is part of a larger API called the Java Naming and Directory Interface (JNDI). We use JNDI to look up an EJB home in an EJB server just like you might use a phone book to find the home number of a friend or business associate.

JNDI is a standard Java extension that provides a uniform API for accessing a wide range of services. In this respect, it is somewhat similar to JDBC, which provides uniform access to different relational databases. Just as JDBC lets you write code that doesn't care whether it's talking to an Oracle database or a Sybase database, JNDI lets you write code that can access different directory and naming services, like LDAP, Novell Netware NDS, CORBA Naming Service, and the naming services provided by EJB servers. EJB servers are required to support JNDI by organizing beans into a directory structure and providing a JNDI driver, called a *service provider*, for accessing that directory structure. Using JNDI, an enterprise can organize its beans, services, data, and other resources in a large virtual directory structure, which can provide a very powerful mechanism for binding together normally disparate systems.

The great thing about JNDI is that it is virtual and dynamic. JNDI is virtual because it allows one directory service to be linked to another through simple URLs. The URLs in JNDI are analogous to HTML links. Clicking on a link in HTML allows a user to load the contents of a web page. The new web page could be downloaded from the same host as the starting page or from a completely different web site—the location of the linked page is transparent to the user. Likewise, using JNDI, you can drill down through directories to files, printers, EJB home objects, and other resources using links that are similar to HTML links. The directories and subdirectories can be located in the same host or can be physically hosted at completely different locations. The user doesn't know or care where the directories are actually located. As a developer or administrator, you can create virtual directories that span a variety of different services over many different physical locations.

JNDI is dynamic because it allows the JNDI drivers (a.k.a. service providers) for specific types of directory services to be loaded at runtime. A driver maps a specific kind of directory service into the standard JNDI class interfaces. Drivers have been created for LDAP, Novell NetWare NDS, Sun Solaris NIS+, CORBA Naming Service, and many other types of naming and directory services. When a link to a different directory service is chosen, the driver for that type of directory service is automatically loaded from the directory's host, if it is not already resident on the user's machine. Automatically downloading JNDI drivers makes it possible for a client to navigate across arbitrary directory services without knowing in advance what kinds of services it is likely to find.

JNDI allows the application client to view the EJB server as a set of directories, like directories in a common filesystem. After the client application locates and obtains a remote reference to the EJB home using JNDI, the client can use the EJB home to obtain a remote reference to a bean. In the TravelAgent bean and the Cabin

bean, which you worked with in Chapter 4, you used the method getInitial-
Context() to get a JNDI InitialContext object, which looked as follows:

```
public static Context getInitialContext() throws javax.naming.NamingException {
    Properties p = new Properties();
    // ... Specify the JNDI properties specific to the vendor.
    return new javax.naming.InitialContext(p);
}
```

An initial context is the starting point for any JNDI lookup—it's similar in concept
to the root of a filesystem. The way you create an initial context is peculiar, but not
fundamentally difficult. You start with a properties table of type Properties. This
is essentially a hash table to which you add various values that determine the kind
of initial context you get.

Of course, as mentioned in Chapter 4, this code will change depending on how
your EJB vendor has implemented JNDI. For Gemstone/J, getInitial-
Context() might look something like this:

```
public static Context getInitialContext() throws Exception {
    Properties p = new Properties();
    p.put(com.gemstone.naming.Defaults.NAME_SERVICE_HOST,"localhost");
    String port = System.getProperty("com.gemstone.naming.NameServicePort",
                                     "10200");
    p.put(com.gemstone.naming.Defaults.NAME_SERVICE_PORT, port);
    p.put(Context.INITIAL_CONTEXT_FACTORY,"com.gemstone.naming.GsCtxFactory");
    return new InitialContext(p);
}
```

For BEA's WebLogic Server, this method would be coded as:

```
public static Context getInitialContext() throws Exception {
    Properties p = new Properties();
    p.put(Context.INITIAL_CONTEXT_FACTORY,
          "weblogic.jndi.T3InitialContextFactory");
    p.put(Context.PROVIDER_URL, "t3://localhost:7001");
    return new InitialContext(p);
}
```

For a more detailed explanation of JNDI, see O'Reilly's *Java™ Enterprise in a Nutshell,* by David Flanagan, Jim Farley, William Crawford, and Kris Magnusson.

The EJB Client-Side API

Enterprise bean developers are required to provide a bean class, two remote interfaces, and for entity beans, a primary key class. Of these types, the remote interfaces and primary key class are visible to the client, while the bean class is not. The
remote interface, home interface, and primary key contribute to the client-side
API in EJB. The methods defined in these types as well as the methods of their

supertypes provide the mechanisms that clients use to interact with an EJB business system.

The following sections examine in more detail the home interface, the remote interface, and the primary key, as well as other types that make up EJB's client-side API. This will provide you with a better understanding of how the client-side API is used and its relationship with the bean class on the EJB server.

EJB 1.1: Java RMI-IIOP Conformance Requirement

Enterprise JavaBeans 1.0 defines its distributed interfaces in terms of Java RMI. RMI assumes that both the client and server are Java applications, so it takes full advantage of Java types as arguments and return values. Enterprise JavaBeans 1.1 also defines its distributed interfaces in terms of Java RMI, but it enforces compliance with CORBA's interface, reference, and value types by requiring that only Java RMI-IIOP types be used. In other words, the underlying protocol can be anything that the vendor wants as long as it supports the types of interfaces and arguments specified by Java RMI-IIOP. In a future version of EJB, Java RMI-IIOP (Java RMI over IIOP) will be the required programming model for accessing beans. Requiring partial support for the Java RMI-IIOP standard ensures that early Java RMI-IIOP adopters are supported and makes for a seamless transition for other vendors in the future.

To be CORBA-compliant, Java RMI-IIOP had to restrict the definition of interfaces and arguments to types that map nicely to CORBA. The restrictions are really not all that bad, and you probably won't even notice them while developing your beans, but it's important to know what they are. The next few paragraphs discuss the Java RMI programming model for both EJB 1.0 and EJB 1.1, and point out the additional restrictions placed on RMI-IIOP types after discussing the restrictions shared by traditional Java RMI and Java RMI-IIOP.

EJB 1.1 and 1.0: The Java RMI Programming Model

The supertypes of the home interface and remote interface, javax.ejb.EJBHome and javax.ejb.EJBObject, both extend java.rmi.Remote. As Remote interface subtypes, they are expected to adhere to the Java RMI specification for Remote interfaces. The Java RMI specification states that every method defined in a Remote interface must throw a java.rmi.RemoteException. The Remote-Exception is used when problems occur with the distributed object communications, like a network failure or inability to locate the object server. In addition, Remote interface types can throw any application-specific exceptions (exceptions defined by the application developer) that are necessary. The following code shows the remote interface to the TravelAgent bean discussed in Chapter 2.

TravelAgent has several remote methods, including bookPassage(). The bookPassage() method can throw a RemoteException (as required), in addition to an application exception, IncompleteConversationalState.

```
public interface TravelAgent extends javax.ejb.EJBObject {

    public void setCruiseID(int cruise) throws RemoteException, FinderException;
    public int getCruiseID() throws RemoteException;

    public void setCabinID(int cabin) throws RemoteException, FinderException;
    public int getCabinID() throws RemoteException;

    public int getCustomerID() throws RemoteException;

    public Ticket bookPassage(CreditCard card, double price)
        throws RemoteException, IncompleteConversationalState;

    public String [] listAvailableCabins(int bedCount)
        throws RemoteException, IncompleteConversationalState;

}
```

Java RMI requires that all parameters and return values be either Java primitive types (int, double, byte, etc.) or objects that implement java.io.Serializable. Serializable objects are passed by copy (a.k.a. passed by value), not by reference, which means that changes in a serialized object on one tier are not automatically reflected on the others. Objects that implement Remote, like Customer, Cruise, and Cabin, are passed as remote references—which is a little different. A remote reference is a Remote interface implemented by a distributed object stub. When a remote reference is passed as a parameter or returned from a method, it is the stub that is serialized and passed by value, not the object server remotely referenced by the stub. In the home interface for the TravelAgent bean, the create() method takes a reference to a Customer bean as its only argument.

```
public interface TravelAgentHome extends javax.ejb.EJBHome {
    public TravelAgent create(Customer customer)
        throws RemoteException, CreateException;
}
```

The customer is a remote reference to a Customer bean that is passed into the create() method. When a remote reference is passed or returned in EJB, the EJB object stub is passed by copy. The copy of the EJB object stub points to the same EJB object as the original stub. This results in both the bean instance and the client having remote references to the same EJB object. So changes made on the client using the remote reference will be reflected when the bean instance uses the same remote reference. Figure 5-1 and Figure 5-2 show the difference between a serializable object and a remote reference argument in Java RMI.

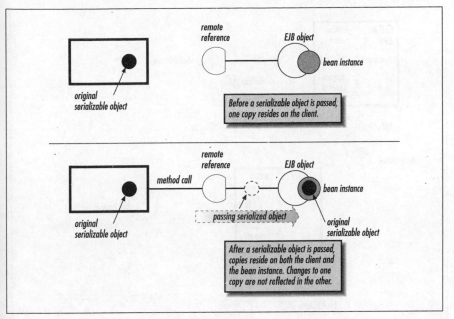

Figure 5-1. Serializable arguments in Java RMI

EJB 1.1: Java RMI-IIOP type restrictions

In addition to the Java RMI programming model discussed earlier, Java RMI-IIOP imposes additional restrictions on the remote interfaces and value types used in EJB 1.1. These restrictions are born of limitations inherit in the Interface Definition Language (IDL) upon which CORBA IIOP is based. The exact nature of these limitations is outside the scope of this book. I have only listed two restrictions because the others, like IDL name collisions, are so rarely encountered that it wouldn't be constructive to mention them.*

- Method overloading is restricted; a remote interface may not *directly* extend two or more interfaces that have methods with the same name (even if their arguments are different). A remote interface may, however, overload its own methods and extend a remote interface with overloaded method names. Overloading is viewed, here, as including overriding. Figure 5-3 illustrates both of these situations.

- Serializable types must not directly or indirectly implement the java.rmi. Remote interface.

---

* To learn more about CORBA IDL and its mapping to the Java language consult *The Common Object Request Broker: Architecture and Specification* and *The Java Language to IDL Mapping* available at the OMG site (*www.omg.org*).

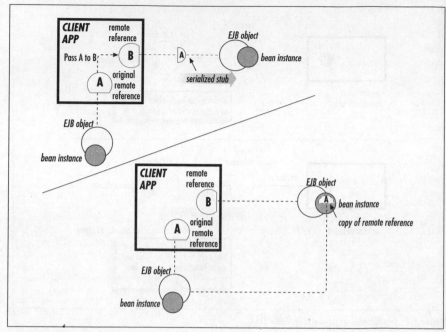

Figure 5-2. Remote reference arguments in Java RMI

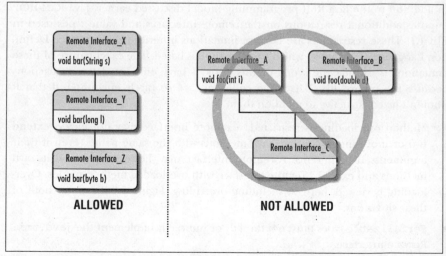

Figure 5-3. Overloading rules for Remote interface inheritance in Java RMI-IIOP

EJB 1.1: Explicit narrowing using PortableRemoteObject

A significant difference between EJB 1.0 and EJB 1.1 is that the new specification requires that remote references be explicitly narrowed using the `javax.rmi.PortableRemoteObject.narrow()` method. The typical practice in Java would be to cast the reference to the more specific type, as follows:

```
javax.naming.Context jndiContext;
...
CabinHome home = (CabinHome)jndiContext.lookup("CabinHome");
```

The `javax.naming.Context.lookup()` method returns an `Object`. In EJB 1.0, which uses simple Java RMI, we can assume that it is legal to cast the return argument to a legal Java type. However, EJB 1.1 must be compatible with Java RMI-IIOP, which means that clients must adhere to limitations imposed by the IIOP protocol. IIOP is not specific to any one programming language. As part of the CORBA standard, it must accommodate many programming languages including C++, Ada, COBOL, and others. All programming languages do *not* support casting, and for this reason casting is *not* native to IIOP. In fact, some languages have no concept of polymorphism or inheritance (COBOL for example), so implicit casting in CORBA is out of the question.

To accommodate all languages, IIOP does not support stubs that implement multiple interfaces. The stub returned in IIOP implements only the interface specified by the return type of the remote method that was invoked. If the return type is `Object`, as is the remote reference returned by the `lookup()` method, the stub will only implement methods specific to the `Object` type.

Of course, some means for converting a remote reference from a more general type to a more specific type is essential in an object-oriented environment. CORBA provides a mechanism for explicitly narrowing references to a specific type. The `javax.rmi.PortableRemoteObject.narrow()` method abstracts this mechanism to provide narrowing in IIOP as well as other protocols. Remember while Java RMI-IIOP defines the reference and argument types, in EJB 1.1 it does not define the underlying protocol. Other protocols besides IIOP may also require explicit narrowing. The `PortableRemoteObject` abstracts the narrowing process so that any protocol can be used.

To narrow the return argument of the `Context.lookup()` method to the appropriate type, we must explicitly ask for a remote reference that implements the interface we want:

```
import javax.rmi.PortableRemoteObject;
...
javax.naming.Context jndiContext;
...
Object ref = jndiContext.lookup("CabinHome");
```

```
CabinHome home = (CabinHome)
    PortableRemoteObject.narrow(ref, CabinHome.class);
```

When the narrow() method has successfully executed, it returns a stub that implements the Remote interface specified. Because the stub is known to implement the correct type, you can now use Java's native casting to narrow the stub to the correct Remote interface. The narrow() method takes two arguments: the remote reference that is to be narrowed and the type it should be narrowed to. The definition of the narrow() method is:*

```
package javax.rmi;

public class PortableRemoteObject extends java.lang.Object {

    public static java.lang.Object narrow(java.lang.Object narrowFrom,
                                           java.lang.Class narrowTo)
    throws java.lang.ClassCastException;
    ...
}
```

The narrow() method only needs to be used when a remote reference to an EJB home or EJB object is returned without a specific Remote interface type. This occurs in six circumstances:

- When an EJB home reference is obtained using the javax.naming.Context. lookup() method:

```
Object ref = jndiContext.lookup("CabinHome");
CabinHome home = (CabinHome) PortableRemoteObject.narrow(ref, CabinHome.class);
```

- When an EJB object reference is obtained using the javax.ejb.Handle. getEJBObject() method:

```
Handle handle = .... // get handle
Object ref = handle.getEJBObject();
Cabin cabin = (Cabin) PortableRemoteObject.narrow(ref,Cabin.class);
```

- When an EJB home reference is obtained using the javax.ejb.HomeHandle. getEJBHome() method:

```
HomeHandle homeHdle = ... // get home handle
EJBHome ref = homeHdle.getEJBHome();
CabinHome home = (CabinHome)
    PortableRemoteObject.narrow(ref, CabinHome.class);
```

- When an EJB home reference is obtained using the javax.ejb.EJBMeta-Data.getEJBHome() method:

---

* Other methods included in the PortableRemoteObject class are not important to EJB application developers. They are intended for Java RMI developers.

```
EJBMetaData metaData = homeHdle.getEJBMetaData();
EJBHome ref = metaData.getEJBHome();
CabinHome home = (CabinHome) PortableRemoteObject.narrow(ref, CabinHome.class);
```

- When an EJB object reference is obtained from a collection returned by a Home interface finder method:

```
ShipHome shipHome = ... // get ship home
Enumeration enum = shipHome.findByCapacity(2000);
while(enum.hasMoreElements()){
    Object ref = enum.nextElement();
    Ship ship = (Ship) PortableRemoteObject.narrow(ref, Ship.class);
    // do something with Ship reference
}
```

- When a wide EJB object type is returned from any business method. Here is a hypothetical example:

```
// Officer extends Crewman
Ship ship = // get Ship remote reference
Crewman crew = ship.getCrewman("Burns", "John", "1st Lieutenant");
Officer burns = (Officer) PortableRemoteObject.narrow(crew, Officer.class);
```

The `PortableRemoteObject.narrow()` method is not required when the remote type is specified in the method signature. This is true of the `create()` methods and find methods that return a single bean. For example, the `create()` and `findByPrimaryKey()` methods defined in the `CabinHome` interface (Chapter 4) do not require the use of `narrow()` because these methods already return the correct EJB object type. Business methods that return the correct type do not need to use the `narrow()` method either, as the following code illustrates:

```
/* The CabinHome.create() method specifies
 * the Cabin remote interface as the return type
 * so explicit narrowing is not needed.*/
Cabin cabin = cabinHome.create(12345);

/* The CabinHome.findByPrimaryKey() method specifies
 * the Cabin remote interface as the return type
 * so explicit narrowing is not needed.*/
Cabin cabin = cabinHome.findByPrimaryKey(12345);

/* The Ship.getCrewman() business method specifies
 * the Crewman remote interface as the return type
 * so explicit narrowing is not needed.*/
Crewman crew = ship.getCrewman("Burns", "John", "1st Lieutenant");
```

The Home Interface

The home interface provides life-cycle operations and metadata for the bean. When you use JNDI to access a bean, you obtain a remote reference, or stub, to the bean's EJB home, which implements the home interface. Every bean type has one home interface, which extends the javax.ejb.EJBHome interface.

Here is the EJBHome interface for EJB 1.1:

```
// EJB 1.1
public interface javax.ejb.EJBHome extends java.rmi.Remote {
    public abstract EJBMetaData getEJBMetaData()
        throws RemoteException;
    public HomeHandle getHomeHandle()      // new in 1.1
        throws RemoteException;
    public abstract void remove(Handle handle)
        throws RemoteException, RemoveException;
    public abstract void remove(Object primaryKey)
        throws RemoteException, RemoveException;
}
```

EJB 1.1 adds the getHomeHandle() method for accessing the HomeHandle, which doesn't exist in EJB 1.0:

```
// EJB 1.0
public interface javax.ejb.EJBHome extends java.rmi.Remote {
    public abstract EJBMetaData getEJBMetaData()
        throws RemoteException;
    public abstract void remove(Handle handle)
        throws RemoteException, RemoveException;
    public abstract void remove(Object primaryKey)
        throws RemoteException, RemoveException;
}
```

Removing beans

The EJBHome.remove() methods are responsible for deleting a bean. The argument is either the javax.ejb.Handle of the bean or, if it's an entity bean, its primary key. The Handle will be discussed in more detail later, but it is essentially a serializable pointer to a specific bean. When either of the EJBHome.remove() methods are invoked, the remote reference to the bean on the client becomes invalid: the stub to the bean that was removed no longer works. If for some reason the bean can't be removed, a RemoveException is thrown.

The impact of the EJBHome.remove() on the bean itself depends on the type of bean. For session beans, the EJBHome.remove() methods end the session's service to the client. When EJBHome.remove() is invoked, the remote reference to the session beans becomes invalid, and any conversational state maintained by the bean is lost. The TravelAgent bean is stateless, so no conversational state exists (more about this in Chapter 7).

When a remove() method is invoked on an entity bean, the remote reference becomes invalid, and any data that it represents is actually deleted from the database. This is a far more destructive activity because once an entity bean is removed, the data that it represents no longer exists. The difference between using a remove() method on a session bean and using remove() on an entity bean is similar to the difference between hanging up on a telephone conversation and actually killing the caller on the other end. Both end the conversation, but the end results are a little different.

The following code fragment is taken from the main() method of a client application that is similar to the clients we created to exercise the Cabin and TravelAgent beans. It shows that you can remove beans using a primary key (entity only) or a handle. Removing an entity bean deletes the entity from the database; removing a session bean results in the remote reference becoming invalid.

```
Context jndiContext = getInitialContext();

// Obtain a list of all the cabins for ship 1 with bed count of 3.

// EJB 1.0: Use native cast instead of narrow()
Object ref = jndiContext.lookup("TravelAgentHome");
TravelAgentHome agentHome = (TravelAgentHome)
    PortableRemoteObject.narrow(ref,TravelAgentHome.class);

TravelAgent agent = agentHome.create();
String list [] = agent.listCabins(1,3);
System.out.println("1st List: Before deleting cabin number 30");
for(int i = 0; i < list.length; i++){
    System.out.println(list[i]);
}

// Obtain the CabinHome and remove cabin 30. Rerun the same cabin list.

// EJB 1.0: Use native cast instead of narrow()
ref = jndiContext.lookup("CabinHome");
CabinHome c_home = (CabinHome)
    PortableRemoteObject.narrow(ref, CabinHome.class);

CabinPK pk = new CabinPK();
pk.id = 30;
c_home.remove(pk);
list = agent.listCabins(1,3);
System.out.println("2nd List: After deleting cabin number 30");
for (int i = 0; i < list.length; i++) {
    System.out.println(list[i]);
}
```

Your output should look something like the following:

```
1st List: Before deleting cabin number 30
1,Master Suite                    ,1
3,Suite 101                       ,1
5,Suite 103                       ,1
7,Suite 105                       ,1
9,Suite 107                       ,1
12,Suite 201                       ,2
14,Suite 203                       ,2
16,Suite 205                       ,2
18,Suite 207                       ,2
20,Suite 209                       ,2
22,Suite 301                       ,3
24,Suite 303                       ,3
26,Suite 305                       ,3
28,Suite 307                       ,3
30,Suite 309                       ,3
2nd List: After deleting cabin number 30
1,Master Suite                    ,1
3,Suite 101                       ,1
5,Suite 103                       ,1
7,Suite 105                       ,1
9,Suite 107                       ,1
12,Suite 201                       ,2
14,Suite 203                       ,2
16,Suite 205                       ,2
18,Suite 207                       ,2
20,Suite 209                       ,2
22,Suite 301                       ,3
24,Suite 303                       ,3
26,Suite 305                       ,3
28,Suite 307                       ,3
```

First, we create a list of cabins, including the cabin with the primary key 30. Then we remove the Cabin bean with this primary key and create the list again. The second time through, cabin 30 is not listed. Because it was removed, the list-Cabin() method was unable to find a cabin with a CabinPK.id equal to 30, so it stopped making the list. The bean, including its data, is no longer in the database.

Bean metadata

EJBHome.getEJBMetaData() returns an instance of javax.ejb.EJBMetaData that describes the home interface, remote interface, and primary key classes, plus whether the bean is a session or entity bean. This type of metadata is valuable to Java tools like IDEs that have wizards or other mechanisms for interacting with a bean from a client's perspective. A tool could, for example, use the class definitions provided by the EJBMetaData with Java reflection to create an environment where deployed beans can be "wired" together by developers. Of course, information such as the JNDI names and URLs of the beans is also needed.

Most application developers rarely use the EJBMetaData. Knowing that it's there, however, is valuable when you need to create automatic code generators or some other automatic facility. In those cases, familiarity with the Reflection API is necessary.* The following code shows the interface definition for EJBMetaData. Any class that implements the EJBMetaData interface must be serializable; it cannot be a stub to a distributed object. This allows IDEs and other tools to save the EJBMetaData for later use.

```java
public interface javax.ejb.EJBMetaData {
    public abstract EJBHome getEJBHome();
    public abstract Class getHomeInterfaceClass();
    public abstract Class getPrimaryKeyClass();
    public abstract Class getRemoteInterfaceClass();
    public abstract boolean isSession();
}
```

The following code shows how the EJBMetaData for the Cabin bean could be used to get more information about the bean. Notice that there is no way to get the bean class using the EJBMetaData; the bean class is not part of the client API and therefore doesn't belong to the metadata.

```java
Context jndiContext = getInitialContext();

// EJB 1.0: Use native cast instead of narrow()
Object ref = jndiContext.lookup("CabinHome");
CabinHome c_home = (CabinHome)
    PortableRemoteObject.narrow(ref, CabinHome.class);

EJBMetaData meta = c_home.getEJBMetaData();

System.out.println(meta.getHomeInterfaceClass().getName());
System.out.println(meta.getRemoteInterfaceClass().getName());
System.out.println(meta.getPrimaryKeyClass().getName());
System.out.println(meta.isSession());
```

This creates output like the following:

```
com.titan.cabin.CabinHome
com.titan.cabin.Cabin
com.titan.cabin.CabinPK
false
```

---

* The Reflection API is outside the scope of this book, but it is covered in *Java™ in a Nutshell*, by David Flanagan (O'Reilly).

In addition to providing the class types of the bean, the EJBMetaData also makes available the EJB home for the bean. By obtaining the EJB home from the EJBMetaData, we can obtain references to the EJB object and perform other functions. In the following code, we use the EJBMetaData to get the primary key class, create a key instance, obtain the EJB home, and from it, get a remote reference to the EJB object for a specific cabin entity:

```
CabinPK pk = (CabinPK)meta.getPrimaryKeyClass().newInstance();
pk.id = 1;

// EJB 1.0: Use native cast instead of narrow()
Object ref = meta.getEJBHome();
CabinHome c_home2 = (CabinHome)
    PortableRemoteObject.narrow(ref,CabinHome.class);

Cabin cabin = c_home2.findByPrimaryKey(pk);
System.out.println(cabin.getName());
```

EJB 1.1: The HomeHandle

EJB 1.1 provides a new object called a HomeHandle, which is accessed by calling the EJBObject.getHomeHandle() method. This method returns a javax.ejb. HomeHandle object, which provides a serializable reference to a bean home. The HomeHandle allows a remote home reference to be stored and used later. It is similar to the javax.ejb.Handle and is discussed in more detail near the end of the chapter.

Creating and finding beans

In addition to the standard javax.ejb.EJBHome methods that all home interfaces inherit, home interfaces also include special *create* and *find* methods for the bean. We have already talked about create and find methods, but a little review will solidify your understanding of the home interface's role in the client-side API. The following code shows the home interface defined for the Cabin bean:

```
public interface CabinHome extends javax.ejb.EJBHome {
    public Cabin create(int id)
        throws CreateException, RemoteException;

    public Cabin findByPrimaryKey(CabinPK pk)
        throws FinderException, RemoteException;
}
```

Create methods throw a CreateException if something goes wrong during the creation process; find methods throw a FinderException if the requested bean can't be located. Since these methods are defined in an interface that subclasses Remote, they must also declare that they throw RemoteException.

The create and find methods are specific to the bean, so it is up to the bean developer to define the appropriate create and find methods in the home interface. CabinHome currently has only one create method that creates a cabin with a specified ID and a find method that looks up a bean given its primary key, but it's easy to imagine methods that would create and find a cabin with particular properties—for example, a cabin with three beds, or a deluxe cabin with blue wallpaper. Unlike entity beans, the home interfaces for session beans do not have find methods. Entity beans represent unique identifiable data within a database and therefore can be found. Session beans, on the other hand, do not represent data: they are created to serve a client application and are not persistent, so there is nothing to find. A find method for a session bean would be meaningless.

The create and find methods defined in the home interfaces are straightforward and can be easily employed by the client. The create methods on the home interface have to match the ejbCreate() methods on the bean class. A create() and ejbCreate() method match when they have the same parameters, when the arguments are of same type and in the same order. This way, when a client calls the create method on the home interface, the call can be delegated to the corresponding ejbCreate() method on the bean instance. The find methods in the home interface work similarly for bean-managed entities. Every find method in the home interface must correspond to an ejbFind() method in the bean itself. Container-managed entities do not implement ejbFind() methods in the bean class; the EJB container supports find methods automatically. You will discover more about how to implement the ebjCreate() and ejbFind() methods in the bean in Chapters 6 and 7.

The Remote Interface

The business methods of an enterprise bean are defined by the remote interface provided by the bean developer. The javax.ejb.EJBObject interface, which extends the java.rmi.Remote interface, is the base class for all remote interfaces.

The following code is the remote interface for the TravelAgent bean that we developed in Chapter 4:

```
public interface TravelAgent extends javax.ejb.EJBObject {

    public String [] listCabins(int shipID, int bedCount)
        throws RemoteException;
}
```

Figure 5-4 shows the TravelAgent interface's inheritance hierarchy.

Remote interfaces are focused on the business problem and do not include methods for system-level operations such as persistence, security, concurrency, or transactions. System-level operations are handled by the EJB server, which relieves the

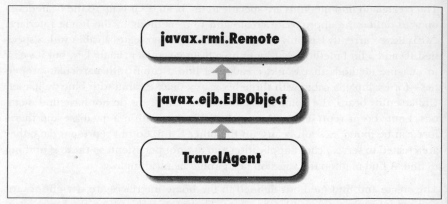

Figure 5-4. Enterprise bean interface inheritance hierarchy

client developer of many responsibilities. All remote interface methods for beans must throw, at the very least, a java.rmi.RemoteException, which identifies problems with distributed communications. In addition, methods in the remote interface can throw as many custom exceptions as needed to indicate abnormal business-related conditions or errors in executing the business method. You will learn more about defining custom exceptions in Chapter 6.

EJBObject, Handle, and Primary Key

All remote interfaces extend the javax.ejb.EJBObject interface, which provides a set of utility methods and return types. These methods and return types are valuable in managing the client's interactions with beans. Here is the definition for the EJBObject interface:

```
public interface javax.ejb.EJBObject extends java.rmi.Remote {
    public abstract EJBHome getEJBHome()
        throws RemoteException;
    public abstract Handle getHandle()
        throws RemoteException;
    public abstract Object getPrimaryKey()
        throws RemoteException;
    public abstract boolean isIdentical(EJBObject obj)
        throws RemoteException;
    public abstract void remove()
        throws RemoteException, RemoveException;
}
```

When the client obtains a reference to the remote interface, it is actually obtaining remote reference to an EJB object. The EJB object implements the remote inter-
by delegating business method calls to the bean class; it provides its own imple-

mentations for the EJBObject methods. These methods return information about the corresponding bean instance on the server. As discussed in Chapter 2, the EJB object is automatically generated when deploying the bean in the EJB server, so the bean developer doesn't need to write an EJBObject implementation.

Getting the EJBHome

The getEJBHome() method returns a remote reference to the EJB home for the bean. The remote reference is returned as a javax.ejb.EJBHome object, which can be narrowed or cast to the specific bean's home interface. This method is useful when an EJB object has left the scope of the EJB home that manufactured it. Because remote references can be passed as references and returned from methods, like any other Java object on the client, a remote reference can quickly find itself in a completely different part of the application from its home. The following code is contrived, but it illustrates how a remote reference can move out of the scope of its home and how getEJBHome() can be used to get a new reference to the EJB home at any time:

```
public static void main(String [] args) {
    try {
        Context jndiContext = getInitialContext();
        // EJB 1.0: Use native cast instead of narrow()
        Object ref = jndiContext.lookup("TravelAgentHome");
        TravelAgentHome home = (TravelAgentHome)
            PortableRemoteObject.narrow(ref,TravelAgentHome.class);

        // Get a remote reference to the bean (EJB object).
        TravelAgent agent = home.create();
        // Pass the remote reference to some method.
        getTheEJBHome(agent);

    } catch (java.rmi.RemoteException re) {re.printStackTrace();}
      catch (Throwable t) {t.printStackTrace();}
}

public static void getTheEJBHome(TravelAgent agent)
    throws RemoteException {

    // The home interface is out of scope in this method,
    // so it must be obtained from the EJB object.
    // EJB 1.0: Use native cast instead of narrow()
    Object ref = agent.getEJBHome();
    TravelAgentHome home = (TravelAgentHome)
        PortableRemoteObject.narrow(ref,TravelAgentHome.class);
    // Do something useful with the home interface.
}
```

Primary key

EJBObject.getPrimaryKey() returns the primary key for a bean. This method is only supported by EJB objects that represent entity beans. Entity beans represent specific data that can be identified using this primary key. Session beans represent tasks or processes, not data, so a primary key would be meaningless. To better understand the nature of a primary key, we need to look beyond the boundaries of the client's view into the EJB container's layer, which was introduced in Chapters 2 and 3.

The EJB container is responsible for persistence of the entity beans, but the exact mechanism for persistence is up to the vendor. In order to locate an instance of a bean in a persistent store, the data that makes up the entity must be mapped to some kind of unique key. In relational databases, data is uniquely identified by one or more column values that can be combined to form a primary key. In an object-oriented database, the key wraps an object ID (OID) or some kind of database pointer. Regardless of the mechanism—which isn't really relevant from the client's perspective—the unique key for an entity bean's data is encapsulated by the primary key, which is returned by the EJBObject.getPrimaryKey() method.

The primary key can be used to obtain remote references to entity beans using the findByPrimaryKey() method on the home interface. From the client's perspective, the primary key object can be used to identify a unique entity bean. Understanding the context of a primary key's uniqueness is important, as the following code shows:

```
Context jndiContext = getInitialContext()

// EJB 1.0: Use native cast instead of narrow()
Object ref = jndiContext.lookup("CabinHome");
CabinHome home = (CabinHome)
    PortableRemoteObject.narrow(ref,CabinHome.class);

Cabin cabin_1 = home.create(101);
CabinPK pk = (CabinPK)cabin_1.getPrimaryKey();
Cabin cabin_2 = home.findByPrimaryKey(pk);
```

In this code, the client creates a Cabin, retrieves the primary key of that Cabin, and then uses the key to get a new reference to the Cabin. Thus, we have two local variables, cabin_1 and cabin_2, which are remote references to EJB objects. These both reference the same Cabin bean, with the same underlying data, because they have the same primary key.

The primary key must be used for the correct bean in the correct container. If, for example, you were to obtain a primary key from a Cabin EJB object and then try to use that key in the findByPrimaryKey() method of a different bean type, like a

Ship bean, it wouldn't work; either it wouldn't compile or you would get a runtime error or FinderException. While this seems fairly obvious, the primary key's relationship to a specific container and home interface is important. The primary key can only be guaranteed to return the same entity if it is used within the container that produced the key. As an example, imagine that a third-party vendor sells the Cabin bean as a product. The vendor sells the Cabin bean to both Titan and to a competitor. Both companies deploy the bean using their own relational databases with their own data. A CabinPK primary key with an id value of 20 in Titan's EJB system will not map to the same Cabin entity in the competitor's EJB system. Both cruise companies have a Cabin bean with an id equal to 20, but they represent different cabins for different ships. The Cabin beans come from different EJB containers, so their primary keys are not equivalent.

Sun Microsystems' *Enterprise JavaBeans™ Specification*, Versions 1.0 and 1.1, describes the primary key and object identity in the following way:

> Every entity EJB object has a unique identity with its home....If two EJB objects have the same home and same primary key, they are considered identical.

A primary key must implement the java.io.Serializable interface. This means that the primary key, regardless of its form, can be obtained from an EJB object, stored on the client using the Java serialization mechanism, and deserialized when needed. When a primary key is deserialized, it can be used to obtain a remote reference to that entity using findByPrimaryKey(), provided that the key is used on the right home interface and container. Preserving the primary key using serialization might be useful if the client application needs to access specific entity beans at a later date. In EJB 1.0, preserving the primary keys is also useful for beans that maintain relationships to other beans. Bean relationships are discussed in more detail in Chapter 9.

The following code shows a primary key that is serialized and then deserialized to reobtain a remote reference to the same bean:

```
// Obtain cabin 101 and set its name.
Context jndiContext = getInitialContext();

// EJB 1.0: Use native cast instead of narrow()
Object ref = jndiContext.lookup("CabinHome");
CabinHome home = (CabinHome)
    PortableRemoteObject.narrow(ref, CabinHome.class);

CabinPK pk_1 = new CabinPK();
pk_1.id = 101;
Cabin cabin_1 = home.findByPrimaryKey(pk_1);
cabin_1.setName("Presidential Suite");
```

```
// Serialize the primary key for cabin 101 to a file.
FileOutputStream fos = new FileOutputStream("pk101.ser");
ObjectOutputStream outStream = new ObjectOutputStream(fos);
outStream.writeObject(pk_1);
outStream.flush();
outStream.close();
pk_1 = null;

// Deserialize the primary key for cabin 101.
FileInputStream fis = new FileInputStream("pk101.ser");
ObjectInputStream inStream = new ObjectInputStream(fis);
CabinPK pk_2 = (CabinPK)inStream.readObject();
inStream.close();

// Re-obtain a remote reference to cabin 101 and read its name.
Cabin cabin_2 = home.findByPrimaryKey(pk_2);
System.out.println(cabin_2.getName());
```

Comparing beans for identity

The EJBObject.isIdentical() method compares two EJB object remote references. It's worth considering why Object.equals() isn't sufficient for comparing EJB objects. An EJB object is a distributed object stub and therefore contains a lot of networking and other state. As a result, references to two EJB objects may be unequal, even if they both represent the same unique bean. The EJBObject. isIdentical() method returns true if two EJB object references represent the same bean, even if the EJB object stubs are different object instances.

The following code shows how this might work. It starts by creating two remote references to the TravelAgent bean. These EJB objects both refer to the same type of bean; comparing them with isIdentical() returns true. The two TravelAgent beans were created separately, but because they are stateless they are considered to be equivalent. If TravelAgent had been a stateful bean (which it becomes in Chapter 7) the outcome would have been very different. Comparing two stateful beans in this manner will result in false because stateful beans have conversational state, which makes them unique. When we use CabinHome.findByPrimaryKey() to locate two EJB objects that refer to the same Cabin entity bean, we know the beans are identical, because we used the same primary key. In this case, isIdentical() also returns true because both EJB object references point to the same entity.

```
Context ctx  = getInitialContext();

// EJB 1.0: Use native cast instead of narrow()
Object ref = ctx.lookup("TravelAgentHome");
TravelAgentHome agentHome =(TravelAgentHome)
    PortableRemoteObject.narrow(ref, TravelAgentHome.class);
```

```
TravelAgent agent_1 = agentHome.create();
TravelAgent agent_2 = agentHome.create();
boolean x = agent_1.isIdentical(agent_2);
// x will equal true; the two EJB objects are equal.

// EJB 1.0: Use native cast instead of narrow()
ref = ctx.lookup("CabinHome");
CabinHome c_home = (CabinHome)
    PortableRemoteObject.narrow(ref, CabinHome.class);

CabinPK pk = new CabinPK();
pk.id = 101;
Cabin cabin_1 = c_home.findByPrimaryKey(pk);
Cabin cabin_2 = c_home.findByPrimaryKey(pk);
x = cabin_1.isIdentical(cabin_2);
// x will equal true; the two EJB objects are equal.
```

The primary key used in the Cabin bean is simple. More complex primary keys require us to override Object.equals() and Object.hashCode() in order for the EJBObject.isIdentical() method to work. Chapter 6 discusses this in more detail.

Removing beans

The EJBObject.remove() method is used to remove the session or entity bean. The impact of this method is the same as the EJBHome.remove() method discussed previously. For session beans, remove() causes the session to be released and the EJB object reference to become invalid. For entity beans, the actual entity data is deleted from the database and the remote reference becomes invalid. The following code shows the EJBObject.remove() method in use:

```
Context jndiContext = getInitialContext();

// EJB 1.0: Use native cast instead of narrow()
Object ref = jndiContext.lookup("CabinHome");
CabinHome c_home = (CabinHome)
    PortableRemoteObject.narrow(ref,CabinHome.class);

CabinPK pk = new CabinPK();
pk.id = 101;
Cabin cabin = c_home.findByPrimaryKey(pk);
cabin.remove();
```

The remove() method throws a RemoveException if for some reason the reference can't be deleted.

The bean handle

The EJBObject.getHandle() method returns a javax.ejb.Handle object. The Handle is a serializable reference to the EJB object. This means that the client can save the Handle object using Java serialization and then deserialize it to reobtain a reference to the same EJB object. This is similar to serializing and reusing the primary key. The Handle allows us to recreate an EJB object remote reference that points to the same *type* of session bean or the same unique entity bean that the handle came from.

Here is the interface definition of the Handle:

```
public interface javax.ejb.Handle {
    public abstract EJBObject getEJBObject()
        throws RemoteException;
}
```

The Handle interface specifies only one method, getEJBObject(). Calling this method returns the EJB object from which the handle was created. Once you've gotten the object back, you can narrow or cast it to the appropriate remote-interface type. The following code shows how to serialize and deserialize the EJB Handle on a client:

```
// Obtain cabin 100.
Context jndiContext = getInitialContext();

// EJB 1.0: Use native cast instead of narrow()
Object ref = jndiContext.lookup("CabinHome");
CabinHome home = (CabinHome)
    PortableRemoteObject.narrow(ref,CabinHome.class);

CabinPK pk_1 = new CabinPK();
pk_1.id = 100;
Cabin cabin_1 = home.findByPrimaryKey(pk_1);

// Serialize the Handle for cabin 100 to a file.
Handle handle = cabin_1.getHandle();
FileOutputStream fos = new FileOutputStream("handle100.ser");
ObjectOutputStream outStream = new ObjectOutputStream(fos);
outStream.writeObject(handle);
outStream.flush();
fos.close();
handle = null;

// Deserialize the Handle for cabin 100.
FileInputStream fis = new FileInputStream("handle100.ser");
ObjectInputStream inStream = new ObjectInputStream(fis);
handle = (Handle)inStream.readObject();
fis.close();
```

```
// Reobtain a remote reference to cabin 100 and read its name.

// EJB 1.0: Use native cast instead of narrow()
ref = handle.getEJBObject();
Cabin cabin_2 = (Cabin)
    PortableRemoteObject.narrow(ref, Cabin.class);

System.out.println(cabin_2.getName());
```

At first glance, the Handle and the primary key appear to do the same thing, but in truth they are very different. Using the primary key requires you to have the correct EJB home—if you no longer have a reference to the EJB home, you must look up the container using JNDI and get a new home. Only then can you call findByPrimaryKey() to locate the actual bean. The following code shows how this might work:

```
// Obtain the primary key from an input stream.
CabinPK primaryKey = (CabinPK)inStream.readObject();

// The JNDI API is used to get a root directory or initial context.
javax.naming.Context ctx = new javax.naming.InitialContext();

// Using the initial context, obtain the EJBHome for the Cabin bean.

// EJB 1.0: Use native cast instead of narrow()
Object ref = ctx.lookup("CabinHome");
CabinHome home = (CabinHome)
    PortableRemoteObject.narrow(ref,CabinHome.class);

// Obtain a reference to an EJB object that represents the entity instance.
Cabin cabin_2 = CabinHome.findByPrimaryKey(primaryKey);
```

The Handle object is easier to use because it encapsulates the details of doing a JNDI lookup on the container. With a Handle, the correct EJB object can be obtained in one method call, Handle.getEJBObject(), rather than using the three method calls required to look up the context, get the home, and find the actual bean.

Furthermore, while the primary key can be used to obtain remote references to unique *entity* beans, it is not available for session beans; a handle can be used with either type of enterprise bean. This makes using a handle more consistent across bean types. Consistency is, of course, good in its own right, but it isn't the whole story. Normally, we think of session beans as not having identifiable instances because they exist for only the life of the client session, but this is not exactly true. We have mentioned (but not yet shown) stateful session beans, which retain state information between method invocations. With stateful session beans, two instances are not equivalent. A handle allows you to work with a stateful session bean, deactivate the bean, and then reactivate it at a later time using the handle.

A client could, for example, be using a stateful session bean to process an order when the process needs to be interrupted for some reason. Instead of losing all the work performed in the session, a handle can be obtained from the EJB object and the client application can be closed down. When the user is ready to continue the order, the handle can be used to obtain a reference to the stateful session EJB object. Note that this process is not as fault tolerant as using the handle or primary key of an entity object. If the EJB server goes down or crashes, the stateful session bean will be lost and the handle will be useless. It's also possible for the session bean to time out, which would cause the container to remove it from service so that it is no longer available to the client.

Changes to the container technology can invalidate both handles and primary keys. If you think your container technology might change, be careful to take this limitation into account. Primary keys obtain EJB objects by providing unique identification of instances in persistent data stores. A change in the persistence mechanism, however, can impact the integrity of the key.

EJB 1.1: HomeHandle

The `javax.ejb.HomeHandle` is similar in purpose to `javax.ejb.Handle`. Just as the `Handle` is used to store and retrieve references to EJB objects, the `HomeHandle` is used to store and retrieve remote references to EJB homes. In other words, the `HomeHandle` can be stored and later used to access an EJB home's remote reference the same way that a `Handle` can be serialized and later used to access an EJB object's remote reference. The `HomeHandle` and the method `EJBHome.getHomeHandle()` are new to EJB 1.1. The following code shows how the `HomeHandle` can be obtained, serialized, and used.

```
// Obtain cabin 100.
Context jndiContext = getInitialContext();

// EJB 1.0: Use native cast instead of narrow()
Object ref = jndiContext.lookup("CabinHome");
CabinHome home = (CabinHome)
    PortableRemoteObject.narrow(ref,CabinHome.class);

// Serialize the HomeHandle for the cabin bean.
HomeHandle homeHandle = home.getHomeHandle();
FileOutputStream fos = new FileOutputStream("handle.ser");
ObjectOutputStream outStream = new ObjectOutputStream(fos);
outStream.writeObject(homeHandle);
outStream.flush();
fos.close();
homeHandle = null;
```

```
// Deserialize the HomeHandle for the cabin bean.
FileInputStream fis = new FileInputStream("handle.ser");
ObjectInputStream inStream = new ObjectInputStream(fis);
homeHandle = (HomeHandle)inStream.readObject();
fis.close();

// EJB 1.0: Use native cast instead of narrow()
EJBHome home = homeHandle.getEJBHome();
CabinHome home2 = (CabinHome)
    PortableRemoteObject.narrow(home,CabinHome.class);
```

Inside the Handle

Different vendors define their concrete implementations of the EJB handle differently. However, thinking about a hypothetical implementation of handles will give you a better understanding of how they work. In this example, we define the implementation of a handle for an entity bean. Our implementation encapsulates the JNDI lookup and use of the home's findByPrimaryKey() method so that any change that invalidates the key invalidates preserved handles that depend on that key. Here's the code for our hypothetical implementation of a Handle:

```
package com.titan.cabin;

import javax.naming.InitialContext;
import javax.naming.Context;
import javax.naming.NamingException;
import javax.ejb.EJBObject;
import javax.ejb.Handle;
import java.rmi.RemoteException;
import java.util.Properties;

public class VendorX_CabinHandle
    implements javax.ejb.Handle, java.io.Serializable {

    private CabinPK primary_key;
    private String home_name;
    private Properties jndi_properties;

    public VendorX_CabinHandle(CabinPK pk, String hn, Properties p) {
        primary_key = pk;
        home_name = hn;
        jndi_properties = p;
    }

    public EJBObject getEJBObject() throws RemoteException {
        try {
            Context ctx = new InitialContext(jndi_properties);
```

```
        // EJB 1.0: Use native cast instead of narrow()
        Object ref = ctx.lookup(home_name);
        CabinHome home =(CabinHome)
            PortableRemoteObject.narrow(ref,CabinHome.class);

        return home.findByPrimaryKey(primary_key);
    } catch (javax.ejb.FinderException fe) {
        throw new RemoteException("Cannot locate EJB object",fe);
    } catch (javax.naming.NamingException ne) {
        throw new RemoteException("Cannot locate EJB object",ne);
    }
  }
}
```

The Handle is less stable than the primary key because it relies on the networking configuration and naming—the IP address of the EJB server and the JNDI name of the bean's home—to remain stable. If the EJB server's network address changes or the name used to identify the home changes, the handle becomes useless.

In addition, some vendors choose to implement a security mechanism in the handle that prevents its use outside the scope of the client application that originally requested it. How this mechanism would work is unclear, but the security limitation it implies should be considered before attempting to use a handle outside the client's scope.

In this chapter:
• *Container-Managed Persistence*
• *Bean-Managed Persistence*
• *The Life Cycle of an Entity Bean*

6

Entity Beans

In Chapter 4, we started developing some simple enterprise beans, skipping over a lot of the details in the process. In this chapter, we'll take a thorough look at the process of developing entity beans. On the surface, some of this material may look familiar, but it is much more detailed and specific to entity beans.

Entity beans model business concepts that can be expressed as nouns. This is a rule of thumb rather than a requirement, but it helps in determining when a business concept is a candidate for implementation as an entity bean. In grammar school you learned that nouns are words that describe a person, place, or thing. The concepts of "person" and "place" are fairly obvious: a person bean might represent a customer or a passenger, and a place bean might represent a city or a port-of-call. Similarly, entity beans often represent "things": real-world objects like ships, cabins, and so on. A bean can even represent a fairly abstract "thing," such as a ticket or a reservation. Entity beans describe both the state and behavior of real-world objects and allow developers to encapsulate the data and business rules associated with specific concepts; a cabin bean encapsulates the data and business rules associated with a cabin, and so on. This makes it possible for data associated with a concept to be manipulated consistently and safely.

In Titan's cruise ship business, we can identify hundreds of business concepts that are nouns and therefore could conceivably be modeled by entity beans. We've already seen a simple Cabin bean in Chapter 4, and we'll develop a Ship bean in this chapter. Titan could clearly make use of a PortOfCall bean, a Passenger bean, and many others. Each of these business concepts represents data that needs to be tracked and possibly manipulated. Entities really represent data in the database, so changes to an entity bean result in changes to the database.

There are many advantages to using entity beans instead of accessing the database directly. Utilizing entity beans to objectify data provides programmers with a simpler mechanism for accessing and changing data. It is much easier, for example, to change a ship's name by calling `ship.setName()` than to execute an SQL command against the database. In addition, objectifying the data using entity beans also provides for more software reuse. Once an entity bean has been defined, its definition can be used throughout Titan's system in a consistent manner. The concept of ship, for example, is used in many areas of Titan's business, including booking, scheduling, and marketing. A Ship bean provides Titan with one complete way of accessing ship information, and thus it ensures that access to the information is consistent and simple. Representing data as entity beans makes development easier and more cost effective.

When a new bean is created, a new record must be inserted into the database and a bean instance must be associated with that data. As the bean is used and its state changes, these changes must be synchronized with the data in the database: entries must be inserted, updated, and removed. The process of coordinating the data represented by a bean instance with the database is called *persistence*.

There are two types of entity beans, and they are distinguished by how they manage persistence. *Container-managed* beans have their persistence automatically managed by the EJB container. The container knows how a bean instance's fields map to the database and automatically takes care of inserting, updating, and deleting the data associated with entities in the database. Beans using *bean-managed* persistence do all this work explicitly: the bean developer must write the code to manipulate the database. The EJB container tells the bean instance when it is safe to insert, update, and delete its data from the database, but it provides no other help. The bean instance does all the persistence work itself.

The next two sections will describe how EJB works with container-managed and bean- managed entity beans.

Container-Managed Persistence

Container-managed entity beans are the simplest to develop because they allow you to focus on the business logic, delegating the responsibility of persistence to the EJB container. When you deploy the bean, you identify which fields in the entity are managed by the container and how they map to the database. Once you have defined the fields that will be automatically managed and how they map to the database, the container generates the logic necessary to save the bean instance's state automatically.

Fields that are mapped to the database are called container-managed fields. Container-managed fields can be any Java primitive type or serializable objects. Most beans will use Java primitive types when persisting to a relational database, since it's easier to map Java primitives to relational data types.

NOTE	EJB 1.1 also allows references to other beans to be container-managed fields. The EJB vendor must support converting bean references (remote or home interface types) from remote references to something that can be persisted in the database and converted back to a remote reference automatically. Vendors will normally convert remote references to primary keys, Handle or HomeHandle objects, or some other proprietary pointer type, which can be used to preserve the bean reference in the database. The container will manage this conversion from remote reference to persistent pointer and back automatically.

The advantage of container-managed persistence is that the bean can be defined independently of the database used to store its state. Container-managed beans can take advantage of a relational database or an object-oriented database. The bean state is defined independently, which makes the bean more reusable and flexible across applications.

The disadvantage of container-managed beans is that they require sophisticated mapping tools to define how the bean's fields map to the database. In some cases, this may be a simple matter of mapping each field in the bean instance to a column in the database or of serializing the bean to a file. In other cases, it may be more difficult. The state of some beans, for example, may be defined in terms of a complex relational database join or mapped to some kind of legacy system such as CICS or IMS.

In Chapter 4, we developed our first container-managed bean, the Cabin bean. During the development of the Cabin bean, we glossed over some important aspects of container-managed entity beans. In this section, we will create a new container-managed entity bean, the Ship bean, but this time we will examine it in detail.

Let's start by thinking about what we're trying to do. An enormous amount of data would go into a complete description of a ship, but for our purposes we will limit the scope of the data to a small set of information. For now, we can say that a ship has the following characteristics or attributes: its name, passenger capacity, and tonnage (i.e., size). The Ship bean will encapsulate this data; we'll need to create a SHIP table in our database to hold this data. Here is the definition for the SHIP table expressed in standard SQL:

```
CREATE TABLE SHIP (ID INT PRIMARY KEY, NAME CHAR(30), CAPACITY INT,
TONNAGE DECIMAL(8,2))
```

When defining any bean, we start by coding the remote interfaces. This focuses our attention on the most important aspect of any bean: its business purpose. Once we have defined the interfaces, we can start working on the actual bean definition.

The Remote Interface

For the Ship bean we will need a Ship remote interface. This interface defines the business methods that clients will use to interact with the bean. When defining the remote interface, we will take into account all the different areas in Titan's system that may want to use the ship concept. Here is the remote interface for Ship:

```
package com.titan.ship;

import javax.ejb.EJBObject;
import java.rmi.RemoteException;

public interface Ship extends javax.ejb.EJBObject {
    public String getName() throws RemoteException;
    public void setName(String name) throws RemoteException;
    public void setCapacity(int cap) throws RemoteException;
    public int getCapacity() throws RemoteException;
    public double getTonnage() throws RemoteException;
    public void setTonnage(double tons) throws RemoteException;
}
```

We put this interface into the com.titan.ship package, which we will use for all the components of the Ship bean. This means that the code should reside in a development directory named *dev/com/titan/ship*. This is the same convention for package and directory names that we used for the Cabin bean.

Set and get methods

The Ship definition uses a series of accessor methods whose names begin with set and get. This is not a required signature pattern, but it is the naming convention used by most Java developers when obtaining and changing the values of object attributes or fields. These methods are often referred to as *setters* and *getters* (a.k.a. mutators and accessors) and the attributes that they manipulate can be called *properties.*[*] These properties should be defined independently of the anticipated storage structure of the data. In other words, you should design the remote interface to model the business concepts, not the underlying data. Just because there's a capacity property doesn't mean that there has to be a capacity field in the bean or the database; the getCapacity() method could conceivably compute the capacity from a list of cabins, by looking up the ship's model and configuration, or with some other algorithm.

---

[*] Although EJB is different from its GUI counterpart, JavaBeans, the concept of accessors and properties are similar. You can learn about this idiom by reading *Developing Java Beans™* by Rob Englander (O'Reilly).

Defining entity properties according to the business concept and not the underlying data is not always possible, but you should try to employ this strategy whenever you can. The reason is two-fold. First, the underlying data doesn't always clearly define the business purpose or concept being modeled by the entity bean. Remote interfaces will be used by developers who know the business, not the database configuration. It is important to them that the entity bean reflect the business concept. Second, defining the properties of the entity bean independent of the data allows the bean and data to evolve separately. This is important because it allows a database implementation to change over time; it also allows for new behavior to be added to the entity bean as needed. If the bean's definition is independent of the data source, the impact of these evolutions is limited.

The Primary Key

A primary key is an object that uniquely identifies an entity bean according to the bean type, home interface, and container context from which it is used.

NOTE   EJB 1.1: In container-managed persistence, a primary key can be a serializable object defined specifically for the bean by the bean developer, or its definition can be deferred until deployment. We will examine deployer-defined primary keys later. For now we will consider primary keys defined by the bean developer.

For our purposes, we will define all primary keys as serializable classes with names that match the pattern *BeanNamePK*. Therefore, the primary key for the Ship bean will be ShipPK. Unlike the remote interface and the home interface, the primary key is a class, and its definition is normally bound to the bean class definition, which we have not yet addressed. Peeking ahead, however, we can make a preliminary definition of a primary key that wraps an integer value called id. Later, we will have to make sure that this field has a corresponding field in the bean class with a matching identifier (name) and data type.

```
package com.titan.ship;

import java.io.Serializable;

public class ShipPK implements java.io.Serializable {

    public int id;

    public ShipPK() {}
    public ShipPK(int value) {
        id = value;
    }
```

```
public boolean equals(Object obj) {
    if (obj == null || !(obj instanceof ShipPK))
        return false;
    else if (((ShipPK)obj).id == id)
        return true;
    else
        return false;
}
public int hashCode(){
    return id;
}

public String toString(){
    return String.valueOf(id);
}
}
```

The primary key defines attributes that can be used to locate a specific bean in the database. In this case, we need only one attribute, id, but in other cases, a primary key may have several attributes, all of which uniquely identify a bean's data.

As discussed in Chapter 4, primary keys should override the equals() and hash-Code() methods of Object to ensure that these method behave properly when invoked. For example, two ShipPK objects with the same id value may not evaluate to the same hash code unless the hashCode() method is overridden as shown in the previous code example. This can cause problems if you store primary keys in a hash table and expect that primary keys for the same entity will evaluate to the same position in the table. In addition, we have overridden the toString() method to return a meaningful value. (The default implementation defined in Object returns the class name of the object appended to the object identity for that name space. Our implementation simply returns the String value of the id, which has more meaning.)

The primary key for the Ship bean is fairly simple. More complex keys—ones with multiple values—will require more intelligent hash code algorithms to ensure as few collisions in a hash table as possible.

The ShipPK class also defines two constructors: a no-argument constructor and an overloaded constructor that sets the id field. The overloaded constructor is a convenience method that reduces the number of steps required to create a primary key. The no-argument constructor is *required* for container-managed persistence. When a new bean is created, the container automatically instantiates the primary key using the Class.newInstance() method, and populates it from the bean class's container-managed fields. A no-argument constructor must exist in order for that to work. You'll learn more about the relationship between the primary key and the bean class later in this section.

The EJB specification requires that all fields in the primary key class be declared public. This requirement ensures that the container can read the fields at runtime via Java reflection. Some EJB servers may be able to read fields with more restrictive access modifiers depending on how the security manager is designed, but making the fields public ensures that fields are always accessible, regardless of the server's vendor. Portability is the key reason that the primary key's fields must be public.

Because the primary key will be used in remote invocations, it must also adhere to the restrictions imposed by Java RMI-IIOP. These are addressed in Chapter 5, but for most cases, you just need to make the primary key serializable.

Both EJB 1.0 and EJB 1.1 specifications allow two types of primary keys: compound and single-field keys. In either case, the primary key must fulfill two criteria: it must be a valid Java RMI type (Java RMI-IIOP value type for EJB 1.1), so it must be serializable; and it must implement equals() and hashCode() methods appropriately.

Compound primary keys

A compound primary key is a class that implements Serializable and contains one or more public fields whose names and types match a subset of the container-managed fields in the bean class. ShipPK is a typical example of a compound primary key. In this class, the ShipPK.id field must map to a ShipBean.id field of type int in the ShipBean class. A compound key may have several fields that map to corresponding fields in the bean class.

Single-field key

The String class and the wrapper classes for the primitive data types can also be used as primary keys. In the case of the ShipBean, for example, we could have specified an Integer type as the primary key:

```
public interface ShipHome extends javax.ejb.EJBHome {
    public Ship findByPrimaryKey(java.lang.Integer key)
        throws FinderException, RemoteException;
    ...
}
```

In this case, there is no explicit primary key class. However, there must still be an identifiable primary key within the bean class itself. That is, there must be a single field in the bean class with the appropriate type. For the ShipBean, we would need to change the id field to be of type java.lang.Integer.

Although primary keys can be primitive wrappers (Integer, Double, Long, etc.), primary keys cannot be primitive types (int, double, long, etc.); some of the

semantics of EJB interfaces prohibit the use of primitives. For example, the
EJBObject.getPrimaryKey() method returns an Object type, thus forcing primary keys to be Objects. As you learn more about the EJB, you'll discover other
reasons that primitives can't be used for single-field keys.

EJB 1.0 support for single-field keys

In EJB 1.0, the specification is unclear about whether or not single-field types
like String or primitive wrapper types are supported. Some EJB 1.0 servers
support them, while others only support compound primary keys. Consult
your vendor documentation to be sure, or use compound primary keys. When
single-field types are supported, there must be only one container-managed
field of that type in the bean class. Otherwise, the container doesn't know to
which field it should map the primary key.

EJB 1.1 support for single-field keys

EJB 1.1 is unambiguous in its support for single-field keys. With single-field
types, you cannot identify the matching field in the bean class by name, since
the primary key is not a named field. Instead, you use the <primkey-field>
tag in the deployment descriptor to specify one of the bean's container-
managed fields as the primary key:

```
<ejb-jar>
 <enterprise-beans>
 <entity>
    <primkey-field>id</primkey-field>
 ...
</ejb-jar>
```

The primkey-field (single-field keys) is not used in the Ship bean example.
The Ship bean uses primary key class, ShipPK, but the use of primkey-field
is explored in more Chapter 10.

EJB 1.1: Undefined primary keys

One objective of EJB is to create a market for third-party components that can be
used independently. Container-managed persistence beans provide an excellent
model for a component market because they make few assumptions about the
underlying database. One problem with container-managed persistence in EJB 1.0
was that the bean developer had to define the primary key before the bean was
deployed. In turn, this requirement forced the developer to make assumptions
about the environment in which the bean would be used, and thus it limited the
bean's portability across databases. For example, a relational database will use a set
of columns in a table as the primary key, to which bean fields map nicely. An
object database, however, uses a completely different mechanism for indexing
objects to which a primary key may not map very well. The same is true for legacy

systems and Enterprise Resource Planing (ERP) systems. To overcome this problem, EJB 1.1 allows the primary key to remain undefined until the bean is deployed. An undefined primary key allows the deployer to choose a system-specific key at deployment time. An object database may generate an Object ID, while an ERP system may generate some other primary key. These keys are generated by the database or backend system automatically. This may require that the CMP bean be altered or extended to support the key, but this is immaterial to the bean developer; she concentrates on the business logic of the bean and leaves the indexing to the container.

To facilitate an undefined primary key, the bean class and its interfaces use the Object type to identify the primary key. The following code shows how the home interface and bean class would be defined for a container-managed bean with an undefined primary key:

```
public interface ShipHome extends EJBHome {
    public Ship findByPrimaryKey(java.lang.Object primaryKey)
        throws RemoteException, FinderException;
...
}
public class ShipBean extends EntityBean {
    public String name;
    public int capacity;
    public double tonnage;

    public java.lang.Object ejbCreate() {
    ...
    }
...
}
```

The use of an undefined primary key means that the bean developer and application developer (client code) must work with a java.lang.Object type and not a specific primary key type, which can be limiting.

The Home Interface

The home interface of any entity bean is used to create, locate, and remove objects from EJB systems. Each entity bean type has its own home interface. The home interface defines two basic kinds of methods: zero or more create methods and one or more find methods.* The create methods act like remote constructors and define how new Ship beans are created. (In our home interface, we only provide a single create() method.) The find method is used to locate a specific ship or ships.

---

* Chapter 9 explains when you should not define any create methods in the home interface.

The following code contains the complete definition of the ShipHome interface:

```
package com.titan.ship;

import javax.ejb.EJBHome;
import javax.ejb.CreateException;
import javax.ejb.FinderException;
import java.rmi.RemoteException;
import java.util.Enumeration;

public interface ShipHome extends javax.ejb.EJBHome {

    public Ship create(int id, String name, int capacity, double tonnage)
        throws RemoteException,CreateException;
    public Ship create(int id, String name)
        throws RemoteException,CreateException;
    public Ship findByPrimaryKey(ShipPK primaryKey)
        throws FinderException, RemoteException;
    public Enumeration findByCapacity(int capacity)
        throws FinderException, RemoteException;
}
```

Enterprise JavaBeans specifies that create methods in the home interface must throw the javax.ejb.CreateException. In the case of container-managed persistence, the container needs a common exception for communicating problems experienced during the create process.

The find methods

With container-managed persistence, implementations of the find methods are generated automatically at deployment time. Different EJB container vendors employ different strategies for defining how the find methods work. Regardless of the implementation, when you deploy the bean, you'll need to do some work to define the rules of the find method. findByPrimaryKey() is a standard method that all home interfaces for entity beans must support. This method locates beans based on the attributes of the primary key. In the case of the Ship bean, the primary key is the ShipPK class, which has one attribute, id. With relational databases, the primary key attributes usually map to a primary key in a table. In the ShipPK, for example, the id attribute maps to the ID primary key column in the SHIP table. In an object-oriented database, the primary key's attributes might point to some other unique identifier.

EJB allows you to specify other find methods in the home interface, in addition to findByPrimaryKey(). All find methods must have names that match the pattern find*lookup-type*. So, for example, if we were to include a find method based on the Ship bean's capacity, it might be called findByCapacity(int capacity). In container-managed persistence, any find method included in the home interface must be explained to the container. In other words, the deployer needs to define how the find method should work in terms that the container understands. This is done at deployment time, using the vendor's deployment tools and syntax specific to the vendor.

Find methods return either the remote-interface type appropriate for that bean, or an instance of java.util.Enumeration.

NOTE   The EJB 1.1 specification also allows multiple references to be returned as a java.util.Collection type, which provides more flexibility to application and bean developers.

Specifying a remote-interface type indicates that the method only locates one bean. The findByPrimaryKey() method obviously returns one remote reference because there is a one-to-one relationship between a primary key's value and an entity. The findByCapacity(int capacity) method, however, could return several remote references, one for every ship that has a capacity equal to the parameter capacity. The possibility of returning several remote references requires the use of the Enumeration type or a Collection type (EJB 1.1 only). Enterprise JavaBeans specifies that any find method used in a home interface must throw the javax.ejb.FinderException. Find methods that return a single remote reference throw a FinderException if an application error occurs and a javax.ejb. ObjectNotFoundException if a matching bean cannot be found. The Object-NotFoundException is a subtype of FinderException and is only thrown by find methods that return single remote references.

EJB 1.1 multi-entity find methods

Find methods that return an Enumeration or Collection type (multi-entity finders) return an empty collection (not a null reference) if no matching beans can be found or throw a FinderException if an application error occurs.

EJB 1.0 multi-entity find methods

Find methods that return an Enumeration return null if no matching beans can be found or throw a FinderException if a failure in the request occurs.

How find methods are mapped to the database for container-managed persistence is not defined in the EJB specification; it is vendor-specific. Consult the documentation provided by your EJB vendor to determine how find methods are defined at deployment time.

Java RMI Return Types, Parameters, and Exceptions

Both the remote interface and home interface extend, indirectly, the java.rmi. Remote interface. Remote interfaces must follow several guidelines, some of which apply to the return types and parameters that are allowed. To be compatible, the *actual* return types and parameter types used in the java.rmi.Remote interfaces must be primitives, String types, java.rmi.Remote types, or serializable types.

There is a difference between *declared* types, which are checked by the compiler, and *actual* types, which are checked by the runtime. The types which may be used in Java RMI are actual types, which are either primitive types, object types implementing (even indirectly) java.rmi.Remote, or object types implementing (even indirectly) java.io.Serializable. The java.util.Enumeration type returned by multi-entity find methods is, for example, is a perfectly valid return type for a remote method, provided that the concrete class implementing Enumeration is Serializable. So Java RMI has *no* special rules regarding declared return types or parameter types. At runtime, a type that is not a java.rmi.Remote type is assumed to be serializable; if it is not, an exception is thrown. The actual type passed cannot be checked by the compiler, it must be checked at the runtime.

Here is a list of the types that can be passed as parameters or returned in Java RMI:

- Primitives: byte, boolean, char, short, int, long, double, float
- Java serializable types: any class that implements or any interface that extends java.io.Serializable
- Java RMI remote types: any class that implements or any interface that extends java.rmi.Remote

All methods defined in remote interfaces must throw java.rmi.Remote-Exception. A RemoteException is thrown by the underlying system (the EJB object) when a communication error or system failure of some kind occurs. Although methods in the remote interface and home interface are required by the compiler to declare that they throw RemoteException, it's not required that the matching methods in the bean class actually throw it.

The ShipBean Class

No bean is complete without its implementation class. Now that we have defined the Ship bean's remote interfaces and primary key, we are ready to define the ShipBean itself. The ShipBean will reside on the EJB server. When a client application or bean invokes a business method on the Ship bean's remote interface, that method invocation is received by the EJB object, which then delegates it to the ShipBean.

When developing any bean, we have to use the bean's remote interfaces as a guide. Business methods defined in the remote interface must be duplicated in the bean class. In container-managed beans, the create methods of the home interface must also have matching methods in the bean class according to the EJB

specification. Finally, callback methods defined by the javax.ejb.EntityBean
interface must be implemented. Here is the code for the ShipBean class. We have
omitted the ejbCreate() method, which will be discussed later because it's different in EJB 1.0 and EJB 1.1:

```java
package com.titan.ship;

import javax.ejb.EntityContext;

public class ShipBean implements javax.ejb.EntityBean {
    public int id;
    public String name;
    public int capacity;
    public double tonnage;

    public EntityContext context;

    /**************************************
    *     ejbCreate() method goes here
    **************************************/

    public void ejbPostCreate(int id, String name, int capacity,
                              double tonnage){
        ShipPK pk = (ShipPK)context.getPrimaryKey();
        // Do something useful with the primary key.
    }

    public void ejbPostCreate(int id, String name) {
        Ship myself = (Ship)context.getEJBObject();
        // Do something useful with the EJBObject reference.
    }
    public void setEntityContext(EntityContext ctx) {
        context = ctx;
    }
    public void unsetEntityContext() {
        context = null;
    }
    public void ejbActivate() {}
    public void ejbPassivate() {}
    public void ejbLoad() {}
    public void ejbStore() {}
    public void ejbRemove() {}

    public String getName() {
        return name;
    }
    public void setName(String n) {
        name = n;
    }
```

```
    public void setCapacity(int cap) {
        capacity = cap;
    }
    public int getCapacity() {
        return capacity;
    }
    public double getTonnage() {
        return tonnage;
    }
    public void setTonnage(double tons) {
        tonnage = tons;
    }
}
```

The Ship bean defines four persistent fields: id, name, capacity, and tonnage. No mystery here: these fields represent the persistent state of the Ship bean; they are the state that defines a unique ship entity in the database. The Ship bean also defines another field, context, which holds the bean's EntityContext. We'll have more to say about this later.

The set and get methods are the business methods we defined for the Ship bean; both the remote interface and the bean class must support them. This means that the signatures of these methods must be exactly the same, except for the javax. ejb.RemoteException. The bean class's business methods aren't required to throw the RemoteException. This makes sense because these methods aren't actually invoked remotely—they're invoked by the EJB object. If a communication problem occurs, the container will throw the RemoteException for the bean automatically.

Implementing the javax.ejb.EntityBean Interface

To make the ShipBean an entity bean, it must implement the javax.ejb. EntityBean interface. The EntityBean interface contains a number of callback methods that the container uses to alert the bean instance of various runtime events:

```
public interface javax.ejb.EntityBean extends javax.ejb.EnterpriseBean {
    public abstract void ejbActivate() throws RemoteException;
    public abstract void ejbPassivate() throws RemoteException;
    public abstract void ejbLoad() throws RemoteException;
    public abstract void ejbStore() throws RemoteException;
    public abstract void ejbRemove() throws RemoteException;
    public abstract void setEntityContext(EntityContext ctx)
        throws RemoteException;
    public abstract void unsetEntityContext() throws RemoteException;
}
```

Each callback method is called at a specific time during the life cycle of a ShipBean. In many cases, container-managed beans, like the ShipBean, don't need to do anything when a callback method is invoked. Container-managed beans have persistence managed automatically, so many of the resources and logic that might be managed by these methods are already handled by the container. Except for the EntityContext methods, we will leave the discussion of these methods for the section on bean-managed persistence. This version of the Ship bean has empty implementations for its callback methods. It is important to note, however, that even a container-managed bean can take advantage of these callback methods if needed; we just don't need them in our ShipBean at this time.

The EntityContext

The first method called after a bean instance is created is setEntityContext(). As the method signature indicates, this method passes the bean instance a reference to a javax.ejb.EntityContext, which is really the bean instance's interface to the container. The definition of EntityContext is as follows:

```
public interface javax.ejb.EntityContext extends javax.ejb.EJBContext {
    public abstract EJBObject getEJBObject() throws IllegalStateException;
    public abstract Object getPrimaryKey() throws IllegalStateException;
}
```

The setEntityContext() method is called prior to the bean instance's entry into the instance pool. In Chapter 3, we discussed the instance pool that EJB containers maintain, where instances of entity and stateless session beans are kept ready to use. EntityBean instances in the instance pool are not associated with any data in the database; their state is not unique. When a request for a specific entity is made by a client, an instance from the pool is chosen, populated with data from the database, and assigned to service the client.

When an entity from the pool is assigned to service a client, the instance is associated with or "wrapped" by an EJB object. The EJB object provides the remote reference, or stub, that implements the bean's remote interface and is used by the client. When the client invokes methods on the stub, the EJB object receives the message and delegates it to the bean instance. The EJB object protects the bean instance from direct contact with the client by intervening in business method invocations to ensure that transactions, security, concurrency, and other primary services are managed appropriately.

The EJB object also maintains the bean instance's identity, which is available from the EntityContext. The EntityContext allows the bean instance to obtain its own primary key and a remote reference to the EJB object. Containers often use a swapping strategy to get maximum use of bean instances. Swapping doesn't impact the client reference to the stub because the stub communicates with the EJB object, not the bean instance. So, as bean instances are assigned to and removed from association with the EJB object server, the server maintains a constant connection to the stub on the client.

When a method is invoked on the EJB object via the stub, a bean instance from the pool is populated with the appropriate data and assigned to the EJB object. When a bean instance is assigned to an EJB object, its EntityContext changes so that the primary key and EJB object obtainable through the EntityContext match the EJB object the bean instance is currently associated with. Because the bean instance's identity changes every time the bean is swapped into a different EJB object, the values returned by the EntityContext change depending on which bean instance it is associated with.

At the end of the bean instance's life, after the bean instance is removed permanently from the instance pool and before the bean instance is garbage collected, the unsetEntityContext() method is called, indicating that the bean instance's EntityContext is no longer implemented by the container.

The Create Methods

When a create method is invoked on the home interface, the EJB home delegates it to the bean instance in the same way that business methods on the remote interface are handled. This means that we need an ejbCreate() method in the bean class that corresponds to each create() method in the home interface. Here are the ejbCreate() methods that we omitted from the source code for the ShipBean class. Note the difference between EJB 1.0 and 1.1:

```
// For EJB 1.1, returns a ShipPK
public ShipPK ejbCreate(int id, String name, int capacity, double tonnage) {
        this.id = id;
        this.name = name;
        this.capacity = capacity;
        this.tonnage = tonnage;
        return null;
}
public ShipPK ejbCreate(int id, String name) {
        this.id = id;
        this.name = name;
        capacity = 0;
        tonnage = 0;
}


// For EJB 1.0: returns void
public void ejbCreate(int id, String name, int capacity, double tonnage) {
        this.id = id;
        this.name = name;
```

```
        this.capacity = capacity;
        this.tonnage = tonnage;
}
    public void ejbCreate(int id, String name) {
        this.id = id;
        this.name = name;
        capacity = 0;
        tonnage = 0;
    }
```

The ejbCreate() method returns void in EJB 1.0 and a null value of type ShipPK for the bean's primary key in EJB 1.1. The end result is the same: in both EJB 1.0 and EJB 1.1, the return value of the ejbCreate() method for a container-managed bean is ignored. EJB 1.1 changed its return value from void to the primary key type to facilitate subclassing; the change was made so that it's easier for a bean-managed bean to extend a container-managed bean. In EJB 1.0, this is not possible because Java won't allow you to overload methods with different return values. By changing this definition so that a bean-managed bean can extend a container-managed bean, the new specification allows vendors to support container-managed persistence by extending the container-managed bean with a generated bean-managed bean—a fairly simple solution to a difficult problem. Bean developers can also take advantage of inheritance to change an existing CMP bean into a BMP bean, which may be needed to overcome difficult persistence problems.

For every create() method defined in the entity bean's home interface, there must be a corresponding ejbPostCreate() method in the bean instance class. In other words, ejbCreate() and ejbPostCreate() methods occur in pairs with matching signatures; there must be one pair for each create() method defined in the home interface.

ejbCreate()

In a container-managed bean, the ejbCreate() method is called just prior to writing the bean's container-managed fields to the database. Values passed in to the ejbCreate() method should be used to initialize the fields of the bean instance. Once the ejbCreate() method completes, a new record, based on the container-managed fields, is written to the database.

Each ejbCreate() method must have parameters that match a create() method in the home interface. The ShipHome, for example, specifies two create() methods. According to the EJB specification, our ShipBean class must therefore have two ejbCreate() methods that match the parameters of the ShipHome create() methods. If you look at the ShipBean class definition and compare it to the ShipHome definition, you can see how the parameters for the create methods match exactly in type and sequence. This enables the container to delegate the create() method on the home interface to the proper ejbCreate() method in the bean instance.

The EntityContext maintained by the bean instance does not provide it with the proper identity until the ejbCreate() method has completed. This means that during the course of the ejbCreate() method, the bean instance doesn't have access to its primary key or EJB object.* The EntityContext does, however, provide the bean with information about the caller's identity, access to its EJB home object, and properties.

| NOTE | In EJB 1.1, the bean can also use the JNDI environment naming context to access other beans and resource managers like javax.sql.DataSource. |

The bean developer must ensure that the ejbCreate() method sets the persistent fields that correspond to the fields of the primary key. When a primary key is defined for a container-managed bean, it must define fields that match one or more of the container-managed (persistent) fields in the bean class. The fields must match with regard to type and name exactly. At runtime, the container will assume that fields in the primary key match some or all of the fields in the bean class. When a new bean is created, the container will use those container-managed fields in the bean class to instantiate and populate a primary key for the bean automatically. In the case of the ShipBean, the container-managed id field corresponds to the ShipPK.id field. When the record is inserted, the ShipBean.id field is used to populate a newly instantiated ShipPK object.

Once the bean's state has been populated and its EntityContext established, an ejbPostCreate() method is invoked. This method gives the bean an opportunity to perform any post-processing prior to servicing client requests.

ejbPostCreate()

The bean identity isn't available to the bean during the call to ejbCreate(), but is available in the ejbPostCreate() method. This means that the bean can access its own primary key and EJB object, which can be useful for initializing the bean instance prior to servicing business method invocations. You can use the ejbPostCreate() method to perform any additional initialization. Each ejbPostCreate() method must have the same parameters as its corresponding ejbCreate() method. The ejbPostCreate() method returns void.

---

* Information that is not specific to the bean identity, such as the environment properties, may be available during the ejbCreate().

It may seem a little silly to define the ejbPostCreate() method with the same parameters as its matching ejbCreate() method, especially in the ShipBean where the instance variables are just as easily retrieved from the bean instance's fields. There are, however, two very good reasons for matching the parameter lists. First, it indicates which ejbPostCreate() method is associated with which ejbCreate() method. This ensures that the container calls the correct ejbPost-Create() method after ejbCreate() is done. Second, it is possible that one of the parameters passed is not assigned to a bean instance field or is only relevant to the ejbPostCreate(). In either case, you would need to duplicate the parameters of the ejbCreate() method to have that information available in the ejbPostCreate() method.

ejbCreate() and ejbPostCreate() sequence of events

To understand how a bean instance gets up and running, we have to think of a bean in the context of its life cycle. Figure 6-1 shows the sequence of events during a portion of the bean's life cycle, as defined by the EJB specification. Every EJB vendor must support this sequence of events.

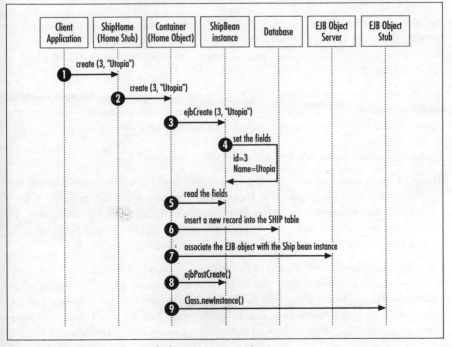

Figure 6-1. The sequence of events for bean instance creation

The process begins when the client invokes one of the create() methods on the bean's EJB home. A create() method is invoked on the EJB home stub (step 1), which communicates the method to the EJB home across the network (step 2). The EJB home plucks a ShipBean instance from the pool and invokes its corresponding ejbCreate() method (step 3).

The create() and ejbCreate() methods pair are responsible for initializing the bean instance so that the container can insert a record into the database. In the case of the ShipBean, the minimal information required to add a new ship to the system is the ship's unique id and a name. These fields are initialized during the ejbCreate() method invocation (step 4).

In a container-managed EntityBean, the container uses the bean instance's public fields (id, name, capacity, and tonnage) to insert a record in the database which it reads from the bean (step 5). Only those fields described as container-managed in the deployment descriptor are accessed automatically. Once the container has read the container-managed fields from the bean instance, it will automatically insert a new record into the database using those fields (step 6). How the data is written to the database is defined when the bean's fields are mapped at deployment time. In our example, a new record is inserted into the SHIP table.

Once the record has been inserted into the database, the bean instance is ready to be assigned to an EJB object (step 7). Once the bean is assigned to an EJB object, the bean's identity is available. This is when the ejbPostCreate() method is invoked (step 8).

Finally, when the ejbPostCreate() processing is complete, the bean is ready to service client requests. The EJB object stub is created and returned to client application, which will use it to invoke business methods on the bean (step 9).

Using ejbLoad() and ejbStore() in container-managed beans

The process of ensuring that the database record and the entity bean instance are equivalent is called *synchronization*. In container-managed persistence, the bean's container-managed fields are automatically synchronized with the database. In most cases, we will not need the ejbLoad() and ejbStore() methods because persistence in container-managed beans is uncomplicated.

Leveraging the ejbLoad() and ejbStore() callback methods in container-managed beans, however, can be useful if more sophisticated logic is needed when synchronizing container-managed fields. Data intended for the database can be reformatted or compressed to conserve space; data just retrieved from the database can be used to calculate derived values for nonpersistent properties.

Imagine a hypothetical bean class that includes an array of Strings that you want to store in the database. Relational databases do not support arrays, so you need to convert the array into some other format. Using the `ejbLoad()` and `ejbStore()` methods in a container-managed bean allows the bean instance to reformat the data as appropriate for the state of the bean and the structure of the database. Here's how this might work:

```
public class HypotheticalBean extends javax.ejb.EntityBean {
    public transient String [] array_of_messages;
    public String messages;

    // Parses the messages into an array_of_messages. This is called on a
    // container-managed bean just after the bean instance is synchronized
    // with the database (right after the bean gets its data).
    public void ejbLoad() {
        StringTokenizer st = new StringTokenizer(messages, "~");
        array_of_messages = new String[st.countTokens()];
        for (int i = 0; st.hasMoreTokens(); i++) {
            array_of_messages[i] = st.nextToken();
        }
    }
    // Creates a '~' delimited string of messages from the
    // array_of_messages. This method is called immediately
    // prior to synchronization of the database with the bean;
    // just before the bean is written to the database.
    public void ejbStore() {
        messages = new String();
        int i = 0;
        for (; i < array_of_messages.length-1;i++) {
            messages += array_of_messages[i]+"~";
        }
        messages += array_of_messages[i];
    }
    // a business method that uses the array_of_messages
    public String [] getMessages() {
        return array_of_messages;
    }
    ...
}
```

Just before the container reads the container-managed field messages, it calls the `ejbStore()` method. This method makes a tilde (~) delimited string from the `array_of_messages` and places the new string in the messages field. This trick formats the messages so the database can store them easily.

Just after the container updates the fields of the HypotheticalBean with fresh data from the database, it calls the `ejbLoad()` method, which parses the tilde-delimited message field and populates the `array_of_messages` with the strings. This reformats the database data into an array that is easier for the HypotheticalBean to return to the client.

EJB 1.1: Deploying the ShipBean

With a complete definition of the Ship bean, including the remote interface,
home interface, and primary key, we are ready to create a deployment descriptor.
The following listing shows the bean's XML deployment descriptor. This deployment descriptor is not significantly different from the descriptor we created for
the Cabin bean in Chapter 4, so it won't be discussed in detail.

```xml
<?xml version="1.0"?>

<!DOCTYPE ejb-jar PUBLIC "-//Sun Microsystems, Inc.//DTD Enterprise
JavaBeans 1.1//EN" "http://java.sun.com/j2ee/dtds/ejb-jar_1_1.dtd">

<ejb-jar>
 <enterprise-beans>
   <entity>
       <description>
            This bean represents a cruise ship.
       </description>
       <ejb-name>ShipBean</ejb-name>
       <home>com.titan.ship.ShipHome</home>
       <remote>com.titan.ship.Ship</remote>
       <ejb-class>com.titan.ship.ShipBean</ejb-class>
       <persistence-type>Container</persistence-type>
       <prim-key-class>com.titan.ship.ShipPK</prim-key-class>
       <reentrant>False</reentrant>

       <cmp-field><field-name>id</field-name></cmp-field>
       <cmp-field><field-name>name</field-name></cmp-field>
       <cmp-field><field-name>capacity</field-name></cmp-field>
       <cmp-field><field-name>tonnage</field-name></cmp-field>
   </entity>
 </enterprise-beans>

<assembly-descriptor>
  <security-role>
    <description>
       This role represents everyone who is allowed full access
       to the Ship bean.
    </description>
    <role-name>everyone</role-name>
  </security-role>

  <method-permission>
    <role-name>everyone</role-name>
    <method>
        <ejb-name>ShipBean</ejb-name>
        <method-name>*</method-name>
    </method>
  </method-permission>
```

```
        <container-transaction>
          <method>
            <ejb-name>ShipBean</ejb-name>
            <method-name>*</method-name>
          </method>
          <trans-attribute>Required</trans-attribute>
        </container-transaction>
      </assembly-descriptor>
    </ejb-jar>
```

Save the Ship bean's deployment descriptor into the *com/titan/ship* directory as *ejb-jar.xml.*

Now that you have put all the necessary files in one directory, creating the JAR file is easy. Position yourself in the *dev* directory that is just above the *com/titan/ship* directory tree, and execute the *jar* utility as you did in Chapter 4:

```
\dev % jar cf ship.jar com/titan/ship/*.class META-INF/ejb-jar.xml
```

```
F:\..\dev>jar cf ship.jar com\titan\ship\*.class META-INF\ejb-jar.xml
```

The c option tells the *jar* utility to create a new JAR file that contains the files indicated in subsequent parameters. It also tells the *jar* utility to stream the resulting JAR file to standard output. The f option tells *jar* to redirect the standard output to a new file named in the second parameter (ship.jar). It's important to get the order of the option letters and the command-line parameters to match.

EJB 1.0: Deploying the ShipBean

If you're using EJB 1.0, you need to create an old-style deployment descriptor, which is a serialized Java object. To create the deployment descriptor, we write a MakeDD application, just as we did in Chapter 4 for the Cabin bean. Other than changing the name of classes, the JNDI name, and the container-managed fields, there isn't much difference between Ship's MakeDD application and the Cabin bean's.

```
package com.titan.ship;

import javax.ejb.deployment.EntityDescriptor;
import javax.ejb.deployment.ControlDescriptor;
import javax.naming.CompoundName;

import java.util.Properties;
import java.io.FileOutputStream;
import java.io.ObjectOutputStream;
import java.lang.reflect.Field;
```

```java
public class MakeDD {

    public static void main(String args []) {
        try {

            if (args.length <1) {
                System.out.println("must specify target directory");
                return;
            }
            EntityDescriptor shipDD = new EntityDescriptor();
            shipDD.setEnterpriseBeanClassName("com.titan.ship.ShipBean");
            shipDD.setHomeInterfaceClassName("com.titan.ship.ShipHome");
            shipDD.setRemoteInterfaceClassName("com.titan.ship.Ship");
            shipDD.setPrimaryKeyClassName("com.titan.ship.ShipPK");

            Class beanClass = ShipBean.class;
            Field [] persistentFields = new Field[4];
            persistentFields[0] = beanClass.getDeclaredField("id");
            persistentFields[1] = beanClass.getDeclaredField("name");
            persistentFields[2] = beanClass.getDeclaredField("capacity");
            persistentFields[3] = beanClass.getDeclaredField("tonnage");
            shipDD.setContainerManagedFields(persistentFields);

            shipDD.setReentrant(false);

            CompoundName jndiName = new CompoundName("ShipHome", new Properties());
            shipDD.setBeanHomeName(jndiName);

            ControlDescriptor cd = new ControlDescriptor();
            cd.setIsolationLevel(ControlDescriptor.TRANSACTION_READ_COMMITTED);
            cd.setMethod(null);
            cd.setRunAsMode(ControlDescriptor.CLIENT_IDENTITY);
            cd.setTransactionAttribute(ControlDescriptor.TX_REQUIRED);
            ControlDescriptor [] cdArray = {cd};
            shipDD.setControlDescriptors(cdArray);

            // Set the name to associate with the enterprise bean
            // in the JNDI name space.

            String fileSeparator =
                System.getProperties().getProperty("file.separator");

            if (! args[0].endsWith(fileSeparator))
                args[0] += fileSeparator;

            FileOutputStream fis = new FileOutputStream(args[0]+"ShipDD.ser");
            ObjectOutputStream oos = new ObjectOutputStream(fis);
            oos.writeObject(shipDD);
            oos.flush();
            oos.close();
            fis.close();
```

```
        } catch (Throwable t){t.printStackTrace();}
   }
}
```

Compile this class and run it:

```
\dev % java com.titan.ship.MakeDD com/titan/ship

F:\..\dev>java com.titan.ship.MakeDD com\titan\ship
```

If you run this application, you should end up with a file called *ShipDD.ser* in the *com/titan/ship* directory. This is your serialized `DeploymentDescriptor` for the Ship bean. We examined the code for this type of `MakeDD` application in detail in Chapter 4, so we won't do it again here.

Next, place the Ship bean in a JAR file using the same process we used for the Cabin and TravelAgent beans in Chapter 4. First, we have to specify a manifest file for the Ship bean, which we will save in the *com/titan/ship* directory:

```
Name: com/titan/ship/ShipDD.ser
Enterprise-Bean: True
```

Now that the manifest is ready, we can JAR the Ship bean so that it's ready for deployment. Again, we use the same process that we used for the Cabin and TravelAgent beans:

```
\dev % jar cmf com/titan/ship/manifest ship.jar \
com/titan/ship/*.class com/titan/ship/*.ser

F:\..\dev>jar cmf com\titan\ship\manifest ship.jar com\titan\ship\*.class
com\titan\ship\*.ser
```

The Ship bean is now complete and ready to be deployed. Use the wizards and deployment utilities provided by your vendor to deploy the Ship bean into the EJB server.

The Client Application

In Chapters 4 and 5, you learned how to write a Java client that uses the EJB client API to access and work with enterprise beans. Here's a simple client that accesses the Ship bean; it creates a single ship, the *Paradise*, that can handle 3,000 passengers:

```
package com.titan.ship;

import javax.naming.InitialContext;
import javax.naming.Context;
import javax.naming.NamingException;
import java.rmi.RemoteException;
import java.util.Properties;
```

```
public class Client_1 {
    public static void main(String [] args) {
        try {
            Context ctx = getInitialContext();

            // EJB 1.0: Use native cast instead of narrow()
            Object ref = ctx.lookup("ShipHome");
            ShipHome home = (ShipHome)
                PortableRemoteObjectnarrow(ref,ShipHome.class);

            Ship ship = home.create(1,"Paradise",3000,100000);
            int t = ship.getCapacity();
            System.out.println("Capacity = " +t);

        } catch (Exception e){e.printStackTrace();}
    }
    public static Context getInitialContext()
        throws javax.naming.NamingException {

        Properties p = new Properties();
        // ... Specify the JNDI properties specific to the vendor.
        return new javax.naming.InitialContext(p);
    }
}
```

Once you have created the ship, you should be able to modify the client to look up the ship using its primary key, as shown in the following code:

```
package com.titan.ship;

import javax.naming.InitialContext;
import javax.naming.Context;
import javax.naming.NamingException;
import java.rmi.RemoteException;
import java.util.Properties;
import java.util.Enumeration;

public class Client_2 {
    public static void main(String [] args){
        try {
            Context ctx = getInitialContext();

            // EJB 1.0: Use native cast instead of narrow().
            Object ref = ctx.lookup("ShipHome");
            ShipHome home = (ShipHome)
                PortableRemoteObject.narrow(ref,ShipHome.class);

            home.create(2,"Utopia",4500,8939);
            home.create(3,"Valhalla",3300,93939);
            ShipPK pk = new ShipPK();
            pk.id = 1;
```

```
            Ship ship = home.findByPrimaryKey(pk);
            ship.setCapacity(4500);
            int capacity = ship.getCapacity();

            Enumeration enum = home.findByCapacity(4500);
            while (enum.hasMoreElements()) {
                // EJB 1.0: Use native cast instead of narrow()
                ref = enum.nextElement();
                Ship aShip = (Ship)
                    PortableRemoteObject.narrow(ref,Ship.class);

                System.out.println(aShip.getName());
            }
        } catch (Exception e){e.printStackTrace();}
    }
    public static Context getInitialContext()
        throws javax.naming.NamingException {
        Properties p = new Properties();
        // ... Specify the JNDI properties specific to the vendor.
        return new javax.naming.InitialContext(p);
    }
}
```

The preceding client code demonstrates that the ship was automatically inserted into the database by the container. Now any changes you make to ship attributes (name, capacity, tonnage) will result in a change to the database.

Spend some time creating, finding, and removing Ships using the client application. You should also explore the use of all the methods in the EJBObject and EJBHome interfaces as you did in Chapter 5 with the Cabin and TravelAgent beans.

Bean-Managed Persistence

Bean-managed persistence is more complicated than container-managed persistence because you must explicitly write the persistence logic into the bean class. In order to write the persistence handling code into the bean class, you must know what type of database is being used and the how the bean class's fields map to that database.

Bean-managed persistence gives you more flexibility in how state is managed between the bean instance and the database. Entity beans that are defined by complex joins, a combination of different databases, or other resources such as legacy systems will benefit from bean-managed persistence. Essentially, bean-managed persistence is the alternative to container-managed persistence when the deployment tools are inadequate for mapping the bean instance's state to the database. It is likely that enterprise developers will use bean-managed persistence for creating custom beans for their business system.

The disadvantage of bean-managed persistence is that more work is required to define the bean. You have to understand the structure of the database and develop the logic to create, update, and remove data associated with an entity. This requires diligence in using the EJB callback methods such as ejbLoad() and ejbStore() appropriately. In addition, you must explicitly develop the find methods defined in the bean's home interface.

Another disadvantage of bean-managed persistence is that it ties the bean to a specific database type and structure. Any changes in the database or in the structure of data require changes to the bean instance's definition; these changes may not be trivial. A bean-managed entity is not as database-independent as a container-managed entity, but it can better accommodate a complex or unusual set of data.*

To understand how bean-managed persistence works, we will modify the Ship bean to use bean-managed persistence. The nice thing about this change is that we do not need to modify any of the client's API. All the changes take place in the ShipBean class and the deployment descriptor.

Making the ShipBean a Bean-Managed Entity

The bulk of the source code for a bean-managed Ship bean is applicable to both EJB 1.1 and EJB 1.0. Changes to accommodate EJB 1.0 containers are indicated by comments in the source code. There are two types of changes required:

- EJB 1.0 requires that a RemoteException be thrown if a system exception occurs. You will notice that a special comment, EJB 1.0: throw new RemoteException(), is placed in the appropriate locations to note this difference. EJB 1.1 requires that the javax.ejb.EJBException be thrown if a system error, like an SQLException, is encountered while executing a method. The EJBException is a subclass of RuntimeException in EJB 1.1, so you don't have to declare it in the method signature.

- Multi-entity find methods in EJB 1.0 are required to return null, if no matching entities are found. This difference is noted in the code of the findByCapacity() method. Multi-entity find methods in EJB 1.1 return an empty Collection or Enumeration if no matching entities are found.

Here is the complete definition of the bean-managed ShipBean:

```
package com.titan.ship;

import javax.naming.Context;
import javax.naming.InitialContext;
import javax.naming.NamingException;
```

---

* Containers that use object-to-relational mapping tools in bean-managed persistence can mitigate this disadvantage.

```java
import javax.ejb.EntityContext;
import java.rmi.RemoteException;
import java.sql.SQLException;
import java.sql.Connection;
import java.sql.PreparedStatement;
import java.sql.DriverManager;
import java.sql.ResultSet;
import javax.sql.DataSource;
import javax.ejb.CreateException;
import javax.ejb.EJBException;
import javax.ejb.FinderException;
import javax.ejb.ObjectNotFoundException;
import java.util.Enumeration;
import java.util.Properties;
import java.util.Vector;

public class ShipBean implements javax.ejb.EntityBean {
    public int id;
    public String name;
    public int capacity;
    public double tonnage;

    public EntityContext context;

    public ShipPK ejbCreate(int id, String name,
            int capacity, double tonnage)
            throws CreateException {
        // EJB 1.0: Also throws RemoteException
        if ((id < 1) || (name == null))
            throw new CreateException("Invalid Parameters");
        this.id = id;
        this.name = name;
        this.capacity = capacity;
        this.tonnage = tonnage;

        Connection con = null;
        PreparedStatement ps = null;
        try {
            con = this.getConnection();
            ps = con.prepareStatement(
                "insert into Ship (id, name, capacity, tonnage) " +
                "values (?,?,?,?)");
            ps.setInt(1, id);
            ps.setString(2, name);
            ps.setInt(3, capacity);
            ps.setDouble(4, tonnage);
            if (ps.executeUpdate() != 1) {
                throw new CreateException ("Failed to add Ship to database");
            }
```

```
        ShipPK primaryKey = new ShipPK();
        primaryKey.id = id;
        return primaryKey;
    }
    catch (SQLException se) {
        // EJB 1.0: throw new RemoteException("", se);
        throw new EJBException (se);
    }
    finally {
        try {
            if (ps != null) ps.close();
            if (con!= null) con.close();
        } catch(SQLException se) {
            se.printStackTrace();
        }
    }
}
public void ejbPostCreate(int id, String name,
    int capacity, double tonnage) {
    // Do something useful with the primary key.
}
public ShipPK ejbCreate(int id, String name )
    throws CreateException {
    // EJB 1.0: Also throws RemoteException
    return ejbCreate(id,name,0,0);
}
public void ejbPostCreate(int id, String name) {
    // Do something useful with the EJBObject reference.
}
public ShipPK ejbFindByPrimaryKey(ShipPK primaryKey)
    throws FinderException, {
    // EJB 1.0: Also throws RemoteException
    Connection con = null;
    PreparedStatement ps = null;
    ResultSet result = null;
    try {
        con = this.getConnection();
        ps = con.prepareStatement(
            "select id from Ship where id = ?");
        ps.setInt(1, primaryKey.id);
        result = ps.executeQuery();
        // Does ship id exist in database?
        if (!result.next()) {
            throw new ObjectNotFoundException(
                "Cannot find Ship with id = "+id);
        }
    } catch (SQLException se) {
        // EJB 1.0: throw new RemoteException("", se);
        throw new EJBException(se);
    }
```

```
      finally {
        try {
          if (result != null) result.close();
          if (ps != null) ps.close();
          if (con!= null) con.close();
        } catch(SQLException se){
          se.printStackTrace();
        }
      }
      return primaryKey;
  }
  public Enumeration ejbFindByCapacity(int capacity)
      throws FinderException {
      // EJB 1.0: Also throws RemoteException
      Connection con = null;
      PreparedStatement ps = null;
      ResultSet result = null;
      try {
        con = this.getConnection();
        ps = con.prepareStatement(
            "select id from Ship where capacity = ?");
        ps.setInt(1,capacity);
        result = ps.executeQuery();
        Vector keys = new Vector();
        while(result.next()) {
          ShipPK shipPk = new ShipPK();
          shipPk.id = result.getInt("id");
          keys.addElement(shipPk);
        }
        // EJB 1.1: always return collection, even if empty.
        return keys.elements();
        // EJB 1.0: return null if collection is empty.
        // return (keys.size() > 0) ? keys.elements() : null;

      }
      catch (SQLException se) {
        // EJB 1.0: throw new RemoteException("",se);
        throw new EJBException (se);
      }
      finally {
        try {
          if (result != null) result.close();
          if (ps != null) ps.close();
          if (con!= null) con.close();
        } catch(SQLException se) {
          se.printStackTrace();
        }
      }
  }
}
```

```java
public void setEntityContext(EntityContext ctx) {
    context = ctx;
}
public void unsetEntityContext() {
    context = null;
}
public void ejbActivate() {}
public void ejbPassivate() {}
public void ejbLoad() {
    // EJB 1.0: throws RemoteException

    ShipPK pk = (ShipPK) context.getPrimaryKey();
    Connection con = null;
    PreparedStatement ps = null;
    ResultSet result = null;
    try {
      con = this.getConnection();
      ps = con.prepareStatement(
          "select name, capacity, tonnage from Ship where id = ?");
      ps.setInt(1,pk.id);
      result = ps.executeQuery();
      if (result.next()){
        id = id;
        name = result.getString("name");
        capacity = result.getInt("capacity");
        tonnage = result.getDouble("tonnage");
      } else {
        /* EJB 1.0: throw new RemoteException();
        */
        throw new EJBException();
      }
    } catch (SQLException se) {
      // EJB 1.0: throw new RemoteException("",se);
      throw new EJBException(se);
    }
    finally {
      try {
        if (result != null) result.close();
        if (ps != null) ps.close();
        if (con!= null) con.close();
      } catch(SQLException se) {
        se.printStackTrace();
      }
    }
}
public void ejbStore() {
// EJB 1.0: throws RemoteException
    Connection con = null;
    PreparedStatement ps = null;
```

```
      try {
        con = this.getConnection();
        ps = con.prepareStatement(
            "update Ship set name = ?, capacity = ?, " +
            "tonnage = ? where id = ?");
        ps.setString(1,name);
        ps.setInt(2,capacity);
        ps.setDouble(3,tonnage);
        ps.setInt(4,id);
        if (ps.executeUpdate() != 1) {
          // EJB 1.0: throw new RemoteException ("ejbStore failed");
          throw new EJBException("ejbStore");
        }
      }
      catch (SQLException se) {
        // EJB 1.0: throw new RemoteException("",se);
        throw new EJBException (se);
      }
      finally {
        try {
          if (ps != null) ps.close();
          if (con!= null) con.close();
        } catch(SQLException se) {
          se.printStackTrace();
        }
      }
  }
  public void ejbRemove() {
      // EJB 1.0: throws RemoteException
      Connection con = null;
      PreparedStatement ps = null;
      try {
        con = this.getConnection();
        ps = con.prepareStatement("delete from Ship where id = ?");
        ps.setInt(1, id);
        if (ps.executeUpdate() != 1) {
          // EJB 1.0 throw new RemoteException("ejbRemove");
          throw new EJBException("ejbRemove");
        }
      }
      catch (SQLException se) {
        // EJB 1.0: throw new RemoteException("",se);
        throw new EJBException (se);
      }
      finally {
        try {
          if (ps != null) ps.close();
          if (con!= null) con.close();
        } catch(SQLException se) {
```

```
                    se.printStackTrace();
                }
            }
        }
        public String getName() {
            return name;
        }
        public void setName(String n) {
            name = n;
        }
        public void setCapacity(int cap) {
            capacity = cap;
        }
        public int getCapacity() {
            return capacity;
        }
      • public double getTonnage() {
            return tonnage;
        }
        public void setTonnage(double tons) {
            tonnage = tons;
        }
        private Connection getConnection() throws SQLException {
            // Implementations for EJB 1.0 and EJB 1.1 shown below
        }
    }
```

Exception Handling

There are three types of exceptions thrown from a bean: application exceptions, which indicate business logic errors, runtime exceptions, and checked subsystem exceptions, which are throw from subsystems like JDBC or JNDI.

Application exceptions

Application exceptions include standard EJB application exceptions and custom application exceptions. The standard EJB application exceptions are `CreateException`, `FinderException`, `ObjectNotFoundException`, `DuplicateKeyException`, and `RemoveException`. These exceptions are thrown from the appropriate methods to indicate that a business logic error has occurred. Custom exceptions are exceptions you develop for specific business problems. You will develop custom exceptions in Chapter 7.

Runtime exceptions

`RuntimeException` types are thrown from the virtual machine itself and indicate that a fairly serious programming error has occurred. Examples include `NullPointerException` and `IndexOutOfBoundsException`. These exceptions are handled by the container automatically and should not be handled inside a bean method.

EJB 1.1 subsystem exceptions

Checked exceptions thrown by other subsystems must be wrapped in an EJBException and rethrown from the method. Several examples of this can be found in the previous example, in which an SQLException that was thrown from JDBC was caught and rethrown as an EJBException. Checked exceptions from other subsystems, such as those thrown from JNDI, JavaMail, JMS, etc., should be handled in the same fashion. The EJBException is a subtype of the RuntimeException, so it doesn't need to be declared in the method's throws clause.

EJB 1.0 subsystem exceptions

Checked exceptions thrown by other subsystems must be wrapped in a RemoteException and rethrown from the method. In the previous example, we caught an SQLException that was thrown by JDBC, and threw our own RemoteException. Checked exceptions, such as those thrown from JNDI, JavaMail, JMS, etc., should be handled in the same fashion.

Exceptions have an impact on transactions and are fundamental to transaction processing. Exceptions are examined in greater detail in Chapter 8.

EntityContext

An EntityContext is given to the bean instance at the beginning of its life cycle, before it's made available to service any clients. The EntityContext should be placed in an instance field of the bean and maintained for the life of the instance.

The setEntityContext() method saves the EntityContext assigned to the bean in the instance field context. As the bean instance is swapped from one EJB object to the next, the information obtainable from the EntityContext reference changes to reflect the EJB object that the instance is assigned to. This is possible because the EntityContext is an interface, not a static class definition. This means that the container can implement the EntityContext with a concrete class that it controls. As the bean instance is swapped from one EJB object to another, some of the information made available through the EntityContext will also change.

Both SessionContext, used by session beans, and EntityContext extend EJBContext. Here is the definition of EntityContext:

```
public interface EntityContext extends EJBContext {
    public EJBObject getEJBObject()
        throws java.lang.IllegalStateException;
    public Object getPrimaryKey()
        throws java.lang.IllegalStateException;
}
```

The superinterface, the EJBContext, defines several methods that provide a lot of information about the bean instance's properties, security, and transactional environment. The next section discusses the EJBContext in more detail. Here we focus on the methods defined in the EntityContext.

The getEJBObject() method returns a remote reference to the bean instance's EJB object. This is the same kind of reference that might be used by an application client or another bean. The purpose of this method is to provide the bean instance with a reference to itself when it needs to perform a loopback operation. A loopback occurs when a bean invokes a method on another bean, passing itself as one of the parameters. Here is a hypothetical example:

```
public class A_Bean extends EntityBean {
    public EntityContext context;
    public void someMethod() {
        B_Bean  b = ... // Get a remote reference to a bean of type B_Bean.
        // EJB 1.0: Use native casting instead of narrow()
        EJBObject obj = context.getEJBObject();
        A_Bean mySelf =  (A_Bean)
            PortableRemoteObject.narrow(obj,A_Bean.class);
      b.aMethod( mySelf );
    }
    ...
}
```

It is illegal for a bean instance to pass a this reference to another bean; instead, it passes its remote reference, which the bean instance gets from its context. As discussed in Chapter 3, loopbacks or reentrant behavior are problematic in EJB and should be avoided by new EJB developers. Session beans also define the get-EJBObject() method in the SessionContext interface; its behavior is exactly the same.

The getEJBHome() method is available to both entity and session beans and is defined in the EJBContext class. The getEJBHome() method returns a remote reference to the EJB home for that bean type. The bean instance can use this method to create new beans of its own type or, in the case of entity beans, to find other bean entities of its own type. Most beans won't need access to their EJB home, but if you need one, getEJBHome() provides a way to get it.

The getPrimaryKey() method allows a bean instance to get a copy of the primary key to which it is currently assigned. Outside of the ejbLoad() and ejbStore() methods, the use of this method, like the getEJBHome() method in the EJBContext, is probably rare, but the EntityContext makes the primary key available for those unusual circumstances when it is needed.

As the context in which the bean instance operates changes, some of the information made available through the EntityContext reference will be changed by the container. This is why the methods in the EntityContext throw the java.lang.

IllegalStateException. The EntityContext is always available to the bean instance, but the instance is not always assigned to an EJB object. When the bean is between EJB objects, it has no EJB object or primary key to return. If the getEJBObject() or getPrimaryKey() methods are invoked when the bean is not assigned to an EJB object (when it is swapped out), they throw an IllegalStateException. Appendix B provides tables for each bean type describing which EJBContext methods can be invoked at what times.

EJB 1.1: EJBContext

The EntityContext extends the javax.ejb.EJBContext class, which is also the base class for the SessionContext used by session beans. The EJBContext defines several methods that provide useful information to a bean at runtime. Here is the definition of the EJBContext interface:

```
package javax.ejb;
public interface EJBContext {

    public EJBHome getEJBHome();

    // security methods
    public java.security.Principal getCallerPrincipal();
    public boolean isCallerInRole(java.lang.String roleName);

    // deprecated methods
    public java.security.Identity getCallerIdentity();
    public boolean isCallerInRole(java.security.Identity role);
    public java.util.Properties getEnvironment();

    // transaction methods
    public javax.transaction.UserTransaction getUserTransaction()
        throws java.lang.IllegalStateException;
    public boolean getRollbackOnly()
        throws java.lang.IllegalStateException;
    public void setRollbackOnly()
        throws java.lang.IllegalStateException;
}
```

The getEJBHome() method returns a reference to the bean's home interface. This is useful if the bean needs to create or find beans of its own type. As an example, if all employees in Titan's system (including managers) are represented by the Employee bean, then a manager employee that needs access to subordinate employees can use the getEJBHome() method to get beans representing the appropriate employees:

```
public class EmployeeBean implements EntityBean {
    int id;
    String firstName;
    ...
```

```
public Enumeration getSubordinates() {
    // EJB 1.0: Use native Java casting instead of narrow()
    Object ref = ejbContext.getEJBHome();
    EmployeeHome home = (EmployeeHome)
        PortableRemoteObject.narrow(ref, EmployeeHome.class);

    Enumeration subordinates = home.findByManagerID(this.id);
    return subordinates;
}
...

}
```

The getCallerPrincipal() method is used to obtain the Principal object representing the client that is currently accessing the bean. The Principal object can, for example, be used by the Ship bean to track the identity of clients making updates:

```
public class ShipBean implements EntityBean {
    String modifiedBy;
    EntityContext context;
    ...
    public void setTonnage(double tons){
        tonnage = tons;
        Principal principal = context.getCallerPrincipal();
        String modifiedBy = principal.getName();
    }
    ...

}
```

The isCallerInRole() method tells you whether the client accessing the bean is a member of a specific role, identified by a role name. This method is useful when more access control is needed than the simple method-based access control can provide. In a banking system, for example, the Teller role might be allowed to make withdrawals, but only a Manager can make withdrawals over $10,000.00. This kind of fine-grained access control cannot be addressed through EJB's security attributes because it involves a business logic problem. Therefore, we can use the isCallerInRole() method to augment the automatic access control provided by EJB. First, let's assume that all Managers also are Tellers. Let's also assume that the deployment descriptor for the Account bean specifies that clients that are members of the Teller role can invoke the withdraw() method. The business logic in the withdraw() method uses isCallerInRole() to further refine access control so that only the Manager role can withdraw over $10,000.00.

```
public class AccountBean implements EntityBean {
    int id;
    double balance;
    EntityContext context;
```

```
public void withdraw(Double withdraw)
throws AccessDeniedException {

    if (withdraw.doubleValue() > 10000) {
        boolean isManager = context.isCallerInRole("Manager");
        if (!isManager) {
            // Only Managers can withdraw more than 10k.
            throw new AccessDeniedException();
        }
    }
    balance = balance - withdraw.doubleValue();

}
...

}
```

The EJBContext contains some deprecated methods that were used in EJB 1.0 but will be abandoned in a future version of the specification. Support for these deprecated methods is optional so that EJB 1.1 servers can host EJB 1.0 beans. EJB servers that do not support the deprecated security methods will throw a RuntimeException. The deprecated security methods are based on EJB 1.0's use of the Identity object instead of the Principal object. The semantics of the deprecated methods are basically the same, but because Identity is an abstract class, it has proven to be too difficult to use. The "EJB 1.0: EJBContext" section goes into detail on how to use the Identity driven security methods. EJB 1.1 beans should use the Principal-based security methods.

The getEnvironment() method has been replaced by the JNDI Environment Naming Context, which is discussed later in the book. Support in EJB 1.1 for the deprecated getEnvironment() method is discussed in detail in Chapter 7.

The transactional methods (getUserTransaction(), setRollbackOnly(), getRollbackOnly()) are described in detail in Chapter 8.

EJB 1.0: EJBContext

In EJB 1.0, the EntityContext serves essentially the same purpose as in EJB 1.1. It extends the javax.ejb.EJBContext class, which is also the base class for the SessionContext used by session beans, and it defines several methods that provide useful information to a bean at runtime. Here is the definition of the EJBContext for Version 1.0:

```
package javax.ejb;
public interface EJBContext {

    public EJBHome getEJBHome();
    public java.util.Properties getEnvironment();
```

```
// security methods
public java.security.Identity getCallerIdentity();
public boolean isCallerInRole(java.security.Identity role);

// transaction methods
public javax.transaction.UserTransaction getUserTransaction()
    throws java.lang.IllegalStateException;
public boolean getRollbackOnly()
    throws java.lang.IllegalStateException;
public void setRollbackOnly()
    throws java.lang.IllegalStateException;
}
```

The getEJBHome() method is used to obtain a reference to the bean's home
interface. Repeating the same example: if all employees in Titan's system (including managers) are represented by the Employee bean, then a manager can access
subordinate employees using the getEJBHome() method:

```
public class EmployeeBean implements EntityBean {
    int id;
    String firstName;
    ...
    public Enumeration getSubordinates() {
        EmployeeHome home = (EmployeeHome) ejbContext.getEJBHome();
        Enumeration subordinates = home.findByManagerID(this.id);
        return subordinates;
    }
    ...
}
```

The EJBContext.getEnvironment() method is used by both session and entity
beans. This method provides the bean instance with a set of properties defined at
deployment; it returns an instance of java.util.Properties, which is a type of
hash table. The bean's deployment descriptor provides the properties, which can
include anything you consider necessary for the bean to function. The environment properties are always available to the bean instance from any method.

Properties are usually used to modify the business behavior at runtime. As an
example, an Account bean used in a banking system might use properties to set a
limit for withdrawals. Here's how the code might look:

```
public class AccountBean implements EntityBean {
    int id;
    double balance;
    EntityContext ejbContext;

    public void withdraw(Double withdraw)
        throws WithdrawLimitException {
```

```
        Properties props = ejbContext.getEnvironment();
        String value = props.getProperty("withdraw_limit");
        Double limit = new Double(value)
        if (withdraw.doubleValue() > limit.doubleValue())
            throw new WithdrawLimitException(limit);
        else
            balance = balance - withdraw.doubleValue();
        }
    }
    ...

}
```

When we create the deployment descriptor for the AccountBean, we set the withdraw_limit property in a Properties object, which in turn defines the environment properties for the entire bean. The following code shows how environment properties are set when creating a deployment descriptor:

```
Properties props = new Properties();
props.put("withdraw_limit","100,000.00");
deploymentDesc.setEnvironmentProperties(props);
```

In this case, we set the withdraw_limit to be $100,000.00. Environment properties can be used for a variety of purposes; setting limits is just one application. In the section "Obtaining a Connection to the Database," you will learn how to use Environment properties to obtain database connections.

The getCallerIdentity() method is used to obtain the java.security. Identity object that represents the client accessing the bean. The Identity object might, for example, be used by the Ship bean to track the identity of the client making updates:

```
public class ShipBean implements EntityBean {
    String modifiedBy;
    EntityContext context;
    ...
    public void setTonnage(double tons) {
        tonnage = tons;
        Identity identity = context.getCallerIdentity();
        String modifiedBy = identity.getName();
    }
    ...
}
```

isCallerInRole() determines whether the client invoking the method is a member of a specific role, identified by a Identity object. We can use the same example that we discussed for EJB 1.1: a bank in which a Teller can make withdrawals, but only a Manager can make withdrawals over $10,000.00. This kind of fine-grained access control cannot be addressed by EJB's security attributes because it's a business logic problem. Therefore, we can use isCallerInRole() to augment

the automatic access control provided by EJB. In the Account bean, the access control attributes specify that only clients that are members of the Teller role can
invoke the withdraw() method. The business logic in the withdraw() method
uses the isCallerInRole() method to further refine access control so that only
Manager role types, which are also a Teller role type, can withdraw over $10,000.00.

```
public class AccountBean implements EntityBean {
    int id;
    double balance;
    EntityContext ejbContext;

    public void withdraw(Double withdraw)
    throws WithdrawLimitException, AccessDeniedException {
        if (withdraw.doubleValue() > 10000) {
            Identity managerRole = new RoleIdentity("Manager");
            boolean isManager = ejbContext.isCallerInRole(managerRole);
            if (!isManager) {
                // Only tellers can withdraw more than 10k.
                throw new AccessDeniedException();
            }
        }
        balance = balance - withdraw.doubleValue();
    }
    ...
}
```

Unfortunately, while the EJB 1.0 specification requires the use of the Identity
type as a role identifier, it doesn't specify how a bean should acquire the
Identity object.* The Identity class is an abstract class, so simply instantiating it
is not possible. In our example, a mysterious RoleIdentity object was instantiated with the name of the role being tested. This provided us with an Identity
object that could be used in the isCallerInRole(Identity role) method. But
where did the RoleIdentity object come from?

The RoleIdentity class is a simple extension of the java.security.Identity
class, and provides us with a simple, concrete implementation of Identity that
we can instantiate with a string name.† Here is the definition of this class:

```
import java.security.Identity;
public class RoleIdentity extends Identity {
    public RoleIdentity(String name) {
        super(name);
```

---

* The remainder of this section appeared first in jGuru's Server-Side Java column "Create forward-
  compatible beans in EJB, Part 2" in *JavaWorld* (*http://www.javaworld.com/javaworld/jw-01-2000/jw-01-ssj-
  ejb2.html*).

† A similar RoleIdentity class was originally defined by Jian Lin in a post to the ejb-interest mailing list
  on September 24, 1999.

```
        }
    }
```

Use of the `RoleIdentity` class works in those EJB servers that limit comparison operations of `Identity` to the name attribute. In other words, these servers simply compare the string values returned by the `getName()` methods of the `Identity` objects.

Some EJB vendors may use more complicated mechanisms for comparing the `Identity` objects. In these cases, you may have to enhance the `RoleIdentity` defined here, or use a vendor-specific mechanism for verifying membership in a role. BEA's WebLogic Server, for example, works well with the `RoleIdentity`, but it also provides a proprietary mechanism for obtaining group `Identity` objects (i.e., roles to which identities belong). The following code fragment shows how the Account bean would be coded to use the WebLogic security API instead of `RoleIdentity`:

```java
public class AccountBean implements EntityBean {
    int id;
    double balance;
    EntityContext ejbContext;

    public void withdraw(Double withdraw)
    throws WithdrawLimitException, AccessDeniedException {
        if (withdraw.doubleValue() > 10000) {
            Identity managerRole = (Identity)
                weblogic.security.acl.Security.getRealm().getGroup("Manager");
            boolean isManager = ejbContext.isCallerInRole(managerRole)
            if (!isManager) {
                // Only tellers can withdraw more than 10k.
                throw new AccessDeniedException();
            }
        }
        balance = balance - withdraw.doubleValue();
    }
    ...
}
```

In general, proprietary APIs like the previous one should be avoided so that the bean remains portable across EJB servers.

The transactional methods (`getUserTransaction()`, `setRollbackOnly()`, `getRollbackOnly()`) are described in detail in Chapter 8.

Obtaining a Connection to the Database

Titan's business system is based on a relational database, so we need to start with access to the database. The JDBC API provides a standard and convenient way for

programs written in Java to access relational databases. We use JDBC throughout
this book and assume that you're already familiar with it.

EJB 1.1: Using JDBC in EJB

To get access to the database we simply request a connection from a DataSource,
which we obtain from the JNDI environment naming context:

```
private Connection getConnection() throws SQLException {
    try {
        Context jndiCntx = new InitialContext();
        DataSource ds =
            (DataSource)jndiCntx.lookup("java:comp/env/jdbc/titanDB");
        return ds.getConnection();
    }
    catch (NamingException ne) {
        throw new EJBException(ne);
    }
}
```

In EJB 1.1, every bean has access to its JNDI environment naming context (ENC),
which is part of the bean-container contract. In the bean's deployment descriptor,
resources such as the JDBC DataSource, JavaMail, and Java Messaging Service can
be mapped to a context (name) in the ENC. This provides a portable model for
accessing these types of resources. In EJB 1.0, standard mechanisms for accessing
JDBC connections and other resources were not defined. Here's the relevant portion of the EJB 1.1 deployment descriptor:

```
<enterprise-beans>
    <entity>
        <resource-ref>
            <description>DataSource for the Titan database</description>
            <res-ref-name>jdbc/titanDB</res-ref-name>
            <res-type>javax.sql.DataSource</res-type>
            <res-auth>Container</res-auth>
        <resource-ref>
        ...
    <entity>
...
<enterprise-beans>
```

The <resource-ref> tag is used for any resource (JDBC, JMS, JavaMail) that is
accessed from the ENC. It describes the JNDI name of the resource (<res-ref-
name>), the factory type (<res-type>), and whether authentication is performed
explicitly by the bean or automatically by the container (<res-auth>). In this
example, we are declaring that the JNDI name "jdbc/titanDB" refers to a
javax.sql.DataSource resource manager, and that authentication to the database is handle automatically by the container. The JNDI name specified in the

<res-ref-name> tag is always relative to the standard JNDI ENC context name, 'java:comp/env'.

When the bean is deployed, the deployer maps the information in the <resource-ref> tag to a live database. This is done in a vendor-specific manner, but the end result is the same. When a database connection is requested using the JNDI name "java:comp/jdbc/titanDB", a DataSource for the Titan database is returned. Consult your vendor's documentation for details on how to map the DataSource to the database at deployment time.

The getConnection() method provides us with a simple and consistent mechanism for obtaining a database connection for our ShipBean class. Now that we have a mechanism for obtaining a database connection, we can use it to insert, update, delete, and find Ship entities in the database.

EJB 1.0: Using JDBC in EJB

To get access to the database, we simply request a connection from the Driver-Manager. To do this, we add a private method to the ShipBean class called getConnection():

```
private Connection getConnection() throws SQLException {
    Properties environmentProps = context.getEnvironment();
    String url = environmentProps.getProperty("jdbcURL");
    return DriverManager.getConnection(url);
}
```

The getConnection() method provides an excellent opportunity to use the EntityContext that was passed to the bean instance at the beginning of its life cycle. We use the EJBContext.getEnvironment() method to obtain properties that help us acquire JDBC connections.

When we create the deployment descriptor for the ShipBean, we use a Properties object to tell the bean what URL to use to obtain a database connection. The following code, taken from the MakeDD class, shows how it's done:

```
Properties props = new Properties();
props.put("jdbcURL","jdbc:<subprotocol>:<subname>");
shipDD.setEnvironmentProperties(props);
```

We create a new instance of Properties, add the "jdbcURL" property, and then call the setEnvironmentProperties() method of the DeploymentDescriptor class to pass the properties to the actual bean when it is deployed. The information in the property table is used in the getConnection() method. This technique solves a nasty problem in an elegant, vendor-independent way: how does the bean make use of vendor-specific resources? The JDBC URL used is vendor-specific and therefore shouldn't be made part of the bean itself. However, when you are deploying a bean, you certainly know what vendor-specific environment you are deploying it in; thus the URL logically belongs to the deployment descriptor. In short, the environment properties lets vendor-specific and environment-specific information be defined in the deployment process, where it belongs, and not during the bean development process.

The getConnection() method provides us with a simple and consistent mechanism for obtaining a database connection for our ShipBean class. Now that we have a mechanism for obtaining a database connection we can use it to insert, update, delete, and find Ship entities in the database.

The ejbCreate() Method

The ejbCreate() methods are called by the container when a client invokes the corresponding create() method on the bean's home. With bean-managed persistence, the ejbCreate() methods are responsible for adding the new entity to the database. This means that the new version of ejbCreate() will be much more complicated than our container-managed version from earlier examples; with container-managed beans, ejbCreate() doesn't have to do much more than initialize a few fields. The EJB specification also states that ejbCreate() methods in bean-managed persistence must return the primary key of the newly created entity. This is another difference between bean-managed and container-managed persistence; in our container-managed beans, ejbCreate() was required to return void.

The following code contains the ejbCreate() method of the ShipBean, modified for bean-managed persistence. Its return type has been changed from void to the Ship bean's primary key, ShipPK. Furthermore, the method uses the JDBC API to insert a new record into the database based on the information passed as parameters. The changes to the original ejbCreate() method are emphasized in bold.

```
public ShipPK ejbCreate(int id, String name,
    int capacity, double tonnage)
        throws CreateException {
        // EJB 1.0: Also throws RemoteException
    if ((id < 1) || (name == null))
        throw new CreateException("Invalid Parameters");
    this.id = id;
    this.name = name;
    this.capacity = capacity;
    this.tonnage = tonnage;

    Connection con = null;
    PreparedStatement ps = null;
    try {
```

```
        con = this.getConnection();
        ps = con.prepareStatement(
            "insert into Ship (id, name, capacity, tonnage) " +
            "values (?,?,?,?)");
        ps.setInt(1, id);
        ps.setString(2, name);
        ps.setInt(3, capacity);
        ps.setDouble(4, tonnage);
        if (ps.executeUpdate() != 1) {
            throw new CreateException ("Failed to add Ship to database");
        }
        ShipPK primaryKey = new ShipPK();
        primaryKey.id = id;
        return primaryKey;
    }
    catch (SQLException se) {
        // EJB 1.0: throw new RemoteException(""se);
        throw new EJBException (se);
    }
    finally {
        try {
            if (ps != null) ps.close();
            if (con!= null) con.close();
        } catch(SQLException se) {
            se.printStackTrace();
        }
    }
}
```

At the beginning of the method, we verify that the parameters are correct, and throw a CreateException if the id is less than 1, or the name is null. This shows how you would typically use a CreateException to report an application logic error.

The ShipBean instance fields are still initialized using the parameters passed to ejbCreate() as before, but now we manually insert the data into the SHIP table in our database. To do so, we use a JDBC PreparedStatement for SQL requests because it makes it easier to see the parameters being used. Alternatively, we could have used a stored procedure through a JDBC CallableStatement or a simple JDBC Statement object. We insert the new bean into the database using an SQL INSERT statement and the values passed into ejbCreate() parameters. If the insert is successful (no exceptions thrown), we create a primary key and return it to the container. If the insert operation is unsuccessful, we throw a new CreateException, which illustrates its use in more ambiguous situation. Failure to insert the record could be construed as an application error or a system failure. In this situation, the JDBC subsystem hasn't thrown an exception, so we shouldn't interpret the inability to insert a record as a failure of the subsystem. Therefore,

we throw a CreateException instead of an EJBException (EJB 1.1) or
RemoteException (EJB 1.0). Throwing a CreateException provides the application the opportunity to recover from the error, a transactional concept that is covered in more detail in Chapter 8.

Behind the scenes, the container uses the primary key and the ShipBean instance
that returned it to provide the client with a remote reference to the new Ship
entity. Conceptually, this means that the ShipBean instance and primary key are
assigned to a newly constructed EJB object, and the EJB object stub is returned to
the client.

Our home interface requires us to provide a second ejbCreate() method with
different parameters. We can save work and write more bulletproof code by making the second method call the first:

```
public ShipPK ejbCreate(int id, String name)
    throws CreateException {
    return ejbCreate(id,name,0,0);
}
```

NOTE   In EJB 1.0, the return type of the ejbCreate() method is void for
          container-managed persistence, while the return type for bean man-
          aged persistence is the primary key type. However, regardless of the
          persistence strategy used, the ejbPostCreate() methods always
          return void.

The ejbLoad() and ejbStore() Methods

Throughout the life of an entity, its data will be changed by client applications. In
the ShipBean, we provide accessor methods to change the name, capacity, and
tonnage of the Ship bean after it has been created. Invoking any of these accessor
methods changes the state of the ShipBean instance, which must be reflected in
the database. It is also necessary to ensure that the state of the bean instance is
always up-to-date with the database.

In container-managed persistence, synchronization between the bean and the
database takes place automatically; the container handles it for you. With bean-
managed persistence, you are responsible for synchronization: the bean must read
and write to the database directly. The container works closely with the bean-
managed entities by advising them when to synchronize their state through the
use of two callback methods: ejbStore() and ejbLoad().

The ejbStore() method is called when the container decides that it is a good
time to write the entity bean's data to the database. The container makes these
decisions based on all the activities it is managing, including transactions, concur-

rency, and resource management. Vendor implementations may differ slightly in when the ejbStore() method is called, but this is not the bean developer's concern. In most cases, the ejbStore() method will be called after a business method has been invoked on the bean. Here is the ejbStore() method for the ShipBean:

```
public void ejbStore() {
// EJB 1.0: throws RemoteException
    Connection con = null;
    PreparedStatement ps = null;
    try {
        con = this.getConnection();
        ps = con.prepareStatement(
            "update Ship set name = ?, capacity = ?, " +
            "tonnage = ? where id = ?");
        ps.setString(1,name);
        ps.setInt(2,capacity);
        ps.setDouble(3,tonnage);
        ps.setInt(4,id);
        if (ps.executeUpdate() != 1) {
        // EJB 1.0: throw new RemoteException ("ejbStore failed");
        throw new EJBException("ejbStore");
        }
    }
    catch (SQLException se) {
        // EJB 1.0: throw new RemoteException("",se);
        throw new EJBException (se);
    }
    finally {
        try {
            if (ps != null) ps.close();
            if (con!= null) con.close();
        } catch(SQLException se) {
            se.printStackTrace();
        }
    }
}
```

Except for the fact that we are doing an update instead of an insert, this method is similar to the ejbCreate() method we coded earlier. A JDBC Prepared-Statement is employed to execute the SQL UPDATE command, and the bean's persistent fields are used as parameters to the request. This method synchronizes the database with the state of the bean.

EJB 1.1 callback methods and exceptions

Notice that we throw an EJBException when a problem occurs. All EJB callback methods declare the EJBException and RemoteException in their throws clause. If you need to throw an exception from one of these callback methods, it must be an EJBException or a subclass. The RemoteException type is included in the method signature to support backward compatibility with EJB 1.0 beans. Throwing the RemoteException from callback methods is deprecated in EJB 1.1, which means that it will not be supported in subsequent versions.

EJB 1.0 callback methods and exceptions

In EJB 1.0, we throw a RemoteException when a problem occurs. All EJB callback methods declare the RemoteException in their throws clause. If you need to throw an exception from one of these callback methods, it must be a RemoteException.

EJB also provides an ejbLoad() method that synchronizes the state of the entity with the database. This method is usually called prior to a new transaction or business method invocation. The idea is to make sure that the bean always represents the most current data in the database, which could be changed by other beans or other non-EJB applications. Here is the ejbLoad() method for a bean-managed ShipBean class:

```
public void ejbLoad() {
// EJB 1.0: throws RemoteException

    ShipPK pk = (ShipPK) context.getPrimaryKey();
    Connection con = null;
    PreparedStatement ps = null;
    ResultSet result = null;
    try {
        con = this.getConnection();
        ps = con.prepareStatement(
            "select name, capacity, tonnage from Ship where id = ?");
        ps.setInt(1,pk.id);
        result = ps.executeQuery();
        if (result.next()) {
            id = id;
            name = result.getString("name");
            capacity = result.getInt("capacity");
            tonnage = result.getDouble("tonnage");
        } else {
            // EJB 1.0: throw new RemoteException();
            throw new EJBException();
        }
    } catch (SQLException se) {
        // EJB 1.0: throw new RemoteException("",se);
        throw new EJBException(se);
    }
    finally {
        try {
```

```
      if (result != null) result.close();
      if (ps != null) ps.close();
      if (con!= null) con.close();
   } catch(SQLException se) {
      se.printStackTrace();
   }
  }
 }
```

To execute the ejbLoad() method we need a primary key. To get a primary key, we query the bean's EntityContext. Note that we don't get the primary key directly from the ShipBean's id field because we cannot guarantee that this field is always valid—the ejbLoad() method might be populating the bean instance's state for the first time, in which case the fields would all be set to the default values. This situation would occur following bean activation. We can guarantee that the EntityContext for the ShipBean is valid because the EJB specification requires that the bean instance EntityContext reference is valid before the ejbLoad() method can be invoked. More about this in the life cycle section later in this chapter.

The ejbRemove() Method

In addition to handling their own inserts and updates, bean-managed entities must also handle their own deletions. When a client application invokes the remove method on the EJB home or EJB object, that method invocation is delegated to the bean-managed entity by calling ejbRemove(). It is the bean developer's responsibility to implement an ejbRemove() method that deletes the entity's data from the database. Here's the ejbRemove() method for our bean-managed ShipBean:

```
public void ejbRemove() {
// EJB 1.0: throws RemoteException
   Connection con = null;
   PreparedStatement ps = null;
   try {
      con = this.getConnection();
      ps = con.prepareStatement("delete from Ship where id = ?");
      ps.setInt(1, id);
      if (ps.executeUpdate() != 1) {
         // EJB 1.0 throw new RemoteException("ejbRemove");
         throw new EJBException("ejbRemove");
      }
   }
   catch (SQLException se) {
      // EJB 1.0: throw new RemoteException("",se);
      throw new EJBException (se);
   }
```

```
        finally {
            try {
                if (ps != null) ps.close();
                if (con!= null) con.close();
            } catch(SQLException se){
                se.printStackTrace();
            }
        }
    }
```

ejbFind() Methods

In bean-managed EntityBeans, the find methods in the home interface must
match the ejbFind methods in the actual bean class. In other words, for each
method named find*lookup-type*() in the home interface, there must be a corresponding ejbFind*lookup-type*() method in the bean implementation with
the same arguments and exceptions. When a find method is invoked on an EJB
home, the container delegates the find*lookup-type*() to a corresponding
ejbFind*lookup-type*() method on the bean instance. The bean-managed entity
is responsible for finding records that match the find requests. In ShipHome, there
are two find methods:

```
public interface ShipHome extends javax.ejb.EJBHome {

    public Ship findByPrimaryKey(ShipPK primaryKey)
        throws FinderException, RemoteException;
    public Enumeration findByCapacity(int capacity)
        throws FinderException, RemoteException;
}
```

And here are the signatures of the corresponding ejbFind methods in the
ShipBean:

```
public class ShipBean extends javax.ejb.EntityBean {

    public ShipPK ejbFindByPrimaryKey(ShipPK primaryKey)
        throws FinderException, RemoteException {}
    public Enumeration ejbFindByCapacity(int capacity)
        throws FinderException, RemoteException {}
}
```

EJB 1.1 return types for find methods

Aside from the names, there's one difference between these two groups of
methods. The find methods in the home interface return either an object
implementing the bean's remote interface—in this case, Ship—or a collection of such objects in the form of a java.util.Enumeration or java.
util.Collection. The ejbFind methods in the bean class return either a primary key for the appropriate bean—in this case, ShipPK—or a collection of

primary keys. The methods that return a single object (whether a remote interface or a primary key) are used whenever you need to look up a single reference to a bean. If you are looking up a group of references (for example, all ships with a certain capacity), you have to use the method that returns either the Collection or Enumeration type. In either case, the container intercepts the primary keys and converts them into remote references for the client.

EJB 1.0 return types for find methods

In EJB 1.0, you are not allowed to write find and ejbFind methods that return arrays, vectors, or other Collection types. The find methods in the home interface return either an object implementing the bean's remote interface—in this case, Ship—or an Enumeration of such objects. The ejbFind methods in the bean class return either a primary key for the appropriate bean or an Enumeration of primary keys. The methods that return a single object (whether a remote interface or a primary key) are used whenever you need to look up a single reference to a bean. If you are looking up a group of references (for example, all ships with a certain capacity), you have to use the method that returns a serializable implementation of Enumeration. In either case, the container intercepts the primary keys and converts them into remote references for the client.

It shouldn't come as a surprise that the object you return—whether it's a primary key or a remote interface—must be appropriate for the type of bean you're defining. For example, you shouldn't put find methods in a Ship bean to look up and return Cabin objects. If you need to return collections of a different bean type, use a business method in the remote interface, not a find method from the home interface.

Both find methods in the ShipBean class methods throw a FinderException if a failure in the request occurs when an SQL exception condition is encountered. The findByPrimaryKey() throws the ObjectNotFoundException if there are no records in the database that match the id argument.

EJB 1.1 empty sets and exceptions

The findByCapacity() method returns an empty collection, and not a null reference, if no SHIP records were found with a matching capacity. Find methods also throw FinderException and EJBException, in addition to any application-specific exceptions that you consider appropriate.

EJB 1.0 empty sets and exceptions

The findByCapacity() method returns a null if no SHIP records were found with a matching capacity. Find methods also throw FinderException and RemoteException. The find methods can also throw any application-specific exceptions that you consider appropriate.

It is mandatory that all entity home interfaces include the method findByPrimaryKey(). This method returns a single remote reference and takes one parameter, the primary key for that bean type. You cannot deploy an entity bean that doesn't include a findByPrimaryKey() method in its home interface.

Following the rules outlined earlier, we can define two ejbFind methods in ShipBean that match the two find methods defined in the ShipHome:

```
public ShipPK ejbFindByPrimaryKey(ShipPK primaryKey)
    throws FinderException, {
    // EJB 1.0: Also throws RemoteException
    Connection con = null;
    PreparedStatement ps = null;
    ResultSet result = null;
    try {
        con = this.getConnection();
        ps = con.prepareStatement(
            "select id from Ship where id = ?");
        ps.setInt(1, primaryKey.id);
        result = ps.executeQuery();
        // does ship id exist in database?
        if (!result.next()){
            throw new ObjectNotFoundException(
                "Cannot find Ship with id = "+id);
        }
    } catch (SQLException se) {
        // EJB 1.0: throw new RemoteException("", se);
        throw new EJBException(se);
    }
    finally {
        try {
            if (result != null) result.close();
            if (ps != null) ps.close();
            if (con!= null) con.close();
        } catch(SQLException se) {se.printStackTrace();}
    }
    return primaryKey;
}
public Enumeration ejbFindByCapacity(int capacity)
    throws FinderException {
    // EJB 1.0: Also throws RemoteException
    Connection con = null;
    PreparedStatement ps = null;    ResultSet result = null;
    try {
        con = this.getConnection();
        ps = con.prepareStatement(
            "select id from Ship where capacity = ?");
        ps.setInt(1,capacity);
        result = ps.executeQuery();
```

```
        Vector keys = new Vector();
        while(result.next()) {
        ShipPK shipPk = new ShipPK();
        shipPk.id = result.getInt("id");
        keys.addElement(shipPk);
        }
        // EJB 1.1: always return collection, even if empty.
        return keys.elements();
        // EJB 1.0: return null if collection is empty.
        // return (keys.size() > 0) ? keys.elements() : null;


    }
    catch (SQLException se) {
        // EJB 1.0: throw new RemoteException("",se);
        throw new EJBException (se);
    }
    finally {
        try {
            if (result != null) result.close();
            if (ps != null) ps.close();
            if (con!= null) con.close();
        } catch(SQLException se){
            se.printStackTrace();
        }
    }
}
```

The mandatory findByPrimaryKey() method uses the primary key to locate the corresponding database record. Once it has verified that the record exists, it simply returns the primary key to the container, which then uses the key to activate a new instance and associate it with that primary key at the appropriate time. If the there is no record associated with the primary key, the method throws a ObjectNotFoundException.

The ejbFindByCapacity() method returns an enumeration of primary keys that match the criteria passed into the method. Again, we construct a prepared statement that we use to execute our SQL query. This time, however, we expect multiple results so we use the java.sql.ResultSet to iterate through the results, creating a vector of primary keys for each SHIP_ID returned.

Find methods are not executed on bean instances that are currently supporting a client application. Only bean instances that are not assigned to an EJB object (instances in the instance pool) are supposed to service find requests, which means that the ejbFind() method in the bean instance has somewhat limited use of its EntityContext. The getPrimaryKey() and getEJBObject() methods will throw exceptions because the bean instance is a pooled instance and is not associated with a primary key or EJBObject. Where do the objects returned by a find

method come from? This seems like a simple enough question, but the answer is
surprisingly complex. Remember that a find method isn't executed by a bean
instance that is actually supporting the client; the container finds an idle bean
instance from the instance pool. The container is responsible for creating the EJB
objects and remote references for the primary keys returned by the ejbFind
method in the bean class. As the client accesses these remote references, bean
instances are swapped into the appropriate EJB objects, loaded with data, and
made ready to service the clients requests.

EJB 1.1: Deploying the Bean-Managed Ship Bean

With a complete definition of the Ship bean, including the remote interface,
home interface, and primary key, we are ready to create a deployment descriptor.
Here is the XML deployment descriptor for EJB 1.1. This deployment descriptor is
not significantly different from the descriptor we created for the container-
managed Ship bean earlier. In this deployment descriptor the `persistence-type`
is `Bean` and there are no container-managed field declarations. We also must
declare the `DataSource` resource factory that we use to query and update the
database.

```xml
<?xml version="1.0"?>

<!DOCTYPE ejb-jar PUBLIC "-//Sun Microsystems, Inc.//DTD Enterprise
JavaBeans 1.1//EN" "http://java.sun.com/j2ee/dtds/ejb-jar_1_1.dtd">

<ejb-jar>
  <enterprise-beans>
    <entity>
      <description>
          This bean represents a cruise ship.
      </description>
      <ejb-name>ShipBean</ejb-name>
      <home>com.titan.ship.ShipHome</home>
      <remote>com.titan.ship.Ship</remote>
      <ejb-class>com.titan.ship.ShipBean</ejb-class>
      <persistence-type>Bean</persistence-type>
      <prim-key-class>com.titan.ship.ShipPK</prim-key-class>
      <reentrant>False</reentrant>

      <resource-ref>
          <description>DataSource for the Titan database</description>
          <res-ref-name>jdbc/titanDB</res-ref-name>
          <res-type>javax.sql.DataSource</res-type>
          <res-auth>Container</res-auth>
      </resource-ref>
```

```
    </entity>
  </enterprise-beans>

  <assembly-descriptor>
    <security-role>
      <description>
        This role represents everyone who is allowed full access
        to the Ship bean.
      </description>
      <role-name>everyone</role-name>
    </security-role>

    <method-permission>
      <role-name>everyone</role-name>
      <method>
        <ejb-name>ShipBean</ejb-name>
        <method-name>*</method-name>
      </method>
    </method-permission>

    <container-transaction>
      <method>
        <ejb-name>ShipBean</ejb-name>
        <method-name>*</method-name>
      </method>
      <trans-attribute>Required</trans-attribute>
    </container-transaction>
  </assembly-descriptor>
</ejb-jar>
```

Save the Ship bean's XML deployment descriptor into the *com/titan/ship* directory
as *ejb-jar.xml* and package it a JAR file:

```
\dev % jar cf ship.jar com/titan/ship/*.class META-INF/ejb-jar.xml

F:\..\dev>jar cf ship.jar com\titan\ship\*.class META-INF\ejb-jar.xml
```

To test this new bean, use the client application that we used to test the container-
managed Ship bean. You will probably need to change the names and IDs of the
ships you create; otherwise, your inserts will cause a database error. In the SQL
statement that we defined to create the SHIP table, we placed a primary key restriction on the ID column of the SHIP table so that only unique ID values can be
inserted. Attempts to insert a record with a duplicate ID will cause an SQL-
Exception to be thrown.

EJB 1.0: Deploying the Bean-Managed Ship Bean

To deploy the bean-managed ShipBean, you can reuse the MakeDD application we
developed earlier to create a serialized DeploymentDescriptor. You will need to

comment out the section that sets the container-managed fields in the
EntityDescriptor, as follows:

```
/* COMMENTED OUT FOR BEAN-MANAGED SHIP BEAN
*******************************************
Class beanClass = ShipBean.class;
Field [] persistentFields = new Field[4];
persistentFields[0] = beanClass.getDeclaredField("id");
persistentFields[1] = beanClass.getDeclaredField("name");
persistentFields[2] = beanClass.getDeclaredField("capacity");
persistentFields[3] = beanClass.getDeclaredField("tonnage");
shipDD.setContainerManagedFields(persistentFields);
*************************
*/
```

Not specifying any container-managed fields tells the EJB deployment tools that
this bean uses bean-managed persistence.

We also need to add some code to set the environment properties for the
ShipBean:

```
Properties props = new Properties();
props.put("jdbcURL","jdbc:subprotocol:subname");
shipDD.setEnvironmentProperties(props);
```

This code defines the property "jdbcURL", which holds the part of the URL that
we need to get a database connection. Replace the URL in this example with whatever is appropriate for the EJB server and JDBC driver that you are using. Our
bean will be able to access the properties defined here through the Entity-
Context and use this URL to get a database connection.

You will need to, consult your EJB vendor's documentation to determine what
JDBC URL is needed for your specific EJB server and database combination. BEA's
WebLogic Server, for example, uses a pooled driver that is accessed using the
JDBC URL, *jdbc:weblogic:jts:ejbPool.* Other EJB servers and database combinations
will use different JDBC URLs.

After running MakeDD to generate the deployment descriptor, use the JAR utility
to archive the Ship bean for deployment. Archiving this version of the Ship bean is
no different than archiving the earlier version.

To test this new bean, use the client application that we used to test the container-
managed Ship bean. You will probably need to change the names and IDs of the
ships you create; otherwise, your inserts will cause a database error. In the SQL
statement that we defined to create the SHIP table, we placed a primary key restriction on the ID column of the SHIP table so that only unique ID values can be
inserted. Attempts to insert a record with a duplicate ID will cause an SQL-
Exception to be thrown.

The Life Cycle of an Entity Bean

To understand how to best develop entity beans, it is important to understand how the container manages them. The EJB specification defines just about every major event in an entity bean's life, from the time it is instantiated to the time it is garbage collected. This is called the *life cycle*, and it provides the bean developer and EJB vendors with all the information they need to develop beans and EJB servers that adhere to a consistent protocol. To understand the life cycle, we will follow an entity instance through several life-cycle events and describe how the container interacts with the entity bean during these events. Figure 6-2 illustrates the life cycle of an entity instance.

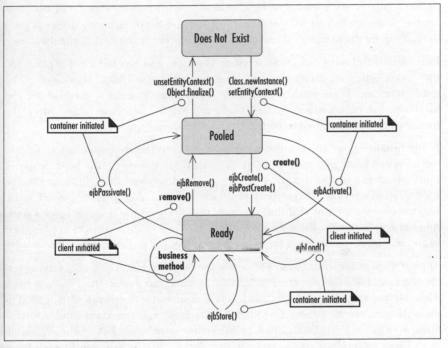

Figure 6-2. Entity bean life cycle

We will examine the life cycle of an entity bean and identify the points at which the container would call each of the methods described in the EntityBean interface. Bean instances must implement the EntityBean interface, which means that invocations of the callback methods are invocations on the bean instance itself.

Does Not Exist

The bean instance begins life as a collection of files. Included in that collection are the bean's deployment descriptor, the remote interface, the home interface, the primary key, and all the supporting classes generated at deployment time. At this stage, no instance of the bean exists.

The Pooled State

When the EJB server is started, it reads the bean's files and instantiates several instances of the bean, which it places in a pool. The instances are created by calling the Class.newInstance() method on the bean class. The newInstance() method creates an instance using the default constructor, which has no arguments.* This means that the persistent fields of the bean instances are set at their default values; the instances themselves do not represent any data in the database.

Immediately following the creation of an instance, and just before it is placed in the pool, the container assigns the instance its EntityContext. The EntityContext is assigned by calling the setEntityContext() method defined in the EntityBean interface and implemented by the bean class. After the instance has been assigned its context, it is entered into the instance pool.

In the instance pool, the bean instance is available to the container as a candidate for serving client requests. Until it is requested, however, the bean instance remains inactive unless it is used to service a find request. Bean instances in the Pooled state typically service find requests, which makes perfectly good sense because they aren't busy and find methods don't rely on the bean instance's state. All instances in the Pooled state are equivalent. None of the instances are assigned to an EJB object, and none of them has meaningful state.

At each stage of the entity bean's life cycle the bean container provides varying levels of access. For example, the EJBContext.getPrimary() method will not work if it's invoked during in the ejbCreate() method, but it does work when called in the ejbPostCreate() method. Other EJBContext methods have similar restrictions, as does the JNDI ENC (EJB 1.1). While this section touches on the accessibility of these methods, a complete table that details what is available in each bean class method (ejbCreate(), ejbActivate(), ejbLoad(), etc.) can be found in Appendix B.

---

* Constructors should never be defined in the bean class. The default no-argument constructor must be available to the container.

The Ready State

When a bean instance is in the Ready State, it can accept client requests. A bean instance moves to the Ready State when the container assigns it to an EJB object. This occurs under two circumstances: when a new entity bean is being created or when the container is activating an entity.

Transitioning from the Pooled state to the Ready State via creation

When a client application invokes the create() method on an EJB home, several operations must take place before the EJB container can return a remote reference (EJB object) to the client. First, an EJB object must be created on the EJB server. Once the EJB object is created, a bean instance is taken from the instance pool and assigned to the EJB object. Next, the create() method, invoked by the client, is delegated to its corresponding ejbCreate() method on the bean instance. After the ejbCreate() method completes, a primary key is created. In container-managed persistence, the container instantiates and populates the key automatically; in bean-managed persistence, the bean instantiates and populates the primary key and returns it from the ejbCreate() method. The key is embedded in the EJB object, providing it with *identity*. Once the EJB object has identity, the bean instance's EntityContext can access information specific to that EJB object, including the primary key and its own remote reference. While the ejbCreate() method is executing, the properties, security, and transactional information is available.

When the ejbCreate() method is done, the ejbPostCreate() method on the bean instance is called. At this time, the bean instance can perform any post-processing that is necessary before making itself available to the client. While the ejbPostCreate() executes, the bean's primary key and access to its own remote reference is available through the EJBContext.

Finally, after the successful completion of the ejbPostCreate() method, the home is allowed to return a remote reference—an EJB object stub—to the client. The bean instance and EJB object are now ready to service method requests from the client. This is one way that the bean instance can move from the Pooled state to the Ready State.

Transitioning from the Pooled state to the Ready State via a find method

When a find method is executed, each bean that is found will be realized by transitioning an instance from the Pooled state to the Ready State. When a bean is found, it is assigned to an EJB object and its remote reference is returned to the client. A found bean follows the same protocol as a passivated bean; it is activated when the client invokes a business method. A found bean can be considered to be a passivated bean and will move into the Ready State through activation as described in the next section.

Transitioning from the Pooled state to the Ready State via activation

The activation process can also move a bean instance from the Pooled state to the Ready State. Activation facilitates resource management by allowing a few bean instances to service many EJB objects. Activation was explained in Chapter 2, but we will revisit the process as it relates to the bean instance's life cycle. Activation presumes that the bean has previously been passivated. More is said about this state transition later; for now, suffice it to say that when a bean instance is passivated, it frees any resources that it does not need and leaves the EJB object for the instance pool. When the bean instance returns to the pool, the EJB object is left without an instance to delegate client requests to. The EJB object maintains its stub connection on the client, so as far as the client is concerned, the entity bean hasn't changed. When the client invokes a business method on the EJB object, the EJB object must obtain a new bean instance. This is accomplished by activating a bean instance.

When a bean instance is activated, it leaves the instance pool (the Pooled State) to be assigned to an EJB object. When a bean instance makes this transition, the bean instance is first assigned to an EJB object. Once assigned to the EJB object, the ejbActivate() method is called—the instance's EntityContext can now provide information specific to the EJB object, but it cannot provide security or transactional information. This callback method can be used in the bean instance to reobtain any resources or perform some other work needed before servicing the client.

When an entity bean instance is activated, nonpersistent fields contain arbitrary values (dirty values) and must be reinitialized in the ejbActivate() method.

In container-managed persistence, persistent fields (container-managed fields) are automatically synchronized with the database after ejbActivate() is invoked and before a business method can be serviced by the bean instance. The order in which these things happen is as follows:

1. ejbActivate() is invoked on the bean instance.

2. Persistent fields are synchronized automatically.

3. ejbLoad() notifies the bean that its persistent fields have been synchronized.

4. Business methods are invoked as needed.

In bean-managed persistence, persistent fields are synchronized by the ejbLoad() method after ejbActivate() has been called and before a business method can be invoked. Here is the order of operations in bean-managed persistence:

1. ejbActivate() is invoked on the bean instance.

2. ejbLoad() is called to let the bean synchronize its persistent fields.

3. Business methods are invoked as needed.

Transitioning from the Ready State to the Pooled state via passivation

A bean can move from the Ready State to the Pooled state via passivation, which is the process of disassociating a bean instance from an EJB object when it is not busy. After a bean instance has been assigned to an EJB object, the EJB container can passivate the instance at any time, provided that the instance is not currently executing a method. As part of the passivation process, the ejbPassivate() method is invoked on the bean instance. This callback method can be used in the instance to release any resources or perform other processing prior to leaving the EJB object. A bean-managed entity instance should not try to save its state to the database in the ejbPassivate() method; this activity is reserved for the ejb-Store() method. The container will invoke ejbStore() to synchronize the bean instance's state with the database prior to passivating the bean. When ejbPassivate() has completed, the bean instance is disassociated from the EJB object server and returned to the instance pool. The bean instance is now back in the Pooled State.

The most fundamental thing to remember is that, for entity beans, passivation is simply a notification that the instance is about to be disassociated from the EJB object. Unlike stateful session beans, an entity bean instance's fields are not serialized and held with the EJB object when the bean is passivated. Whatever values are held in the instance's fields when it was assigned to the EJB object will be carried with it to its next assignment.

Transitioning from the Ready State to the Pooled state via removal

A bean instance also moves from the Ready State to the Pooled state when it is removed. This occurs when the client application invokes one of the remove() methods on the bean's EJB object or EJB home. With entity beans, invoking a remove method means that the entity's data is deleted from the database. Once the entity's data has been deleted from the database, it is no longer a valid entity. The EntityContext can provide the EJB object with identity information during the execution of the ejbRemove() method. Once the ejbRemove() method has finished, the bean instance is moved back to the instance pool and out of the

Ready State. It is important that the ejbRemove() method release any resources that would normally be released by ejbPassivate(), which is not called when a bean is removed. This can be done by invoking the ejbPassivate() method within the ejbRemove() method body.

Life in the Ready State

A bean is in the Ready State when it is associated with an EJB object and is ready to service requests from the client. When the client invokes a business method, like Ship.getName(), on the bean's remote reference (EJB object stub), the method invocation is received by the EJB object server and delegated to the bean instance. The instance performs the method and returns the results. As long as the bean instance is in the Ready State, it can service all the business methods invoked by the client. Business methods can be called zero or more times in any order.

The ejbLoad() and ejbStore() methods, which synchronize the bean instance's state with the database, can be called only when the bean is in the Ready State. These methods can be called in any order, depending on the vendor's implementation. Some vendors call ejbLoad() before every method invocation and ejbStore() after every method invocation, depending on the transactional context. Other vendors call these methods less frequently.

In bean-managed persistence, the ejbLoad() method should always use the EntityContext.getPrimaryKey() to obtain data from the database and not trust any primary key or other data that the bean has stored in one of its fields. (This is how we implemented it in the bean-managed version of the Ship bean.) It should be assumed, however, that the state of the bean is valid when calling the ejbStore() method.

In container-managed persistence, the ejbLoad() method is always called immediately following the synchronization of the bean's container-managed fields with the database—in other words, right after the container updates the state of the bean instance with data from the database. This provides an opportunity to perform any calculations or reformat data before the instance can service business method invocations from the client. The ejbStore() method is called just before the database is synchronized with the state of the bean instance—just before the container writes the container-managed fields to the database. This provides the container-managed bean instance with an opportunity to change the data in the container-managed fields prior to their persistence to the database.

In bean-managed persistence, the ejbLoad() and ejbStore() methods are called when the container deems it appropriate to synchronize the bean's state with the database. These are the only callback methods that should be used to synchronize the bean's state with the database. Do not use ejbActivate(), ejbPassivate(), setEntityContext(), or unsetEntityContext() to access the database for the purpose of synchronization. The ejbCreate() and ejb-Remove() methods, however, can be used to insert and delete (respectively) the entity's data from the database.

End of the Life Cycle

A bean instance's life ends when the container decides to remove it from the pool and allow it to be garbage collected. This happens under a few different circumstances. If the container decides to reduce the number of instances in the pool—usually to conserve resources—it releases one or more bean instances and allows them to be garbage collected. The ability to adjust the size of the instance pool allows the EJB server to manage its resources—the number of threads, available memory, etc.—so that it can achieve the highest possible performance. This behavior is typical of a CTM.

When an EJB server is shut down, most containers will release all the bean instances so that they can be safely garbage collected. Finally, some containers may decide to release an instance that is behaving unfavorably or an instance that has suffered from some kind of unrecoverable error that makes it unstable. A bean could be behaving unfavorably if, for example, it has a bug that causes it to enter an endless loop or create an unusually large number of objects.

When a entity bean instance leaves the instance pool to be garbage collected, the unsetEntityContext() method is invoked by the container to alert the bean instance that it is about be destroyed. This callback method lets the bean release any resources it maintains in the pool and dereference the EntityContext (usually by setting it to null). Once the bean's unsetEntityContext() method has been called and it is removed from the pool, it will be garbage collected.

The bean instance's finalize() method may or may not be invoked following the unsetEntityContext() method. A bean should not rely on its finalize() method, since each vendor will handle dereferenced instances differently: some may garbage collect an instance immediately, and others may postpone garbage collection indefinitely.

7

Session Beans

As you learned in Chapter 6, entity beans provide an object-oriented interface that makes it easier for developers to create, modify, and delete data from the database. Entity beans make developers more productive by encouraging reuse and by reducing development costs. A concept like a Ship can be reused throughout a business system without having to redefine, recode, or retest the business logic and data access defined by the Ship bean.

However, entity beans are not the entire story. We have also seen another kind of enterprise bean: the session bean. Session beans fill the gaps left by entity beans. They are useful for describing interactions between other beans (workflow) or for implementing particular tasks. Unlike entity beans, session beans don't represent shared data in the database, but they can access shared data. This means that we can use session beans to read, update, and insert data. For example, we might use a session bean to provide lists of information, such as a list of all available cabins. Sometimes we might generate the list by interacting with entity beans, like the cabin list we developed in the TravelAgent bean in Chapter 4. More frequently, session beans will generate lists by accessing the database directly.

So when do you use an entity bean and when do you use a session bean to directly access data? Good question! As a rule of thumb, an entity bean is developed to provide a safe and consistent interface to a set of shared data that defines a concept. This data may be updated frequently. Session beans access data that spans concepts, is not shared, or is usually read-only.

In addition to accessing data directly, session beans can represent *workflow*. Workflow describes all the steps required to accomplish a particular task, such as booking passage on a ship or renting a video. Session beans are part of the same business API as entity beans, but as workflow components, they serve a different purpose. Session beans can manage the interactions between entity beans, describing how they work together to accomplish a specific task. The relationship between session beans and entity beans is like the relationship between a script for a play and the actors that perform the play. Where entity beans are the actors and props, the session bean is the script. Actors and props without a script can each serve a function individually, but only in the context of a script can they tell a story. In terms of our example, it makes no sense to have a database full of cabins, ships, passengers, and other objects if we can't create interactions between them, like booking a passenger for a cruise.

Session beans are divided into two basic types: *stateless* and *stateful*. A *stateless* session bean is a collection of related services, each represented by a method; the bean maintains no state from one method invocation to the next. When you invoke a method on a stateless session bean, it executes the method and returns the result without knowing or caring what other requests have gone before or might follow. Think of a stateless session bean as a set of procedures or batch programs that execute a request based on some parameters and return a result. Stateless session beans tend to be general-purpose or reusable, such as a software service.

A *stateful* session bean is an extension of the client application. It performs tasks on behalf of the client and maintains state related to that client. This state is called *conversational state* because it represents a continuing conversation between the stateful session bean and the client. Methods invoked on a stateful session bean can write and read data to and from this conversational state, which is shared among all methods in the bean. Stateful session beans tend to be specific to one scenario. They represent logic that might have been captured in the client application of a two-tier system.

Session beans, whether they are stateful or stateless, are not persistent like entity beans. In other words, session beans are not saved to the database. Stateful session beans are dedicated to one client and may have a preset timeout period. In EJB 1.0, the timeout period, which is specified in the deployment descriptor, is defined in seconds and is applied between business method invocations by the client. Each time a business method is invoked, the timeout clock is reset.* In EJB 1.1, the bean deployer declares the timeout in a vendor-dependent manner. Timeouts are no longer included in the deployment descriptor.

If the client fails to use the stateful bean before it times out, the bean instance is destroyed and the remote reference is invalidated. This prevents the stateful session bean from lingering long after a client has shut down or otherwise finished

---

* This was not clearly defined in the EJB 1.0 specification. As a result, some vendors incorrectly measure the timeout period from the creation of the bean by the client, and the timeout period is not reset between method invocations. Consult your vendor's documentation to determine which strategy your vendor employs.

using it. A client can also explicitly remove a stateful session bean by calling one of its remove methods.

Stateless session beans have longer lives because they don't retain any conversational state and are not dedicated to one client, but they still aren't saved in a database because they don't represent any data. Once a stateless session bean has finished a method invocation for a client, it can be reassigned to any other EJB object to service a new client. A client can maintain a connection to a stateless session bean's EJB object, but the bean instance itself is free to service requests from anywhere. Because it doesn't contain any state information, there's no difference between one client and the next. Stateless session beans may also have a timeout period and can be removed by the client, but the impact of these events is different than with a stateful session bean. With a stateless session bean, a timeout or remove operation simply invalidates the remote reference for that client; the bean instance is not destroyed and is free to service other client requests.

The Stateless Session Bean

A stateless session bean is relatively easy to develop and also very efficient. Stateless session beans require few server resources because they are neither persistent nor dedicated to one client. Because they aren't dedicated to one client, many EJB objects can use just a few instances of a stateless bean. A stateless session bean does not maintain conversational state relative to the EJB object it is servicing, so it can be swapped freely between EJB objects. As soon as a stateless instance services a method invocation, it can be swapped to another EJB object immediately. Because there is no conversational state, a stateless session bean doesn't require passivation or activation, further reducing the overhead of swapping. In short, they are lightweight and fast!

Stateless session beans often perform services that are fairly generic and reusable. The services may be related, but they are not interdependent. This means that everything a stateless session bean method needs to know has to be passed via the method's parameters. The only exception to this rule is information obtainable from the SessionContext and in EJB 1.1, the JNDI ENC. This provides an interesting limitation. Stateless session beans can't remember anything from one method invocation to the next, which means that they have to take care of the entire task in one method invocation.

Stateless session beans are EJB's version of the traditional transaction processing applications, which are executed using a procedure call. The procedure executes from beginning to end and then returns the result. Once the procedure is done, nothing about the data that was manipulated or the details of the request are remembered. There is no state.

These restrictions don't mean that a stateless session bean can't have instance variables and therefore some kind of internal state. There's nothing that prevents you from keeping a variable that tracks the number of times a bean has been called or that tracks data for debugging. An instance variable can even hold a reference to a live resource like a URL connection for writing debugging data, verifying credit cards, or anything else that might be useful. However, it's important to remember that this state can never be visible to a client. A client can't assume that the same bean instance will service it every time. If these instance variables have different values in different bean instances, their values will appear to change randomly as stateless session beans are swapped from one client to another. Therefore, any resources that you reference in instance variables should be generic. For example, each bean instance might reasonably record debugging messages in a different file—that might be the only way to figure out what was happening on a large server with many bean instances. The client doesn't know or care where debugging output is going. However, it would be clearly inappropriate for a stateless bean to remember that it was in the process of making a reservation for Madame X—the next time it is called, it may be servicing another client entirely.

Stateless session beans can be used for report generation, batch processing, or some stateless services like validating a credit card. Another good application would be a StockQuote bean that returns a stock's current price. Any activity that can be accomplished in one method call is a good candidate for the high-performance stateless session bean.

Downloading the Missing Pieces

Both the TravelAgent bean and the ProcessPayment beans, which we develop in this chapter, depend on other entity beans, some of which we developed earlier in this book and several that you can download from O'Reilly's web site. The Cabin was developed in Chapter 4, but we still need several other beans to develop this example. The other beans are the Cruise, Customer, and Reservation beans. The source code for these beans is available with the rest of the examples for this book at the O'Reilly download site. Instructions for downloading code are available in the preface of this book.

Before you can use these beans, you will need to create some new tables in your database. Here are the table definitions that the new entity beans will need. The Cruise bean maps to the CRUISE table:

```
CREATE TABLE CRUISE
(
    ID          INT PRIMARY KEY,
    NAME        CHAR(30),
    SHIP_ID     INT
)
```

The Customer bean maps to the CUSTOMER table:

```
CREATE TABLE CUSTOMER
(
    ID              INT PRIMARY KEY,
    FIRST_NAME      CHAR(30),
    LAST_NAME       CHAR(30),
    MIDDLE_NAME     CHAR(30)
)
```

The Reservation bean maps to the RESERVATION table:

```
CREATE TABLE RESERVATION
(
    CUSTOMER_ID     INT,
    CABIN_ID        INT,
    CRUISE_ID       INT,
    PRICE           NUMERIC
)
```

Once you have created the tables, deploy these beans as container-managed entities in your EJB server and test them to ensure that they are working properly.

The ProcessPayment Bean

Chapters 2 and 3 discussed the TravelAgent bean, which had a business method
called bookPassage(). This bean demonstrated how a session bean manages
workflow. Here is the code for bookPassage():

```
public Ticket bookPassage(CreditCard card, double price)
    throws IncompleteConversationalState {// EJB 1.0: also throws RemoteException

    if (customer == null || cruise == null || cabin == null) {
        throw new IncompleteConversationalState();
    }
    try {
        ReservationHome resHome = (ReservationHome)
            getHome("ReservationHome",ReservationHome.class);
        Reservation reservation =
        resHome.create(customer, cruise, cabin, price);
        ProcessPaymentHome ppHome = (ProcessPaymentHome)
            getHome("ProcessPaymentHome",ProcessPaymentHome.class);
        ProcessPayment process = ppHome.create();
        process.byCredit(customer, card, price);

        Ticket ticket = new Ticket(customer, cruise, cabin, price);
        return ticket;
    } catch (Exception e) {
        // EJB 1.0: throw new RemoteException("",e);
```

```
        throw new EJBException(e);
    }
}
```

In the next section, we will develop a complete definition of the TravelAgent bean, including the logic of the bookPassage() method. At this point, however, we are interested in the ProcessPayment bean, which is a stateless bean used by the TravelAgent bean. The TravelAgent bean uses the ProcessPayment bean to charge the customer for the price of the cruise.

The process of charging customers is a common activity in Titan's business systems. Not only does the reservation system need to charge customers, but so do Titan's gift shops, boutiques, and other related businesses. The process of charging a customer for services is common to many systems, so it has been encapsulated in its own bean.

Payments are recorded in a special database table called PAYMENT. The PAYMENT data is batch processed for accounting purposes and is not normally used outside of accounting. In other words, the data is only inserted by Titan's system; it's not read, updated, or deleted. Because the process of making a charge can be completed in one method, and because the data is not updated frequently or shared, a stateless session bean has been chosen for processing payments. Several different forms of payment can be used: credit card, check, or cash. We will model these payment forms in our stateless ProcessPayment bean.

PAYMENT: *The database table*

The ProcessPayment bean accesses an existing table in Titan's system called the PAYMENT table. Create a table in your database called PAYMENT with this definition:

```
CREATE TABLE PAYMENT
(
    customer_id     NUMERIC,
    amount          DECIMAL(8,2),
    type            CHAR(10),
    check_bar_code  CHAR(50),
    check_number    INTEGER,
    credit_number   NUMERIC,
    credit_exp_date DATE
)
```

ProcessPayment: *The remote interface*

A stateless session bean, like any other bean, needs a remote interface. We obviously need a byCredit() method because the TravelAgent bean uses it. We can also identify two other methods that we'll need: byCash() for customers paying cash and byCheck() for customers paying with a personal check.

Here is a complete definition of the remote interface for the ProcessPayment bean:

```
package com.titan.processpayment;

import java.rmi.RemoteException;
import java.util.Date;
import com.titan.customer.Customer;

public interface ProcessPayment extends javax.ejb.EJBObject {

    public boolean byCheck(Customer customer, Check check, double amount)
        throws RemoteException, PaymentException;

    public boolean byCash(Customer customer, double amount)
        throws RemoteException, PaymentException;

    public boolean byCredit(Customer customer, CreditCard card, double amount)
        throws RemoteException, PaymentException;
}
```

Remote interfaces in session beans follow the same rules as the entity beans. Here we have defined the three business methods, byCheck(), byCash(), and byCredit(), which take information relevant to the form of payment used and return a boolean value that indicates the success of the payment. In addition to the required RemoteException, these methods can throw an application-specific exception, the PaymentException. The PaymentException is thrown if any problems occur while processing the payment, such as a low check number or an expired credit card. Notice, however, that nothing about the ProcessPayment interface is specific to the reservation system. It could be used just about anywhere in Titan's system. In addition, each method defined in the remote interface is completely independent of the others. All the data that is required to process a payment is obtained through the method's arguments.

As an extension of the javax.ejb.EJBObject interface, the remote interface of a session bean inherits the same functionality as the remote interface of an entity bean. However, the getPrimaryKey() method throws a RemoteException, since session beans do not have a primary key to return:*

```
public interface javax.ejb.EJBObject extends java.rmi.Remote {
    public abstract EJBHome getEJBHome()
        throws RemoteException;
    public abstract Handle getHandle()
```

---

* The exact behavior of primary key related operations on session beans is undefined in EJB 1.0. Because it is undefined, certain vendors may choose to return null or throw a different exception when these methods are invoked. The behavior described here, however, is the recommended behavior for EJB 1.0–compliant servers and is the required behavior in EJB 1.1.

```
     throws RemoteException;
  public abstract Object getPrimaryKey()
     throws RemoteException;
  public abstract boolean isIdentical(EJBObject obj)
     throws RemoteException;
  public abstract void remove()
     throws RemoteException, RemoveException;
}
```

The getHandle() method returns a serializable handle object, just like the getHandle() method in the entity bean. For stateless session beans, this handle can be serialized and reused any time, as long as the stateless bean type is still available in the container that generated the handle.

NOTE   Unlike stateless session beans, stateful session beans are only available through the handle for as long as that specific bean instance is kept alive on the EJB server. If the client explicitly destroys the stateful session bean using one of the remove() methods, or if the bean times out, the instance is destroyed and the handle becomes invalid. As soon as the server removes a stateful session bean, its handle is no longer valid and will throw a RemoteException when its getEJB-Object() is invoked.

A remote reference to the bean can be obtained from the handle by invoking its getEJBObject() method:

```
public interface javax.ejb.Handle {
   public abstract EJBObject getEJBObject()
      throws RemoteException;
}
```

We've placed the ProcessPayment bean in its own package, which means it has its own directory in our development tree, *dev/com/titan/processpayment.* That's where we'll store all the code and compile class files for this bean.

Dependent classes: The CreditCard and Check classes

The ProcessPayment bean's remote interface uses two classes in its definition that are particularly interesting: the CreditCard and Check classes. The definitions for these classes are as follows:

```
/* CreditCard.java */
package com.titan.processpayment;

import java.util.Date;

public class CreditCard implements java.io.Serializable {
   final static public String MASTER_CARD = "MASTER_CARD";
```

```
    final static public String VISA = "VISA";
    final static public String AMERICAN_EXPRESS = "AMERICAN_EXPRESS";
    final static public String DISCOVER = "DISCOVER";
    final static public String DINERS_CARD = "DINERS_CARD";

    public long number;
    public Date expiration;
    public String type;

    public CreditCard(long nmbr, Date exp, String typ) {
        number = nmbr;
        expiration = exp;
        type = typ;
    }
}

/* Check.java */
package com.titan.processpayment;

public class Check implements java.io.Serializable {
    String checkBarCode;
    int checkNumber;
    public Check(String barCode, int number) {
        checkBarCode = barCode;
        checkNumber = number;
    }
}
```

If you examine the class definitions of the CreditCard and Check classes, you will see that they are not enterprise beans. They are simply serializable Java classes. These classes provide a convenient mechanism for transporting and binding together related data. CreditCard, for example, binds all the credit card data together in once class, making it easier to pass the information around as well as making our interfaces a little cleaner.

It may be surprising that these classes aren't entity beans, and there's certainly no restriction in the specification preventing you from implementing them that way. However, just because something can be an entity bean doesn't mean that it has to be, and in this case, there are good reasons for this design decision. Making everything an entity bean is unnecessary and will hurt the performance of your EJB application. Remember that supporting an entity bean requires a lot of overhead on the server's part. When that overhead isn't necessary, it's best avoided. Fine-grained, dependent objects like Check and CreditCard don't make practical entity beans, because they are not shared or changed over time and they are dependent on the Customer to provide them with context. The use of dependent classes should be limited to pass-by-value objects, which is explored in more detail in Chapter 9.

PaymentException: An application exception

Any remote interface, whether it's for an entity bean or a session bean, can throw application exceptions, in addition to the required RemoteException. Application exceptions are created by the bean developer and should describe a business logic problem—in this particular case, a problem making a payment. Application exceptions should be meaningful to the client, providing an explanation of the error that is both brief and relevant.

It's important to understand what exceptions to use and when to use them. The RemoteException indicates subsystem-level problems and is used by the RMI facility. Likewise, exceptions like javax.naming.NamingException and java.sql.SQLException are thrown by other Java subsystems; usually these should not be thrown explicitly by your beans. The Java Compiler requires that you use try/catch blocks to capture checked exceptions like these.

EJB 1.1 subsystem exceptions

When a checked exception from a subsystem (JDBC, JNDI, JMS, etc.) is caught by a bean method, it should be rethrown as an EJBException or an application exception. You would rethrow a checked exception as an EJBException if it represented a system-level problem; checked exceptions are rethrown as application exceptions when they result from business logic problems. Your beans incorporate your business logic; if a problem occurs in the business logic, that problem should be represented by an application exception. When an EJBException is thrown, it's first processed by the container, and then a RemoteException is thrown to the client.

EJB 1.0 subsystem exceptions

When a checked exception from a subsystem (JDBC, JNDI, JMS, etc.) is caught by a bean method, it should be rethrown as a RemoteException or an application exception. You would rethrow a checked exception as a RemoteException if it represented a system-level problem; checked exceptions are rethrown as application exceptions when they result from business logic problems. Your beans incorporate your business logic; if a problem occurs in the business logic, that problem should be represented by an application exception.

In either EJB 1.0 or EJB 1.1, if an unchecked exception, like java.lang.NullPointerException, is thrown by the bean instance, the container automatically throws a RemoteException to the client.

The PaymentException describes a specific business problem, so it is an application exception. Application exceptions extend java.lang.Exception. If you choose to include any instance variables in the exception, they should all be serializable. Here is the definition of ProcessPayment application exception:

```
package com.titan.processpayment;

public class PaymentException extends java.lang.Exception {
    public PaymentException() {
        super();
    }
    public PaymentException(String msg) {
        super(msg);
    }
}
```

ProcessPaymentHome: The home interface

The home interface of all stateless session beans contains one create() method with no arguments. This is a requirement of the EJB specification. It is illegal to define create() methods with arguments, because stateless session beans don't maintain conversational state that needs to be initialized. There are no find methods in session beans, because session beans do not have primary keys and do not represent data in the database. Here is the definition of the home interface for the ProcessPayment bean:

```
package com.titan.processpayment;

import java.rmi.RemoteException;
import javax.ejb.CreateException;

public interface ProcessPaymentHome extends javax.ejb.EJBHome {
    public ProcessPayment create()
        throws RemoteException, CreateException;
}
```

The CreateException is mandatory, as is the RemoteException. The Create-Exception can be thrown by the bean itself to indicate an application error in creating the bean. A RemoteException is thrown when other system errors occur, for example, when there is a problem with network communication or when an unchecked exception is thrown from the bean class.

The ProcessPaymentHome interface, as an extension of the javax.ejb.EJB-Home, offers the same EJBHome methods as entity beans. The only difference is that remove(Object primaryKey) doesn't work because session beans don't have primary keys. If EJBHome.remove(Object primaryKey) is invoked on a session bean (stateless or stateful), a RemoteException is thrown.* Logically, this method should never be invoked on the home interface of a session bean.

---

* The exact behavior of the EJBHome.remove(ObjectprimaryKey) in session beans is undefined in EJB 1.0. The recommended behavior in EJB 1.0 is to throw a RemoteException, which is the specified behavior in the EJB 1.1 specification. Check your vendor's documentation to determine how this behavior was implemented for EJB 1.0 containers.

Here are the definitions of the EJBHome interface for EJB 1.1 and EJB 1.0:

```
// EJBHome interface, EJB 1.1
public interface javax.ejb.EJBHome extends java.rmi.Remote {
    public abstract HomeHandle getHomeHandle()
        throws RemoteException;
    public abstract EJBMetaData getEJBMetaData()
        throws RemoteException;
    public abstract void remove(Handle handle)
        throws RemoteException, RemoveException;
    public abstract void remove(Object primaryKey)
        throws RemoteException, RemoveException;
}
```

```
// EJBHome interface, EJB 1.0
public interface javax.ejb.EJBHome extends java.rmi.Remote {
    public abstract EJBMetaData getEJBMetaData()
        throws RemoteException;
    public abstract void remove(Handle handle)
        throws RemoteException, RemoveException;
    public abstract void remove(Object primaryKey)
        throws RemoteException, RemoveException;
}
```

The home interface of a session bean can return the EJBMetaData for the bean, just like an entity bean. EJBMetaData is a serializable object that provides information about the bean's interfaces. The only difference between the EJBMetaData for a session bean and an entity bean is that the getPrimaryKeyClass() on the session bean's EJBMetaData throws a java.lang.RuntimeException when invoked:*

```
public interface javax.ejb.EJBMetaData {
    public abstract EJBHome getEJBHome();
    public abstract Class getHomeInterfaceClass();
    public abstract Class getPrimaryKeyClass();
    public abstract Class getRemoteInterfaceClass();
    public abstract boolean isSession();
    public abstract boolean isStateless();  // EJB 1.0 only
}
```

ProcessPaymentBean: The bean class

As stated earlier, the ProcessPayment bean accesses data that is not generally shared by systems, so it is an excellent candidate for a stateless session bean. This bean really represents a set of independent operations that can be invoked and

---

* The exact behavior of the MetaData.getPrimaryKeyClass() method is undefined for session beans in EJB 1.0. The recommended behavior in EJB 1.0 is to throw a runtime exception, which is the specified behavior in the EJB 1.1 specification.

then thrown away—another indication that it's a good candidate for a stateless session bean. Here is the complete definition of our ProcessPaymentBean class:

```
package com.titan.processpayment;
import com.titan.customer.*;

import java.sql.*;
import java.rmi.RemoteException;
import javax.ejb.SessionContext;

import javax.naming.InitialContext;
import javax.sql.DataSource;
import javax.ejb.EJBException;
import javax.naming.NamingException;

public class ProcessPaymentBean implements javax.ejb.SessionBean {

    final public static String CASH = "CASH";
    final public static String CREDIT = "CREDIT";
    final public static String CHECK = "CHECK";

    public SessionContext context;

    public void ejbCreate() {
    }

    public boolean byCash(Customer customer, double amount)
    throws PaymentException{// EJB 1.0: also throws RemoteException
        return process(getCustomerID(customer),amount,
                        CASH,null,-1,-1,null);
    }

    public boolean byCheck(Customer customer, Check check, double amount)
    throws PaymentException{// EJB 1.0: also throws RemoteException
        int minCheckNumber = getMinCheckNumber();
        if (check.checkNumber > minCheckNumber) {
            return process(getCustomerID(customer), amount, CHECK,
                            check.checkBarCode,check.checkNumber,-1,null);
        }
        else {
            throw new PaymentException(
                "Check number is too low. Must be at least "+minCheckNumber);
        }
    }
    public boolean byCredit(Customer customer, CreditCard card, double amount)
    throws PaymentException {// EJB 1.0: also throws RemoteException
        if (card.expiration.before(new java.util.Date())) {
            throw new PaymentException("Expiration date has passed");
        }
```

```
        else {
            return process(getCustomerID(customer), amount, CREDIT, null,
                        -1, card.number,
                        new java.sql.Date(card.expiration.getTime())));
        }
    }
    private boolean process(long customerID, double amount, String type,
                        String checkBarCode, int checkNumber,
                        long creditNumber, java.sql.Date creditExpDate)
        throws PaymentException{// EJB 1.0: also throws RemoteException

        Connection con = null;

        PreparedStatement ps = null;

        try {
            con = getConnection();
            ps = con.prepareStatement
                ("INSERT INTO payment (customer_id, amount, type,"+
                "check_bar_code,check_number,credit_number,"+
                "credit_exp_date) VALUES (?,?,?,?,?,?,?)");
            ps.setLong(1,customerID);
            ps.setDouble(2,amount);
            ps.setString(3,type);
            ps.setString(4,checkBarCode);
            ps.setInt(5,checkNumber);
            ps.setLong(6,creditNumber);
            ps.setDate(7,creditExpDate);
            int retVal = ps.executeUpdate();
            if (retVal!=1) {
                // EJB 1.0: throw new RemoteException("Payment insert failed");
                throw new EJBException("Payment insert failed");
            }

            return true;
        } catch(SQLException sql) {
            // EJB 1.0: throw new RemoteException("",sql);
            throw new EJBException(sql);
        } finally {
            try {
                if (ps != null) ps.close();
                if (con!= null) con.close();
            } catch(SQLException se){se.printStackTrace();}
        }
    }
}
public void ejbActivate() {}
public void ejbPassivate() {}
public void ejbRemove() {}
public void setSessionContext(SessionContext ctx) {
```

```
            context = ctx;
        }
    private int getCustomerID(Customer customer) {
    // EJB 1.0: throws RemoteException
        try {// EJB 1.0: remove try/catch
            return ((CustomerPK)customer.getPrimaryKey()).id;
        } catch(RemoteException re) {
            throw new EJBException(re);
        }
    }

    private Connection getConnection() throws SQLException {
        // Implementations for EJB 1.0 and EJB 1.1 shown below
    }
    private int getMinCheckNumber() {
        // Implementations for EJB 1.0 and EJB 1.1 shown below
    }
}
```

The three payment methods all use the private helper method process(), which
does the work of adding the payment to the database. This strategy reduces the
possibility of programmer error and makes the bean easier to maintain. The
process() method simply inserts the payment information into the PAYMENT
table. The use of JDBC in this method should be familiar to you from your work
on the bean-managed Ship bean in Chapter 6. The JDBC connection is obtained
from the getConnection() method; here are the EJB 1.1 and EJB 1.0 versions of
this method:

```
// getConnection() for EJB 1.1
private Connection getConnection() throws SQLException {
    try {
        InitialContext jndiCntx = new InitialContext();
        DataSource ds = (DataSource)
            jndiCntx.lookup("java:comp/env/jdbc/titanDB");
        return ds.getConnection();
    } catch(NamingException ne){throw new EJBException(ne);}
}

// getConnection() for EJB 1.0
private Connection getConnection() throws SQLException {
    return DriverManager.getConnection(
        context.getEnvironment().getProperty("jdbcURL"));
}
```

Both the byCheck() and the byCredit() methods contain some logic to validate
the data before processing it. The byCredit() method checks to ensure that the
credit card's expiration data does not precede the current date. If it does, a
PaymentException is thrown.

The byCheck() method checks to ensure that the check is above a minimum number, as determined by a property that's defined when the bean is deployed. If the check number is below this value, a PaymentException is thrown. The property is obtained from the getMinCheckNumber() method. In EJB 1.1, we can use the JNDI ENC to read the value of the minCheckNumber property. In 1.0, we read this property from the SessionContext:

```
// getMinCheckNumber() for EJB 1.1: uses JNDI ENC
private int getMinCheckNumber() {
        try {
            InitialContext jndiCntx = new InitialContext( );
            Integer value = (Integer)
                jndiCntx.lookup("java:comp/env/minCheckNumber");
            return value.intValue();
        } catch(NamingException ne){throw new EJBException(ne);}
}

// getMinCheckNumber() for EJB 1.0
private int getMinCheckNumber() {
    String min_check_string =
        context.getEnvironment().getProperty("minCheckNumber");
    return Integer.parseInt(min_check_string);
}
```

Thus, we are using an environment property, set in the deployment descriptor, to change the business behavior of a bean. It is a good idea to capture thresholds and other limits in the environment properties of the bean rather than hardcoding them. This gives you greater flexibility. If, for example, Titan decided to raise the minimum check number, you would only need to change the bean's deployment descriptor, not the class definition. (You could also obtain this type of information directly from the database.)

EJB 1.1: Accessing environment properties

In EJB 1.1, the bean container contract has been extended to include the JNDI environment naming context (JNDI ENC). The JNDI ENC is a JNDI name space that is specific to each bean type. This name space can be referenced from within any bean, not just entity beans, using the name "java:comp/env". The enterprise naming context provides a flexible, yet standard, mechanism for accessing properties, other beans, and resources from the container.

We've already seen the JNDI ENC several times. In Chapter 6, we used it to access a resource factory, the DataSource. The ProcessPaymentBean also uses the JNDI ENC to access a DataSource in the getConnection() method; further, it uses the ENC to access an environment property in the getMinCheckNumber()

method. This section examines the use of the JNDI ENC to access environment properties.

Named properties can be declared in a bean's deployment descriptor. The bean accesses these properties at runtime by using the JNDI ENC. Properties can be of type String or one of several primitive wrapper types including Integer, Long, Double, Float, Byte, Boolean, and Short. By modifying the deployment descriptor, the bean deployer can change the bean's behavior without changing its code. As we've seen in the ProcessPayment bean, we could change the minimum check number that we're willing to accept by modifying the minCheckNumber property at deployment. Two ProcessPayment beans deployed in different containers could easily have different minimum check numbers, as shown in the following example:

```
<ejb-jar>
    <enterprise-beans>
        <session>
            <env-entry>
                <env-entry-name>minCheckNumber</env-entry-name>
                <env-entry-type>java.lang.Integer</env-entry-type>
                <env-entry-value>2000</env-entry-value>
            </env-entry>
            ...
        </session>
        ...
    <enterprise-beans>
    ...
</ejb-jar>
```

EJB 1.1: EJBContext

The EJBContext.getEnvironment() method is optional in EJB 1.1, which means that it may or may not be supported. If it is not functional, the method will throw a RuntimeException. If it is functional, it returns only those values declared in the deployment descriptor as follows (where minCheckNumber is the property name):

```
<ejb-jar>
    <enterprise-beans>
        <session>
            <env-entry>
        .       <env-entry-name>ejb10-properties/minCheckNumber</env-entry-name>
                <env-entry-type>java.lang.String</env-entry-name>
                <env-entry-value>20000</env-entry-value>
            </env-entry>
            ...
        </session>
        ...
```

```
    </enterprise-beans>
    ...
 </ejb-jar>
```

The ejb10-properties subcontext specifies that the property minCheckNumber is available from both JNDI ENC context "java:comp/env/ejb10-properties/minCheckNumber" (as a String value), and from the getEnvironment() method.

Only those properties declared under the ejb10-properties subcontext are available via the EJBContext. Furthermore, such properties are only available through the EJBContext in containers that choose to support the EJB 1.0 getEnvironment() method; all other containers will throw a RuntimeException.

EJB 1.1: The ProcessPayment bean's deployment descriptor

Deploying the ProcessPayment bean presents no significant problems. It's essentially the same as deploying the Ship or Cabin beans, except that the ProcessPayment bean has no primary key or persistent fields. Here is the XML deployment descriptor for the ProcessPayment bean:

```
<?xml version="1.0"?>

<!DOCTYPE ejb-jar PUBLIC "-//Sun Microsystems, Inc.//DTD Enterprise
JavaBeans 1.1//EN" "http://java.sun.com/j2ee/dtds/ejb-jar_1_1.dtd">

<ejb-jar>
 <enterprise-beans>
   <session>
     <description>
         A service that handles monetary payments.
     </description>
     <ejb-name>ProcessPaymentBean</ejb-name>
     <home>com.titan.processpayment.ProcessPaymentHome</home>
     <remote>com.titan.processpayment.ProcessPayment</remote>
     <ejb-class>com.titan.processpayment.ProcessPaymentBean</ejb-class>
     <session-type>Stateless</session-type>
     <transaction-type>Container</transaction-type>
     <env-entry>
         <env-entry-name>minCheckNumber</env-entry-name>
         <env-entry-type>java.lang.Integer</env-entry-type>
         <env-entry-value>2000</env-entry-value>
     </env-entry>
     <resource-ref>
         <description>DataSource for the Titan database</description>
         <res-ref-name>jdbc/titanDB</res-ref-name>
         <res-type>javax.sql.DataSource</res-type>
         <res-auth>Container</res-auth>
     </resource-ref>
```

```
    </session>
  </enterprise-beans>

  <assembly-descriptor>
    <security-role>
      <description>
        This role represents everyone who is allowed full access
        to the ProcessPayment bean.
      </description>
      <role-name>everyone</role-name>
    </security-role>

    <method-permission>
      <role-name>everyone</role-name>
      <method>
        <ejb-name>ProcessPaymentBean</ejb-name>
        <method-name>*</method-name>
      </method>
    </method-permission>

    <container-transaction>
      <method>
        <ejb-name>ProcessPaymentBean</ejb-name>
        <method-name>*</method-name>
      </method>
      <trans-attribute>Required</trans-attribute>
    </container-transaction>
  </assembly-descriptor>
</ejb-jar>
```

EJB 1.0: The ProcessPayment bean's deployment descriptor

The DeploymentDescriptor for the ProcessPayment bean is created and serialized using an application called MakeDD, which is basically the same as the one used to create the *TravelAgentDD.ser* file in Chapter 4:

```
package com.titan.processpayment;

import javax.ejb.deployment.*;
import javax.naming.CompoundName;

import java.util.*;
import java.io.*;

public class MakeDD {

    public static void main(String args []) {
        try {
```

```
        if (args.length <1) {
            System.out.println("must specify target directory");
            return;
        }

        SessionDescriptor paymentDD = new SessionDescriptor();
        paymentDD.setRemoteInterfaceClassName(
            "com.titan.processpayment.ProcessPayment");
        paymentDD.setHomeInterfaceClassName(
            "com.titan.processpayment.ProcessPaymentHome");
        paymentDD.setEnterpriseBeanClassName(
            "com.titan.processpayment.ProcessPaymentBean");
        paymentDD.setSessionTimeout(60);
        paymentDD.setStateManagementType(
            SessionDescriptor.STATELESS_SESSION);

        Properties props = new Properties();
        props.put("jdbcURL","jdbc:subprotocol:subname");

        props.put("minCheckNumber","1000");
        paymentDD.setEnvironmentProperties(props);

        ControlDescriptor cd = new ControlDescriptor();
        cd.setIsolationLevel(ControlDescriptor.TRANSACTION_READ_COMMITTED);
        cd.setMethod(null);
        cd.setRunAsMode(ControlDescriptor.CLIENT_IDENTITY);
        cd.setTransactionAttribute(ControlDescriptor.TX_REQUIRED);
        ControlDescriptor [] cdArray = {cd};
        paymentDD.setControlDescriptors(cdArray);

        CompoundName jndiName =
            new CompoundName("ProcessPaymentHome", new Properties());
        paymentDD.setBeanHomeName(jndiName);

        String fileSeparator =
            System.getProperties().getProperty("file.separator");
        if (! args[0].endsWith(fileSeparator))
            args[0] += fileSeparator;

        FileOutputStream fis =
            new FileOutputStream(args[0]+"ProcessPaymentDD.ser");
        ObjectOutputStream oos = new ObjectOutputStream(fis);
        oos.writeObject(paymentDD);
        oos.flush();
        oos.close();
        fis.close();
        } catch(Throwable t) {t.printStackTrace();}
    }
}
```

The class names, the JNDI name, and the environment properties are the only differences between the two descriptors. We create a properties table, add two properties to it, and call setEnvironmentProperties() to install the table. The two properties are "jdbcURL", which tells the bean how to contact the database, and "minCheckNumber", which tells the bean the minimum check number that it is allowed to accept. You will need to replace the value associated with the "jdbcURL" environment property with a JDBC URL specific to your EJB server and database.

In this context, it's important to notice that the state management type that we specify for this bean is STATELESS_SESSION. In the deployment descriptor for the TravelAgent bean, this was a piece of black magic that we didn't really explain in Chapter 4. Now we know what it means. This informs the container that the bean instance can be swapped between method invocations from EJB object to EJB object; it doesn't need to maintain conversational state.

Deploy the ProcessPayment bean and make some payments. You should also attempt to make payments in such a way that an application exception is thrown. You could, for example, submit a check payment with a check number that is too low or a credit card payment with an expiration date that has passed.

The Life Cycle of a Stateless Session Bean

Just as the entity bean has a well-defined life cycle, so does the stateless session bean. The stateless session bean's life cycle has two states: the *Does Not Exist* state and the *Method-Ready Pool*. The Method-Ready Pool is similar to the instance pool used for entity beans. This is one of the significant life-cycle differences between stateless and stateful session beans; stateless beans define instance pooling in their life cycle and stateful beans do not.* Figure 7-1 illustrates the states and transitions that a stateless session bean instance goes through in its lifetime.

Does Not Exist

When a bean instance is in the Does Not Exist state, it is not an instance in the memory of the system. In other words, it has not been instantiated yet.

---

* Some vendors do *not* pool stateless instances, but may instead create and destroy instances with each method invocation. This is an implementation-specific decision that shouldn't impact the specified life cycle of the stateless bean instance.

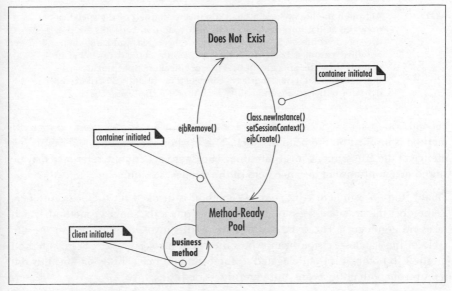

Figure 7-1. Stateless session bean life cycle

The Method-Ready Pool

Stateless bean instances enter the Method-Ready Pool as the container needs them. When the EJB server is first started, it will probably create a number of stateless bean instances and enter them into the Method-Ready Pool. (The actual behavior of the server depends on the implementation.) When the number of stateless instances servicing client requests is insufficient, more can be created and added to the pool.

Transitioning to the Method-Ready Pool

When an instance transitions from the Does Not Exist state to the Method-Ready Pool, three operations are performed on it. First, the bean instance is instantiated by invoking the `Class.newInstance()` method on the stateless bean class.

WARNING   Bean classes, entity and session alike, must never define construc-
            tors. Take care of initialization needs within `ejbCreate()` and other
            callback methods available through the bean class's `Enterprise-`
            `Bean` interface (`EntityBean` or `SessionBean`). The container
            instantiates instances of the bean class using `Class.new-`
            `Instance()`, which requires a no-argument constructor.

Second, the `SessionBean.setSessionContext(SessionContext context)`
method is invoked on the bean instance. This is when the instance receives its reference to the `EJBContext` for its lifetime. The `SessionContext` reference may be
stored in a nontransient instance field of the stateless session bean.*

Finally, the no-argument `ejbCreate()` method is invoked on the bean instance.
Remember that a stateless session bean only has one `ejbCreate()` method, which
takes no arguments. The `ejbCreate()` method is invoked only once in the life
cycle of the stateless session bean; when the client invokes the `create()` method
on the EJB home, it is not delegated to the bean instance. This is significantly different from both entity beans and stateful session beans.

Stateless session beans are not subject to activation, so they can maintain open
connections to resources for their entire life cycle.† The `ejbRemove()` method
should close any open resources before the stateless session bean is evicted from
memory at the end of its life cycle. More about `ejbRemove()` later in this section.

Life in the Method-Ready Pool

Once an instance is in the Method-Ready Pool, it is ready to service client requests.
When a client invokes a business method on an EJB object, the method call is delegated to any available instance in the Method-Ready Pool. While the instance is
executing the request, it is unavailable for use by other EJB objects. Once the
instance has finished, it is immediately available to any EJB object that needs it.
This is slightly different from the instance pool for entity beans, described in
Chapter 6. In the entity instance pool, a bean instance might be swapped in to ser-

---

* The EJB 1.0 specification is not clear on whether an `EJBContext` should be stored in a transient or
  nontransient field in the bean instance. The recommended approach is to use nontransient, but some
  vendors will preserve an `EJBContext` reference's binding to the instance only if it is set as a transient
  field. Consult your vendor for its implementation-specific requirements. EJB 1.1 explicitly states that
  the `EJBContext` must *not* be referenced in a transient field.

† The duration of a stateless bean instance's life is assumed to be very long. However, some EJB servers
  may actually destroy and create instances with every method invocation, making this strategy less attractive. Consult your vendor's documentation for details on how your EJB server handles stateless
  instances.

vice an EJB object for several method invocations. Stateless session instances are only dedicated to an EJB object for the duration of the method.

Although vendors can choose different strategies to support stateless session beans, it's likely that vendors will use an instance-swapping strategy similar to that used for entity beans (the strategy utilized by entity beans is described in Chapter 6). However, the swap is very brief, lasting only as long as the business method needs to execute. When an instance is swapped in, its SessionContext changes to reflect the context of its EJB object and the client invoking the method. The bean instance may be included in the transactional scope of the client's request, and it may access SessionContext information specific to the client request, for example, the security and transactional methods. Once the instance has finished servicing the client, it is disassociated from the EJB object and returned to the Method-Ready Pool.

Stateless session beans are not subject to activation and never have their ejbActivate() or ejbPassivate() callback methods invoked. The reason is simple: stateless instances have no conversational state that needs to preserved. (*Stateful* session beans do depend on activation, as we'll see later.)

Clients that need a remote reference to a stateless session bean begin by invoking the create() method on the bean's EJB home:

```
// EJB 1.0: Use native cast
Object ref = jndiConnection.lookup("ProcessPaymentHome");
ProcessPaymentHome home = (ProcessPaymentHome)
    PortableRemoteObject.narrow(ref,ProcessPaymentHome.class);

ProcessPayment pp = home.create();
```

Unlike the entity bean and stateful session bean, invoking the create() method does not result in a call to the bean's ejbCreate() method. In stateless session beans, calling the EJB home's create() method results in the creation of an EJB object for the client, but that is all. The ejbCreate() method of a stateless session bean is only invoked once in the life cycle of an instance—when it is transitioning from the Does Not Exist state to the Method-Ready Pool. It isn't reinvoked every time a client requests a remote reference to the bean.

Transitioning out of the Method-Ready Pool: The death of a stateless bean instance

Bean instances leave the Method-Ready Pool for the Does Not Exist state when the server no longer needs the instance. This occurs when the server decides to reduce the total size of the Method-Ready Pool by evicting one or more instances from memory. The process begins by invoking the ejbRemove() method on the instance. At this time, the bean instance should perform any cleanup operations, like closing open resources. The ejbRemove() method is only invoked once in the life cycle of a stateless session bean's instance—when it is about to transition to the Does Not Exist state. When a client invokes one of the remove() methods on a stateless session bean's remote or home interface, it is not delegated to the bean instance. The client's invocations of this method simply invalidates the stub and releases the EJB object; it notifies the container that the client no longer needs the bean. The container itself invokes the ejbRemove() method on the stateless instance, but only at the end of the instance's life cycle. Again, this is very different from both stateful session beans and entity beans, which suffer more destructive consequences when the client invokes a remove method. During the ejbRemove() method, the SessionContext (and JNDI ENC for EJB 1.1) is still available to the bean instance. Following the execution of the ejbRemove() method, the bean is dereferenced and eventually garbage collected.

The Stateful Session Bean

Stateful session beans offer an alternative that lies between entity beans and stateless session beans. Stateful session beans are dedicated to one client for the life of the bean instance; a stateful session bean acts on behalf of a client as its agent. They are not swapped among EJB objects or kept in an instance pool like entity and stateless bean instances. Once a stateful session bean is instantiated and assigned to an EJB object, it is dedicated to that EJB object for its entire life cycle.*

Stateful session beans maintain conversational state, which means that the instance variables of the bean class can cache data relative to the client between method invocations. This makes it possible for methods to be interdependent, so that changes made by methods to the bean's state can affect the result of subsequent method invocations. In contrast, the stateless session beans we have been talking about do not maintain conversational state. Although stateless beans may have instance variables, these fields are not specific to one client. A stateless instance is swapped among many EJB objects, so you can't predict which instance will service a method call. With stateful session beans, every method call from a client is serviced by the same instance (at least conceptually), so the bean instance's state can be predicted from one method invocation to the next.

Although stateful session beans maintain conversational state, they are not themselves persistent like entity beans. Entity beans represent data in the database; their persistent fields are written directly to the database. Stateful session beans, like stateless beans, can access the database but do not represent data in the data-

---

* This is a conceptual model. Some EJB containers may actually use instance swapping with stateful session beans but make it appear as if the same instance is servicing all requests. Conceptually, however, the same stateful session bean instance services all requests.

base. In addition, session beans are not used concurrently like entity beans. If you have an entity EJB object that wraps an instance of the ship called *Paradise*, for example, all client requests for that ship will be coordinated through the same EJB object.* With session beans, the EJB object is dedicated to one client—session beans are not used concurrently.

Stateful session beans are often thought of as extensions of the client. This makes sense if you think of a client as being made up of operations and state. Each task may rely on some information gathered or changed by a previous operation. A GUI client is a perfect example: when you fill in the fields on a GUI client you are creating conversational state. Pressing a button executes an operation that might fill in more fields, based on the information you entered previously. The information in the fields is conversational state.

Stateful session beans allow you to encapsulate the business logic and the conversational state of a client and move it to the server. Moving this logic to the server thins the client application and makes the system as a whole easier to manage. The stateful session bean acts as an agent for the client, managing processes or *workflow* to accomplish a set of tasks; it manages the interactions of other beans in addition to direct data access over several operations to accomplish a complex set of tasks. By encapsulating and managing workflow on behalf of the client, stateful beans present a simplified interface that hides the details of many interdependent operations on the database and other beans from the client.

The TravelAgent Bean

The TravelAgent bean, which we have already seen, is a stateful session bean that encapsulates the process of making a reservation on a cruise. We will develop this bean further to demonstrate how stateful session beans can be used as workflow objects.

TravelAgent: The remote interface

In Chapter 4, we developed an early version of the TravelAgent interface that contained a single business method, listCabins(). We are going to remove the listCabins() method and redefine the TravelAgent bean so that it behaves like a workflow object. Later in the chapter, we will add a modified listing method for obtaining a more specific list of cabins for the user.

---

* This is a conceptual model. Some EJB containers may actually use separate EJB objects for concurrent access to the same entity, relying on the database to control concurrency. Conceptually, however, the end result is the same.

As a stateful session bean that models workflow, TravelAgent manages the interactions of several other beans while maintaining conversational state. The following code contains the modified `TravelAgent` interface:

```
package com.titan.travelagent;

import java.rmi.RemoteException;
import javax.ejb.FinderException;
import com.titan.cruise.Cruise;
import com.titan.customer.Customer;
import com.titan.processpayment.CreditCard;

public interface TravelAgent extends javax.ejb.EJBObject {

    public void setCruiseID(int cruise)
        throws RemoteException, FinderException;
    public int getCruiseID() throws RemoteException,
                                IncompleteConversationalState;

    public void setCabinID(int cabin)
        throws RemoteException, FinderException;
    public int getCabinID() throws RemoteException,
                                IncompleteConversationalState;
    public int getCustomerID() throws RemoteException,
                                IncompleteConversationalState;

    public Ticket bookPassage(CreditCard card, double price)
        throws RemoteException, IncompleteConversationalState;
}
```

The purpose of the TravelAgent bean is to make cruise reservations. To accomplish this task, the bean needs to know which cruise, cabin, and customer make up the reservation. Therefore, the client using the TravelAgent bean needs to gather this kind of information before making the booking. The `TravelAgent` remote interface provides methods for setting the IDs of the cruise and cabin that the customer wants to book. We can assume that the cabin ID came from a list and that the cruise ID came from some other source. The customer is set in the `create()` method of the home interface—more about this later.

Once the customer, cruise, and cabin are chosen, the TravelAgent bean is ready to process the reservation. This operation is performed by the `bookPassage()` method, which needs the customer's credit card information and the price of the cruise. `bookPassage()` is responsible for charging the customer's account, reserving the chosen cabin in the right ship on the right cruise, and generating a ticket for the customer. How this is accomplished is not important to us at this point; when we are developing the remote interface, we are only concerned with the business definition of the bean. We will discuss the implementation when we talk about the bean class.

Like the CreditCard and Check classes used in the ProcessPayment bean, the Ticket class that bookPassage() returns is defined as a pass-by-value object. It can be argued that a ticket should be an entity bean since it is not dependent and may be accessed outside the context of the TravelAgent bean. However, determining how a business object is used can also dictate whether it should be a bean or simply a class. The Ticket object, for example, could be digitally signed and emailed to the client as proof of purchase. This wouldn't be feasible if the Ticket object had been an entity bean. Enterprise beans are only referenced through their remote interfaces and are not passed by value, as are serializable objects such as Ticket, CreditCard, and Check. As an exercise in pass-by-value, we define the Ticket as a simple serializable object instead of a bean:

```
package com.titan.travelagent;

import com.titan.cruise.Cruise;
import com.titan.cabin.Cabin;
import com.titan.customer.Customer;
import java.rmi.RemoteException;

public class Ticket implements java.io.Serializable {
    public int cruiseID;
    public int cabinID;
    public double price;
    public String description;

    public Ticket(Customer customer, Cruise cruise, Cabin cabin, double price)
            throws javax.ejb.FinderException, RemoteException,
            javax.naming.NamingException {

        description = customer.getFirstName()+" "+customer.getMiddleName()+
        " " + customer.getLastName() +
        " has been booked for the " + cruise.getName().trim() +
        " cruise on ship " + cruise.getShipID() + ".\n" +
        " Your accommodations include " + cabin.getName().trim() +
        " a " + cabin.getBedCount() +
        " bed cabin on deck level " + cabin.getDeckLevel() +
        ".\n Total charge = " + price;
    }

    public String toString() {
        return description;
    }
}
```

Note that the bookPassage() method throws an application-specific exception, the IncompleteConversationalState. This exception is used to communicate business problems encountered while booking a customer on a cruise. The IncompleteConversationalState exception indicates that the TravelAgent bean didn't have enough information to process the booking. The Incomplete-ConversationalState application exception class is defined below:

```
package com.titan.travelagent;

public class IncompleteConversationalState extends java.lang.Exception {
    public IncompleteConversationalState(){super();}
    public IncompleteConversationalState(String msg){super(msg);}
}
```

TravelAgentHome: The home interface

Starting with the TravelAgentHome interface that we developed in Chapter 4, we can modify the create() method to take a remote reference to the customer who is making the reservation:

```
package com.titan.travelagent;

import java.rmi.RemoteException;
import javax.ejb.CreateException;
import com.titan.customer.Customer;

public interface TravelAgentHome extends javax.ejb.EJBHome {

    public TravelAgent create(Customer cust)
        throws RemoteException, CreateException;
}
```

The create() method in this home interface requires that a remote reference to a Customer bean be used to create the TravelAgent bean. Because there are no other create() methods, you can't create a TravelAgent bean if you don't know who the customer is. The Customer bean reference provides the TravelAgent bean with some of the conversational state it will need to process the bookPassage() method.

Taking a peek at the client view

Before settling on definitions for your remote interface and home interface, it is a good idea to figure out how the bean will be used by clients. Imagine that the TravelAgent bean is used by a Java applet with GUI fields. The GUI fields capture the customer's preference for the type of cruise and cabin. We start by examining the code used at the beginning of the reservation process:

```
Context jndiContext = getInitialContext();
// EJB 1.0: Use native cast instead of narrow().
```

```
Object ref = jndiContext.lookup("CustomerHome");
CustomerHome customerHome =(CustomerHome)
    PortableRemoteObject.narrow(ref, CustomerHome.class);

String ln = tfLastName.getText();
String fn = tfFirstName.getText();
String mn = tfMiddleName.getText();
Customer customer = customerHome.create(nextID, ln, fn, mn);

// EJB 1.0: Use native cast instead of narrow()
ref = jndiContext.lookup("TravelAgentHome");
TravelAgentHome home = (TravelAgentHome)
    PortableRemoteObject.narrow(ref, TravelAgentHome.class);

TravelAgent agent = home.create(customer);
```

This snippet of code creates a new Customer bean based on information the travel agent gathered over the phone. The Customer reference is then used to create a TravelAgent bean. Next, we gather the cruise and cabin choices from another part of the applet:

```
int cruise_id = Integer.parseInt(textField_cruiseNumber.getText());
int cabin_id = Integer.parseInt(textField_cabinNumber.getText());
agent.setCruiseID(cruise_id);
agent.setCabinID(cabin_id);
```

The user chooses the cruise and cabin that the customer wishes to reserve. These IDs are set in the TravelAgent bean, which maintains the conversational state for the whole process.

At the end of the process, the travel agent completes the reservation by processing the booking and generating a ticket. Because the TravelAgent bean has maintained the conversational state, caching the Customer, Cabin, and Cruise information, only the credit card and price are needed to complete the transaction:

```
long cardNumber = Long.parseLong(textField_cardNumber.getText());
Date date =
    dateFormatter.format(textField_cardExpiration.getText());
String cardBrand = textField_cardBrand.getText();
CreditCard card = new CreditCard(cardNumber,date,cardBrand);
double price =
    double.valueOf(textField_cruisePrice.getText()).doubleValue();
Ticket ticket = agent.bookPassage(card,price);
PrintingService.print(ticket);
```

We can now move ahead with development; this summary of how the client will use the TravelAgent bean confirms that our remote interface and home interface definitions are workable.

TravelAgentBean: The bean class

We now implement all the behavior expressed in the new remote interface and home interface for the TravelAgent bean. Here is a partial definition of the new TravelAgentBean; the getHome() method and, for EJB 1.0, the getJNDIContext() method will be added as we go along:*

```
package com.titan.travelagent;

import com.titan.cabin.*;
import com.titan.cruise.*;
import com.titan.customer.*;
import com.titan.processpayment.*;
import com.titan.reservation.*;

import java.sql.*;
import javax.sql.DataSource;
import java.util.Vector;
import java.rmi.RemoteException;
import javax.naming.NamingException;
import javax.ejb.EJBException;

public class TravelAgentBean implements javax.ejb.SessionBean {

    public Customer customer;
    public Cruise cruise;
    public Cabin cabin;

    public javax.ejb.SessionContext ejbContext;
    // EJB 1.0: jndiContext should be declared transient
    public javax.naming.Context jndiContext;

    public void ejbCreate(Customer cust) {
        customer = cust;
    }
    public int getCustomerID()
        throws IncompleteConversationalState {
        // EJB 1.0: also throws RemoteException
        try { // EJB 1.0: remove try/catch
            if (customer == null)
                throw new IncompleteConversationalState();
            return ((CustomerPK)customer.getPrimaryKey()).id;
        } catch(RemoteException re) {
            throw new EJBException(re);
        }
    }
}
```

---

* If you're modifying the bean developed in Chapter 4, remember to delete the listCabin() method. We will add a new implementation of that method later in this chapter.

```
public int getCruiseID()
    throws IncompleteConversationalState {
    // EJB 1.0: also throws RemoteException
    try { // EJB 1.0: remove try/catch
        if (cruise == null)
            throw new IncompleteConversationalState();
        return ((CruisePK)cruise.getPrimaryKey()).id;
    } catch(RemoteException re) {
        throw new EJBException(re);
    }

}

public int getCabinID()
    throws IncompleteConversationalState {
    // EJB 1.0: also throws RemoteException
    try { // EJB 1.0: remove try/catch
        if (cabin==null)
            throw new IncompleteConversationalState();
        return ((CabinPK)cabin.getPrimaryKey()).id;
    } catch(RemoteException re) {
        throw new EJBException(re);
    }
}
public void setCabinID(int cabinID)
    throws javax.ejb.FinderException { // EJB 1.0: also throws RemoteException
    try { // EJB 1.0: remove try/catch
        CabinHome home = (CabinHome)getHome("CabinHome",CabinHome.class);
        CabinPK pk = new CabinPK();
        pk.id=cabinID;
        cabin = home.findByPrimaryKey(pk);
    } catch(RemoteException re) {
        throw new EJBException(re);
    }
}
public void setCruiseID(int cruiseID)
    throws javax.ejb.FinderException { // EJB 1.0: also throws RemoteException
    try { // EJB 1.0: remove try/catch
        CruiseHome home = (CruiseHome)getHome("CruiseHome", CruiseHome.class);
        cruise = home.findByPrimaryKey(new CruisePK(cruiseID));
    } catch(RemoteException re) {
        throw new EJBException(re);
    }
}

public Ticket bookPassage(CreditCard card, double price)
    throws IncompleteConversationalState {
    // EJB 1.0: also throws RemoteException
```

```
        if (customer == null || cruise == null || cabin == null) {
            throw new IncompleteConversationalState();
        }
        try {
            ReservationHome resHome = (ReservationHome)
                getHome("ReservationHome",ReservationHome.class);
            Reservation reservation =
                resHome.create(customer, cruise, cabin, price);
            ProcessPaymentHome ppHome = (ProcessPaymentHome)
                getHome("ProcessPaymentHome",ProcessPaymentHome.class);
            ProcessPayment process = ppHome.create();
            process.byCredit(customer, card, price);

            Ticket ticket = new Ticket(customer,cruise,cabin,price);
            return ticket;
        } catch(Exception e) {
            // EJB 1.0: throw new RemoteException("",e);
            throw new EJBException(e);
        }
    }
    public void ejbRemove() {}
    public void ejbActivate() {}

    public void ejbPassivate() {
        /*
        EJB 1.0: Close the JNDI Context and set to null.
        try {
            jndiContext.close();
        } catch(NamingException ne) {}
        jndiContext = null;
        */
    }
    public void setSessionContext(javax.ejb.SessionContext cntx) {
        // EJB 1.0: throws RemoteException
        ejbContext = cntx;
        try {
          jndiContext = new javax.naming.InitialContext();
        } catch(NamingException ne) {
            // EJB 1.0: throw new RemoteException("",ne);
            throw new EJBException(ne);
        }
    }
    protected Object getHome(String name, Class type)
    {// EJB 1.0: throws RemoteException
        // EJB 1.1 and EJB 1.0 specific implementations
    }
}
```

There is a lot of code to digest, so we will approach it in small pieces. First, let's examine the ejbCreate() method:

```
public class TravelAgentBean implements javax.ejb.SessionBean {

    public Customer customer;
    public Cruise cruise;
    public Cabin cabin;

    public javax.ejb.SessionContext ejbContext;
    // EJB 1.0: jndiContext should be declared transient
    public javax.naming.Context jndiContext;

    public void ejbCreate(Customer cust) {
        customer = cust;
    }
```

When the bean is created, the remote reference to the Customer bean is passed to the bean instance and maintained in the customer field. The customer field is part of the bean's conversational state. We could have obtained the customer's identity as an integer ID and constructed the remote reference to the Customer bean in the ejbCreate() method. However, we passed the reference directly to demonstrate that remote references to beans can be passed from a client application to a bean. They can also be returned from the bean to the client and passed between beans on the same EJB server or between EJB servers.

References to the SessionContext and JNDI context are held in fields called ejbContext and jndiContext. Prefixing the names of these context types helps avoid confusion.

EJB 1.1: the jndiContext

When a bean is passivated in EJB 1.1, the JNDI ENC must be maintained as part of the bean's conversational state. This means that the JNDI context should not be transient, as was the case in EJB 1.0. In EJB 1.1, once a field is set to reference the JNDI ENC, the reference remains valid for the life of the bean. In the TravelAgentBean, we set the field jndiContext to reference the JNDI ENC when the SessionContext is set a the beginning of the bean's life cycle:

```
public void setSessionContext(javax.ejb.SessionContext cntx) {
    // EJB 1.0: throws RemoteException
    ejbContext = cntx;
    try {
        jndiContext = new InitialContext();
    } catch(NamingException ne) {
        // EJB 1.0: throw new RemoteException("",ne);
        throw new EJBException(ne);
    }
}
```

EJB 1.1 makes special accommodations for references to SessionContext, the JNDI ENC, references to other beans (remote and home interface types) and the JTA UserTransaction type, which is discussed in detail in Chapter 8. The container must maintain any instance fields that reference objects of these types as part of the conversational state, even if they are not serializable. (In EJB 1.0, references to most of these special types had to be closed or set to null in the ejbPassivate() method.) All other fields must be serializable or null when the bean is passivated.

Open resources such as sockets or JDBC connections must be closed whenever the bean is passivated. In stateful session beans, open resources will not be maintained for the life of the bean instance. When a stateful session bean is passivated, any open resource can cause problems with the activation mechanism.

EJB 1.0: the jndiContext

In EJB 1.0, references to a JNDI context are not considered part of the bean's conversational state; the JNDI context is an open resource that must be referenced by a transient field and should be closed when the bean is passivated. In the TravelAgentBean, the jndiContext is obtained through the method getJndiContext():

```
protected javax.naming.Context getJndiContext()
    throws javax.naming.NamingException {

    if (jndiContext != null)
        return jndiContext;

    // ... Specify the JNDI properties specific to the vendor.

    jndiContext = new InitialContext(p);
    return jndiContext; }
```

The InitialContext, obtained by the getJndiContext() method, is saved in the instance variable jndiContext. This reduces the number of times the InitialContext needs to be created.* However, because the JNDI context is an open resource, it must be closed whenever the bean is passivated. When a stateful session bean is passivated, any open resource can cause problems with the activation mechanism. TravelAgentBean uses the ejbPassivate() notification method to close the JNDI context and set the jndiContext variable to null:

```
public void ejbPassivate() {
    try {
```

---

* The advantage gained by maintaining the connection will be marginal if the container calls ejbPassivate() after every method call—which some implementations do.

```
        jndiContext.close();
    } catch(NamingException ne) {}
    jndiContext = null;
}
```

The TravelAgent bean has methods for setting the desired cruise and cabin. These methods take integer IDs as arguments and retrieve references to the appropriate Cruise or Cabin bean from the appropriate home interface. These references are also a part of the TravelAgent bean's conversational state:

```
public void setCabinID(int cabinID)
throws javax.ejb.FinderException { // EJB 1.0: also throws RemoteException
    try { // EJB 1.0: remove try/catch
        CabinHome home = (CabinHome)getHome("CabinHome",CabinHome.class);
        CabinPK pk = new CabinPK();
        pk.id=cabinID;
        cabin = home.findByPrimaryKey(pk);
    } catch(RemoteException re) {
        throw new EJBException(re);
    }
}
public void setCruiseID(int cruiseID)
throws javax.ejb.FinderException { // EJB 1.0: also throws RemoteException
    try { // EJB 1.0: remove try/catch
        CruiseHome home = (CruiseHome)getHome("CruiseHome", CruiseHome.class);
        cruise = home.findByPrimaryKey(new CruisePK(cruiseID));
    } catch(RemoteException re) {
        throw new EJBException(re);
    }
}
```

It may seem strange that we set these values using the integer IDs, but we keep them in the conversational state as remote references. Using the integer IDs for these objects is simpler for the client, which doesn't work with their remote references. In the client code, we got cabin and cruise IDs from text fields. Why make the client obtain a remote reference to the Cruise and Cabin beans when an ID is simpler? In addition, using the ID is cheaper than passing a network reference in terms of network traffic. We need the EJB object references to these bean types in the bookPassage() method, so we use their IDs to obtain actual remote references. We could have waited until the bookPassage() method was invoked before reconstructing the remote references, but this way we keep the bookPassage() method simple.

The method getHome(), used in both set methods, is a convenience method defined in the TravelAgentBean. It hides the details of obtaining a remote reference to an EJB home object.

EJB 1.1: accessing EJB references

In EJB 1.1, the JNDI ENC can be used to obtain a reference to the home interface of other beans. Using the ENC lets you avoid hardcoding vendor-specific
JNDI properties into the bean—a common problem in EJB 1.0. In other
words, the JNDI ENC allows EJB references to be network and vendor independent.

In the `TravelAgentBean`, the `getHome()` method uses the `jndiContext` reference to obtain references to the Cabin, Ship, ProcessPayment, and Cruise
home objects:

```
protected Object getHome(String name,Class type) {
    try {
        Object ref = jndiContext.lookup("java:comp/env/ejb/"+name);
        return PortableRemoteObject.narrow(ref, type);
    } catch(NamingException ne) {
        throw new EJBException(ne);
    }
}
```

EJB 1.1 recommends that all EJB references be bound to the `"java:comp/
env/ejb"` context, which is the convention followed here. In the TravelAgent
bean, we pass in the name of the home object we want and append it to the
`"java:comp/env/ejb"` context to do the lookup.

The deployment descriptor provides a special set of tags for declaring EJB references. Here's how the `<ejb-ref>` tag and its subelements are used:

```
<ejb-ref>
    <ejb-ref-name>ejb/CabinHome</ejb-ref-name>
    <ejb-ref-type>Entity</ejb-ref-type>
    <home>com.titan.cabin.CabinHome</home>
    <remote>com.titan.cabin.Cabin</remote>
</ejb-ref>
```

The `<ejb-ref>` tag and its subelements should be self explanatory: they
define a name for the bean within the ENC, declare the bean's type, and give
the names of its remote and home interfaces. When a bean is deployed, the
deployer maps the `<ejb-ref>` elements to actual beans in a way specific to the
vendor. The `<ejb-ref>` elements can also be linked by the application assembler to beans in the same deployment (a subject covered in detail in
Chapter 10, which is about the XML deployment descriptors).

EJB 1.0: accessing EJB references

In EJB 1.0, beans access other beans in exactly the same way that application
clients access beans: you use JNDI to look up the bean's home interface. To
accomplish this, the JNDI `InitialContext` must be created and initialized
with properties specific to the EJB vendor.

The TravelAgent bean uses the getJndiContext() method and the Deploy-mentDescriptor environment properties to obtain references to other beans. The getHome() method should be implemented as follows:

```
protected Object getHome(String name, Class type) throws RemoteException {
    try {
        String jndiName =
            ejbContext.getEnvironment().getProperty(name);
        return getJndiContext().lookup(jndiName);
    } catch(NamingException ne) {
        throw new RemoteException("Could not lookup ("+name+")",ne);
    }
}
```

The last point of interest in our bean definition is the bookPassage() method. This method leverages the conversational state accumulated by the ejbCreate() method and the methods (setCabinID(), setCruiseID()) to process a reservation for a customer on a cruise:

```
public Ticket bookPassage(CreditCard card, double price)
throws IncompleteConversationalState{// EJB 1.0: also throws RemoteException

    if (customer == null || cruise == null || cabin == null) {
        throw new IncompleteConversationalState();
    }
    try {
        ReservationHome resHome =
            (ReservationHome) getHome("ReservationHome",ReservationHome.class);
        Reservation reservation =
            resHome.create(customer, cruise, cabin, price);
        ProcessPaymentHome ppHome = (ProcessPaymentHome)
            getHome("ProcessPaymentHome",ProcessPaymentHome.class);
        ProcessPayment process = ppHome.create();
        process.byCredit(customer, card, price);

        Ticket ticket = new Ticket(customer, cruise, cabin, price);
        return ticket;
    } catch(Exception e) {
        // EJB 1.0: throw new RemoteException("",e);
        throw new EJBException(e);
    }
}
```

This method exemplifies the workflow concept. It uses several beans, including the Reservation bean, the ProcessPayment bean, the Customer bean, the Cabin bean, and the Cruise bean to accomplish one task: book a customer on a cruise. Deceptively simple, this method encapsulates several interactions that ordinarily

might have been performed on the client. For the price of one bookPassage()
call from the client, the TravelAgent bean performs many operations:

1. Look up and obtain a remote reference to the Reservation bean's EJB home.

2. Create a new Reservation bean resulting in a database insert.

3. Look up and obtain a remote reference to the ProcessPayment bean's EJB
   home.

4. Create a new ProcessPayment bean.

5. Charge the customer's credit card using the ProcessPayment bean.

6. Generate a new Ticket with all the pertinent information describing the customer's purchase.

From a design standpoint, encapsulating the workflow in a stateful session bean
means a less complex interface for the client and more flexibility for implementing changes. We could, for example, easily change the bookPassage() method to
include a check for overlapped booking (when a customer books passage on two
different cruises that overlap). If Titan's customers often book passage on cruises
that overlap, we could add logic to bookPassage() to detect the problem. This
type of enhancement would not change the remote interface, so the client application wouldn't need modification. Encapsulating workflow in stateful session beans
allows the system to evolve over time without impacting clients.

In addition, the type of clients used can change. One of the biggest problems with
two-tier architectures—besides scalability and transactional control—is that the
business logic is intertwined with the client logic. This makes it difficult to reuse
the business logic in a different kind of client. With stateful session beans this is
not a problem, because stateful session beans are an extension of the client but are
not bound to the client's presentation. Let's say that our first implementation of
the reservation system used a Java applet with GUI widgets. The TravelAgent bean
would manage conversational state and perform all the business logic while the
applet focused on the GUI presentation. If, at a later date, we decide to go to a
thin client (HTML generated by a Java servlet, for example), we would simply
reuse the TravelAgent bean in the servlet. Because all the business logic is in the
stateful session bean, the presentation (Java applet or servlet or something else)
can change easily.

The TravelAgent bean also provides transactional integrity for processing the customer's reservation. As explained in Chapter 3, if any one of the operations within
the body of the bookPassage() method fails, all the operations are rolled back so
that none of the changes are accepted. If the credit card can't be charged by the
ProcessPayment bean, the newly created Reservation bean and its associated

record are removed. The transactional aspects of the TravelAgent bean are explained in detail in Chapter 8.

Why use a Reservation entity bean?

Although the Reservation bean is an entity bean, understanding its design and purpose is important to understanding how and why it's used within the TravelAgent bean. For this reason, we will depart momentarily from our discussion of session beans, and the TravelAgent bean in particular, to expand our understanding of the Reservation bean. (The code for this bean is available on the O'Reilly web site. See the preface for details.)

The Reservation bean represents an immutable record in the database: a reservation. It records an event in the history of the reservation system. If you examine the Reservation bean closely, you will discover that you cannot modify its contents once it is created. This means it can't be changed, although it can be deleted. So why make it an entity bean at all? Why not simply write records into the database?

Titan discovered that customers were averaging two calls to confirm their reservations between the time they made the reservation and the time they actually went on the trip. This is a lot of calls when you consider that ships book 2,000 to 3,000 passengers each. Titan also discovered that about 15% of its reservations are canceled. Canceling a reservation means deleting a record, which can be tricky business. In short, Titan was accessing reservation information a lot, mostly to confirm data, but also to delete reservations for cancellations. To provide consistent and safe access to reservation data, Titan created a Reservation bean. This helped encapsulate the logic for creating, reading, and deleting reservation data, so that it could be reused in several different kinds of workflow. In addition to the TravelAgent session, the ConfirmReservation and CancelReservation beans also use the Reservation bean (we don't create bean types like these in this book). These other stateful session beans have different workflow and reuse the Reservation bean differently. Encapsulating the reservation record as an entity bean ensures consistent and safe access to sensitive data.

Another advantage of the Reservation bean is that it can help prevent double booking—when two different customers book the same cabin on the same cruise. There is a gap between the time the customer chooses a cabin and cruise and the time when bookPassage() is invoked. During this time, some other reservation agent could book the same cabin and cruise for a different customer. To prevent a double booking, we can place a unique index on the CABIN_ID and CRUISE_ID in the RESERVATION table. Any attempt to add a new record—by creating a Reservation bean—with the same CABIN_ID and CRUISE_ID will result in an SQL-Exception, effectively preventing a double booking.

EJB provides its own strategy for handling duplicate records through the DuplicateKeyException. The DuplicateKeyException is a type of Create-Exception that is thrown by the create() methods of the home interfaces for entity beans if the bean cannot be created because a bean with that same primary key already exists. The Reservation bean's primary key is defined as follows:

```
package com.titan.reservation;
public class ReservationPK implements java.io.Serializable {

    public int cruiseID;
    public int cabinID;

    public ReservationPK(){}
    public ReservationPK(int crsID, int cbnID) {
        cruiseID = crsID;
        cabinID = cbnID;
    }
    ...// equals() & hashCode() methods not shown
}
```

Notice that the cruiseID and cabinID combination is used to define the uniqueness of a Reservation entity. With container-managed persistence, the Duplicate-KeyException is thrown automatically; with bean-managed persistence, we need to capture the SQLException resulting from the attempted insert and throw the DuplicateKeyException explicitly. Either way, the DuplicateKeyException causes the bookPassage() method to fail, preventing the customer from double booking. In our example, we capture the DuplicateKeyException and rethrow it as a DoubleBookedException, which is more understandable from the client's perspective.

If we have a Reservation bean, why do we need a TravelAgent bean? Good question! The TravelAgent bean uses the Reservation bean to create a reservation, but it also has to charge the customer and generate a ticket. These are not activities that are specific to the Reservation bean, so they need to be captured in a stateful session bean that can manage workflow and transactional scope. In addition, the TravelAgent bean also provides listing behavior, which spans concepts in Titan's system. It would have been inappropriate to include any of these other behaviors in the Reservation entity bean.

listAvailableCabins(): Listing behavior

As promised, we are going to bring back the cabin-listing behavior we played around with in Chapter 4. This time, however, we are not going to use the Cabin bean to get the list; instead, we will access the database directly. Accessing the database directly is a double-edged sword. On one hand, we don't want to access the database directly if entity beans exist that can access the same information. Entity beans provide a safe and consistent interface for a particular set of data. Once an entity bean has been tested and proven, it can be reused throughout the system, substantially reducing data integrity problems. The Reservation bean is an example of that kind of usage. In addition, entity beans can pull together disjointed data and apply additional business logic such as validation, limits, and security to ensure that data access follows the business rules.

But entity beans cannot define every possible data access needed, and they shouldn't. One of the biggest problems with entity beans is that they tend to become bloated over time. A development effort that relies too heavily on entity beans will create beans that have more functionality than is normally needed. Huge entity beans with dozens of methods are a sure sign of poor design. Entity beans should be focused on providing data access to a very limited, but conceptually bound, set of data. You should be able to update, read, and insert records or data specific to that concept. Data access that spans concepts, however, should not be encapsulated in one entity bean. An example of this is listing behavior.

Systems always need listing behavior to present clients with choices. In the reservation system, for example, customers will want to choose a cabin from a list of *available* cabins. The word *available* is key to the definition of this behavior. The Cabin bean can provide us with a list of cabins, but not available cabins. That's because a cabin doesn't know if it is available; it only knows the details that describe it. The question of whether a cabin is available or not is relevant to the process using it— in this case TravelAgent—but is not relevant to the cabin itself. As an analogy, an automobile entity would not care what road it's on; it is only concerned with characteristics that describe its state and behavior. An automobile-tracking system would be concerned with the location of individual automobiles.

To get availability information, we need to compare the list of cabins on our ship to the list of cabins that have already been reserved. The listAvailable-Cabins() method does exactly that. It uses a complex SQL query to produce a list of cabins that have not yet been reserved for the cruise chosen by the client:

```
public String [] listAvailableCabins(int bedCount)
    throws IncompleteConversationalState { // EJB 1.0: also throws RemoteException

    if (cruise == null) throw new IncompleteConversationalState();

    Connection con = null;
    PreparedStatement ps = null;;
    ResultSet result = null;
    try {
        int cruiseID = ((CruisePK)cruise.getPrimaryKey()).id;
        int shipID = cruise.getShipID();
        con = getConnection();
        ps = con.prepareStatement(
```

```
                        "select ID, NAME, DECK_LEVEL  from CABIN "+
                        "where SHIP_ID = ? and ID NOT IN "+
                        "(SELECT CABIN_ID FROM RESERVATION WHERE CRUISE_ID = ?)");

            ps.setInt(1,shipID);
            ps.setInt(2,cruiseID);
            result = ps.executeQuery();
            Vector vect = new Vector();
            while(result.next()) {
                StringBuffer buf = new StringBuffer();
                buf.append(result.getString(1));
                buf.append(',');
                buf.append(result.getString(2));
                buf.append(',');
                buf.append(result.getString(3));
                vect.addElement(buf.toString());
            }
            String [] returnArray = new String[vect.size()];
            vect.copyInto(returnArray);
            return returnArray;
        }
        catch (Exception e) {
            // EJB 1.0: throw new RemoteException("",e);
            throw new EJBException(e);
        }
        finally {
            try {
                if (result != null) result.close();
                if (ps != null) ps.close();
                if (con!= null) con.close();
            }catch(SQLException se){se.printStackTrace();}
        }
    }
}
```

As you can see, the SQL query is complex. It could have been defined in a bean-managed Cabin bean using a method like Cabin.findAvailable-Cabins(Cruise cruise) but this would be a poor design choice. First, the Cabin bean would need to access the RESERVATION table, which is not a part of its definition. Entity beans should focus on only the data that defines them.

It might make a little more sense to make this behavior a find method of the Cruise bean. One can imagine a method like Cruise.findAvailableCabins(). You can certainly argue that a cruise should be aware of its own reservations. But this behavior is not very reusable. In other words, this kind of listing behavior is only used in the reservation system. Making it part of the Cruise bean's behavior suggests that is universally useful, which it's not.

The listAvailableCabins() method returns an array of String objects. This is important because we could have opted to return an collection of Cabin remote references, but we didn't. The reason is simple: we want to keep the client application as lightweight as possible. A list of String objects is much more lightweight than the alternative, a collection of remote references. In addition, a collection of remote references means that client would be working with many stubs, each with its own connection to EJB objects on the server. By returning a lightweight string array, we reduce the number of stubs on the client, which keeps the client simple and conserves resources on the server.

To make this method work, you need to create a getConnection() method for obtaining a database connection and add it to the TravelAgentBean:

```
// EJB 1.1: getConnection()
private Connection getConnection() throws SQLException {
    try {
        DataSource ds = (DataSource)jndiContext.lookup(
            "java:comp/env/jdbc/titanDB");
        return ds.getConnection();
    } catch(NamingException ne) {throw new EJBException(ne);}
}

// EJB 1.0: getConnection()
private Connection getConnection() throws SQLException {
    return DriverManager.getConnection(
        ejbContext.getEnvironment().getProperty("jdbcURL"));
}
```

Change the remote interface for TravelAgent to include the listAvailableCabins() method as shown in the following code:

```
public interface TravelAgent extends javax.ejb.EJBObject {

    public void setCruiseID(int cruise)
        throws RemoteException, FinderException;
    public int getCruiseID() throws RemoteException;

    public void setCabinID(int cabin) throws RemoteException, FinderException;
    public int getCabinID() throws RemoteException;
    public int getCustomerID() throws RemoteException;

    public Ticket bookPassage(CreditCard card, double price)
        throws RemoteException, IncompleteConversationalState;

    public String [] listAvailableCabins(int bedCount)
        throws RemoteException, IncompleteConversationalState;
}
```

EJB 1.1: The TravelAgent deployment descriptor

Use the following XML deployment descriptor when deploying the TravelAgent bean. The most important difference between this descriptor and the deployment descriptor used for the ProcessPayment bean is the `<session-type>` tag, which states that this bean is stateful, and the use of the `<ejb-ref>` elements to describe beans that are referenced through the ENC:

```xml
<?xml version="1.0"?>

<!DOCTYPE ejb-jar PUBLIC "-//Sun Microsystems, Inc.//DTD Enterprise
JavaBeans 1.1//EN" "http://java.sun.com/j2ee/dtds/ejb-jar_1_1.dtd">

<ejb-jar>
  <enterprise-beans>
    <session>
      <description>
          Acts as a travel agent for booking passage on a ship.
      </description>
      <ejb-name>TravelAgentBean</ejb-name>
      <home>com.titan.travelagent.TravelAgentHome</home>
      <remote>com.titan.travelagent.TravelAgent</remote>
      <ejb-class>com.titan.travelagent.TravelAgentBean</ejb-class>
      <session-type>Stateful</session-type>
      <transaction-type>Container</transaction-type>

      <ejb-ref>
          <ejb-ref-name>ejb/ProcessPaymentHome</ejb-ref-name>
          <ejb-ref-type>Session</ejb-ref-type>
          <home>com.titan.processpayment.ProcessPaymentHome</home>
          <remote>com.titan.processpayment.ProcessPayment</remote>
      </ejb-ref>
      <ejb-ref>
          <ejb-ref-name>ejb/CabinHome</ejb-ref-name>
          <ejb-ref-type>Entity</ejb-ref-type>
          <home>com.titan.cabin.CabinHome</home>
          <remote>com.titan.cabin.Cabin</remote>
      </ejb-ref>
      <ejb-ref>
          <ejb-ref-name>ejb/CruiseHome</ejb-ref-name>
          <ejb-ref-type>Entity</ejb-ref-type>
          <home>com.titan.cruise.CruiseHome</home>
          <remote>com.titan.cruise.Cruise</remote>
      </ejb-ref>
      <ejb-ref>
          <ejb-ref-name>ejb/CustomerHome</ejb-ref-name>
          <ejb-ref-type>Entity</ejb-ref-type>
          <home>com.titan.customer.CustomerHome</home>
          <remote>com.titan.customer.Customer</remote>
```

```
        </ejb-ref>
        <ejb-ref>
            <ejb-ref-name>ejb/ReservationHome</ejb-ref-name>
            <ejb-ref-type>Entity</ejb-ref-type>
            <home>com.titan.reservation.ReservationHome</home>
            <remote>com.titan.reservation.Reservation</remote>
        </ejb-ref>

        <resource-ref>
            <description>DataSource for the Titan database</description>
            <res-ref-name>jdbc/titanDB</res-ref-name>
            <res-type>javax.sql.DataSource</res-type>
            <res-auth>Container</res-auth>
        </resource-ref>

    </session>
</enterprise-beans>

<assembly-descriptor>
  <security-role>
    <description>
        This role represents everyone who is allowed full access
        to the TravelAgent bean.
    </description>
    <role-name>everyone</role-name>
  </security-role>

  <method-permission>
    <role-name>everyone</role-name>
    <method>
        <ejb-name>TravelAgentBean</ejb-name>
        <method-name>*</method-name>
    </method>
  </method-permission>

  <container-transaction>
    <method>
        <ejb-name>TravelAgentBean</ejb-name>
        <method-name>*</method-name>
    </method>
    <trans-attribute>Required</trans-attribute>
  </container-transaction>
</assembly-descriptor>
</ejb-jar>
```

Once you have generated the deployment descriptor, *jar* the TravelAgent bean
and deploy it in your EJB server. You will also need to deploy the Reservation,
Cruise, and Customer beans that you downloaded earlier. Based on the business

methods in the remote interface of the TravelAgent bean and your past experiences with the Cabin, Ship, and ProcessPayment beans, you should be able to create your own client application to test this code.

EJB 1.0: The TravelAgent deployment descriptor

For EJB 1.0, we need to make one change to the deployment descriptor for the TravelAgent bean that we created in Chapter 4. We need to change the state management type from stateless to stateful. Here is the new definition of the MakeDD class used to generate the deployment descriptor for the TravelAgent bean:

```
package com.titan.travelagent;

import javax.ejb.deployment.*;
import javax.naming.CompoundName;
import java.util.*;
import java.io.*;

public class MakeDD {

    public static void main(String args []) {
        try {
            if (args.length <1) {
                System.out.println("must specify target directory");
                return;
            }

            SessionDescriptor sd = new SessionDescriptor();

            sd.setEnterpriseBeanClassName(
                "com.titan.travelagent.TravelAgentBean");
            sd.setHomeInterfaceClassName(
                "com.titan.travelagent.TravelAgentHome");
            sd.setRemoteInterfaceClassName(
                "com.titan.travelagent.TravelAgent");

            sd.setSessionTimeout(60);
            sd.setStateManagementType(SessionDescriptor.STATEFUL_SESSION);

            ControlDescriptor cd = new ControlDescriptor();
            cd.setIsolationLevel(ControlDescriptor.TRANSACTION_READ_COMMITTED);
            cd.setMethod(null);
            cd.setRunAsMode(ControlDescriptor.CLIENT_IDENTITY);
            cd.setTransactionAttribute(ControlDescriptor.TX_REQUIRED);
            ControlDescriptor [] cdArray = {cd};
            sd.setControlDescriptors(cdArray);

            // Set enterprise bean's environment properties.
            Properties ep = new Properties();
            ep.put("CruiseHome","CruiseHome");
```

```
         ep.put("CabinHome","CabinHome");
         ep.put("ReservationHome","ReservationHome");
         ep.put("ProcessPaymentHome","ProcessPaymentHome");
         ep.put("ShipHome","ShipHome");
         ep.put("jdbcURL","jdbc:subprotocol:subname");
         sd.setEnvironmentProperties(ep);

         Properties jndiProps = new Properties();
         CompoundName jndiName =
             new CompoundName("TravelAgentHome",jndiProps);
         sd.setBeanHomeName(jndiName);

         String fileSeparator =
             System.getProperties().getProperty("file.separator");
         if (! args[0].endsWith(fileSeparator))
             args[0] += fileSeparator;

         FileOutputStream fis =
             new FileOutputStream(args[0]+"TravelAgentDD.ser");
         ObjectOutputStream oos = new ObjectOutputStream(fis);
         oos.writeObject(sd);
         oos.flush();
         oos.close();
         fis.close();
         } catch(Throwable t) {t.printStackTrace();}
     }
}
```

In addition to changing the state management type, we added several environment properties that help us to locate the beans that the TravelAgent bean needs to work with.

Once you have generated the deployment descriptor, *jar* the TravelAgent bean and deploy it in your EJB server. You will also need to deploy the Reservation, Cruise, and Customer beans that you downloaded earlier. Based on the business methods in the remote interface of the TravelAgent bean and your past experiences with the Cabin, Ship, and ProcessPayment beans, you should be able to create your own client application to test this code.

The Life Cycle of a Stateful Session Bean

The biggest difference between the stateful session bean and the other bean types is that stateful session beans don't use instance pooling. Stateful session beans are dedicated to one client for their entire life, so there is no swapping or pooling of instances.* Instead of pooling instances, stateful session beans are simply evicted

---

* Some vendors use pooling with stateful session beans, but that is a proprietary implementation and shouldn't impact the specified life cycle of the stateful session bean.

from memory to conserve resources. The EJB object remains connected to the client, but the bean instance is dereferenced and garbage collected during inactive periods. This means that a stateful bean must be passivated before it is evicted to preserve the conversational state of the instance, and it must be activated to restore the state when the EJB object becomes active again.

The bean's perception of its life cycle depends on whether or not it implements a special interface called `javax.ejb.SessionSynchronization`. This interface defines an additional set of callback methods that notify the bean of its participation in transactions. A bean that implements `SessionSynchronization` can cache database data across several method calls before making an update. We have not discussed transactions in any detail yet, so we will not consider this view of the stateful session bean's life cycle until Chapter 8. This section describes the life cycle of stateful session beans that do not implement the `SessionSynchron-ization` interface.

The life cycle of a stateful session bean has three states: Does Not Exist, Method-Ready, and Passivated. This sounds a lot like a stateless session bean, but the Method-Ready state is significantly different from the Method-Ready Pool of stateless beans. Figures 7-2 and 7-3 show the state diagrams for stateful session beans in EJB 1.1 and EJB 1.1.

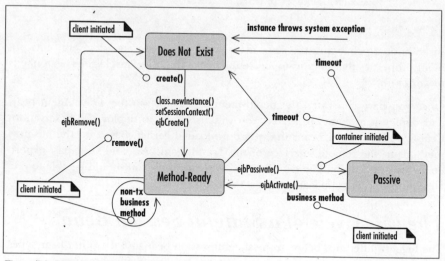

Figure 7-2. EJB 1.1 stateful session bean life cycle

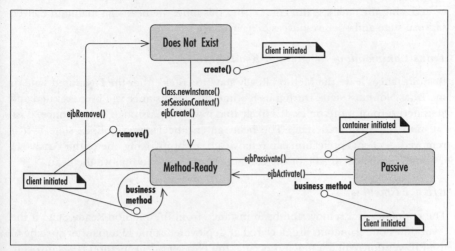

Figure 7-3. EJB 1.0 stateful session bean life cycle

Does Not Exist

Like the entity bean and stateless session bean, when a bean instance is in the Does Not Exist state, it is not an instance in the memory of the system. In other words, it has not been instantiated yet.

The Method-Ready State

Transitioning to the Method-Ready state

When a client invokes the create() method on an EJB home of a stateful session bean, its life cycle begins. When the create() method is received by the container, the container invokes newInstance() on the bean class, creating a new instance of the bean. At this point, the bean instance is assigned to its EJB object. Next, the container invokes setSessionContext() on the instance, handing it its reference to the SessionContext, which it must maintain for life. Finally, the container invokes the ejbCreate() method on the instance that matches the create() method invoked by the client. Once ejbCreate() has completed, the container returns the EJB object's remote reference to the client. The instance is now in the Method-Ready State and is ready to service business methods invoked by the client on the bean's remote reference.

Life in the Method-Ready state

While in the Method-Ready State, the bean instance is free to receive method invocations from the client, which may involve controlling the workflow of other beans or accessing the database directly. During this time, the bean can maintain conversational state and open resources in its instance variables.

Transitioning out of the Method-Ready state

Bean instances leave the Method-Ready state to enter either the Passivated state or the Does Not Exist state. During its lifetime, a bean instance will be passivated and activated zero or more times. It's likely that it will be passivated at least once, passing into the Passivated state. The bean enters the Does Not Exist state if it is removed. A client application can remove a bean by invoking one of the remove() methods on the client API, or the container can choose to remove the bean.

EJB 1.1 timeouts

The container can remove the bean instance from the Method-Ready State if the bean times out. Timeouts are declared at deployment time in a manner specific to the EJB vendor. When a timeout occurs, the ejbRemove() method is *not* invoked. A stateful bean cannot time out while a transaction is in progress.

EJB 1.0 timeouts

The container removes the bean if it times out (the timeout period is set in the deployment descriptor). When a bean is removed, its ejbRemove() method is invoked, giving the bean instance an opportunity to close any open resources and invoke remove() on any session beans it has referenced.

Passivated State

During the lifetime of a stateful session bean, there may be periods of inactivity, when the bean instance is not servicing methods from the client. To conserve resources, the container can passivate the bean instance while it is inactive by preserving its conversational state and evicting the bean instance from memory.

When a stateful bean is passivated, the instance fields are read and then written to the secondary storage associated with the EJB object. When the stateful session bean has been successfully passivated, the instance is evicted from memory; it is destroyed.

When a bean is about to be passivated, its ejbPassivate() method is invoked, alerting the bean instance that it is about to enter the Passivated state. At this time, the bean instance should close any open resources and set all nontransient, non-serializable fields to null. This will prevent problems from occurring when the bean is serialized. Transient fields will simply be ignored.

EJB 1.1 passivation issues

A bean's conversational state may consist of only primitive values, objects that are serializable, and the following special types:

- `javax.ejb.SessionContext`
- `javax.ejb.EJBHome` (home interface types)
- `javax.ejb.EJBObject` (remote interface types)
- `javax.jta.UserTransaction` (bean transaction interface)
- `javax.naming.Context` (only when it references the JNDI ENC)

The types in this list (and their subtypes) are handled specially by the passivation mechanism. They don't need to be serializable; they will be maintained through passivation and restored automatically to the bean instance when it is activated.

A bean instance's conversational state will be written to secondary storage to preserve it when the instance is passivated and destroyed. Containers can use standard Java serialization to preserve the bean instance, or some other mechanism that achieves the same result. Some vendors, for example, will simply read the values of the fields and store them in a cache. The container is required to preserve remote references to other beans with the conversational state. When the bean is activated, the container must restore any bean references automatically. The container must also restore any references to the special types listed earlier.

Fields declared `transient` will not be preserved when the bean is passivated. Except for the special types listed earlier, all fields that are nontransient and nonserializable must be set to `null` before the instance is passivated or else the container will destroy the bean instance, making it unavailable for continued use by the client. References to special types must automatically be preserved with the serialized bean instance by the container so that they can be reconstructed when the bean is activated.

A bean instance can time out while it is passivated. If a timeout occurs, the container will discard the instance, returning it to the Does Not Exist state. The `ejbRemove()` method will *not* be called on an instance that times out.

EJB 1.0 passivation issues

With the exception of the `SessionContext` and remote references to other beans, conversational state must be primitive values or objects that are serializable. This is because the bean instance's conversational state will be written to secondary storage to preserve it when the instance is destroyed. Containers can use standard Java serialization to preserve the bean instance, or some other mechanism that achieves the same result. Some vendors, for example, will simply read the values of the fields and store them in a cache. The container is required to preserve remote references to other beans with the conversational state. When the bean is activated, the container must restore any bean references automatically. The container must also restore the `Session-Context` reference automatically.*

Nonserializable object references and variables labeled as `transient` will not be preserved when the bean is passivated. Fields that are nontransient and nonserializable must be set to `null` before the instance is passivated or the container can destroy the bean, making it unavailable for continued use by the client. References to beans and the `SessionContext` must be automatically preserved with the serialized bean instance by the container so that they can be reconstructed when the bean is activated.

When the client makes a request on an EJB object whose bean is passivated, the container activates the instance. This involves deserializing the bean instance and reconstructing the `SessionContext` reference and bean references held by the instance before it was passivated. When a bean's conversational state has been successfully activated, the `ejbActivate()` method is invoked. The bean instance should open any resources needed and initialize the value of any transient fields within the `ejbActivate()` method. Once `ejbActivate()` is complete, the bean is back in the Method-Ready state and available to service client requests delegated by the EJB object.

The activation of a bean instance follows the rules of Java serialization. The exception to this is transient fields. In Java serialization, transient fields are set to their default values when an object is deserialized; primitive numbers become zero, Booleans `false`, and object references `null`. In EJB, transient fields do not have to be set to their initial values; therefore, they could contain arbitrary values when the bean is activated. The value held by transient fields following activation is unpredictable across vendor implementations, so don't depend on them to be initialized. Instead, use `ejbActivate()` to reset their values.

EJB 1.1 system exceptions

Whenever a system exception is thrown by a bean method, the container invalidates the EJB object and destroys the bean instance. The bean instance moves directly to the Does Not Exist state and the `ejbRemove()` method is *not* invoked.

A system exception is any nonapplication exception including `RemoteException`, `EJBException`, and any unchecked exceptions. Checked exceptions thrown from

---

* References to `SessionContext` or `EntityContext` in a bean class should not be transient. At the time of this writing, however, at least one major vendor *required* that references to `SessionContext` in session beans be transient. This is a proprietary requirement and is noncompliant with the specification.

subsystems are usually wrapped in an EJBException and rethrown as system exceptions. A checked exception thrown by a subsystem does not need to be handled this way if the bean can safely recover from the exception. In most cases, however, the subsystem exception should be rethrown as a EJBException.

8

In this chapter:
- *ACID Transactions*
- *Declarative Transaction Management*
- *Isolation and Database Locking*
- *Non-Transactional Beans*
- *Explicit Transaction Management*
- *Exceptions and Transactions*
- *Transactional Stateful Session Beans*

Transactions

ACID Transactions

To understand how transactions work, we will revisit the TravelAgent bean, a stateful session bean that encapsulates the process of making a cruise reservation for a customer. Here is the TravelAgent's bookPassage() method:

```
public Ticket bookPassage(CreditCard card, double price)
    throws IncompleteConversationalState {
    // EJB 1.0: also throws RemoteException

    if (customer == null || cruise == null || cabin == null){
        throw new IncompleteConversationalState();
    }
    try {
        ReservationHome resHome =
            (ReservationHome) getHome("ReservationHome",ReservationHome.class);
        Reservation reservation =
        resHome.create(customer, cruise, cabin, price);
        ProcessPaymentHome ppHome = (ProcessPaymentHome)
            getHome("ProcessPaymentHome",ProcessPaymentHome.class);
        ProcessPayment process = ppHome.create();
        process.byCredit(customer, card, price);

        Ticket ticket = new Ticket(customer,cruise,cabin,price);
        return ticket;
```

```
    } catch(Exception e) {
        // EJB 1.0: throw new RemoteException("",e);
        throw new EJBException(e);
    }
}
```

The TravelAgent bean is a fairly simple session bean, and its use of other beans is a typical example of business object design and workflow. Unfortunately, good business object design is not enough to make these beans useful in an industrial-strength application. The problem is not with the definition of the beans or the workflow; the problem is that a good design doesn't, in and of itself, guarantee that the TravelAgent's bookPassage() method represents a good *transaction*. To understand why, we will take a closer look at what a transaction means and what criteria a transaction must meet to be considered reliable.

In business, a transaction usually involves an exchange between two parties. When you purchase an ice cream cone, you exchange money for food; when you work for a company, you exchange skill and time for money (which you use to buy more ice cream). When you are involved in these exchanges, you monitor the outcome to ensure that you don't get "ripped off." If you give the ice cream vendor a $20 bill, you don't want him to drive off without giving you your change; you want to make sure that your paycheck reflects all the hours that you worked. By monitoring these commercial exchanges, you are attempting to ensure the reliability of the transactions; you are making sure that the transaction meets everyone's expectations.

In business software, a transaction embodies the concept of a commercial exchange. A business system transaction (transaction for short) is the execution of a *unit-of-work* that accesses one or more shared resources, usually databases. A unit-of-work is a set of activities that relate to each other and must be completed together. The reservation process is a unit-of-work made up of several activities: recording a reservation, debiting a credit card, and generating a ticket together make up a unit-of-work.

Transactions are part of many different types of systems. In each transaction, the objective is the same: to execute a unit-of-work that results in a reliable exchange. Here are some examples of other types of business systems that employ transactions:

ATM
> The ATM (automatic teller machine) you use to deposit, withdraw, and transfer funds, executes these units-of-work as transactions. In an ATM withdrawal, for example, the ATM checks to make sure you don't overdraw and then debits your account and spits out some money.

Online book order

You've probably purchased many of your Java books from an online book-seller—maybe even this book. This type of purchase is also a unit-of-work that takes place as a transaction. In an online book purchase, you submit your credit card number, it is validated, and then a charge is made for price of the book, and an order to ship you the book is sent to the bookseller's warehouse.

Medical system

In a medical system, important data—some of it critical—is recorded about patients every day, including information about clinical visits, medical procedures, prescriptions, and drug allergies. The doctor prescribes the drug, then the system checks for allergies, contraindications, and appropriate dosages. If all tests pass, then the drug can be administered. The tasks just described make up a unit-of-work in a medical system. A unit-of-work in a medical system may not be financial, but it's just as important. A failure to identify a drug allergy in a patient could be fatal.

As you can see, transactions are often complex and usually involve the manipulation of a lot of data. Mistakes in data can cost money, or even a life. Transactions must therefore preserve data integrity, which means that the transaction must work perfectly every time or not be executed at all. This is a pretty tall order, especially for complex systems. As difficult as this requirement is, however, when it comes to commerce there is no room for error. Units-of-work that involve money, or anything of value, always require the utmost reliability because errors impact the revenues and the well-being of the parties involved.

To give you an idea of the accuracy required by transactions, think about what would happen if a transactional system suffered from seemingly infrequent errors. ATMs provide customers with convenient access to their bank accounts and represent a significant percentage of the total transactions in personal banking. The number of transactions handled by ATMs are simple but numerous, providing us with a great example of why transactions must be error proof. Let's say that a bank has 100 ATMs in a metropolitan area, and each ATM processes 300 transactions (deposits, withdrawals, or transfers) a day for a total of 30,000 transactions per day. If each transaction, on average, involves the deposit, withdrawal, or transfer of about $100, about three million dollars would move through the ATM system per day. In the course of a year, that's a little over a billion dollars:

$$(365 \text{ days}) \times (100 \text{ ATMs}) \times (300 \text{ transactions}) \times (\$100.00) = \$1,095,000,000.00$$

How well do the ATMs have to perform in order for them to be considered reliable? For the sake of argument, let's say that ATMs execute transactions correctly 99.99% of the time. This seems to be more than adequate: after all, only one out of every ten thousand transactions executes incorrectly. But over the course of a year, if you do the math, that could result in over $100,000 in errors!

$1,095,000,000.00 × .01% = $109,500.00

Obviously, this is an oversimplification of the problem, but it illustrates that even a small percentage of errors is unacceptable in high-volume or mission-critical systems. For this reason, experts in the field of transaction services have identified four characteristics of a transaction that must be followed in order to say that a system is safe. Transactions must be atomic, consistent, isolated, and durable (ACID)—the four horsemen of transaction services. Here's what each term means:

Atomic

> To be atomic, a transaction must execute completely or not at all. This means that every task within a unit-of-work must execute without error. If any of the tasks fails, the entire unit-of-work or transaction is *aborted*, meaning that changes to the data are undone. If all the tasks execute successfully, the transaction is *committed*, which means that the changes to the data are made permanent or durable.

Consistent

> Consistency is a transactional characteristic that must be enforced by both the transactional system and the application developer. Consistency refers to the integrity of the underlying data store. The transactional system fulfills its obligation in consistency by ensuring that a transaction is atomic, isolated, and durable. The application developer must ensure that the database has appropriate constraints (primary keys, referential integrity, and so forth) and that the unit-of-work, the business logic, doesn't result in inconsistent data (data that is not in harmony with the real world it represents). In an account transfer, for example, a debit to one account must equal the credit to the other account.

Isolated

> A transaction must be allowed to execute without interference from other processes or transactions. In other words, the data that a transaction accesses cannot be affected by any other part of the system until the transaction or unit-of-work is completed.

Durable

> Durability means that all the data changes made during the course of a transaction must be written to some type of physical storage before the transaction is successfully completed. This ensures that the changes are not lost if the system crashes.

To get a better idea of what these principles mean, we will examine the Travel-Agent bean in terms of the four ACID properties.

Is the TravelAgent Bean Atomic?

Our first measure of the TravelAgent bean's reliability is its atomicity: does it ensure that the transaction executes completely or not at all? What we are really concerned with are the critical tasks that change or create information. In the bookPassage() method, a Reservation bean is created, the ProcessPayment bean debits a credit card, and a Ticket object is created. All of these tasks must be successful for the entire transaction to be successful.

To understand the importance of the atomic characteristic, you have to imagine what would happen if even one of the subtasks failed to execute. If, for example, the creation of a Reservation failed but all other tasks succeeded, your customer would probably end up getting bumped from the cruise or sharing the cabin with a stranger. As far as the travel agent is concerned, the bookPassage() method executed successfully because a Ticket was generated. If a ticket is generated without the creation of a reservation, the state of the business system becomes inconsistent with reality because the customer paid for a ticket but the reservation was not recorded. Likewise, if the ProcessPayment bean fails to charge the customer's credit card, the customer gets a free cruise. He may be happy, but management isn't. Finally, if the Ticket is never created, the customer would have no record of the transaction and probably wouldn't be allowed onto the ship.

So the only way bookPassage() can be completed is if all the critical tasks execute successfully. If something goes wrong, the entire process must be aborted. Aborting a transaction requires more than simply not finishing the tasks; in addition, all the tasks that did execute within the transaction must be undone. If, for example, the creation of the Reservation bean and ProcessPayment.byCredit() method succeeded but the creation of the Ticket failed, then the Reservation record and payment records must not be added to the database.

Is the TravelAgent Bean Consistent?

In order for a transaction to be consistent, the state of the business system must make sense after the transaction has completed. In other words, the *state* of the business system must be consistent with the reality of the business. This requires that the transaction enforce the atomic, isolated, and durable characteristics of the transaction, and it also requires diligent enforcement of integrity constraints by the application developer. If, for example, the application developer fails to include the credit card charge operation in the bookPassage() method, the customer would be issued a ticket but would never be charged. The data would be inconsistent with the expectation of the business—a customer should be charged for passage. In addition, the database must be set up to enforce integrity constraints. For example, it should not be possible for a record to be added to the

RESERVATION table unless the CABIN_ID, CRUISE_ID, and CUSTOMER_ID foreign keys map to corresponding records in the CABIN, CRUISE, and CUSTOMER tables, respectively. If a CUSTOMER_ID is used that doesn't map to a CUSTOMER record, referential integrity should cause the database to throw an error message.

Is the TravelAgent Bean Isolated?

If you are familiar with the concept of thread synchronization in Java or row-locking schemes in relational databases, isolation will be a familiar concept. To be isolated, a transaction must protect the data that it is accessing from other transactions. This is necessary to prevent other transactions from interacting with data that is in transition. In the TravelAgent bean, the transaction is isolated to prevent other transactions from modifying the beans that are being updated. Imagine the problems that would arise if separate transactions were allowed to change any entity bean at any time—transactions would walk all over each other. You could easily have several customers book the same cabin because their travel agents happened to make their reservations at the same time.

The isolation of data accessed by beans doesn't mean that the entire application shuts down during a transaction. Only those entity beans and data directly affected by the transaction are isolated. In the TravelAgent bean, for example, the transaction isolates only the Reservation bean created. There can be many Reservation beans in existence; there's no reason these other beans can't be accessed by other transactions.

Is the TravelAgent Bean Durable?

To be durable, the funds transfer must write all changes and new data to a permanent data store before it can be considered successful. While this may seem like a no-brainer, often it isn't what happens in real life. In the name of efficiency, changes are often maintained in memory for long periods of time before being saved on a disk drive. The idea is to reduce disk accesses—which slow systems down—and only periodically write the cumulative effect of data changes. While this approach is great for performance, it is also dangerous because data can be lost when the system goes down and memory is wiped out. Durability requires the system to save all updates made within a transaction as the transaction successfully completes, thus protecting the integrity of the data.

In the TravelAgent bean, this means that the new RESERVATION and PAYMENT records inserted are made persistent before the transaction can complete successfully. Only when the data is made durable are those specific records accessible through their respective beans from other transactions. Hence, durability also plays a role in isolation. A transaction isn't finished until the data is successfully recorded.

Ensuring that transactions adhere to the ACID principles requires careful design. The system has to monitor the progress of a transaction to ensure that it does all its work, that the data is changed correctly, that transactions don't interfere with each other, and that the changes can survive a system crash. Engineering all this functionality into a system is a lot of work, and not something you would want to reinvent for every business system you worked on. Fortunately, EJB is specifically designed to support transactions automatically, making the development of transactional systems easier. The rest of this chapter examines how EJB supports transactions implicitly (through declarative transaction attributes) and explicitly (through the Java Transaction API).

Declarative Transaction Management

One of the primary advantages of Enterprise JavaBeans is that it allows for declarative transaction management. Without this feature, transactions must be controlled using explicit transaction demarcation. This involves the use of fairly complex APIs like the OMG's OTS (Object Transaction Service) or its Java implementation, JTS (Java Transaction Service). Explicit demarcation is difficult for developers to use at best, particularly if you are new to transactional systems. In addition, explicit transaction demarcation requires that the transactional code be written within the business logic, which reduces the clarity of the code and more importantly creates inflexible distributed objects. Once transaction demarcation is "hardcoded" into the business object, changes in transaction behavior require changes to the business logic itself. We talk more about explicit transaction management and EJB later in this chapter.

With EJB's declarative transaction management, the transactional behavior of beans can be controlled using the deployment descriptor, which sets transaction attributes for individual bean methods. This means that the transactional behavior of a bean within an application can be changed easily without changing the bean's business logic. In addition, a bean deployed in one application can be defined with very different transactional behavior than the same bean deployed in a different application. Declarative transaction management reduces the complexity of transactions for bean developers and application developers and makes it easier for you to create robust transactional applications.

Transaction Scope

Transaction scope is a crucial concept for understanding transactions. In this context, transaction scope means those beans—both session and entity—that are participating in a particular transaction.

In the bookPassage() method of the TravelAgent bean, all the beans involved are a part of the same transaction scope. The scope of the transaction starts when a client invokes the TravelAgent bean's bookPassage() method. Once the transaction scope has started, it is *propagated* to both the newly created Reservation bean and the ProcessPayment bean:

```
public Ticket bookPassage(CreditCard card, double price)
    throws IncompleteConversationalState{// EJB 1.0: also throws RemoteException

    if (customer == null || cruise == null || cabin == null) {
        throw new IncompleteConversationalState();
    }
    try {
        ReservationHome resHome =
            (ReservationHome) getHome("ReservationHome",ReservationHome.class);
        Reservation reservation =
        resHome.create(customer, cruise, cabin, price);
        ProcessPaymentHome ppHome = (ProcessPaymentHome)
            getHome("ProcessPaymentHome",ProcessPaymentHome.class);
        ProcessPayment process = ppHome.create();
        process.byCredit(customer, card, price);

        Ticket ticket = new Ticket(customer,cruise,cabin,price);
        return ticket;
    } catch(Exception e) {
        // EJB 1.0: throw new RemoteException("",e);
        throw new EJBException(e);
    }
}
```

As you know, a transaction is a unit-of-work that is made up of one or more tasks. In a transaction, all the tasks that make up the unit-of-work must succeed for the entire transaction to succeed; the transaction must be atomic. If any task fails, the updates made by all the other tasks in the transaction will be rolled back or undone. In EJB, tasks are expressed as bean methods, and a unit-of-work consists of every bean method invoked in a transaction. The scope of a transaction includes every bean that participates in the unit-of-work.

It is easy to trace the scope of a transaction by following the thread of execution. If the invocation of the bookPassage() method begins a transaction, then logically, the transaction ends when the method completes. The scope of the bookPassage() transaction would include the TravelAgent, Reservation, and ProcessPayment beans—every bean touched by the bookPassage() method. A transaction is propagated to a bean when that bean's method is invoked and included in the scope of a transaction.

A transaction can end if an exception is thrown while the bookPassage() method is executing. The exception could be thrown from one of the other beans or from the bookPassage() method itself. An exception may or may not cause a rollback, depending on its type. More about exceptions and transactions later.

The thread of execution isn't the only factor that determines whether a bean is included in the scope of a transaction; the bean's transaction attributes also play a role. Determining whether a bean participates in the transaction scope of any unit-of-work is accomplished either implicitly using EJB's transaction attributes or explicitly using the Java Transaction API (JTA).

Transaction Attributes

As an application developer, you do *not* normally need to control transactions explicitly when using an EJB server. EJB servers can manage transactions implicitly, based on the transaction attributes established for beans at deployment time. The ability to specify how business objects participate in transactions through attribute-based programming is a common characteristic of CTMs, and one of the most important features of the EJB component model.

When an enterprise bean is deployed, you can set its runtime transaction attribute in the deployment descriptor to one of several values. Table 8-1 shows the transaction attributes, the XML attribute values used to specify these transaction attributes in an EJB 1.1 deployment descriptor, and the constants that represent these attributes in an EJB 1.0 deployment descriptor. We'll discuss the meaning of these attributes later in the chapter.

Table 8-1. Transaction Attributes

Transaction Attribute	EJB 1.1 Text Value	EJB 1.0 Constant
Not Supported	NotSupported	TX_NOT_SUPPORTED
Supports	Supports	TX_SUPPORTS
Required	Required	TX_REQUIRED
Requires New	RequiresNew	TX_REQUIRES_NEW
Mandatory	Mandatory	TX_MANDATORY
Never (1.1)	Never	
Bean Managed (1.0)		TX_BEAN_MANAGED

NOTE　　The transaction attributes are declared differently in EJB 1.1 and EJB 1.0. In EJB 1.1, they are text values declared without spaces between words as shown in the "EJB 1.1 Text Value" column. In the EJB 1.0 deployment descriptors, transaction attributes are upper-case constants as shown in the "EJB 1.0 Constant" column. In this book we use the natural language format shown in the first column of Table 8-1 (words are separated by spaces), which maps to either the EJB 1.1 or EJB 1.0 declarations.

Using transaction attributes simplifies building transactional applications by reducing the risks associated with improper use of transactional protocols like JTA (discussed later in this chapter). It's more efficient and easier to use transaction attributes than to control transactions explicitly.

It is possible to set a transaction attribute for the entire bean (in which case, it applies to all methods) or to set different transaction attributes for individual methods. The former is much simpler and less error prone, but setting attributes at the method level offers more flexibility. The code fragments in the following sections show how the default transaction attribute of a bean can be set in the bean's deployment descriptor.

EJB 1.1: Setting a transaction attribute

In EJB 1.1, a <container-transaction> element specifies the transaction attributes for the beans described in the deployment descriptor:

```
<ejb-jar>
  ...
  <assembly-descriptor>
    ...
    <container-transaction>
       <method>
           <ejb-name>TravelAgentBean</ejb-name>
           <method-name> * </method-name>
       </method>
       <trans-attribute>Required</trans-attribute>
    </container-transaction>
    <container-transaction>
       <method>
           <ejb-name>TravelAgentBean</ejb-name>
           <method-name>listAvailableCabins</method-name>
       </method>
       <trans-attribute>Supports</trans-attribute>
    </container-transaction>
    ...
  </assembly-descriptor>
  ...
</ejb-jar>
```

This deployment descriptor specifies the transaction attributes for the TravelAgent bean. The <container-transaction> element specifies a method and the transaction attribute that should be applied to that method. The first <container-transaction> element specifies that all methods by default have a transaction attribute of Required; the * is a wildcard that indicates all of the methods of the TravelAgent bean. The second <container-transaction> element overrides the default setting to specify that the listAvailableCabins() method will have a Supports transaction attribute. Note that we have to specify which bean we're referring to with the <ejb-name> element; an XML deployment descriptor can cover many beans.

EJB 1.0: Setting a transaction attribute

EJB 1.0 uses a control descriptor object within the deployment descriptor to set transaction attributes:

```
ControlDescriptor cd = new ControlDescriptor();
cd.setMethod(null);
cd.setTransactionAttribute(ControlDescriptor.TX_NOT_SUPPORTED);
ControlDescriptor [] cdArray = {cd};
sd.setControlDescriptors(cdArray);
```

The null argument to setMethod() means that the ControlDescriptor applies to the entire bean. To set the transaction attributes for a specific method, change the argument passed into setMethod() from null to a java.lang.reflect.Method object representing a business method in the bean class. Here is an example of how this might work:

```
ControlDescriptor cd = new ControlDescriptor();
Class [] parameters = new Class[0];
Method method = ShipBean.class.getDeclaredMethod("getName",parameters);
cd.setMethod(method);
cd.setTransactionAttribute(ControlDescriptor.TX_NOT_SUPPORTED);
ControlDescriptor [] cdArray = {cd};
sd.setControlDescriptors(cdArray);
```

Transaction Attributes Defined

Here are the definitions of the transaction attributes identified in the table of transaction attributes (Table 8-1). In a few of the definitions, we say that the client transaction is *suspended*. This means that the transaction is not propagated to the bean method being invoked; propagation of the transaction is temporarily halted until the bean method returns.

Not Supported

Invoking a method on a bean with this transaction attribute suspends the transaction until the method is completed. This means that the transaction scope is not propagated to the *Not Supported* bean or any of the beans it calls. Once the method on the *Not Supported* bean is done, the original transaction resumes its execution.

Figure 8-1 shows that a *Not Supported* bean does not propagate the client transaction when one of its methods is invoked.

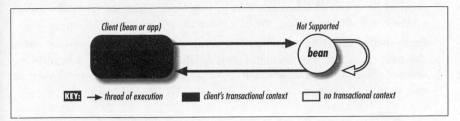

Figure 8-1. Not Supported attribute

Supports

This attribute means that the bean method will be included in the transaction scope if it is invoked within a transaction. In other words, if the bean or client that invokes the *Supports* bean is part of a transaction scope, the *Supports* bean and all beans accessed by that bean become part of the original transaction. However, the *Supports* bean doesn't have to be part of a transaction and can interact with clients and beans that are not included in a transaction scope.

Figure 8-2(a) shows the *Supports* bean being invoked by a transactional client and propagating the transaction. Figure 8-2(b) shows the *Supports* bean being invoked from a non-transactional client.

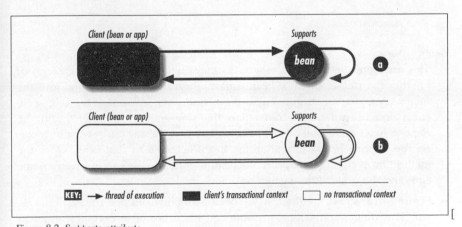

Figure 8-2. Supports attribute

Required

This attribute means that the bean method must be invoked within the scope of a transaction. If the calling client or bean is part of a transaction, the *Required* bean is automatically included in its transaction scope. If, however, the calling client or bean is not involved in a transaction, the *Required* bean starts its own new transaction. The new transaction's scope covers only the

Required bean and all beans accessed by that bean. Once the method invoked on the *Required* bean is done, the new transaction's scope ends.

Figure 8-3(a) shows the *Required* bean being invoked by a transactional client and propagating the transaction. Figure 8-3(b) shows the *Required* bean being invoked from a non-transactional client, which causes the *Required* bean to start its own transaction.

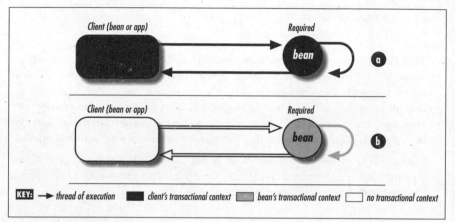

Figure 8-3. Required attribute

Requires New

> This attribute means that a new transaction is always started. Regardless of whether the calling client or bean is part of a transaction, a method with the *Requires New* attribute begins a new transaction when invoked. If the calling client is already involved in a transaction, that transaction is suspended until the *Requires New* bean's method call returns. The new transaction's scope only covers the *Requires New* bean and all the beans accessed by that bean. Once the method invoked on the *Requires New* bean is done, the new transaction's scope ends and the original transaction resumes.

> Figure 8-4(a) shows the *Requires New* bean being invoked by a transactional client. The client's transaction is suspended while the bean executes under its own transaction. Figure 8-4(b) shows the *Requires New* bean being invoked from a non-transactional client; the *Requires New* executes under its own transaction.

Mandatory

> This attribute means that the bean method must always be made part of the transaction scope of the calling client. If the calling client or bean is not part

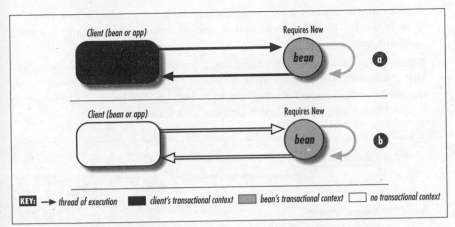

Figure 8-4. Requires New attribute

of a transaction, the invocation will fail, throwing a `javax.transaction.`
`TransactionRequiredException`.

Figure 8-5(a) shows the `Mandatory` bean being invoked by a transactional client and propagating the transaction. Figure 8-5(b) shows the *Mandatory* bean being invoked from a non-transactional client; the method throws the `Trans-actionRequiredException` because there is no transaction scope.

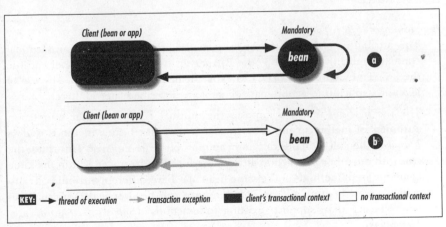

Figure 8-5. Mandatory attribute

Never (EJB 1.1 only)

This attribute means that the bean method must never be invoked within the scope of a transaction. If the calling client or bean is part of a transaction, the

Never bean will throw a `RemoteException`. If, however, the calling client or bean is not involved in a transaction, the *Never* bean will execute normally without a transaction.

Figure 8-6(a) shows the *Never* bean being invoked by a non-transactional client. Figure 8-6(b) shows the *Never* bean being invoked by transactional client; the method throws the `RemoteException` because the method can never be invoked by a client or bean that is included in a transaction.

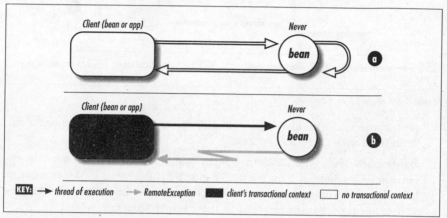

Figure 8-6. Never attribute

Bean Managed (EJB 1.0 only)

This attribute means that the bean or method doesn't have its transactional context implicitly managed by the EJB server. Instead, the developer can use the Java Transaction API (JTA) to explicitly manage transactions. The use of JTA and explicit transaction management are described later in this chapter.

The use of *Bean Managed* imposes the unusual restriction that transaction attributes of methods cannot be mixed. If one of a bean's methods is *Bean Managed*, then all methods of that bean must be *Bean Managed*. This is not the case with the other transaction attributes, which can be mixed within the same bean: different methods of the same bean may have different attributes. Transactions created within a *Bean Managed* bean can be propagated normally to other beans that support existing transactions (*Supports*, *Required*, and *Mandatory*).

How are bean-managed transactions supported in EJB 1.1? We'll discuss this in more detail later in the chapter. For the time being, it's enough to say that only session beans are allowed to manage transactions explicitly; entity beans cannot. The deployment descriptor of a session bean can have a transaction-type element that specifies whether the bean manages its own transactions.

Figure 8-7(a) shows the *Bean Managed* bean being invoked by a transactional client. The client's transaction is suspended while the bean executes under its own transaction. Figure 8-7(b) shows the *Bean Managed* bean being invoked from a non-transactional client; the *Bean Managed* bean executes under its own transaction.

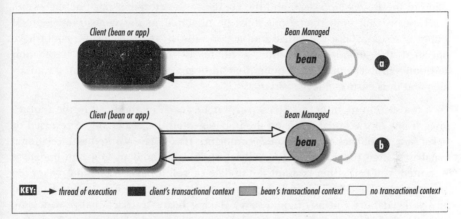

Figure 8-7. Bean Managed attribute

Transaction Propagation

To illustrate the impact of transaction attributes on bean methods, we'll look once again at the bookPassage() method of the TravelAgent bean created in Chapter 7:

```
public Ticket bookPassage(CreditCard card, double price)
throws IncompleteConversationalState{// EJB 1.0: also throws RemoteException

    if (customer == null || cruise == null || cabin == null) {
        throw new IncompleteConversationalState();
    }
    try {
        ReservationHome resHome =
            (ReservationHome) getHome("ReservationHome",ReservationHome.class);
        Reservation reservation =
        resHome.create(customer, cruise, cabin, price);
        ProcessPaymentHome ppHome = (ProcessPaymentHome)
            getHome("ProcessPaymentHome",ProcessPaymentHome.class);
        ProcessPayment process = ppHome.create();
        process.byCredit(customer, card, price);
```

```
            Ticket ticket = new Ticket(customer,cruise,cabin,price);
            return ticket;
        } catch(Exception e) {
            // EJB 1.0: throw new RemoteException("",e);
            throw new EJBException(e);
        }
    }
```

In order for bookPassage() to execute as a successful transaction, both the creation of the Reservation bean and the charge to the customer must be successful. This means that both operations must be included in the same transaction. If either operation fails, the entire transaction fails. In these beans, we could have specified the *Required* transaction attribute as the default. This transaction attribute enforces our desired policy that all beans must execute within a transaction and thus ensures data consistency.

As a transaction monitor, an EJB server watches each method call in the transaction. If any of the updates fail, all the updates to all the beans will be reversed or *rolled back*. A rollback is like an *undo* command. If you have worked with relational databases, then the concept of a rollback should be familiar. Once an update is executed, you can either commit the update or roll it back. A commit makes the changes requested by the update permanent; a rollback aborts the update and leaves the database in its original state. Making beans transactional provides the same kind of rollback/commit control. For example, if the Reservation bean cannot be created, the charge made by the ProcessPayment bean is rolled back. Transactions make updates an all-or-nothing proposition. This ensures that the unit-of-work, like the bookPassage() method, executes as intended, and it prevents inconsistent data from being written to databases.

In cases where the container implicitly manages the transaction, the commit and rollback decisions are handled automatically. When transactions are managed explicitly within a bean or by the client, the responsibility falls on the bean or application developer to commit or roll back a transaction. Explicit demarcation of transactions is covered in detail later in this chapter.

Let's assume that the TravelAgent bean is created and used on a client as follows:

```
TravelAgent agent = agentHome.create(customer);
agent.setCabinID(cabin_id);
agent.setCruiseID(cruise_id):
try {
    agent.bookPassage(card,price);
} catch(Exception e) {
    System.out.println("Transaction failed!");
}
```

Furthermore, let's assume that the bookPassage() method has been given the transaction attribute *Requires New*. In this case, the client that invokes the bookPassage() method is not itself part of a transaction. When bookPassage() is invoked on the TravelAgent bean, a new transaction is created, as required by the *Requires New* attribute. This means that the TravelAgent bean registers itself with the EJB server's transaction manager, which will manage the transaction automatically. The transaction manager coordinates transactions, propagating the transaction scope from one bean to the next to ensure that all beans touched by a transaction are included in the transaction's unit-of-work. That way, the transaction manager can monitor the updates made by each bean and decide, based on the success of those updates, whether to commit all changes made by all beans to the database or roll them all back. If a *system exception* is thrown by the bookPassage() method, the transaction is automatically rolled back. We will talk more about exceptions later in this chapter.

NOTE   In EJB 1.0, where the transaction scope begins and ends with the bookPassage() method, an application exception thrown by bookPassage() also causes a transaction rollback.

When the byCredit() method is invoked within the bookPassage() method, the ProcessPayment bean registers with the manager under the transactional context that was created for the TravelAgent bean; the transactional context is propagated to the ProcessPayment bean. When the new Reservation bean is created, it is also registered with the manager under the same transaction. When all the beans are registered and their updates made, the transaction manager checks to ensure that their updates will work. If all the updates will work, then the manager allows the changes to become permanent. If one of the beans reports an error or fails, any changes made by either the ProcessPayment or Reservation bean are rolled back by the manager. Figure 8-8 illustrates the propagation and management of the TravelAgent bean's transactional context.

In addition to managing transactions in its own environment, an EJB server can coordinate with other transactional systems. If, for example, the ProcessPayment bean actually came from a different EJB server than the TravelAgent bean, the two EJB servers would cooperate to manage the transaction as one unit-of-work. This is called a *distributed transaction.**

A distributed transaction is a great deal more complicated, requiring what is called a *two-phase commit* (2-PC or TPC). 2-PC is a mechanism that allows transactions to be managed across different servers and databases. The details of a 2-PC are beyond the scope of this book, but a system that supports it will not require any

---

* Not all EJB servers support distributed transactions.

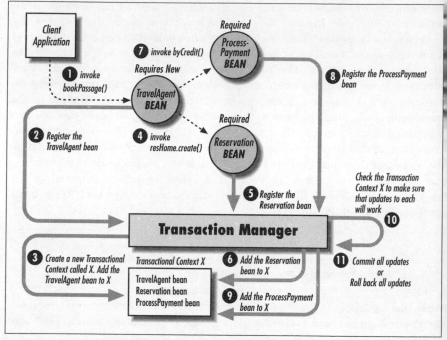

Figure 8-8. Managing the TravelAgent bean's transactional context

extra operations by a bean or application developer. If distributed transactions are supported, the protocol for propagating transactions, as discussed earlier, will be supported. In other words, as an application or bean developer, you should not notice a difference between local and distributed transactions.

Isolation and Database Locking

Transaction isolation (the "I" in ACID) is a critical part of any transactional system. This section explains isolation conditions, database locking, and transaction isolation levels. These concepts are important when deploying any transactional system.

Dirty, Repeatable, and Phantom Reads

Transaction isolation is defined in terms of isolation conditions called *dirty reads*, *repeatable reads*, and *phantom reads*. These conditions describe what can happen when two or more transactions operate on the same data.*

---

* Isolation conditions are covered in detail by the ANSI SQL-92 Specification, Document Number: ANSI X3.135-1992 (R1998).

To illustrate these conditions, let's think about two separate client applications using their own instances of the TravelAgent to access the same data—specifically, a cabin record with the primary key of 99. These examples revolve around the RESERVATION table, which is accessed by both the bookPassage() method (through the Reservation bean) and the listAvailableCabins() method (through JDBC). It might be a good idea to go back to Chapter 7 and review how the RESERVATION table is accessed through these methods. This will help you to understand how two transactions executed by two different clients can impact each other. Assume that both methods have a transaction attribute of *Required*.

Dirty reads

A dirty read occurs when the first transaction reads uncommitted changes made by a second transaction. If the second transaction is rolled back, the data read by the first transaction becomes invalid because the rollback undoes the changes. The first transaction won't be aware that the data it has read has become invalid. Here's a scenario showing how a dirty read can occur (illustrated in Figure 8-9):

1. Time 10:00:00: Client 1 executes the TravelAgent.bookPassage() method on its bean. Along with the Customer and Cruise beans, Client 1 had previously chosen Cabin 99 to be included in the reservation.

2. Time 10:00:01: Client 1 creates a Reservation bean within the bookPassage() method. The Reservation bean's create() method inserts a record into the RESERVATION table, which reserves Cabin 99.

3. Time 10:00:02: Client 2 executes TravelAgent.listAvailableCabins(). Cabin 99 has been reserved by Client 1, so it is *not* in the list of available cabins that are returned from this method.

4. Time 10:00:03: Client 1 executes the ProcessPayment.byCredit() method within the bookPassage() method. The byCredit() method throws an exception because the expiration date on the credit card has passed.

5. Time 10:00:04: The exception thrown by the ProcessPayment bean causes the entire bookPassage() transaction to be rolled back. As a result, the record inserted into the RESERVATION table when the Reservation bean was created is not made durable (it is removed). Cabin 99 is now available.

Client 2 is now using an invalid list of available cabins because Cabin 99 is available but is not included in the list. This would be serious if Cabin 99 was the last available cabin because Client 2 would inaccurately report that the cruise was booked. The customer would presumably try to book a cruise on a competing cruise line.

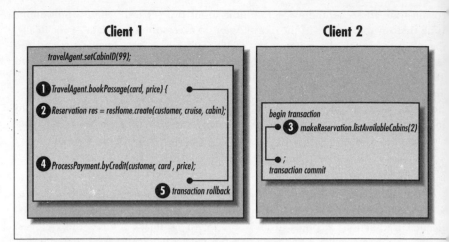

Figure 8-9. A dirty read

Repeatable reads

A repeatable read is when the data read is guaranteed to look the same if read again during the same transaction. Repeatable reads are guaranteed in one of two ways: either the data read is locked against changes or the data read is a snapshot that doesn't reflect changes. If the data is locked, then it cannot be changed by any other transaction until this transaction ends. If the data is a snapshot, then other transactions can change the data, but these changes won't be seen by this transaction if the read is repeated. Here's an example of a repeatable read (illustrated in Figure 8-10):

1. Time 10:00:00: Client 1 begins an explicit `javax.transaction.User-Transaction`.

2. Time 10:00:01: Client 1 executes `TravelAgent.listAvailableCabins(2)`, asking for a list of available cabins that have two beds. Cabin 99 *is* in the list of available cabins.

3. Time 10:00:02: Client 2 is working with an interface that manages Cabin beans. Client 2 attempts to change the bed count on Cabin 99 from 2 to 3.

4. Time 10:00:03: Client 1 re-executes the `TravelAgent.listAvailableCabins(2)`. Cabin 99 is *still* in the list of available cabins.

This example is somewhat unusual because it uses `javax.transaction.User-Transaction`. This class is covered in more detail later in this chapter; essentially it allows a client application to control the scope of a transaction explicitly. In this case, Client 1 places transaction boundaries around both calls to listAvailable-

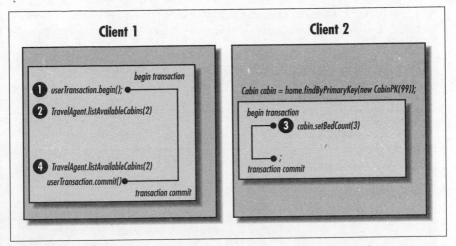

Figure 8-10. Repeatable read

Cabins(), so that they are a part of the same transaction. If Client 1 didn't do this, the two listAvailableCabins() methods would have executed as separate transactions and our repeatable read condition would not have occurred.

Although Client 2 attempted to change the bed count for Cabin 99 to 3, Cabin 99 still shows up in the Client 1 call to listAvailableCabins() when a bed count of 2 is requested. This is because either Client 2 was prevented from making the change (because of a lock), or Client 2 was able to make the change, but Client 1 is working with a snapshot of the data that doesn't reflect that change.

A *nonrepeatable read* is when the data retrieved in a subsequent read within the same transaction can return different results. In other words, the subsequent read can see the changes made by other transactions.

Phantom reads

Phantom reads occur when new records added to the database are detectable by transactions that started prior to the insert. Queries will include records added by other transactions after their transaction has started. Here's a scenario that includes a phantom read (illustrated in Figure 8-11):

1. Time 10:00:00: Client 1 begins an explicit javax.transaction.User-Transaction.

2. Time 10:00:01: Client 1 executes TravelAgent.listAvailableCabins(2), asking for a list of available cabins that have two beds. Cabin 99 *is* in the list of available cabins.

3. Time 10:00:02: Client 2 executes bookPassage() and creates a Reservation bean. The reservation inserts a new record into the RESERVATION table, reserving cabin 99.

4. Time 10:00:03: Client 1 re-executes the TravelAgent.listAvailableCabins(2). Cabin 99 is no longer in the list of available cabins.

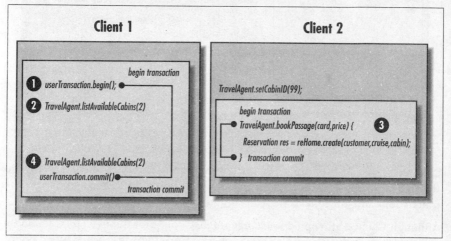

Figure 8-11. Phantom read

Client 1 places transaction boundaries around both calls to listAvailable-Cabins(), so that they are a part of the same transaction. In this case, the reservation was made between the listAvailableCabins() queries in the same transaction. Therefore, the record inserted in the RESERVATION table didn't exist when the first listAvailableCabins() method is invoked, but it does exist and is visible when the second listAvailableCabins() method is invoked. The record inserted is a *phantom record*.

Database Locks

Databases, especially relational databases, normally use several different locking techniques. The most common are *read locks*, *write locks*, and *exclusive write locks*. (I've taken the liberty of adding "snapshots," although this isn't a formal term.) These locking mechanisms control how transactions access data concurrently. Locking mechanisms impact the read conditions that were just described. These types of locks are simple concepts that are not directly addressed in the EJB specification. Database vendors implement these locks differently, so you should understand how your database addresses these locking mechanisms to best predict how the isolation levels described in this section will work.

Read locks

Read locks prevent other transactions from changing data read during a transaction until the transaction ends, thus preventing nonrepeatable reads. Other transactions can read the data but not write it. The current transaction is also prohibited from making changes. Whether a read lock locks only the records read, a block of records, or a whole table depends on the database being used.

Write locks

Write locks are used for updates. A write lock prevents other transactions from changing the data until the current transaction is complete. A write lock allows dirty reads, by other transactions and by the current transaction itself. In other words, the transaction can read its own uncommitted changes.

Exclusive write locks

Exclusive write locks are used for updates. An exclusive write lock prevents other transactions from reading or changing data until the current transaction is complete. An exclusive write lock prevents dirty reads by other transactions. Other transactions are not allowed to read the data while it is exclusively locked. Some databases do not allow transactions to read their own data while it is exclusively locked.

Snapshots

Some databases get around locking by providing every transaction with its own *snapshot* of the data. A snapshot is a frozen view of the data that is taken when the transaction begins. Snapshots can prevent dirty reads, nonrepeatable reads, and phantom reads. Snapshots can be problematic because the data is not real-time; it is old the instant the snapshot is taken.

Transaction Isolation Levels

Transaction isolation is defined in terms of the isolation conditions (*dirty reads, repeatable reads,* and *phantom reads*). Isolation levels are commonly used in database systems to describe how locking is applied to data within a transaction.* The following terms are usually used to discuss isolation levels:

Read Uncommitted

The transaction can read uncommitted data (data changed by a different transaction that is still in progress).

Dirty reads, nonrepeatable reads, and phantom reads can occur. Bean methods with this isolation level can read uncommitted change.

---

* Isolation conditions are covered in detail by ANSI SQL-92 Specification, Document Number: ANSI X3. 135-1992 (R1998).

Read Committed

> The transaction cannot read uncommitted data; data that is being changed by a different transaction cannot be read.
>
> Dirty reads are prevented; nonrepeatable reads and phantom reads can occur. Bean methods with this isolation level cannot read uncommitted data.

Repeatable Read

> The transaction cannot change data that is being read by a different transaction.
>
> Dirty reads and nonrepeatable reads are prevented; phantom reads can occur. Bean methods with this isolation level have the same restrictions as *Read Committed* and can only execute repeatable reads.

Serializable

> The transaction has exclusive read and update privileges to data; different transactions can neither read nor write the same data.
>
> Dirty reads, nonrepeatable reads, and phantom reads are prevented. This isolation level is the most restrictive.

These isolation levels are the same as those defined for JDBC. Specifically, they map to the static final variables in the `java.sql.Connection` class. The behavior modeled by the isolation levels in the connection class is the same as the behavior described here.

The exact behavior of these isolation levels depends largely on the locking mechanism used by the underlying database or resource. How the isolation levels work depends in large part on how your database supports them.

EJB 1.1 transaction isolation control

In EJB 1.1, isolation levels are not controlled through declarative attributes, as was the case in EJB 1.0. In EJB 1.1, the deployer sets transaction isolation levels if the container manages the transaction. The bean developer sets the transaction isolation level if the bean manages the transaction. Up to this point we have only discussed container-managed transactions; bean-managed transactions are discussed later in this chapter.

EJB 1.0 transaction isolation control

EJB 1.0 describes four isolation levels that can be assigned to the methods of a bean in the `ControlDescriptor`. We did this several times when we created control descriptors for all the beans we developed in this book. Here is a snippet of code from the MakeDD class used to create the *TravelAgentDD.ser* in Chapter 7, showing how we set the isolation level:

```
ControlDescriptor cd = new ControlDescriptor();
cd.setIsolationLevel(ControlDescriptor.TRANSACTION_SERIALIZABLE);
cd.setMethod(null);
ControlDescriptor [] cdArray = {cd};
sd.setControlDescriptors(cdArray);
```

In our example so far, we have always used the isolation level ControlDescrip-tor.TRANSACTION_SERIALIZABLE, the most restrictive isolation level. Table 8-2 shows the transaction isolation levels and their corresponding attribute in the ControlDescriptor class.

Table 8-2. Isolation Level Attributes in EJB 1.0

Isolation Level	ControlDescriptor Constant
Read Committed	TRANSACTION_READ_COMMITTED
Read Uncommitted	TRANSACTION_READ_UNCOMMITTED
Repeatable Read	TRANSACTION_REPEATABLE_READ
Serializable	TRANSACTION_SERIALIZABLE

You are allowed to specify isolation levels on a per-method basis, but this flexibility comes with an important restriction: all methods invoked in the same transaction must have the same isolation level. You can't mix isolation levels within transactions at runtime.

Balancing Performance Against Consistency

Generally speaking, as the isolation levels become more restrictive, the performance of the system decreases because more restrictive isolation levels prevent transactions from accessing the same data. If isolation levels are very restrictive, like *Serializable*, then all transactions, even simple reads, must wait in line to execute. This can result in a system that is very slow. EJB systems that process a large number of concurrent transactions and need to be very fast will therefore avoid the *Serializable* isolation level where it is not necessary, since it will be prohibitively slow.

Isolation levels, however, also enforce consistency of data. More restrictive isolation levels help ensure that invalid data is not used for performing updates. The old adage "garbage in, garbage out" applies here. The *Serializable* isolation level ensures that data is never accessed concurrently by transactions, thus ensuring that the data is always consistent.

Choosing the correct isolation level requires some research about the database you are using and how it handles locking. You must also balance the performance needs of your system against consistency. This is not a cut-and-dried process, because different applications use data differently.

Although there are only three ships in Titan's system, the beans that represent them are included in most of Titan's transactions. This means that many, possibly hundreds, of transactions will be accessing these Ship beans at the same time. Access to Ship beans needs to be fast or it becomes a bottleneck, so we do not want to use very restrictive isolation levels. At the same time, the ship data also needs to be consistent; otherwise, hundreds of transactions will be using invalid data. Therefore, we need to use a strong isolation level when making changes to ship information. To accommodate these conflicting requirements, we can apply different isolation levels to different methods.

Most transactions use the Ship bean's get methods to obtain information. This is *read-only* behavior, so the isolation level for the get methods can be very low, such as *Read Uncommitted*. The set methods of the ship bean are almost never used; the name of the ship probably wouldn't change for years. However, the data changed by the set methods must be isolated to prevent dirty reads by other transactions, so we will use the most restrictive isolation level, *Serializable*, on the ship's set methods. By using different isolation levels on different business methods, we can balance consistency against performance.

EJB 1.1: Controlling isolation levels

Different EJB servers allow different levels of granularity for setting isolation levels; some servers defer this responsibility to the database. In some servers, you may be able to set different isolation levels for different methods, while other products may require the same isolation level for all methods in a bean, or possibly even all beans in the container. You will need to consult your vendor's documentation to find out the level of control your server offers.

Bean-managed transactions in stateful session beans, however, allow the bean developer to specify the transaction isolation level using the API of the resource providing persistent storage. The JDBC API, for example, provides a mechanism for specifying the isolation level of the database connection. The following code shows how this is done. Bean-managed transactions are covered in more detail later in this chapter.

```
DataSource source = (javax.sql.DataSource)
    jndiCntxt.lookup("java:comp/env/jdbc/titanDB");

Connection con = source.getConnection();
con.setTransactionIsolation(Connection.TRANSACTION_SERIALIZABLE);
...
```

You can set the isolation level to be different for different databases within the same transaction, but all beans that use the same database in a transaction should use the same isolation level.

EJB 1.0: Controlling isolation levels

The following code, taken from a deployment descriptor for a Ship bean, shows one way to assign these isolation levels:

```
Method [] methods = new Method[6];

Class [] parameters = new Class[0];
methods[ 0 ] = ShipBean.class.getDeclaredMethod("getName",parameters);
methods[ 1 ] = ShipBean.class.getDeclaredMethod("getTonnage",parameters);
methods[ 2 ] = ShipBean.class.getDeclaredMethod("getCapacity",parameters);

parameters = new Class[1];

parameters[0] = String.class;
methods[ 3 ] = ShipBean.class.getDeclaredMethod("setName",parameters);
parameters[0] = Double.TYPE;
methods[ 4 ] = ShipBean.class.getDeclaredMethod("setTonnage",parameters);
parameters[0] = Integer.TYPE;
methods[ 5 ] = ShipBean.class.getDeclaredMethod("setCapacity",parameters);

ControlDescriptor [] cds = new ControlDescriptor[methods.length];

for (int i = 0; i < methods.length; i++) {
    cds[i] = new ControlDescriptor(methods[i]);
    if (methods[i].getReturnType() == Void.TYPE) {
        // Set methods all return void.
        cds[i].setIsolationLevel(
            ControlDescriptor.TRANSACTION_SERIALIZABLE);
    }
    else {
        // Get methods don't return void.
        cds[i].setIsolationLevel(
            ControlDescriptor.TRANSACTION_READ_UNCOMMITTED);
    }
    cds[i].setRunAsMode(ControlDescriptor.CLIENT_IDENTITY);
    cds[i].setTransactionAttribute(ControlDescriptor.TX_REQUIRED);
}

    shipDD.setControlDescriptors(cds);
```

This code takes all the set methods in the Ship interface that are used to make updates (setName(), setCapacity(), setTonnage()) and gives them an isolation level of TRANSACTION_SERIALIZABLE. For the get methods (getName(), getCapacity(), getTonnage()), which are used for reading data, the isolation level is set to TRANSACTION_READ_UNCOMMITTED.

NOTE   Remember that all bean methods invoked in the same transaction
              must have the same isolation level.

Understanding the effect of isolation levels on your code's behavior is crucial to balancing performance against consistency. In EJB 1.0, all the bean methods invoked within the same transaction must have the same isolation level. In the TravelAgent bean, for example, every method invoked on every bean within the scope of the bookPassage() method must have the same transaction isolation level. Any method invoked with a different isolation level will throw a java.rmi. RemoteException. Therefore, mixing isolation levels across beans (specifying different isolation levels for different beans within your application) must be done with care and only in those circumstances when methods with different isolation levels will never need to be executed in the same transaction.

Non-Transactional Beans

Beans that reside outside a transaction scope normally provide some kind of stateless service that doesn't directly manipulate data in a data store. While these types of beans may be necessary as utilities during a transaction, they do not need to meet the stringent ACID requirements of a transaction.

Consider a non-transactional stateless session bean, the QuoteBean, that provides live stock quotes. This bean may respond to a request from a transactional bean involved in a stock purchase transaction. The success or failure of the stock purchase, as a transaction, will not impact the state or operations of the QuoteBean, so it doesn't need to be part of the transaction. Beans that are involved in transactions are subjected to the isolated ACID property, which means that their services *cannot* be shared during the life of the transaction. Making a bean transactional is an expensive runtime activity. Declaring a bean to be non-transactional (i.e., *Not Supported*) leaves it out of the transaction scope, which improves the performance and availability of that service.

Explicit Transaction Management

NOTE   Although this section covers JTA, it is strongly recommended that
              you do not attempt to manage transactions explicitly. Through trans-
              action attributes, EJB provides a comprehensive and simple mecha-
              nism for delimiting transactions at the method level and propagat-
              ing transactions automatically. Only developers with a thorough
              understanding of transactional systems should attempt to use JTA
              with EJB.

In EJB, implicit transaction management is provided on the bean method level so that we can define transactions that are delimited by the scope of the method being executed. This is one of the primary advantages of EJB over cruder distributed object implementations: it reduces complexity and therefore programmer error. In addition, declarative transaction demarcation, as used in EJB, separates the transactional behavior from the business logic; a change to transactional behavior does not require changes to the business logic. In rare situations, however, it may be necessary to take control of transactions explicitly. To do this, it is necessary to have a much more complete understanding of transactions.

Explicit management of transactions is complex and is normally accomplished using the OMG's OTS (Object Transaction Service) or the Java implementation of OTS, JTS (Java Transaction Service). OTS and JTS provide APIs that allow developers to work with transaction managers and resources (databases) directly. While the JTS implementation of OTS is robust and complete, it is not the easiest API to work with; it requires clean and intentional control over the bounds of enrollment in transactions.

Enterprise JavaBeans supports a much simpler API, the Java Transaction API (JTA), for working with transactions.* This API is implemented by the javax. transaction package. JTA actually consists of two components: a high-level transactional client interface and a low-level X/Open XA interface. We are concerned with the high-level client interface since that is the one accessible to the beans and is the recommended transactional interface for client applications. The low-level XA interface is used by the EJB server and container to automatically coordinate transactions with resources like databases.

As an application and bean developer, you will not work with the XA interface in JTA. Instead, your use of explicit transaction management will focus on one very simple interface: javax.transaction.UserTransaction. UserTransaction provides an interface to the transaction manager that allows the application developer to manage the scope of a transaction explicitly. Here is an example of how explicit demarcation might be used in a bean or client application:

```
// EJB 1.0: Use native casting instead of narrow()
Object ref = getInitialContext().lookup("travelagent.Home");
TravelAgentHome home = (TravelAgentHome)
    PortableRemoteObject.narrow(ref,TravelAgentHome.class);

TravelAgent tr1 = home.create(customer);
tr1.setCruiseID(cruiseID);
tr1.setCabinID(cabin_1);
```

* Enterprise JavaBeans 1.0 originally specified JTS as the transitional API for explicit demarcation. JTA, which was released after EJB, is the preferred API in both EJB 1.0 and EJB 1.1. Both JTS and JTA, however, use the UserTransaction interface, and so the information here is applicable to servers that support either API.

```
TravelAgent tr2 = home.create(customer);
tr2.setCruiseID(cruiseID);
tr2.setCabinID(cabin_2);

javax.transaction.UserTransaction tran = ...; // Get the UserTransaction.
tran.begin();
tr1.bookPassage(visaCard,price);
tr2.bookPassage(visaCard,price);
tran.commit();
```

The client application needs to book two cabins for the same customer—in this case, the customer is purchasing a cabin for himself and his children. The customer doesn't want to book either cabin unless he can get both, so the client application is designed to include both bookings in the same transaction. Explicitly marking the transaction's boundaries through the use of the javax. transaction.UserTransaction object does this. Each bean method invoked by the current thread between the UserTransaction.begin() and UserTransaction.commit() method is included in the same transaction scope, according to transaction attribute of the bean methods invoked.

Obviously this example is contrived, but the point it makes is clear. Transactions can be controlled directly, instead of depending on method scope to delimit them. The advantage of using explicit transaction demarcation is that it gives the client control over the bounds of a transaction. The client, in this case, may be a client application or another bean.* In either case, the same javax.transaction.UserTransaction is used, but it is obtained from different sources depending on whether it is needed on the client or in a bean class.

EJB 1.1: how client applications obtain the UserTransaction object

Java 2 Enterprise Edition (J2EE) specifies how a client application can obtain a UserTransaction object using JNDI. Here's how a client obtains a UserTransaction object if the EJB 1.1 container is part of a J2EE system:

```
...
Context jndiCntx = new InitialContext();
UserTransaction tran =
    (UserTransaction)jndiCntx.lookup("java:comp/UserTransaction");

utx.begin();
...
utx.commit();
...
```

J2EE and its relationship with EJB 1.1 is covered in more detail in Chapter 11.

---

* Only beans declared as managing their own transactions (bean-managed transaction beans) can use the UserTransaction interface.

EJB 1.0: how client applications obtain the UserTransaction object

EJB 1.0 doesn't specify how client applications should obtain a reference to a `UserTransaction`. Many vendors make the `UserTransaction` available to the client application through JNDI. Here's how a client application obtains a `UserTransaction` using JNDI:

```
UserTransaction ut = (UserTransaction)
        jndiContext.lookup("javax.transaction.UserTransaction");
```

EJB servers may use other mechanisms, such as a proprietary API or casting the home interface into a `UserTransaction`.

Beans can also manage transactions explicitly. In EJB 1.1, only session beans with the `<transaction-type>` value of "Bean" can be bean-managed transaction beans. Entity beans can never be bean-managed transaction beans. Beans that manage their own transactions do not declare transaction attributes for their methods. Here's how an EJB 1.1 session bean declares that it will manage transactions explicitly:

```
<ejb-jar>
 <enterprise-beans>
  ...
  <session>
   ...
   <transaction-type>Bean</transaction-type>
   ...
```

In EJB 1.0, only beans with the transaction attribute TX_BEAN_MANAGED for its methods are considered bean-managed transaction beans. Entity beans as well as session beans can manage their own transactions.

To manage its own transaction, a bean needs to obtain a `UserTransaction` object. A bean obtains a reference to the `UserTransaction` from the EJB-Context, as shown below:

```
public class HypotheticalBean extends SessionBean {
  SessionContext ejbContext;

  public void someMethod() {
   try {
   UserTransaction ut = ejbContext.getUserTransaction();
   ut.begin();

   // Do some work.

   ut.commit();
   } catch(IllegalStateException ise) {...}
     catch(SystemException se) {...}
     catch(TransactionRolledbackException tre) {...}
```

```
catch(HeuristicRollbackException hre) {...}
catch(HeuristicMixedException hme) {...}
```

An EJB 1.1 bean can access the UserTransaction from the EJBContext as shown
in the previous example or from the JNDI ENC as shown in the following example. Both methods are legal and proper in EJB 1.1. The bean performs the lookup
using the "java:comp/env/UserTransaction" context:

```
InitialContext jndiCntx = new InitialContext();
UserTransaction tran = (UserTransaction)
    jndiCntx.lookup("java:comp/env/UserTransaction");
```

Transaction Propagation in Bean-Managed Transactions

With stateless session beans (and entity beans in EJB 1.0), transactions that are
managed using the UserTransaction must be started and completed within the
same method, as shown previously. In other words, UserTransaction transactions cannot be started in one method and ended in another. This makes sense
because both entity and stateless session bean instances are shared across many
clients.

With stateful session beans, however, a transaction can begin in one method and
be committed in another because a stateful session bean is only used by one client. This allows a stateful session bean to associate itself with a transaction across
several different client-invoked methods. As an example, imagine the TravelAgent
bean as a bean-managed transaction bean. In the following code, the transaction is
started in the setCruiseID() method and completed in the bookPassage()
method. This allows the TravelAgent bean's methods to be associated with the
same transaction.

```
public class TravelAgentBean implements javax.ejb.SessionBean {

    public Customer customer;
    public Cruise cruise;
    public Cabin cabin;
    public javax.ejb.SessionContext ejbContext;
    ...
    public void setCruiseID(int cruiseID)
    throws javax.ejb.FinderException{
    // EJB 1.0: also throws RemoteException

        try {
            ejbContext.getUserTransaction().begin();

            CruiseHome home = (CruiseHome)getHome("CruiseHome", CruiseHome.class);
            cruise = home.findByPrimaryKey(new CruisePK(cruiseID));
```

```
        } catch(Exception re) {
            // EJB 1.0: throw new RemoteException("",re);
            throw new EJBException(re);
        }
    }

    public Ticket bookPassage(CreditCard card, double price)
        throws IncompleteConversationalState { // EJB 1.0: also throws RemoteException

        try {
            if (ejbContext.getUserTransaction().getStatus() !=
                javax.transaction.Status.STATUS_ACTIVE) {
                // EJB 1.0: throw new RemoteException("Transaction is not active");
                throw new EJBException("Transaction is not active");
            }
        } catch(javax.transaction.SystemException se) {
            // EJB 1.0: throw new RemoteException("",se);
            throw new EJBException(se);
        }

        if (customer == null || cruise == null || cabin == null) {
            throw new IncompleteConversationalState();
        }
        try {
            ReservationHome resHome = (ReservationHome)
                getHome("ReservationHome",ReservationHome.class);
            Reservation reservation =
            resHome.create(customer, cruise, cabin, price);
            ProcessPaymentHome ppHome = (ProcessPaymentHome)
                getHome("ProcessPaymentHome",ProcessPaymentHome.class);
            ProcessPayment process = ppHome.create();
            process.byCredit(customer, card, price);

            Ticket ticket = new Ticket(customer,cruise,cabin,price);
            ejbContext.getUserTransaction().commit();
            return ticket;
        } catch(Exception e) {
            // EJB 1.0: throw new RemoteException("",e);
            throw new EJBException(e);
        }
    }
    ...
}
```

Repeated calls to the EJBContext.getUserTransaction() method return a reference to the same UserTransaction object. The container is required to retain the association between the transaction and the stateful bean instance across multiple client calls until the transaction terminates.

In the bookPassage() method, we can check the status of the transaction to ensure that it's still active. If the transaction is no longer active, we throw an exception. The use of the getStatus() method is covered in more detail later in this chapter.

When a bean-managed transaction method is invoked by a client that is already involved in a transaction, the client's transaction is suspended until the bean method returns. This suspension occurs whether the bean-managed transaction bean explicitly starts its own transaction within the method or, in the case of stateful beans, the transaction was started in a previous method invocation. The client transaction is always suspended until the bean-managed transaction method returns.

NOTE   Transaction control across methods is strongly discouraged because
            it can result in improperly managed transactions and long-lived
            transactions that lock up resources.

Heuristic Decisions

Transactions are normally controlled by a *transaction manager* (often the EJB server) that manages the ACID characteristics across several beans, databases, and servers. This transaction manager uses a *two-phase commit* (2-PC) to manage transactions. 2-PC is a protocol for managing transactions that commits updates in two stages. 2-PC is complex and outside the scope of this book, but basically it requires that servers and databases cooperate to ensure that all the data is made durable together. Some EJB servers support 2-PC while others don't, and the value of this transaction mechanism is a source of some debate. The important point to remember is that a transaction manager controls the transaction; based on the results of a poll against the resources (databases and other servers), it decides whether all the updates should be committed or rolled back. A *heuristic decision* is when one of the resources makes a unilateral decision to commit or roll back without permission from the transaction manager. Once a heuristic decision has been made, the atomicity of the transaction is lost and possible data integrity errors can occur.

UserTransaction, discussed in the next section, throws a couple of different exceptions related to heuristic decisions; these are included in the following discussion.

UserTransaction

UserTransaction is a Java interface that is defined in the following code. In EJB 1.0, the EJB server is only required to support the functionality of this interface and the Status interface discussed here. EJB servers are not required to support the rest of JTA, nor are they required to use JTS for their transaction service. The UserTransaction is defined as follows:

```
public interface javax.transaction.UserTransaction
{
    public abstract void begin()
        throws IllegalStateException, SystemException;
    public abstract void commit()
        throws IllegalStateException, SystemException,
            TransactionRolledbackException,
                HeuristicRollbackException, HeuristicMixedException;
    public abstract int getStatus();
    public abstract void rollback()
        throws IllegalStateException, SecurityException, SystemException;
    public abstract void setRollbackOnly()
        throws IllegalStateException, SystemException;
    public abstract void setTransactionTimeout(int seconds)
        throws SystemException;
}
```

Here's what the methods defined in this interface do:

begin()

Invoking the begin() method creates a new transaction. The thread that executes the begin() method is immediately associated with the new transaction. The transaction is propagated to any bean that supports existing transactions. The begin() method can throw one of two checked exceptions. IllegalStateException is thrown when begin() is called by a thread that is already associated with a transaction. You must complete any transactions associated with that thread before beginning a new transaction. SystemException is thrown if the transaction manager (the EJB server) encounters an unexpected error condition.

commit()

The commit() method completes the transaction that is associated with the current thread. When commit() is executed, the current thread is no longer associated with a transaction. This method can throw several checked exceptions. IllegalStateException is thrown if the current thread is not associated with a transaction. SystemException is thrown if the transaction manager (the EJB server) encounters an unexpected error condition. TransactionRolledbackException is thrown when the entire transaction is rolled back instead of committed; this can happen if one of the resources was unable to perform an update or if the UserTransaction.rollBackOnly() method was called. HeuristicRollbackException indicates that heuristic decisions were made by one or more resources to roll back the transaction. HeuristicMixedException indicates that heuristic decisions were made by resources to both roll back and commit the transaction; some resources decided to roll back while others decided to commit.

`rollback()`

The `rollback()` method is invoked to roll back the transaction and undo updates. The `rollback()` method can throw one of three different checked exceptions. `SecurityException` is thrown if the thread using the `User-Transaction` object is not allowed to roll back the transaction. `Illegal-StateException` is thrown if the current thread is not associated with a transaction. `SystemException` is thrown if the transaction manager (the EJB server) encounters an unexpected error condition.

`setRollBackOnly()`

This method is invoked to mark the transaction for rollback. This means that, whether or not the updates executed within the transaction succeed, the transaction must be rolled back when completed. This method can be invoked by any `TX_BEAN_MANAGED` bean participating in the transaction or by the client application. The `setRollBackOnly()` method can throw one of two different checked exceptions. `IllegalStateException` is thrown if the current thread is not associated with a transaction. `SystemException` is thrown if the transaction manager (the EJB server) encounters an unexpected error condition.

`setTransactionTimeout(int seconds)`

This method sets the life span of a transaction: how long it will live before timing out. The transaction must complete before the transaction timeout is reached. If this method is not called, the transaction manager (EJB server) automatically sets the timeout. If this method is invoked with a value of 0 seconds, the default timeout of the transaction manager will be used. This method must be invoked after the `begin()` method. `SystemException` is thrown if the transaction manager (EJB server) encounters an unexpected error condition.

`getStatus()`

The `getStatus()` method returns an integer that can be compared to constants defined in the `javax.transaction.Status` interface. This method can be used by a sophisticated programmer to determine the status of a transaction associated with a `UserTransaction` object. `SystemException` is thrown if the transaction manager (EJB server) encounters an unexpected error condition.

Status

`Status` is a simple interface that contains no methods, only constants. Its sole purpose is to provide a set of constants that describe the current status of a transactional object—in this case, the `UserTransaction`:

```
interface javax.transaction.Status
{
    public final static int STATUS_ACTIVE;
    public final static int STATUS_COMMITTED;
    public final static int STATUS_COMMITTING;
    public final static int STATUS_MARKED_ROLLBACK;
    public final static int STATUS_NO_TRANSACTION;
    public final static int STATUS_PREPARED;
    public final static int STATUS_PREPARING;
    public final static int STATUS_ROLLEDBACK;
    public final static int STATUS_ROLLING_BACK;
    public final static int STATUS_UNKNOWN;
}
```

The value returned by getStatus() tells the client using the UserTransaction the status of a transaction. Here's what the constants mean:

STATUS_ACTIVE

An active transaction is associated with the UserTransaction object. This status is returned after a transaction has been started and prior to a transaction manager beginning a 2-PC commit. (Transactions that have been suspended are still considered active.)

STATUS_COMMITTED

A transaction is associated with the UserTransaction object; the transaction has been committed. It is likely that heuristic decisions have been made; otherwise, the transaction would have been destroyed and the STATUS_NO_TRANSACTION constant would have been returned instead.

STATUS_COMMITTING

A transaction is associated with the UserTransaction object; the transaction is in the process of committing. The UserTransaction object returns this status if the transaction manager has decided to commit but has not yet completed the process.

STATUS_MARKED_ROLLBACK

A transaction is associated with the UserTransaction object; the transaction has been marked for rollback, perhaps as a result of a UserTransaction.setRollbackOnly() operation invoked somewhere else in the application.

STATUS_NO_TRANSACTION

No transaction is currently associated with the UserTransaction object. This occurs after a transaction has completed or if no transaction has been created. This value is returned rather than throwing an IllegalStateException.

STATUS_PREPARED

A transaction is associated with the UserTransaction object. The transaction has been prepared, which means that the first phase of the two-phase commit process has completed.

STATUS_PREPARING

A transaction is associated with the UserTransaction object; the transaction is in the process of preparing, which means that the transaction manager is in the middle of executing the first phase of the two-phase commit.

STATUS_ROLLEDBACK

A transaction is associated with the UserTransaction object; the outcome of the transaction has been identified as a rollback. It is likely that heuristic decisions have been made; otherwise, the transaction would have been destroyed and the STATUS_NO_TRANSACTION constant would have been returned.

STATUS_ROLLING_BACK

A transaction is associated with the UserTransaction object; the transaction is in the process of rolling back.

STATUS_UNKNOWN

A transaction is associated with the UserTransaction object; its current status cannot be determined. This is a transient condition and subsequent invocations will ultimately return a different status.

EJBContext Rollback Methods

Only beans that manage their own transactions have access to the User-Transaction from the EJBContext. To provide other types of beans with an interface to the transaction, the EJBContext interface provides the methods setRollbackOnly() and getRollbackOnly().

The setRollbackOnly() method gives a bean the power to veto a transaction. This power can be used if the bean detects a condition that would cause inconsistent data to be committed when the transaction completes. Once a bean invokes the setRollbackOnly() method, the current transaction is marked for rollback and cannot be committed by any other participant in the transaction—including the container.

The getRollbackOnly() method returns true if the current transaction has been marked for rollback. This can be used to avoid executing work that wouldn't be committed anyway. If, for example, an exception is thrown and captured within a bean method, this method can be used to determine whether the exception caused the current transaction to be rolled back. If it did, there is no sense in continuing the processing. If it didn't, the bean has an opportunity to correct the problem and retry the task that failed. Only expert bean developers should attempt to retry tasks within a transaction. Alternatively, if the exception didn't cause a rollback (getRollbackOnly() returns false), a rollback can be forced using the setRollbackOnly() method.

Beans that manage their own transaction must *not* use the setRollbackOnly() and getRollbackOnly() methods of the EJBContext. These beans should use the getStatus() and rollback() methods on the UserTransaction object to check for rollback and force a rollback respectively.

EJB 1.1: *Exceptions and Transactions*

Application Exceptions Versus System Exceptions

In EJB 1.1, an application exception is any exception that does *not* extend java. lang.RuntimeException or the java.rmi.RemoteException. System exceptions are java.lang.RuntimeException and java.rmi.RemoteException types and subtypes, including EJBException.

Transactions are *automatically* rolled back if a system exception is thrown from a bean method. Transactions are *not automatically* rolled back if an application exception is thrown. If you remember these two rules, you will be well prepared to deal with exceptions and transactions in EJB 1.1.

The bookPassage() method provides a good illustration of an application exception and how it's used. The following code shows the bookPassage() method with the relevant exception handling in bold:

```
public Ticket bookPassage(CreditCard card, double price)
    throws IncompleteConversationalState {

    if (customer == null || cruise == null || cabin == null) {
        throw new IncompleteConversationalState();
    }
    try {
        ReservationHome resHome = (ReservationHome)
            getHome("ReservationHome",ReservationHome.class);
        Reservation reservation =
        resHome.create(customer, cruise, cabin, price);
        ProcessPaymentHome ppHome = (ProcessPaymentHome)
            getHome("ProcessPaymentHome",ProcessPaymentHome.class);
        ProcessPayment process = ppHome.create();
        process.byCredit(customer, card, price);

        Ticket ticket = new Ticket(customer,cruise,cabin,price);
        return ticket;
```

```
        } catch(Exception e) {
            throw new EJBException(e);
        }
    }
```

System exceptions

System exceptions are RuntimeExceptions, RemoteExceptions, and their sub-types. The EJBException is a subclass of the RuntimeException, so it's considered a system exception.

System exceptions always cause a transaction to roll back when thrown from a bean method. Any RuntimeException (NullPointerException, IndexOutOf-BoundsException, etc.) thrown within the bookPassage() method is handled by the container automatically, and also results in a transaction rollback. In Java, RuntimeException types do not need to be declared in the throws clause of the method signature or handled using try/catch blocks; they are automatically thrown from the method.

System exceptions thrown from within beans always cause the current transaction to roll back. If the method in which the exception occurs started the transaction, the transaction is rolled back. If the transaction started from a client that invoked the method, the client's transaction is marked for rollback and cannot be committed.

System exceptions are handled automatically by the container, which will always:

* Roll back the transaction

* Log the exception to alert the system administrator

* Discard the bean instance

* Throw a RemoteException or one of its subtypes

Exceptions thrown from the callback methods (ejbLoad(), ejbActivate(), etc.) are treated the same as exceptions thrown from business methods.

While EJB 1.1 requires that system exceptions be logged, it does not specify how exceptions should be logged or the format of the log file. The exact mechanism for recording the exception and reporting it to the system administrator is left to the vendor.

When a system exception occurs, the bean instance is discarded, which means that it's dereferenced and garbage collected. The container assumes that the bean instance may have corrupt variables or otherwise be unstable, and is therefore unsafe to use.

The impact of discarding a bean instance depends on the bean's type. In the case of stateless session beans and entity beans, the client does not notice that the instance was discarded. These types of beans are not dedicated to a particular client; they are swapped in and out of an instance pool, so any instance can service a new request. With stateful session beans, however, the impact on the client is severe. Stateful session beans are dedicated to a single client and maintain conversational state. Discarding a stateful bean instance destroys the instance's conversation state and invalidates the client's reference to the bean. When stateful session instances are discarded, subsequent invocations of the bean's methods by the client result in a NoSuchObjectException, a subclass of the RemoteException.*

When a system exception occurs and the instance is discarded, a RemoteException is always thrown to the client. If the client started the transaction, which was then propagated to the bean, a system exception (thrown by the bean method) will be caught by the container and rethrown as a javax.transaction. TransactionRolledbackException. The TransactionRolledbackException is a subtype of the RemoteException; it's a more explicit indication to the client that a rollback occurred. In all other cases, whether the bean is container-managed or bean-managed, a system exception thrown from within the bean method will be caught by the container and rethrown as a RemoteException. A system exception always results in a rollback of the transaction.

Application exceptions

An application exception is normally thrown in response to a business logic error, as opposed to a system error. They are always delivered directly to the client, without being repackaged as RemoteExceptions. They do not typically cause transactions to roll back; the client usually has an opportunity to recover after an application exception is thrown.

The bookPassage() method throws an application exception called IncompleteConversationalState; this is an application exception because it does not extend RuntimeException or RemoteException. The IncompleteConversationalState exception is thrown if one of the arguments passed into the bookPassage() method is null. (Application errors are frequently used to report validation errors like this.) In this case, the exception is thrown before tasks are started, and is clearly not the result of a subsystem (JDBC, Java RMI, JNDI, etc.) failure.

Because it is an application exception, throwing the IncompleteConversationalState exception does not result in a transaction rollback. The exception is

---

* Although the instance is always discarded with a RuntimeException, the impact on the remote reference may vary depending on the vendor.

thrown before any work is done, avoiding unnecessary processing by the bookPassage() method and providing the client (the bean or application that invoked the bookPassage() method) with an opportunity to recover and possibly retry the method call with valid arguments.

The ProcessPayment bean also throws an application exception, PaymentException, to indicate that a validation error has occurred. In the bookPassage() method, we have always allowed this exception to be captured by the try/catch block and rethrown as a EJBException, which would result in a transaction rollback. An alternative would be to rearrange the sequence of events a little and allow the bookPassage() method to throw the PaymentException. This approach would allow more concise reporting of the business error to the client and, if organized correctly, would avoid a transaction rollback. Upon catching the PaymentException, the client could attempt to recover by retrying the bookPassage() method with the valid payment arguments. The following code shows a revised bookPassage() method that illustrates this strategy. Notice that the payment is processed before the reservation and that more explicit exception handling allows the PaymentException (thrown by the byCredit() method) to escape the try/catch block, so it can be thrown by the bookPassage() method.

```
public Ticket bookPassage(CreditCard card, double price)
    throws IncompleteConversationalState, PaymentException {

    if (customer == null || cruise == null || cabin == null){
        throw new IncompleteConversationalState();
    }
    try {
        ProcessPaymentHome ppHome = (ProcessPaymentHome)
            getHome("ProcessPaymentHome",ProcessPaymentHome.class);
        ProcessPayment process = ppHome.create();

        process.byCredit(customer, card, price);

        ReservationHome resHome = (ReservationHome)
            getHome("ReservationHome", ReservationHome.class);

        Reservation reservation =
            resHome.create(customer, cruise, cabin, price);

        Ticket ticket = new Ticket(customer,cruise,cabin,price);
        return ticket;
    } catch(RemoteException re) {
        throw new EJBException(re);
    } catch(NamingException ne) {
        throw new EJBException(ne);
    } catch(CreateException ce) {
        throw new EJBException(ce);
```

```
        } catch(FinderException fe) {
            throw new EJBException(fe);
        }
    }
```

Business methods defined in the remote interface can throw any kind of application exception. These application exceptions must be declared in the method signatures of the remote interface and in the corresponding method in the bean class.

The EJB create, find, and remove methods can also throw several exceptions defined in the javax.ejb package: CreateException, DuplicateKey-Exception, FinderException, ObjectNotFoundException, and Remove-Exception. These exceptions are also considered application exceptions: they are delivered to the client as is, without being repackaged as RemoteExceptions. Furthermore, these exceptions don't necessarily cause a transaction to roll back, giving the client the opportunity to retry the operation. These exceptions may be thrown by the beans themselves; in the case of container managed persistence (CMP), the container can also throw any of these exceptions while handling the bean's create, find, or remove methods (ejbCreate(), ejbFind...(), and ejbRemove()). The container might, for example, throw a CreateException if the container encounters a bad argument while attempting to insert a record for a container-managed bean. A bean developer can always choose to throw a standard application exception from the appropriate method regardless of how persistence is managed.

Here is a detailed explanation of the five standard application exceptions and the situations in which they are thrown:

CreateException

The CreateException is thrown by the create() method in the remote interface. This exception can be thrown by the container if the container is managing persistence, or it can be thrown explicitly by the bean developer in the ejbCreate() or ejbPostCreate() methods. This exception indicates that an application error has occurred (invalid arguments, etc.) while the bean was being created. If the container throws this exception, it *may or may not* roll back the transaction. Explicit transaction methods must be used to determine the outcome. Bean developers should roll back the transaction before throwing this exception only if data integrity is a concern.

DuplicateKeyException

The DuplicateKeyException is an subtype of the CreateException; it is thrown by the create() method in the remote interface. This exception can be thrown by the container, if the container is managing persistence, or it can be thrown explicitly by the bean developer in the ejbCreate() method. This exception indicates that a bean with the same primary key already exists in the database. The transaction is typically *not* rolled back by the bean provider or container before throwing this exception.

FinderException

The FinderException is thrown by the find methods in the home interface. This exception can be thrown by the container, if the container is managing persistence, or it can be thrown explicitly by the bean developer in the ejbFind...() methods. This exception indicates that an application error occurred (invalid arguments, etc.) while the container attempted to find the beans. Do not use this method to indicate that entities were not found. Multi-entity find methods return an empty collection if no entities were found; single-entity find methods throw an ObjectNotFoundException to indicate that no object was found. The transaction is typically *not* rolled back by the bean provider or container before throwing this exception.

ObjectNotFoundException

The ObjectNotFoundException is thrown from a single-entity find method to indicate that the container couldn't find the requested entity. This exception can be thrown by the container if the container is managing persistence, or it can be thrown explicitly by the bean developer in the ejbFind...() methods. This exception should *not* be thrown to indicate a business logic error (invalid arguments, etc.). Use the FinderException to indicate business logic errors in single-entity find methods. The ObjectNotFound-Exception is only thrown by single-entity find methods to indicate that the entity requested was not found. Find methods that return multiple entities should return an empty collection if nothing is found. The transaction is typically *not* rolled back by the bean provider or container before throwing this exception.

RemoveException

The RemoveException is thrown from the remove() methods in the remote and home interfaces. This exception can be thrown by the container, if the container is managing persistence, or it can be thrown explicitly by the bean developer in the ejbRemove() method. This exception indicates that an application error has occurred while the bean was being removed. The transaction *may or may not* have been rolled back by the container before throwing this exception. Explicit transaction methods must be used to determine the outcome. Bean developers' should roll back the transaction before throwing the exception only if data integrity is a concern.

Table 8-3 summarizes the interactions between different types of exceptions and transactions.

Table 8-3. Exception Summary

Transaction Scope	Transaction Type Attributes	Exception Thrown	Container's Action	Client's View
Client Initiated Transaction Transaction is started by the client (application or bean) and is propagated to the bean method.	transaction-type = Container transaction-attribute = Required | Mandatory | Supports |	Application Exception	If the bean invoked setRollbackOnly(), then mark the client's transaction for rollback. Rethrow the Application Exception.	Receives the Application Exception. The client's transaction may or may not have been marked for rollback.
		System Exception	Mark the client's transaction for rollback. Log the error. Discard the instance. Rethrow the Transaction-RollbackException.	Receives the TransactionRollback-Exception The client's transaction has been rolled back.
Container Initiated Transaction The transaction started when the bean's method was invoked and will end when method completes.	transaction-type = Container transaction-attribute = Required | RequiresNew	Application Exception	If the bean called setRoll-backOnly(), then roll back the transaction and rethrow the Application Exception. If the bean didn't explicitly roll back the transaction, then attempt to commit the transaction and rethrow the Application Exception.	Receives the Application Exception. The bean's transaction may or may not have been rolled back. The client's transaction is not affected.
		System Exception	Roll back the transaction. Log the error. Discard the instance. Rethrow RemoteException.	Receives the RemoteException. The bean's transaction was rolled back. The client's transaction is not affected.

Table 8-3. *Exception Summary (continued)*

Transaction Scope	Transaction Type Attributes	Exception Thrown	Container's Action	Client's View
Bean is not part of a transaction The bean was invoked but does not propagate the client's transaction and does not start its own transaction.	transaction-type = Container transaction-attribute = Never | NotSupported | Supports |	Application Exception	Rethrow the Application Exception.	Receives the Application Exception. The client's transaction is not affected.
		System Exception	Log the error. Discard the instance. Rethrow RemoteException.	Receives the RemoteException. The client's transaction is not affected.
Bean Managed Transaction. The stateful or stateless session bean uses the EJBContext to explicitly manage its own transaction	transaction-type = bean transaction-attribute = Bean-managed transaction beans do not use transaction attributes.	Application Exception	Rethrow the Application Exception.	Receives the Application Exception. The client's transaction is not affected.
		System Exception	Roll back the transaction. Log the error. Discard the instance. Rethrow RemoteException.	Receives the RemoteException. The client's transaction is not affected.

EJB 1.0: Exceptions and Transactions

In EJB 1.0, the impact of exceptions on transactions largely depends on who initiates the transaction. A transaction that is started automatically when a bean method is invoked is a container-initiated transaction. Specifying the TX_REQUIRES_NEW transaction attribute, for example, always results in a container-initiated transaction. A TX_REQUIRED method invoked by a non-transactional client also results in a container-initiated transaction. A transaction that is started explicitly using JTA (on the client or in a TX_BEAN_MANAGED bean) is not a container-initiated transaction.

With container-initiated transactions, any exception thrown during a transaction can cause the transaction to roll back. The impact of an exception thrown during a transaction depends on the type of exception (checked or unchecked) and the transaction attribute of the bean method throwing the exception. This section examines the different combinations of exceptions (checked or unchecked) and transaction attributes and their combined affect on transactional outcomes.

Container-Initiated Transactions

Any exception (application exception, unchecked exception, or Remote-Exception) *not* handled within the scope of the container-initiated transaction causes the container to roll back the entire transaction.

NOTE   An exception that is not handled within the scope of container-initiated transaction is an exception that is propagated, through the call stack, beyond the bean method that started the container-initiated transaction.

As an example, take another look at the bookPassage() method from the TravelAgent bean:

```
public Ticket bookPassage(CreditCard card, double price)
    throws IncompleteConversationalState, RemoteException {

    if (customer == null || cruise == null || cabin == null){
        throw new IncompleteConversationalState();
    }
    try {
        ReservationHome resHome = (ReservationHome)
            getHome("ReservationHome",ReservationHome.class);
        Reservation reservation =
        resHome.create(customer, cruise, cabin, price);
        ProcessPaymentHome ppHome = (ProcessPaymentHome)
            getHome("ProcessPaymentHome",ProcessPaymentHome.class);
```

```
        ProcessPayment process = ppHome.create();
        process.byCredit(customer, card, price);

        Ticket ticket = new Ticket(customer,cruise,cabin,price);
        return ticket;
    } catch(Exception e) {
        throw new RemoteException("",e);
    }
}
```

The beans (Reservation and ProcessPayment) accessed by the bookPassage() method have a transaction attribute of TX_REQUIRED. This means that the transaction associated with the bookPassage() method will be propagated to the methods called on the ProcessPayment and Reservation beans. If bookPassage() has a transaction attribute of TX_REQUIRES_NEW, then we can assume that it will always be called in the scope of a container-initiated transaction; when bookPassage() is invoked, a new container-initiated transaction is created.

In container-initiated transactions, any application exception thrown within the scope of the container-initiated transaction does not cause a rollback. This provides the bean with an opportunity to recover and retry an operation. However, an application exception that is *not* handled within the scope of the container-initiated transaction does cause the transaction to be rolled back.

This can be demonstrated by redefining the bookPassage() method:

```
public Ticket bookPassage(CreditCard card, double price)
    throws IncompleteConversationalState {
 // EJB 1.0: also throws RemoteException

    if (customer == null || cruise == null || cabin == null) {
        throw new IncompleteConversationalState();
    }
    try {
        ReservationHome resHome = (ReservationHome)
            getHome("ReservationHome",ReservationHome.class);
        Reservation reservation =
        resHome.create(customer, cruise, cabin, price);
        ProcessPaymentHome ppHome = (ProcessPaymentHome)
            getHome("ProcessPaymentHome",ProcessPaymentHome.class);
        ProcessPayment process = ppHome.create();

        try {
            process.byCredit(customer, card, price);
        } catch(PaymentException pe) {
            // Attempt to recover.
        }

        Ticket ticket = new Ticket(customer,cruise,cabin,price);
        return ticket;
```

```
    } catch(Exception e){
        // EJB 1.0: throw new RemoteException("",e);
        throw new EJBException(e);
    }
}
```

Here, the byCredit() method of the ProcessPayment bean has been wrapped in its own exception-handling logic; we can imagine some sophisticated code in the catch block that evaluates the problem and attempts to reinvoke the method. In this case, the PaymentException thrown by the byCredit() method does not cause the bookPassage() container-initiated transaction to be rolled back because the application exception is thrown from within the container-initiated scope. However, if an IncompleteConversationalState exception is thrown by the bookPassage() method itself, the transaction will be rolled back. Once an exception is thrown by the bookPassage() method, and therefore *not* handled within the scope of the container-initiated transaction, the transaction will be rolled back.

These rules for application exceptions also apply to RemoteException types. If a RemoteException is thrown by a bean or by some other resource (JNDI, for example), that exception does not automatically cause a rollback. Rollback only occurs if the remote exception is *not* handled within of the scope of the container-initiated transaction.

Client-Initiated Transactions

When a transaction is propagated from a client to a bean, the client defines the scope of the transaction. This means that application exceptions and Remote-Exceptions thrown by the beans do not automatically cause the transaction to be rolled back. Again, consider the possibility that the byCredit() method throws an application exception. If the client initiated the transaction, it's the client's responsibility to determine whether the operation can be retried and to roll back if appropriate. Similarly, if the bookPassage() method had a transaction attribute of TX_REQUIRED or TX_SUPPORTS and was invoked from a client-initiated transaction (perhaps the client uses JTA), then any application exception or RemoteException thrown from within the bookPassage() method will not automatically cause a rollback. The client must handle the exception and determine for itself if a rollback is appropriate.

Bean-Managed Transactions

The effect of exceptions is different on bean-managed transactions (TX_BEAN_MANAGED). With TX_BEAN_MANAGED entity beans and stateless session beans, any exception thrown by the bean method causes the transaction to be rolled back by the container. Remember that with TX_BEAN_MANAGED, transactions must begin and be completed within the same method. If an exception unexpectedly ends the method, the container rolls back the transaction.

With TX_BEAN_MANAGED stateful session beans, only unchecked exceptions thrown by bean methods cause the container to roll back the transaction. Any other exception thrown by the bean method, whether it be an application exception or RemoteException, does not affect the transaction. This can cause major headaches if the exception is thrown before an intended commit was reached. For this reason, beans that manage their own transactions must be extremely careful about exception handling. The EJBContext rollback methods can be used in these situations.

Unchecked Exceptions

Regardless of the method's transaction attribute (unless it's TX_NOT_SUPPORTED), an unchecked exception causes the transaction to be rolled back, regardless of whether the transaction is container-initiated, client-initiated, or bean-managed. Unchecked exceptions thrown by a bean in the scope of a transaction always cause a rollback. In addition, the container intercepts the unchecked exception and rethrows it to the bean's client as a javax.transaction.TransactionRolledbackException.*

Transactional Stateful Session Beans

As you saw in Chapter 7, session beans can interact directly with the database as easily as they can manage the workflow of other beans. The ProcessPayment bean, for example, makes inserts into the PAYMENT table when the byCredit() method is invoked. The TravelAgent bean queries the database directly when the listAvailableCabins() method is invoked. With stateless session beans like ProcessPayment, there is no conversational state, so each method invocation must make changes to the database immediately. With stateful session beans, however, we may not want to make changes to the database until the transaction is complete. Remember, a stateful session bean can be just one participant out of many in a transaction, so it may be advisable to postpone database updates until the entire transaction is committed or to avoid updates if it's rolled back.

There are several different scenarios in which a stateful session bean would want to cache changes before applying them to the database. In Chapter 9, we will take a look at modeling entity business concepts in stateful session beans that implement the SessionSynchronization interface. These sessions may have their methods

---

* Bean methods with the TX_SUPPORTS attribute that are invoked by non-transactional clients are not included in this policy. They simply throw the unchecked exception as a RemoteException.

invoked many times before writing to the database. For example, think of a shopping cart implemented by a stateful session bean that accumulates several items for purchase. If the bean implements `SessionSynchronization`, it can cache the items and only write them to the database when the transaction is complete.

The `javax.ejb.SessionSynchronization` interface allows a session bean to receive additional notification of the session's involvement in transactions. The addition of these transaction callback methods by the `SessionSynchronization` interface expands the bean's awareness of its life cycle to include a new state, the *Transactional Method-Ready state*. This third state, although not discussed in Chapter 7, is always a part of the life cycle of a transactional stateful session bean. Implementing the `SessionSynchronization` interface simply makes it visible to the bean. Figures 8-12 and 8-13 show the stateful session bean with the additional state in EJB 1.1 and EJB 1.0.

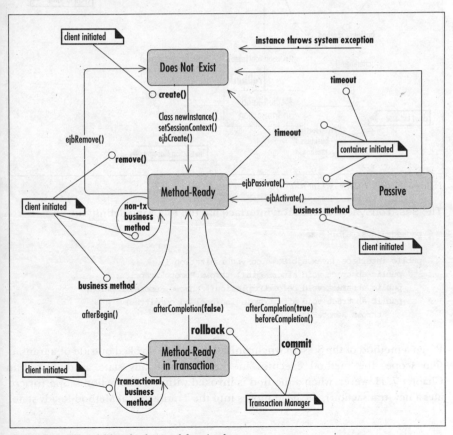

Figure 8-12. EJB 1.1 life cycle of a stateful session bean

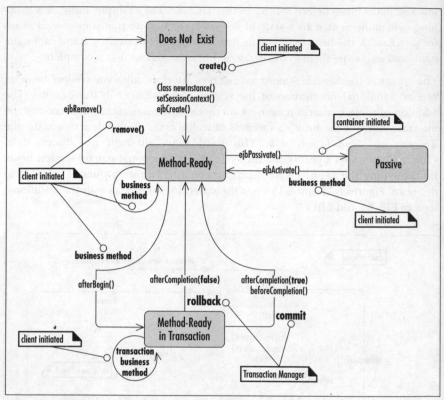

Figure 8-13. EJB 1.0 life cycle of a stateful session bean

The SessionSynchronization interface has the following definition:

```
package javax.ejb;

public interface javax.ejb.SessionSynchronization {
    public abstract void afterBegin() throws RemoteException;
    public abstract void beforeCompletion() throws RemoteException;
    public abstract void afterCompletion(boolean committed)
        throws RemoteException;
}
```

When a method of the SessionSynchronization bean is invoked outside of a transaction scope, the method executes in the Method-Ready state as discussed in Chapter 7. However, when a method is invoked within a transaction scope (or creates a new transaction), the bean moves into the Transactional Method-Ready state.

The Transactional Method-Ready State

Transitioning into the Transactional Method-Ready state

When a transactional method is invoked on a bean, the bean becomes part of the transaction. This causes the afterBegin() callback method defined in the SessionSynchronization interface to be invoked. This method should take care of reading any data from the database and storing the data in the bean's instance fields. The afterBegin() method is called before the EJB object delegates the business method invocation to the bean instance.

Life in the Transactional Method-Ready state

When the afterBegin() callback method is done, the business method originally invoked by the client is executed on the bean instance. Any subsequent business methods invoked within the same transaction will be delegated directly to the bean instance.

Once a stateful session bean is a part of a transaction—whether it implements SessionSynchronization or not—it cannot be accessed by any other transactional context. This is true regardless of whether the client tries to access the bean with a different context or the bean's own method creates a new context. If, for example, a method with a transaction attribute of *Requires New* is invoked, the new transactional context causes an error to be thrown. Since the attributes *Not Supported* and *Never* (EJB 1.1 only) imply a different transactional context (no context), invoking a method with thesex attributes also causes an error. A stateful session bean cannot be removed while it is involved in a transaction. This means that invoking ejbRemove() while the bean is in the middle of a transaction will cause an error to be thrown.

At some point, the transaction in which the bean has been enrolled will come to an end. If the transaction is committed, the bean will be notified through its beforeCompletion() method. At this time, the bean should write its cached data to the database. If the transaction is rolled back, the beforeCompletion() method will not be invoked, avoiding the pointless effort of writing changes that won't be committed to the database.

The afterCompletion() method is always invoked, whether the transaction ended successfully with a commit or unsuccessfully with a rollback. If the transaction was a success—which means that beforeCompletion() was invoked—the committed parameter of the afterCompletion() method will be true. If the transaction was unsuccessful, committed will be false.

It may be desirable to reset the stateful session bean's instance variables to some initial state if the afterCompletion() method indicates that the transaction was rolled back.

9

Design Strategies

The previous eight chapters have presented the core EJB technology. What's left is a grab bag of miscellaneous issues: how do you solve particular design problems, how do you work with particular kinds of databases, and topics of that nature.

Hash Codes in Compound Primary Keys

Chapter 6 discusses the necessity of overriding the `Object.hashCode()` and `Object.equals()` methods in the primary key class. As an example, we used the primary key for the Ship bean, `ShipPK`. This is a simple primary key with a single integer field, `id`. Therefore, our `hashCode()` and `equals()` methods were very simple; `hashCode()` just returned the `id` field as the hash value. With complex primary keys that have several fields, overriding the `Object.equals()` method remains trivial. However, the `Object.hashCode()` method is more complicated because an integer value that can serve as a suitable hash code must be created from several fields.

One solution is to concatenate all the values into a `String` and use the `String` object's `hashCode()` method to create a hash code value for the whole primary key. The `String` class has a decent hash code algorithm that generates a fairly well distributed and repeatable hash code value from any set of characters. The following code shows how to create such a hash code for a hypothetical primary key:

```
public class HypotheticalPrimaryKey implements java.io.Serializable {
    public int primary_id;
```

```
       public short secondary_id;
       public java.util.Date date;
       public String desc;

       public int hashCode() {

           StringBuffer strBuff = new StringBuffer();
           strBuff.append(primary_id);
           strBuff.append(secondary_id);
           strBuff.append(date);
           strBuff.append(desc);
           String str = strBuff.toString();
           int hashCode = str.hashCode();
           return hashCode;
       }
       // the constructor, equals, and toString methods follow
   }
```

A StringBuffer cuts down on the number of objects created, since String concatenation is expensive. The code could be improved by saving the hash code in a private variable and returning that value in subsequent method calls; this way, the hash code is only calculated once in the life of the instance.

Well-Distributed Versus Unique Hash Codes

A Hashtable is designed to provide fast lookups by binding an object to a key. Given any object's key, looking the object up in a hash table is a very quick operation. For the lookup, the key is converted to an integer value using the key's hashCode() method.

Hash codes do not need to be unique, only well-distributed. By "well-distributed," we mean that given any two keys, the chances are very good that the hash codes for the keys will be different. A well-distributed hash code algorithm reduces, but does not eliminate, the possibility that different keys evaluate to the same hash code. When keys evaluate to the same hash code, they are stored together and uniquely identified by their equals() method. If you look up an object using a key that evaluates to a hash code that is shared by several other keys, the Hashtable locates the group of objects that have been stored with the same hash code; then it uses the key's equals() method to determine which key (and hence, which object) you want. (That's why you have to override the equals() method in primary keys, as well as the hashCode() method.) Therefore, the emphasis in designing a good hash code algorithm is on producing codes that are well-distributed rather than unique. This allows you to design an index for associating keys with objects that is easy to compute, and therefore fast.

Passing Objects by Value

Passing objects by value is tricky with Enterprise JavaBeans. Two simple rules will keep you out of most problem areas: objects that are passed by value should be fine-grained dependent objects or wrappers used in bulk accessors, and dependent objects should be immutable.

Dependent Objects

Dependent objects are objects that only have meaning within the context of another business object. They typically represent fairly fine-grained business concepts, like an address, phone number, or order item. For example, an address has little meaning when it is not associated with a business object like Person or Organization. It depends on the context of the business object to give it meaning. Such an object can be thought of as a wrapper for related data. The fields that make up an address (street, city, state, and Zip) should be packaged together in a single object called Address. In turn, the Address object is usually an attribute or property of another business object; in EJB, we would typically see an Address or some other dependent object as a property of an entity bean.

Here's a typical implementation of an Address:

```
public class Address implements java.io.Serializable {

    private String street;
    private String city;
    private String state;
    private String zip;

    public Address(String str, String cty, String st, String zp) {
        street = str;
        city = cty;
        state = st;
        zip = zp;
    }
    public String getStreet() {return street;}
    public String getCity() {return city;}
    public String getState() {return state;}
    public String getZip() {return zip;}
}
```

We want to make sure that clients don't change an Address's fields. The reason is quite simple: the Address object is a copy, not a remote reference. Changes to Address objects are not reflected in the entity from which it originated. If the client were to change the Address object, those changes would not be reflected in the database. Making the Address immutable helps to ensure that clients do not mistake this fine-grained object for a remote reference, thinking that a change to an address property is reflected on the server.

NOTE	Some EJB 1.0 servers that use early versions of CORBA IIOP do not support passing objects by value. With these vendors, dependent objects must declare their fields as public. Of course, since the fields are public, the client can modify them directly. In these cases you need to trust your client programmers to exercise some discipline in the way they use the Address object.

To change an address, the client is required to remove the Address object and add a new one with the changes. This enforces the idea that the dependent object is not a remote object and that changes to its state are not reflected on the server. Here is the remote interface to a hypothetical Employee bean that aggregates address information:

```
public interface Employee extends javax.ejb.EJBObject {
    public Address [] getAddresses() throws RemoteException;
    public void removeAddress(Address adrs) throws RemoteException;
    public void addAddress(Address adrs) throws RemoteException;
    // ... Other business methods follow.
}
```

In this interface, the Employee can have many addresses, which are obtained as a collection of pass-by-value Address objects. To remove an address, the target Address is passed back to the bean in the removeAddress() method. The bean class then removes the matching Address object from its persistent fields. To add an address, an Address object is passed to the bean by value.

Dependent objects may be persistent fields, or they may be properties that are created as needed. The following code demonstrates both strategies using the Address object. In the first listing, the Address object is a persistent field, while in the second the Address object is a property that doesn't correspond to any single field; we create the Address object as needed but don't save it as part of the bean. Instead, the Address object corresponds to four persistent fields: street, city, state, and zip.

```
// Address as a persistent field
public class Person extends javax.ejb.EntityBean {
    public Address address;
    public Address getAddress(){
        return address;
    }
    public void setAddress(Address addr){
        address = addr;
    }
}
```

```
        }

        // Address as a property
        public class Person extends javax.ejb.EntityBean {

            public String street;
            public String city;
            public String state;
            public String zip;

            public Address getAddress(){
                return new Address(street, city, state, zip);
            }
            public void setAddress(Address addr){
                street = addr.street;
                city = addr.city;
                state = addr.state;
                zip = addr.zip;
            }
            ....
        }
```

When a dependent object is used as a property, it can be synchronized with the persistent fields in the accessor methods themselves or in the ejbLoad() and ejbStore() methods. Both strategies are acceptable.

This discussion of dependent objects has been full of generalizations, and thus may not be applicable to all situations. That said, it is recommended that only very fine-grained, dependent, immutable objects should be passed by value. All other business concepts should be represented as beans—entity or session. A very fine-grained object is one that has very little behavior, consisting mostly of get and set methods. A dependent object is one that has little meaning outside the context of its aggregator. An immutable object is one that provides only get methods and thus cannot be modified once created.

Validation Rules in Dependent Objects

Dependent objects make excellent homes for format validation rules. Format validation ensures that a simple data construct adheres to a predetermined structure or form. As an example, a Zip Code always has a certain format. It must be composed of digits; it must be five or nine digits in length; and if it has nine digits, it must use a hyphen as a separator between the fifth and sixth digits. Checking to see that a Zip Code follows these rules is format validation.

One problem that all developers face is deciding where to put validation code. Should data be validated at the user interface (UI), or should it be done by the bean that uses the data? Validating the data at the UI has the advantage of conserving network resources and improving performance. Validating data in the bean, on the middle tier, ensures that the logic is reusable across user interfaces. Dependent objects provide a logical compromise that allows data to be validated on the client, but remain independent of the UI. By placing the validation logic in the constructor of a dependent object, the object automatically validates data when it is created. When data is entered at the UI (GUI, Servlet, JSP, or whatever) it can be validated by the UI using its corresponding dependent object. If the data is valid, the dependent object is created; if the data is invalid, the constructor throws an exception.

The following code shows a dependent object that represents a Zip Code. It adheres to the rules for a dependent object as I have defined them, and also includes format validation rules in the constructor.

```
public class ZipCode implements java.io.Serializable {

    private String code;
    private String boxNumber;

    public ZipCode(String zipcode) throws ValidationException {
        if (zipcode == null)
            throw new ValidationException("Zip code cannot be null");
        else if (zipcode.length()==5 && ! isDigits(zipcode))
            throw new ValidationException("Zip code must be all digits");
        else if (zipcode.length()==10 )
            if (zipcode.charAt(5) == '-' ) {
                code = zipcode.substring(0,5);
                if (isDigits( code )){
                    boxNumber = zipcode.substring(6);
                    if (isDigits( boxNumber ))
                        return;
                }
            }
        throw new ValidationException("Zip code must be of form #####-####");
    }
    private boolean isDigits(String str) {
        for (int i = 0; i < str.length(); i++){
            char chr = str.charAt(i);
            if ( ! Character.isDigit(chr)) {
                return false;
            }
        }
        return true;
    }
    public String getCode() { return code; }

    public String getBoxNumber() { return boxNumber; }
```

```
    public String toString() {
       return code+'-'+boxNumber;
    }
  }
```

This simple example illustrates that format validation can be performed by dependent objects when the object is constructed at the user interface or client. Any format validation errors are reported immediately, without requiring any interaction with the middle tier of the application. In addition, any business object that uses ZipCode automatically gains the benefit of the validation code, making the validation rules reusable (and consistent) across beans. Placing format validation in the dependent object is also a good coding practice because it makes the dependent object responsible for its own validation; responsibility is a key concept in object-oriented programming. Of course, dependent objects are only useful for validation if the Enterprise JavaBeans implementation supports pass-by-value. Some of the EJB 1.0 CORBA-based systems only support a crude form of pass-by-value that uses CORBA structures, which prevents you from using dependent objects that incorporate validation rules.

As an alternative to using dependent objects, format validation can be performed by the accessors of enterprise beans. If, for example, a customer bean has accessors for setting and obtaining the Zip Code, the accessors could incorporate the validation code. While this is more efficient from a network perspective—passing a String value is more efficient than passing a dependent object by value—it is less reusable than housing format validation rules in dependent objects.

Bulk Accessors

Most entity beans have several persistent fields that are manipulated through accessor methods. Unfortunately, the one-to-one nature of the accessor idiom can result in many invocations when editing an entity, which translates into a lot of network traffic even for simple edits. Every field you want to modify requires a method invocation, which in turn requires you to go out to the network. One way to reduce network traffic when editing entities is to use bulk accessors. This strategy packages access to several persistent fields into one bulk accessor. Bulk accessors provide get and set methods that work with structures or simple pass-by-value objects. The following code shows how a bulk accessor could be implemented for the Cabin bean:

```
// CabinData DataObject
public class CabinData {
    public String name;
    public int deckLevel;
    public int bedCount;
    public CabinData() {
    }
```

```
        public CabinData(String name, int deckLevel, int bedCount) {
            this.name = name;
            this.deckLevel = deckLevel;
            this.bedCount = bedCount;
        }
    }

    // CabinBean using bulk accessors
    public class CabinBean implements javax.ejb.EntityBean {
        public int id;
        public String name;
        public int deckLevel;
        public int ship;
        public int bedCount;
        // bulk accessors
        public CabinData getData() {
            return new CabinData(name,deckLevel,bedCount);
        }
        public void setData(CabinData data) {
            name = data.name;
            deckLevel = data.deckLevel;
            bedCount = data.bedCount;
        }
        // simple accessors and entity methods
        public String getName() {
            return name;
        }
        public void setName(String str) {
            name = str;
        }
        // more methods follow
    }
```

The getData() and setData() methods allow several fields to be packaged into
a simple object and passed between the client and bean in one method call. This is
much more efficient than requiring three separate calls to set the name, deck
level, and bed count.

Rules-of-thumb for bulk accessors

Data objects are not dependent objects

Data objects and dependent objects serve clearly different purposes, but they
may appear at first to be the same. Where dependent objects represent business concepts, data objects do not; they are simply an efficient way of packaging an entity's fields for access by clients. Data objects may package dependent objects along with more primitive attributes, but they are not dependent
objects themselves.

Data objects are simple structures

Keep the data objects as simple as possible; ideally, they should be similar to a simple struct in C. In other words, the data object should not have any business logic at all; it should only have fields. All the business logic should remain in the entity bean, where it is centralized and easily maintained. In addition, some EJB systems based on CORBA 2.0 may not be capable of passing complex objects by value.

In order to keep the semantics of a C struct, data objects should not have accessor (get and set) methods for reading and writing their fields. The CabinData class doesn't have accessor methods; it only has fields and a couple of constructors. The lack of accessors reinforces the idea that the data object exists only to bundle fields together, not to "behave" in a particular manner. As a design concept, we want the data object to be a simple structure devoid of behavior; it's a matter of form following function. The exception is the multi-argument constructor, which is left as a convenience for the developer.

Bulk accessors bundle related fields

The bulk accessors can pass a subset of the entity's data. Some fields may have different security or transaction needs, which require that they be accessed separately. In the CabinBean, only a subset of the fields (name, deckLevel, bedCount) are passed in the data object. The id field is not included for several reasons: it doesn't describe the business concept, it's already found in the primary key, and the client should not edit it. The ship field is not passed because it should only be updated by certain individuals; the identities authorized to change this field are different from the identities allowed to change the other fields. Similarly, access to the ship may fall under a different transaction isolation level than the other fields (e.g., *Serializable* versus *Read Committed*).

In addition, it's more efficient to design bulk accessors that pass logically related fields. In entity beans with many fields, it is possible to group certain fields that are normally edited together. An employee bean, for example, might have several fields that are demographic in nature (address, phone, email) that can be logically separated from fields that are specific to benefits (compensation, 401K, health, vacation). Logically related fields can have their own bulk accessor; you might even want several bulk accessors in the same bean:

```
public interface Employee extends javax.ejb.EJBObject {

    public EmployeeBenefitsData getBenefitsData()
        throws RemoteException;
```

```
public void setBenefitsData(EmployeeBenefitsData data)
   throws RemoteException;

public EmployeeDemographicData getDemographicData()
   throws RemoteException;

public void setDemographicData(EmployeeDemographicData data)
   throws RemoteException;

// more simple accessors and other business methods follow

}
```

Retain simple accessors

Simple accessors (get and set methods for single fields) should not be abandoned when using bulk accessors. It is still important to allow editing of single fields. It's just as wasteful to use a bulk accessor to change one field as it is to change several fields using simple accessors.

Entity Objects

The pass-by-value section earlier gave you some good ground rules for when and how to use pass-by-value in EJB. Business concepts that do not meet the dependent object criteria should be modeled as either session or entity beans. It's easy to mistakenly adopt a strategy of passing business objects that would normally qualify as entity beans (Customer, Ship, and City) by value to the clients. Overzealous use of bulk accessors that pass data objects loaded with business behavior is bad design. The belief is that passing the entity objects to the client avoids unnecessary network traffic by keeping the set and get methods local. The problem with this approach is object equivalence. Entities are supposed to represent the actual data on the database, which means that they are shared and always reflect the current state of the data. Once an object is resident on the client, it is no longer representative of the data. It is easy for a client to end up with many dirty copies of the same entity, resulting in inconsistent processing and representation of data.

While it's true that the set and get methods of entity objects can introduce a lot of network traffic, implementing pass-by-value objects instead of using entity beans is not the answer. The network problem can be avoided if you stick to the design strategy elaborated throughout this book: remote clients interact primarily with session beans, not entity beans. You can also reduce network traffic significantly by using bulk accessors, provided that these accessors only transfer structures with no business logic. Finally, try to keep the entity beans on the server encapsulated in workflow defined by session beans. This eliminates the network traffic associated with entities, while ensuring that they always represent the correct data.

Improved Performance with Session Beans

In addition to defining the interactions among entity beans and other resources (workflow), session beans have another substantial benefit: they improve performance. The performance gains from using session beans are related to the concept of *granularity*. Granularity describes the scope of a business component, or how much business territory the component covers. As you learned previously, very fine-grained dependent business objects are usually modeled as pass-by-value objects. At a small granularity, you are dealing with entity beans like Ship or Cabin. These have a scope limited to a single concept and can only impact the data associated with that concept. Session beans represent large, coarse-grained components with a scope that covers several business concepts—all the business concepts or processes that the bean needs in order to accomplish a task. In distributed business computing, you rely on fine-grained components like entity beans to ensure simple, uniform, reusable, and safe access to data. Coarse-grained business components like session beans capture the interactions of entities or business processes that span multiple entities so that they can be reused; in doing so, they also improve performance on both the client and the server. As a rule of thumb, client applications should do most of their work with coarse-grained components like session beans, and with limited direct interaction with entity beans.

To understand how session beans improve performance, we have to address the most common problems cited with distributed component systems: network traffic, latency, and resource consumption.

Network Traffic and Latency

One of the biggest problems of distributed component systems is that they generate a lot of network traffic. This is especially true of component systems that rely solely on entity-type business components, such as EJB's EntityBean component. Every method call on a remote reference begins a remote method invocation loop, which sends information from the stub to the server and back to the stub. The loop requires data to be streamed to and from the client, consuming bandwidth. If we built a reservation system for Titan Cruise Lines, we would probably use several entity beans like Ship, Cabin, Cruise, and Customer. As we navigate through these fine-grained beans, requesting information, updating their states, and creating new beans, we generate network traffic. One client probably doesn't generate very much traffic, but multiply that by thousands of clients and we start to develop problems. Eventually, thousands of clients will produce so much network traffic that the system as a whole will suffer.

Another aspect of network communications is *latency*. Latency is the delay between the time we execute a command and the time it completes. With enterprise beans there is always a bit of latency due to the time it takes to communicate requests via the network. Each method invocation requires a RMI loop that takes time to travel from the client to the server and back to the client. A client that uses many beans will suffer from a time delay with each method invocation. Collectively, the latency delays can result in very slow clients that take several seconds to respond to each user action.

Accessing coarse-grained session beans from the client instead of fine-grained entity beans can substantially reduce problems with network bandwidth and latency. In Chapter 6, we developed the `bookPassage()` method on the Travel-Agent bean. The `bookPassage()` method encapsulates the interactions of entity beans that would otherwise have resided on the client. For the network cost of one method invocation on the client (`bookPassage()`), several tasks are performed on the EJB server. Using session beans to encapsulate several tasks reduces the number of remote method invocations needed to accomplish a task, which reduces the amount of network traffic and latency encountered while performing these tasks.

Resource Consumption

Make decisions about whether to access data directly or through entity beans with care. Listing behavior that is specific to a workflow should be provided by direct data access from a session bean. Methods like `listAvailableCabins()` in the TravelAgent bean use direct data access because it is less expensive than creating a find method in the Cabin bean that returns a list of Cabin beans. Every bean that the system has to deal with requires resources; by avoiding the use of components where their benefit is questionable, we can improve the performance of the whole system. A CTM is like a powerful truck, and each business component it manages is like a small weight. A truck is much better at hauling around a bunch of weights than an lightweight vehicle like a bicycle, but piling too many weights on the truck will make it just as ineffective as the bicycle. If neither vehicle can move, which one is better?

Striking a Balance

We don't want to abandon the use of entity business components, because they provide several advantages over traditional two-tier computing. They allow us to encapsulate the business logic and data of a business concept so that it can be used consistently and reused safely across applications. In short, entity business components are better for accessing business state because they simplify data access.

At the same time, we don't want to overuse entity beans on the client. Instead, we want the client to interact with coarse-grained session beans that encapsulate the interactions of small-grained entity beans. There are situations where the client application should interact with entity beans directly. If a client application needs to edit a specific entity—change the address of a customer, for example—exposing the client to the entity bean is more practical than using a session bean. If, however, a task needs to be performed that involves the interactions of more than one entity bean—transferring money from account to another, for example—then a session bean should be used.

When a client application needs to perform a very specific operation on an entity, like an update, it makes sense to make the entity available to client directly. If the client is performing a task that spans business concepts or otherwise involves more then one entity, that task should be modeled in a session bean as a workflow. A good design will emphasize the use of coarse-grained session beans as workflow and limit the number of activities that require direct client access to entity beans.

Listing Behavior

Chapter 7 spends some time discussing the TravelAgent bean's listAvailable-Cabins() method as an example of a method that returns a list of tabular data. This section provides several different strategies for implementing listing behavior in your beans.

Tabular data is data that is arranged into rows and columns. Tabular data is often used to let application users select or inspect data in the system. Enterprise Java-Beans lets you use find methods to list entity beans, but this mechanism is not a silver bullet. In many circumstances, find methods that return remote references are a heavyweight solution to a lightweight problem. For example, Table 9-1 shows the schedule for a cruise.

Table 9-1. Hypothetical Cruise Schedule

Cruise ID	Port-of-Call	Arrive	Depart
233	San Juan	June 4, 1999	June 5, 1999
233	Aruba	June 7, 1999	June 8, 1999
233	Cartagena	June 9, 1999	June 10, 1999
233	San Blas Islands	June 11, 1999	June 12, 1999

It would be possible to create a Port-Of-Call entity object that represents every destination, and then obtain a list of destinations using a find method, but this would be overkill. Recognizing that the data is not shared and only useful in this one circumstance, we would rather present the data as a simple tabular listing.

In this case, we will present the data to the bean client as an array of String objects, with the values separated by a character delimiter. Here is the method signature used to obtain the data:.

```
public interface Schedule implements javax.ejb.EJBObject {
    public String [] getSchedule(int ID) throws RemoteException;
}
```

And here is the structure of the String values returned by the getSchedule() method:

```
233; San Juan; June 4, 1999; June 5, 1999
233; Aruba; June 7, 1999; June 8, 1999
233; Cartegena; June 9, 1999; June 10, 1999
233; San Blas Islands; June 11, 1999; June 12, 1999
```

The data could also be returned as a multidimensional array of strings, in which each column represents one field. This would certainly make it easier to reference each data item, but would also complicate navigation.

One disadvantage to using the simple array strategy is that Java is limited to single type arrays. In other words, all the elements in the array must be of the same type. We use an array of Strings here because it has the most flexibility for representing other data types. We could also have used an array of Objects or even a Vector. The problem with using an Object array or a Vector is that there is no typing information at runtime or development time.

Implementing lists as arrays of structures

Instead of returning a simple array, a method that implements some sort of listing behavior can also return an array of structures. For example, to return the cruise ship schedule data illustrated in Table 9-1, you could return an array of schedule structures. The structures are simple Java objects with no behavior (i.e., no methods) that are passed in an array. The definition of the structure and the bean interface that would be used are:

```
// Definition of the bean that uses the Structure
public interface Schedule implements javax.ejb.EJBObject {
    public CruiseScheduleItem [] getSchedule(int ID) throws RemoteException;
}

// Definition of the Structure
public class CruiseScheduleItem {
    public int cruiseID;
    public String portName;
    public java.util.Date arrival;
    public java.util.Date departure;
}
```

Using structures allows the data elements to be of different types. In addition, the structures are self describing: it is easy to determine the structure of the data in the tabular set based on its class definition.

Implementing lists as ResultSets

A more sophisticated and flexible way to implement a list is to provide a pass-by-value implementation of the `java.sql.ResultSet` interface. Although it is defined in the JDBC package (`java.sql`) the `ResultSet` interface is semantically independent of relational databases; it can be used to represent any set of tabular data. Since the `ResultSet` interface is familiar to most enterprise Java developers, it is an excellent construct for use in listing behavior. Using the `ResultSet` strategy, the signature of the `getSchedule()` method would be:

```
public interface Schedule implements javax.ejb.EJBObject {
    public ResultSet getSchedule(int cruiseID) throws RemoteException;
}
```

In some cases, the tabular data displayed at the client may be generated using standard SQL through a JDBC driver. If the circumstances permit, you may choose to perform the query in a session bean and return the result set directly to the client through a listing method. However, there are many cases in which you don't want to return a `ResultSet` that comes directly from JDBC drivers. A `ResultSet` from a JDBC 1.x driver is normally connected directly to the database, which increases network overhead and exposes your data source to the client. In these cases, you can implement your own `ResultSet` object that uses arrays or vectors to cache the data. JDBC 2.0 provides a cached `javax.sql.RowSet` that looks like a `ResultSet`, but is passed by value and provides features like reverse scrolling. You can use the `RowSet`, but don't expose behavior that allows the result set to be updated. Data updates should only be performed by bean methods.

In some cases, the tabular data comes from several data sources or nonrelational databases. In these cases, you can query the data using the appropriate mechanisms within the listing bean, and then reformat the data into your `ResultSet` implementation. Regardless of the source of data, you still want to present it as tabular data using a custom implementation of the `ResultSet` interface.

Using a `ResultSet` has a number of advantages and disadvantages. First, the advantages:

Consistent interface for developers

> The `ResultSet` interface provides a consistent interface that developers are familiar with and that is consistent across different listing behaviors. Developers don't need to learn several different constructs for working with tabular data; they use the same `ResultSet` interface for all listing methods.

Consistent interface for automation

The `ResultSet` interface provides a consistent interface that allows software algorithms to operate on data independent of its content. A builder can be created that constructs an HTML or GUI table based on any set of results that implements the `ResultSet`.

Metadata operations

The `ResultSet` interface defines several metadata methods that provide developers with runtime information describing the result set they are working with.

Flexibility

The `ResultSet` interface is independent of the data content, which allows tabular sets to change their schema independent of the interfaces. A change in schema does not require a change to the method signatures of the listing operations.

And now, the disadvantages of using a `ResultSet`:

Complexity

The `ResultSet` interface strategy is much more complex than returning a simple array or an array of structures. It normally requires you to develop a custom implementation of the `ResultSet` interface. If properly designed, the custom implementation can be reused across all your listing methods, but it's still a significant development effort.

Hidden structure at development time

Although the `ResultSet` can describe itself through metadata at runtime, it cannot describe itself at development time. Unlike a simple array or an array of structures, the `ResultSet` interface provides no clues at development time about the structure of the underlying data. At runtime, metadata is available, but at development time, good documentation is required to express the structure of the data explicitly.

Bean Adapters

One of the most awkward aspects of the EJB bean interface types is that, in some cases, the callback methods are never used or are not relevant to the bean at all. A simple container-managed entity bean might have empty implementations for its `ejbLoad()`, `ejbStore()`, `ejbActivate()`, `ejbPassivate()`, or even its `setEntityContext()` methods. Stateless session beans provide an even better example of unnecessary callback methods: they must implement the `ejbActivate()` and `ejbPassivate()` methods even though these methods are never invoked!

To simplify the appearance of the bean class definitions, we can introduce *adapter classes* that hide callback methods that are never used or that have minimal implementations. Here is an adapter for the entity bean that provides empty implementations of all the EntityBean methods:

```
public class EntityAdapter implements javax.ejb.EntityBean {
    public EntityContext ejbContext;

    public void ejbActivate(){}
    public void ejbPassivate(){}
    public void ejbLoad(){}
    public void ejbStore(){}
    public void ejbRemove(){}

    public void setEntityContext(EntityContext ctx) {
        ejbContext = ctx;
    }
    public void unsetEntityContext() {
        ejbContext = null;
    }
    public EntityContext getEJBContext() {
        return ejbContext;
    }
}
```

We took care of capturing the EntityContext for use by the subclass. We can do this because most entity beans implement the context methods in exactly this way. We simply leverage the adapter class to manage this logic for our subclasses.

The bean class then extends this adapter class. Here's a modified version of the CabinBean class that uses the EntityAdapter to reduce the clutter of empty callback methods. Compare this definition of the CabinBean with the one from Chapter 2.

```
public class CabinBean extends EntityAdapter {

    public int id;
    public String name;
    public int deckLevel;
    public int shipID;
    public int bedCount;

    public int getShipID() {
        return shipID;
    }
    public void setShipID(int ship) {
        shipID = ship;
    }
    public CabinPK ejbCreate(int id) {
```

```
            // EJB 1.0 return type is void
            this.id = id;
            return null;
    }
    public void ejbPostCreate(int id) {
            // Do nothing. Required.
    }
    public String getName() {
            return name;
    }
    public void setName(String str) {
            name = str;
    }
    public int getBedCount() {
            return bedCount;
    }
    public void setBedCount(int bc) {
            bedCount = bc;
    }
    public int getDeckLevel() {
            return deckLevel;
    }
    public void setDeckLevel(int level) {
            deckLevel = level;
    }
}
```

If a callback method is deemed necessary, it can simply be overridden by a method in the bean class.

A similar Adapter class can be created for stateless session beans:

```
public class SessionAdapter implements javax.ejb.SessionBean {
    public SessionContext ejbContext;

    public void ejbActivate() {}
    public void ejbPassivate() {}
    public void ejbRemove() {}

    public void setSessionContext(SessionContext ctx) {
            ejbContext = ctx;
    }
    public SessionContext getEJBContext() {
            return ejbContext;
    }
}
```

Don't use these adapter classes when you need to override more than one or two of their methods. If you need to implement several of the callback methods, your code will be clearer if you don't use the adapter class. The adapter class also impacts the inheritance hierarchy of the bean class. If later you would like to implement a different superclass, one that captures business logic, the class inheritance would need to be modified.

Implementing a Common Interface

This book discourages implementing the remote interface in the bean class. This makes it a little more difficult to enforce consistency between the business methods defined in the remote interface and the corresponding methods on the bean class. There are good reasons for not implementing the remote interface in the bean class, but there is also a need for a common interface to ensure that the bean class and remote interface define the same business methods. This section describes a design alternative that allows you to use a common interface to ensure consistency between the bean class and the remote interface.

Why the Bean Class Shouldn't Implement the Remote Interface

There should be no difference, other than the missing java.rmi.RemoteException, between the business methods defined in the ShipBean and their corresponding business methods defined in the Ship interface. EJB requires you to match the method signatures so that the remote interface can accurately represent the bean class on the client. Why not implement the remote interface com.titan.Ship in the ShipBean class to ensure that these methods are matched correctly?

EJB allows a bean class to implement its remote interface, but this practice is discouraged for a couple of very good reasons. First, the remote interface is actually an extension of the javax.ejb.EJBObject interface, which you learned about in Chapter 5. This interface defines several methods that are implemented by the EJB container when the bean is deployed. Here is the definition of the javax.ejb.EJBObject interface:

```
public interface javax.ejb.EJBObject extends java.rmi.Remote {
    public abstract EJBHome getEJBHome();
    public abstract Handle getHandle();
    public abstract Object getPrimaryKey();
    public abstract boolean isIdentical(EJBObject obj);
    public abstract void remove();
}
```

The methods defined here are implemented and supported by the EJB object for use by client software and are not implemented by the javax.ejb.EntityBean class. In other words, these methods are intended for the remote interface's implementation, not the bean instance's. The bean instance implements the business methods defined in the remote interface, but it does so indirectly. The EJB object receives all the method invocations made on the remote interface; those that are business methods (like the getName or setCapacity methods in Ship) are delegated to the bean instance. The other methods, defined by the EJBObject, are handled by the container and are never delegated to the bean instance.

Just for kicks, change the ShipBean definition so that it implements the Ship interface as show here:

```
public class ShipBean implements Ship {
```

When you recompile the ShipBean, you should have five errors stating that the ShipBean must be declared abstract because it doesn't implement the methods from the javax.ejb.EJBObject. EJB allows you to implement the remote interface, but in so doing you clutter the bean class's definition with a bunch of methods that have nothing to do with its functionality. You can hide these methods in an adapter class; however, using an adapter for methods that have empty implementations is one thing, but using an adapter for methods that shouldn't be in the class at all is decidedly bad practice.

Another reason that beans should not implement the remote interface is that a client can be an application on a remote computer or it can be another bean. Beans as clients are very common. When calling a method on an object, the caller sometimes passes itself as one of the parameters.* In normal Java programming, an object passes a reference to itself using the this keyword. In EJB, however, clients, even bean clients, are only allowed to interact with the remote interfaces of beans. When one bean calls a method on another bean, it is not allowed to pass the this reference; it must obtain its own remote reference from its context and pass that instead. The fact that a bean class doesn't implement its remote interface prevents you from passing the this reference and forces you to get a reference to the interface from the context. The bean class won't compile if you attempt to use this as a remote reference. For example, assume that the ShipBean needs to call someMethod(Ship ship). It can't simply call someMethod(this) because ShipBean doesn't implement Ship. If, however, the bean instance implements the remote interface, you could mistakenly pass the bean instance reference using the this keyword to another bean.

Beans should always interact with the remote references of other beans so that method invocations are intercepted by the EJB objects. Remember that the EJB objects apply security, transaction, concurrency, and other system-level constraints

---

* This is frequently done in loopbacks where the invokee will need information about the invoker. Loopbacks are discouraged in EJB because they require reentrant programming, which should be avoided.

to method calls before they are delegated to the bean instance; the EJB object works with the container to manage the bean at runtime.

The proper way to obtain a bean's remote reference, within the bean class, is to use the EJBContext. Here is an example of how this works:

```
public class HypotheticalBean extends EntityBean {
    public EntityContext ejbContext;
    public void someMethod() throws RemoteException {

        Hypothetical mySelf = (Hypothetical) ejbContext.getEJBObject();

        // Do something interesting with the remote reference.
    }
    // More methods follow.
}
```

The Business Interface Alternative

Although it is undesirable for the bean class to implement its remote interface, we can define an intermediate interface that is used by both the bean class and the remote interface to ensure consistent business method definitions. We will call this intermediate interface the *business interface.*

The following code contains an example of a business interface defined for the Ship bean, called ShipBusiness. All the business methods formerly defined in the Ship interface are now defined in the ShipBusiness interface. The business interface defines all the business methods, including every exception that will be thrown from the remote interface when used at runtime:

```
package com.titan.ship;
import java.rmi.RemoteException;

public interface ShipBusiness {
    public String getName() throws RemoteException;
    public void setName(String name) throws RemoteException;
    public void setCapacity(int cap) throws RemoteException;
    public int getCapacity() throws RemoteException;
    public double getTonnage() throws RemoteException;
    public void setTonnage(double tons) throws RemoteException;
}
```

Once the business interface is defined, it can be extended by the remote interface. The remote interface extends both the ShipBusiness and the EJBObject interfaces, giving it all the business methods and the EJBObject methods that the container will implement at deployment time:

```
package com.titan.ship;
import javax.ejb.EJBObject;
```

```
public interface Ship extends ShipBusiness, javax.ejb.EJBObject {
}
```

Finally, we can implement the business interface in the bean class as we would any other interface:

```
public class ShipBean implements ShipBusiness, javax.ejb.EntityBean {
    public int id;
    public String name;
    public int capacity;
    public double tonnage;

    public String getName() {
        return name;
    }
    public void setName(String n) {
        name = n;
    }
    public void setCapacity(int cap) {
        capacity = cap;
    }
    public int getCapacity() {
        return capacity;
    }
    public double getTonnage() {
        return tonnage;
    }
    public void setTonnage(double tons) {
        tonnage = tons;
    }

    // More methods follow...
}
```

In the case of the ShipBean class, we choose not to throw the RemoteException. Classes that implement interfaces can choose not to throw exceptions defined in the interface. They cannot, however, add exceptions. This is why the business interface must declare that its methods throw the RemoteException and all application exceptions. The remote interface should not modify the business interface definition. The bean class can choose not to throw the RemoteException, but it must throw all the application-specific exceptions.

The business interface is an easily implemented design strategy that will make it easier to develop beans. This book recommends that you use the business interface strategy in your own implementations. Remember not to pass the business interface in method calls; always use the bean's remote interface in method parameters and as return types.

Entity Beans Without Create Methods

If an entity bean is never meant to be created by a client, you can simply not implement a create() method on the home interface. This means that the entity in question can only be obtained using the find() methods on the home interface. Titan might implement this strategy with their Ship beans, so that new ships must be created by directly inserting a record into the database—a privilege that might be reserved for the database administrator. They wouldn't want some crazed travel agent inserting random ships into their cruise line.

Entity Bean Relationships

Business systems frequently define relationships between entity beans. These relationships can be complex or simple. The concept of a cabin and its relationship to a ship embodies both simple and complex relationships. A cabin always belongs to a particular ship—a relationship that's obviously fairly simple. From the ship's perspective, the relationship is more complex: a ship has many cabins and must maintain a relationship to all of them.

This section explores how to write entity beans that use container-managed persistence and maintain relationships with other beans. This information will be most useful to EJB 1.0 developers. EJB 1.0 does not allow references to other beans to be container-managed. This means that a bean needs to manage persistence for references to other beans within its own code.

If you're using EJB 1.1, you can probably ignore this section, particularly if your server has robust support for the persistence of bean references. While EJB 1.1 allows bean references to be container-managed fields, a few EJB 1.1 servers may not be able to persist relationships between beans. This section will be useful to developers using these limited EJB 1.1 servers. EJB 1.1 developers using bean-managed persistence may also find the strategies in this section useful.

However, since this is predominately a EJB 1.0 problem, the code in this section has been left in the EJB 1.0 style. EJB 1.1 developers must make minor changes to the code for it to work in EJB 1.1 servers.

Simple Associations

In Titan Cruises, the business concept of a cabin models the real-world cabins that are in all of Titan's ships. Regardless of the ship, cabins all have certain attributes that we want to capture in the Cabin business concept: cabin name, deck level, and so forth. Important to this discussion is the cabin's relationship to its ship. How do we model and implement this simple relationship?

There are several alternatives, which can be grouped into two general categories: implementation-specific and non-implementation-specific. Both categories have their own strengths and weaknesses, which we will explore later in this section.

Let's start by defining the Cabin bean's remote interface. We add methods that allow the cabin to set and get the Ship as a bean, rather than by its ID. The advantage of this approach is that it encapsulates the Ship bean's unique identifier and deals with business concepts as beans, not database-dependent IDs.

```
package com.titan.cabin;
import com.titan.ship.Ship;
import java.rmi.RemoteException;

public interface Cabin extends javax.ejb.EJBObject {
    public Ship getShip() throws RemoteException;
    public void setShip(Ship ship) throws RemoteException;

    public String getName() throws RemoteException;
    public void setName(String str) throws RemoteException;
    public int getDeckLevel() throws RemoteException;
    public void setDeckLevel(int level) throws RemoteException;
    public int getBedCount() throws RemoteException;
    public void setBedCount(int bc) throws RemoteException;
}
```

Maintaining the database mapping

The simplest strategy for managing the cabin-to-ship relationship would be to support the relationship as defined in the database. In the relational database, the CABIN table includes a foreign key to the SHIP table's primary key, called SHIP_ID. In its current definition, we maintain the database mapping by preserving the SHIP_ID as an integer value. We can modify the behavior slightly by using the Ship bean in the get and set methods rather than the ID:

```
public class CabinBean implements javax.ejb.EntityBean {

    public int id;
    public String name;
    public int deckLevel;
    public int bedCount;
    public int ship_id;
    public Ship ship;

    public javax.ejb.EntityContext ejbContext;
    public transient javax.naming.Context jndiContext;

    public Ship getShip() throws RemoteException {
        try {
```

```
            if (ship != null)
                return ship;
            else {
                ShipHome home = (ShipHome)getHome("jndiName_ShipHome");
                ship = home.findByPrimaryKey(new ShipPK(ship_id));
                return ship;
            }
        } catch(javax.ejb.FinderException fe) {
            throw new RemoteException("Invalid Ship",fe);
        }
    }
    public void setShip(Ship ship) throws RemoteException {
        ship_id = ((ShipPK)ship.getPrimaryKey()).id;
        this.ship = ship;
    }
    protected Object getHome(String name) throws RemoteException {
        try {
            String jndiName =
                ejbContext.getEnvironment().getProperty(name);
            return getJndiContext().lookup(jndiName);
        } catch(javax.naming.NamingException ne) {
            throw new RemoteException("Could not lookup ("+name+")",ne);
        }
    }
    private javax.naming.Context getJndiContext()
        throws javax.naming.NamingException {
        if (jndiContext != null)
            return jndiContext;

        Properties p = new Properties();

        // ... Specify the JNDI properties specific to the vendor.

        jndiContext = new InitialContext(p);
        return jndiContext;
    }
    public void ejbActivate() {
        ship = null;
    }
}
```

From the client's standpoint, the Cabin bean now models its relationship to the Ship bean as a business concept and not as a database ID. The advantage of this approach is that we maintain the database mapping defined by the CABIN table while hiding the mapping from the client. The disadvantage is that the bean must frequently dereference the ship's primary key whenever a client invokes the getShip() method. If the entity bean has been deactivated since the ship's remote reference was last obtained, the reference will need to be reobtained.

After you've deployed this new version of the Cabin bean, you can use a client application to see if your code works. You can use code like this in your client:

```
Context ctx = getInitialContext();
CabinHome cabinHome = (CabinHome)ctx.lookup("CabinHome");
CabinPK pk = new CabinPK();
pk.id = 1;
Cabin cab = cabinHome.findByPrimaryKey(pk);
System.out.println(cab.getName());
Ship ship = cab.getShip();
System.out.println(ship.getName());
```

Mapping serializable to VARBINARY

With the Cabin bean, the use of the database mappings is the most straightforward approach to preserving the Cabin bean's relationship to the Ship bean. With other relationships, a relational database foreign key may not already exist. In this case, we need to preserve the relationship in the form of primary keys or handles.

Both primary keys and handles are serializable, so they can be preserved in a relational database as the JDBC type VARBINARY. The data type in the actual database will vary; some databases use BLOB while others use a different data type to indicate variable-length binary data. These data types are typically used for storing arbitrary binary data-like images. If you are using an existing database and need to preserve a nonrelational association between entities, you must update the table structure to include a VARBINARY type column.

Whether we use the primary key or the handle, we need to obtain it from the Ship bean and preserve it in the database. To do this, we use Java serialization to convert the primary key or handle into a byte array, which we can then save in the database as binary data. We can convert this data back into a usable key or handle as needed. One way to do this is to define a couple of simple methods that can take any Serializable object and make it into a byte array and convert it back. These methods are defined as follows:

```
public byte [] serialize(Object obj) throws IOException {
    ByteArrayOutputStream byteStream = new ByteArrayOutputStream();
    ObjectOutputStream oos = new ObjectOutputStream(byteStream);
    oos.writeObject(obj);
    return byteStream.toByteArray();
}
public Object deserialize(byte [] byteArray)
    throws IOException,ClassNotFoundException {
    ByteArrayInputStream byteStream = new ByteArrayInputStream(byteArray);
    ObjectInputStream oos = new ObjectInputStream(byteStream);
    return oos.readObject();
}
```

Preserving the primary key

If you can't preserve a foreign database ID, you can preserve the primary key directly. We can use the serialize() method defined earlier in setShip(Ship ship) to preserve the primary key of the Ship bean in the database:

```
public class CabinBean implements javax.ejb.EntityBean {

    public int id;
    public String name;
    public int deckLevel;
    public byte [] shipBinary;
    public int bedCount;
    public Ship ship;

    public javax.ejb.EntityContext ejbContext;
    public transient javax.naming.Context jndiContext;

    public Ship getShip() throws RemoteException {
      try {
        if (ship != null)
            return ship;
        else {
            ShipHome home = (ShipHome)getHome("jndiName_ShipHome");
            ShipPK pk = (ShipPK)deserialize(shipBinary);
            ship = home.findByPrimaryKey(pk);
                return ship;
        }
      } catch(Exception e) {
          throw new RemoteException("Invalid Ship",e);
      }
    }
    public void setShip(Ship ship) throws RemoteException {
        try {
        Object pk = ship.getPrimaryKey();
            shipBinary = serialize(pk);
            this.ship = ship;
        } catch(Exception e) {
            throw new RemoteException("Ship not set",e);
        }
    }
}
```

We have replaced the ship_id field with shipBinary. Remember, we are now looking at situations where the relationship between entities cannot be modeled in a relational database. When the CabinBean class is persisted to the database, the shipBinary field is written to the database with the primary key's serialized value. If the bean uses container-managed persistence, the shipBinary field will need to be mapped to the BLOB or binary column of the table. If the bean uses bean-managed persistence, the JDBC API will simply return a binary data type from the appropriate column.

Preserving the handle

Using the handle to preserve simple relationships is almost exactly the same as using the primary key. To preserve the handle, we can use the same shipBinary field that we used to save the primary key strategy; we only need to make a couple of simple changes to the setShip() and getShip() methods:

```
public Ship getShip() throws RemoteException {
    try {
      if (ship != null)
          return ship;
      else {
          Handle handle = (Handle)deserialize(shipBinary);
          ship = (Ship)handle.getEJBObject();
          return ship;
      }
    } catch (Exception e) {
      throw new RemoteException("Invalid Ship",e);
    }
}
public void setShip(Ship ship) throws RemoteException {
    try {
        Object handle = ship.getHandle();
        shipBinary = serialize(handle);
        this.ship = ship;
    } catch (Exception e) {
        throw new RemoteException("Ship not set",e);
    }
}
```

In many cases, serializing the handle is simpler then using the primary key. This version of the getShip() method is much simpler: you don't need to reconstruct the primary key, and the getInitialContext() method is no longer needed. However, the use of handles over primary keys should be done with care. Handles are simpler, but also more volatile. A change in the container, naming, networking, or security can cause the handle to become invalid.

This strategy is especially useful when the primary key is more complex than our simple ShipPK. If the primary key is made up of several fields, for example, using a binary format provides more benefits.

Native Java persistence

Some database products support native persistence of Java objects. These might be object databases or even relational databases that can store Java objects. Entity

beans that use native persistence are the simplest to develop because there is no
need to convert fields to byte streams so they can be stored in the database. In the
following listing, the CabinBean class has been changed so that it uses native Java
persistence with the Ship bean's primary key:

```java
public class CabinBean implements javax.ejb.EntityBean {

    public int id;
    public String name;
    public int deckLevel;
    public ShipPK shipPK;
    public int bedCount;
    public Ship ship;

    public javax.ejb.EntityContext ejbContext;
    public transient javax.naming.Context jndiContext;

    public Ship getShip() throws RemoteException {
      try {
        if (ship != null)
            return ship;
        else {
            ShipHome home = (ShipHome)getHome("jndiName_ShipHome");
            ship = home.findByPrimaryKey(shipPK);
            return ship;
        }
      } catch(Exception e) {
         throw new RemoteException("Invalid Ship",e);
      }
    }
    public void setShip(Ship ship) throws RemoteException {
       try {
          shipPK = (ShipPK)ship.getPrimaryKey();
          this.ship = ship;
       } catch(Exception e) {
           throw new RemoteException("Ship not set",e);
       }
    }
    ...
}
```

Complex Entity Relationships

Situations in which an entity has a relationship to several other entities of a particular type are as common as simple relationships. An example of a complex relationship is a ship. In the real world, a ship may contain thousands of cabins. To
develop a Ship bean that models the relationship between a real-world ship and its
cabins, we can use the same strategies that we discussed earlier. The most impor-

tant difference is that we're now discussing one-to-many associations rather than one-to-one. Before we get started, let's add a couple of new methods to the Ship bean's remote interface:

```
package com.titan.ship;

import com.titan.cabin.Cabin;
import javax.ejb.EJBObject;
import java.rmi.RemoteException;

public interface Ship extends javax.ejb.EJBObject {
    public Cabin [] getCabins() throws RemoteException;
    public void addCabin(Cabin cabin) throws RemoteException;
    public String getName() throws RemoteException;
    public void setName(String name) throws RemoteException;
    public void setCapacity(int cap) throws RemoteException;
    public int getCapacity() throws RemoteException;
    public double getTonnage() throws RemoteException;
    public void setTonnage(double tonnage) throws RemoteException;
}
```

The Ship bean's remote interface indicates that it is associated with many Cabin beans, which makes perfectly good sense as a business concept. The application developer using the Ship remote interface is not concerned with how the Cabin beans are stored in the Ship bean. Application developers are only concerned with using the two new methods, which allow them to obtain a list of cabins assigned to a specific ship and to add new cabins to the ship when appropriate.

One-to-many database mapping

The database structure provides a good relational model for mapping multiple cabins to a single ship. In the relational database, the CABIN table contains a foreign key called ship_id, which we used previously to manage the cabin's relationship to the ship.

As a foreign key, the ship_id provides us with a simple relational mapping from a ship to many cabins using an SQL join:

```
"select ID from CABIN where SHIP_ID = "+ship_id
```

Nothing complicated about that. Unfortunately, this relationship cannot be done conveniently with container-managed persistence, because we would need to map a collection to the join, which is not as straightforward as mapping a single entity field to a database field. More advanced object-to-relational mapping software will simplify this task, but these advanced tools are not always available and have their own limitations. If your EJB server doesn't support object-to-relational mapping, you will need an alternative solution. One alternative is to use bean-managed persistence to leverage the database mapping. If, however, your EJB server supports JavaBlend™ or some other object-to-relational technology, you may still be able to use container-managed persistence with a one-to-many database mapping.

If you examine the SHIP table definition, there is no column for storing a list of cabins, so we will not store this relationship directly in the SHIP table. Instead, we use a Vector called cabins to store this relationship temporarily. Every time the bean's ejbLoad() method is called, it populates the vector with cabin IDs, as it does all the other fields. Here are the getCabins() and ejbLoad() methods of the ShipBean class, with the changes for managing the vector of cabin IDs in bold:

```
public class ShipBean implements ShipBusiness, javax.ejb.EntityBean {
    public int id;
    public String name;
    public int capacity;
    public double tonnage;
    public Vector cabins;

    private EntityContext ejbContext;
    private transient Context jndiContext;

    public Cabin [] getCabins() throws RemoteException {
        try {
            Cabin [] cabinArray = new Cabin[cabins.size()];
            CabinHome home = (CabinHome)getHome("jndiName_CabinHome");
            for (int i = 0; i < cabinArray.length; i++) {
                CabinPK pk = (CabinPK)cabins.elementAt(i);
                cabinArray[i] = home.findByPrimaryKey(pk);
            }
            return cabinArray;
        } catch(Exception e) {
            throw new RemoteException("Cannot get cabins",e);
        }
    }
    public void ejbLoad() throws RemoteException {
        try {
            ShipPK pk = (ShipPK) ejbContext.getPrimaryKey();
            loadUsingId(pk.id);
        } catch(FinderException fe) {
            throw new RemoteException();
        }
    }
    private void loadUsingId(int id)
            throws RemoteException, FinderException {
        Connection con = null;
        PreparedStatement ps = null;
        ResultSet result = null;
        try {
```

```
                con = getConnection();
                ps = con.prepareStatement(
                  "select name, capacity, tonnage from Ship where id = ?");
                ps.setInt(1,id);
                result = ps.executeQuery();
                if (result.next()) {
                  this.id = id;
                  this.name = result.getString("name");
                  this.capacity = result.getInt("capacity");
                  this.tonnage = result.getDouble("tonnage");
                } else {
                  throw new FinderException("Cannot find Ship with id = "+id);
                }
                result.close();

                ps = con.prepareStatement(
                    "select ID from CABIN where SHIP_ID = ?");
                ps.setInt(1,id);
                result = ps.getResultSet();
                cabins = new Vector();
                while(result.next()) {
                  CabinPK pk = new CabinPK(result.getInt(1));
                  cabins.addElement(pk);
                }
              }
              catch (SQLException se) {
                throw new RemoteException (se.getMessage());
              }
              finally {
                try {
                  if (result != null) result.close();
                  if (ps != null) ps.close();
                  if (con!= null) con.close();
                } catch(SQLException se) {
                  se.printStackTrace();
                }
              }
          }
          ...
        }
```

Mapping serializable to VARBINARY

Using byte arrays and Java serialization works with complex relationships just as
well as it did with simple relationships. In this case, however, we are serializing
some kind of collection instead of a single reference. If, for example, the Ship
bean were container-managed, the ejbLoad() and ejbStore() methods could
be used to convert our cabins vector between its representation as a Vector and

a byte array. The following code illustrates how this could work with container-managed persistence; it applies equally well to Cabin primary keys or Cabin bean Handle objects:

```
public class ShipBean implements ShipBusiness, javax.ejb.EntityBean {
    public int id;
    public String name;
    public int capacity;
    public double tonnage;
    public Vector cabins;
    public byte [] cabinBinary;

    public void ejbLoad() throws RemoteException {
        try {
          if (cabinBinary != null)
            cabins = (java.util.Vector)deserialize(cabinBinary);
        } catch(Exception e) {
            throw new RemoteException("Invalid Cabin aggregation ",e);
        }
    }
    public void ejbStore() throws RemoteException {
        try {
          if (cabins != null)
              cabinBinary = serialize(cabins);
        } catch(Exception e) {
            throw new RemoteException("Invalid Cabin aggregation",e);
        }
    }
    public byte [] serialize(Object obj) throws IOException {
        ByteArrayOutputStream byteStream = new ByteArrayOutputStream();
        ObjectOutputStream oos = new ObjectOutputStream(byteStream);
        oos.writeObject(obj);
        return byteStream.toByteArray();
    }
    public Object deserialize(byte [] byteArray)
          throws IOException,ClassNotFoundException {
        ByteArrayInputStream byteStream =
            new ByteArrayInputStream(byteArray);
        ObjectInputStream oos = new ObjectInputStream(byteStream);
        return oos.readObject();
    }
    ...
}
```

Native Java persistence

As with the simple relationships, preserving complex relationships is the easiest with native Java persistence. The ShipBean definition is much simpler because the cabins vector can be stored directly, without converting it to a binary format.

Using this strategy, we can opt to preserve the `CabinPK` types or Cabin bean handles for the aggregated Cabin beans.

Object-to-Relational Mapping Tools

Some EJB vendors provide object-to-relational mapping tools that, using wizards, can create object representations of relational databases, generate tables from objects, or map existing objects to existing tables. These tools are outside the scope of this book because they are proprietary in nature and cannot generally be used to produce beans that can be used across EJB servers. In other words, in many cases, once you have begun to rely on a mapping tool to define a bean's persistence, you might not be able to migrate your beans to a different EJB server; the bean definition is bound to the mapping tool.

Mapping tools can make bean developers much more productive, but you should consider the implementation-specific details of your tool before using it. If you will need to migrate your application to a bigger, faster EJB server in the future, make sure that the mapping tool you use is supported in other EJB servers.

Some products that perform object-to-relational mapping use JDBC. The Object People's TOPLink and Watershed's ROF are examples of this type of product. These products provide more flexibility for mapping objects to a relational database and are not as dependent on the EJB server. However, EJB servers must support these products in order for them to be used, so again let caution guide your decisions about using these products.

When Entity Beans Are Not an Option

A couple of EJB 1.0 servers do not support entity beans. This is a legitimate choice, since support for entity beans is not required in EJB 1.0.* This section provides some strategies for developing systems that only use session beans for EJB 1.0 developers.

Entity bean support is required in EJB 1.1. If you're using EJB 1.1, you can skip this section.

Emulating Entity Beans with Session Beans

Session beans that implement the `SessionSynchronization` interface (discussed in Chapter 8) can emulate some of the functionality of bean-managed entity beans. This approach provides a couple of advantages. First, these session

---

* Support for entity beans is required in Version 1.1 of EJB.

beans can represent entity business concepts like entity beans; second, dependency on vendor-specific object-to-relational mapping tools is avoided.

Unfortunately, session beans were never designed to represent data directly in the database, so using them as a replacement for entity beans is problematic. Entity beans fulfill this duty nicely because they are transactional objects. When the attributes of a bean are changed, the changes are reflected in the database automatically in a transactionally safe manner. This cannot be duplicated in stateful session beans because they are transactionally aware but are not transactional objects. The difference is subtle but important. Stateful session beans are not shared like entity beans. There is no concurrency control when two clients attempt to access the same bean at the same time. In the case of the stateful session beans, each client gets its own instance, so many copies of the same session bean representing the same entity data can be in use concurrently. Database isolation can prevent some problems, but the danger of obtaining and using dirty data is high.

Other problems include the fact that session beans emulating entity beans cannot have find() methods in their home interfaces. Entity beans support find() methods as a convenient way to locate data. Find methods could be placed in the session bean's remote interface, but this would be inconsistent with the EJB component model. Also, a stateful session bean must use the SessionSynchronization interface to be transactionally safe, which requires that it only be used in the scope of the client's transaction. This is because methods like ejbCreate() and ejbRemove() are not transactional. In addition, ejbRemove() has a significantly different function in session beans than in entity beans. Should ejbRemove() end the conversation, delete data, or both?

Weighing all the benefits against the problems and risks of data inconsistency, it is recommended that you do not use stateful session beans to emulate entity beans. If your EJB server doesn't support entity beans, use the direct access or object-to-relational mapping options.

Limiting Session Beans to Workflow

Direct database access with JDBC

Perhaps the most straightforward and most portable option for using a server that only supports session beans is direct database access. We did some of this with the ProcessPayment bean and the TravelAgent bean in Chapter 7. When entity beans are not an option, we simply take this a step further. The following code is an example of the TravelAgent bean's bookPassage() method, coded with direct JDBC data access instead of using entity beans:

```
public Ticket bookPassage(CreditCard card, double price)
        throws RemoteException, IncompleteConversationalState {
```

```
        if (customerID == 0 || cruiseID == 0 || cabinID == 0) {
            throw new IncompleteConversationalState();
        }
        Connection con = null;
        PreparedStatement ps = null;;
        try {
            con = getConnection();

            // Insert reservation.
            ps = con.prepareStatement("insert into RESERVATION "+
                "(CUSTOMER_ID, CRUISE_ID, CABIN_ID, PRICE) values (?,?,?,?)");
            ps.setInt(1, customerID);
            ps.setInt(2, cruiseID);
            ps.setInt(3, cabinID);
            ps.setDouble(4, price);
            if (ps.executeUpdate() != 1) {
            throw new RemoteException (
                "Failed to add Reservation to database");
            }
            // Insert payment.
            ps = con.prepareStatement("insert into PAYMENT "+
                "(CUSTOMER_ID, AMOUNT, TYPE, CREDIT_NUMBER, CREDIT_EXP_DATE) "+
                "values(?,?,?,?,?)");
            ps.setInt(1, customerID);
            ps.setDouble(2, price);
            ps.setString(3, card.type);
            ps.setLong(4, card.number);
            ps.setDate(5, new java.sql.Date(card.experation.getTime()));
            if (ps.executeUpdate() != 1) {
            throw new RemoteException (
                "Failed to add Reservation to database");
            }
            Ticket ticket = new Ticket(customerID,cruiseID,cabinID,price);
            return ticket;

        } catch (SQLException se) {
          throw new RemoteException (se.getMessage());
        }
        finally {
          try {
            if (ps != null) ps.close();
            if (con!= null) con.close();
          } catch(SQLException se){
            se.printStackTrace();
          }
        }
    }
```

No mystery here: we have simply redefined the TravelAgent bean so that it works directly with the data through JDBC rather than using entity beans. This method is transactionally safe because an exception thrown anywhere within the method will cause all the database inserts to be rolled back. Very clean and simple.

The idea behind this strategy is to continue to model workflow or processes with session beans. The TravelAgent bean models the process of making a reservation. Its conversational state can be changed over the course of a conversation, and safe database changes can be made based on the conversational state.

Direct access with object-to-relational mapping tools

Object-to-relational mapping provides another mechanism for "direct" access to data in a stateful session bean. The advantage of object-to-relational mapping tools is that data can be encapsulated as object-like entity beans. So, for example, an object-to-relational mapping approach could end up looking very similar to our entity bean design. The problem with object-to-relational mapping is that most tools are proprietary and may not be reusable across EJB servers. In other words, the object-to-relational tool may bind you to one brand of EJB server. Object-to-relational mapping tools are, however, a much more expedient, safe, and productive mechanism to obtaining direct database access when entity beans are not available.

Avoid Chaining Stateful Session Beans

In developing session-only systems you will be tempted to use stateful session beans from inside other stateful session beans. While this appears to be a good modeling approach, it's problematic. Chaining stateful session beans can lead to problems when beans time out or throw exceptions that cause them to become invalid. Figure 9-1 shows a chain of stateful session beans, each of which maintains conversational state that other beans depend on to complete an operation encapsulated by bean A.

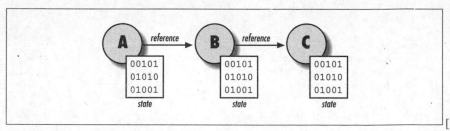

Figure 9-1. Chain of stateful session beans

If any one of the beans in this chain times out, say bean B, the conversational state trailing that bean is lost. If this conversational state was built up over a long time, considerable work can be lost. The chain of stateful session beans is only as strong as its weakest link. If one bean times out or becomes invalid, the entire conversational state on which bean A depends becomes invalid. Avoid chaining stateful session beans.

Using stateless session beans from within stateful session beans is not a problem, because a stateless session bean does not maintain any conversational state. Use stateless session beans from within stateful session beans as much as you need.

Using a stateful session bean from within a stateless session bean is almost nonsensical because the benefit of the stateful session bean's conversational state cannot be leveraged beyond the scope of the stateless session bean's method.

10

XML Deployment Descriptors

What Is an XML Deployment Descriptor?

One of the biggest changes between EJB 1.0 and 1.1 is the introduction of XML deployment descriptors. In EJB 1.0, deployment descriptors were serialized Java objects; you wrote a program that set up an appropriate `DeploymentDescriptor`, and then serialized that object. This approach was clumsy at best, even for experienced developers. XML deployment descriptors are much easier to edit, even without special tools for editing XML files. An XML deployment descriptor is simple enough that it's easy to create a descriptor using nothing more than your favorite text editor, be it Notepad, Emacs, or vi.

This chapter discusses what goes into an XML deployment descriptor; it teaches you how to write deployment descriptors for your beans. Keep in mind that you may never need to write a deployment descriptor by hand; most vendors of integrated development tools and EJB servers will provide tools for creating the descriptor automatically. Even if you have such a tool available, however, you should be familiar enough with deployment descriptors to be able to read them on your own.

This chapter doesn't attempt to teach you how to read or write correct XML. There are many books on the subject; a good quick reference is *XML Pocket Reference* by Bob Eckstein (O'Reilly). Very briefly, XML looks like HTML, but with different tag names and different attributes inside the tags. You won't see `<h1>` and `<p>` inside a deployment descriptor; you'll see tags like `<ejb-jar>`. But otherwise, if you expect an XML document to look like HTML, you're most of the way toward reading it. The tag names and attribute names for an XML document are defined by a special document called a DTD (Document Type Definition). Therefore, for XML deployment descriptors, there is a DTD that defines the tags and attributes that can be used in the document; the DTD for EJB 1.1 deployment descriptors is available online at *http://java.sun.com/j2ee/dtds/ejb-jar_1_1.dtd.*

There are a few other important differences between XML and HTML. XML is much more strict; many things that are acceptable in HTML are errors in XML. This shouldn't make a difference if you're just reading a deployment descriptor, but if you're writing one, you have to be careful. Two differences are particularly important: XML is case sensitive. You can't mix upper- and lowercase in your tag names. HTML doesn't care about the difference between <h1> and <H1>, but XML does. All of the tags and attributes used in deployment descriptors are lower case. In addition, XML will not forgive you if you don't supply closing tags. In HTML, it was okay to write <p>...<p>, without ever putting in </p> to end the paragraph. XML never allows you to be sloppy. Whenever you have a tag, there must always be a closing tag.

And that's about it. These few paragraphs don't even qualify as a quick introduction to XML, but the basic ideas are very simple, and that's really all you should need to get going.

The Contents of a Deployment Descriptor

We've discussed XML deployment descriptors throughout this book. At this point, you probably know enough to write deployment descriptors on your own. However, it's still worthwhile to take a tour through a complete deployment descriptor. Here's the deployment descriptor for the Cabin bean, which we created in Chapter 4. It contains most of the tags that are needed to describe entity beans, and session beans aren't much different. We'll use this deployment descriptor to guide our discussion in the following sections.

```
<?xml version="1.0"?>

<!DOCTYPE ejb-jar PUBLIC "-//Sun Microsystems, Inc.//DTD Enterprise
JavaBeans 1.1//EN" "http://java.sun.com/j2ee/dtds/ejb-jar_1_1.dtd">

<ejb-jar>
  <enterprise-beans>
    <entity>
      <description>
            This Cabin enterprise bean entity represents a cabin on
            a cruise ship.
      </description>
      <ejb-name>CabinBean</ejb-name>
```

```
            <home>com.titan.cabin.CabinHome</home>
            <remote>com.titan.cabin.Cabin</remote>
            <ejb-class>com.titan.cabin.CabinBean</ejb-class>
            <persistence-type>Container</persistence-type>
            <prim-key-class>com.titan.cabin.CabinPK</prim-key-class>
            <reentrant>False</reentrant>

            <cmp-field><field-name>id</field-name></cmp-field>
            <cmp-field><field-name>name</field-name></cmp-field>
            <cmp-field><field-name>deckLevel</field-name></cmp-field>
            <cmp-field><field-name>ship</field-name></cmp-field>
            <cmp-field><field-name>bedCount</field-name></cmp-field>
        </entity>
    </enterprise-beans>

    <assembly-descriptor>
        <security-role>
            <description>
                This role represents everyone who is allowed full access
                to the cabin bean.
            </description>
            <role-name>everyone</role-name>
        </security-role>

        <method-permission>
            <role-name>everyone</role-name>
            <method>
                <ejb-name>CabinBean</ejb-name>
                <method-name>*</method-name>
            </method>
        </method-permission>

        <container-transaction>
            <method>
                <ejb-name>CabinBean</ejb-name>
                <method-name>*</method-name>
            </method>
            <trans-attribute>Required</trans-attribute>
        </container-transaction>
    </assembly-descriptor>
</ejb-jar>
```

The Document Header

All XML documents start with a few tags that provide general information about
the document itself. The first tag specifies the version of XML that is in use:

```
<?xml version="1.0"?>
```

This tag identifies the document as an XML document that adheres to Version 1.0 of the XML specification.

The next tag specifies the DTD that defines the document:

```
<!DOCTYPE ejb-jar PUBLIC "-//Sun Microsystems, Inc.//DTD Enterprise
JavaBeans 1.1//EN" "http://java.sun.com/j2ee/dtds/ejb-jar_1_1.dtd">
```

This tag provides the URL from which you (or, more important, tools processing the deployment descriptor) can download the document. The DTD can be used to validate the XML document; this means that the EJB server deploying the bean can download the DTD and use it to prove that your deployment descriptor is correct (i.e., that it is organized correctly uses the right tag names, and that all the tags and attributes have appropriate parameters).

This tag also identifies the name of the document's root element, which is ejb-jar. The <ejb-jar> tag marks the beginning of the document proper.

The Descriptor's Body

The body of any XML document begins and ends with the tag for the document's "root element," which is defined by the DTD. For a deployment descriptor, the root element is named ejb-jar, and looks like this:

```
<ejb-jar>
... other elements ...
</ejb-jar>
```

All other elements must be nested within the ejb-jar element. You can place the following kinds of elements within ejb-jar:

<description> (optional)

The description element can be used to provide a description of this deployment descriptor. This element can be used in many contexts within a deployment descriptor: to describe the descriptor as a whole, to describe particular beans, to describe particular security roles, etc. The Cabin bean deployment descriptor doesn't use a description element for the deployment descriptor as a whole, but it does provide a description for the Cabin bean itself.

<display-name> (optional)

The display-name element is used by tools (like a deployment wizard) that are working with the deployment descriptor. It provides a convenient visual label for the entire JAR file and individual bean components.

<small-icon> and <large-icon> (optional)

These elements point to files within the JAR file that provide icons that a deployment wizard or some other tool can use to represent the JAR file. Icons must be image files in either the JPEG or GIF format. Small icons must be 16 × 16 pixels; large icons must be 32 × 32 pixels. These icon elements are also used in the entity and session elements to represent individual bean components.

<enterprise-beans> *(one required)*

The enterprise-beans element contains descriptions of the bean or beans that are contained in this JAR file. A deployment descriptor must have one, and only one, enterprise-beans element. Within this element, entity and session elements describe the individual beans.

<ejb-client-jar> *(optional)*

The ejb-client-jar provides the path of the client JAR, which normally contains all the classes (including stubs, remote and home interface classes, etc.) that the client will need to access the beans defined in the deployment descriptor. How client JAR files are organized and delivered to the client is not specified—consult your vendor's documentation.

<assembly-descriptor> *(optional)*

The application assembler or bean developer adds an assembly-descriptor element to the deployment descriptor to define how the beans are used in an actual application. The assembly-descriptor contains a number of elements that define the security roles used to access the bean, the method permissions that govern which roles can call different methods, and transactional attributes.

All of these elements are quite simple, except for the enterprise-beans element and the assembly-descriptor element. These two elements contain a lot of other material nested within them. We'll look at the enterprise-beans element first.

Describing Beans

The beans contained in a JAR file are described within the deployment descriptor's enterprise-beans element. So far, we've only talked about deployment descriptors for a single bean, but there's no reason that you can't package several beans in a JAR file and describe them all within a single deployment descriptor. We could, for example, have deployed the TravelAgent, ProcessPayment, Cruise, Customer, and Reservation beans in the same JAR file. The deployment descriptor would look something like this:

```
<?xml version="1.0"?>
<!DOCTYPE ejb-jar PUBLIC "-//Sun Microsystems, Inc.//DTD Enterprise
JavaBeans 1.1//EN" "http://java.sun.com/j2ee/dtds/ejb-jar_1_1.dtd">

<ejb-jar>
 <description>
```

```
    This Deployment includes all the beans needed to make a reservation:
    TravelAgent, ProcessPayment, Reservation, Customer, Cruise, and Cabin.
</description>
<enterprise-beans>
  <session>
     <ejb-name>TravelAgentBean</ejb-name>
     <remote>com.titan.travelagent.TravelAgent</remote>
     ...
  </session>
  <entity>
     <ejb-name>CustomerBean</ejb-name>
     <remote>com.titan.customer.Customer</remote>
     ...
  </entity>
  <session>
     <ejb-name>ProcessPaymentBean</ejb-name>
     <remote>com.titan.processpayment.ProcessPayment</remote>
     ...
  </session>
  ...
</enterprise-beans>
<assembly-descriptor>
...
</assembly-descriptor>
...
</ejb-jar>
```

In this descriptor, the enterprise-beans element contains two session elements and one entity element describing the three beans. Other elements within the entity and session elements provide detailed information about the beans; as you can see, the ejb-name element defines the bean's name. We'll discuss all of the things that can go into a bean's description later.

Multiple bean deployments have the advantage that they can share assembly information, which is defined in the assembly-descriptor element that follows the enterprise-beans element. In other words, beans can share security and transactional declarations, making it simpler to deploy them consistently. For example, deployment is easier if the same logical security roles control access to all the beans, and it's easiest to guarantee that the roles are defined consistently if they are defined in one place. It's also easier to ensure that the transactional attributes are applied consistently to all beans because you can declare them all at the same time.

Session and Entity Beans

The session and entity elements, which are used to describe session and entity beans, usually contain many elements nested within them, but the lists of allowable subelements are similar. Therefore, we'll discuss the session and entity elements together.

Like the ebj-jar element itself, a session or an entity element can optionally have description, display-name, small-icon, and large-icon elements. These are fairly self-explanatory and, in any case, mean the same as they did for the ejb-jar element. The description lets you provide a comment that describes the bean; the display-name is used by deployment tools to represent the bean; and the two icons are used to represent the bean in visual environments. The icons must point to JPEG or GIF images within the JAR file.

The other elements are more interesting:

<ejb-name> *(one required)*
This is the name of the bean component. It is used in the methodx element to scope method declarations to the correct bean. Throughout this book, we use ejb-names of the form "*Name*Bean" as the ejb-name for bean. Other common conventions use the ejb-names of the form "*Name*EJB" or "The*Name*."

<home> *(one required)*
This is the fully qualified class name of the bean's home interface.

<remote> *(one required)*
This is the fully qualified class name of the bean's remote interface.

<ejb-class> *(one required)*
This is the fully qualified class name of the bean class.

<primkey-field> *(optional; entity beans only)*
This element is used to specify the primary key field for entity beans that use container-managed persistence. Its value is the name of the field that is used as the primary key. It is not used if the bean has a custom primary key or if the entity bean manages its own persistence. This element is discussed in more detail in the section "Specifying Primary Keys," later in this chapter.

<prim-key-class> *(one required; entity beans only)*
This element specifies the class of the primary key for entity beans. Its value is the fully qualified name of the primary key class; it makes no difference whether you're using a custom compound primary key like the CabinPK, or a simple primkey-field like an Integer, String, Date, etc. If you defer definition of the primary key class to the deployer, specify the type as java.lang. Object in this element.

<persistence-type> *(one required; entity beans only)*
The persistence-type element declares that the entity bean uses either container-managed persistence or bean-managed persistence. This element can have one of two values: Container or Bean.

<reentrant> *(one required; entity beans only)*
The reentrant element declares that the bean either allows loopbacks (reentrant invocations) or not. This element can have one of two values: True or

`False`. `True` means that the bean allows loopbacks; `False` means that the bean throws an exception if a loopback occurs.

`<cmp-field>` *(zero or more; entity beans only)*

This element is used in entity beans with container-managed persistence. A `cmp-field` element must exist for each container-managed field in the bean class. Each `cmp-field` element may include a `description` element and must include a `field-name` element. The description is an optional comment describing the field. The `field-name` is required and must be the name of one of the bean's fields. The container will manage persistence for the given field. The following portion of a descriptor shows several `cmp-field` declarations for the Cabin bean:

```
<cmp-field>
  <description>This is the primary key</description>
  <field-name>id</field-name>
</cmp-field>
<cmp-field>
  <field-name>name</field-name>
</cmp-field>
<cmp-field>
  <field-name>deckLevel</field-name>
</cmp-field>
<cmp-field>
  <field-name>ship</field-name>
</cmp-field>
<cmp-field>
  <field-name>bedCount</field-name>
</cmp-field>
```

`<env-entry>` *(zero or more)*

This element declares an environment entry that is available through the JNDI ENC. The use of environment entries in a bean and a deployment descriptor is discussed further in the section "Environment Entries."

`<ejb-ref>` *(zero or more)*

This element declares a bean reference that is available through the JNDI ENC. The mechanism for making bean references available through the ENC is described in more detail later, in the section "References to Other Beans."

`<resource-ref>` *(zero or more)*

This element declares a reference to a connection factory that is available through the JNDI ENC. An example of a resource factory is the `javax.sql.DataSource`, which is used to obtain a connection to a database. This element is discussed in detail in the section "References to External Resources," later in this chapter.

`<security-role-ref>` *(zero or more)*

The `security-role-ref` element is used to declare security roles in the deployment descriptor, and map them into the security roles in effect for the bean's runtime environment. This element is described in more detail in the section "Security Roles."

`<session-type>` *(one required; session beans only)*

The `session-type` element declares that a session bean is either stateful or stateless. This element can have one of two values: `Stateful` or `Stateless`.

`<transaction-type>` *(one required; session beans only)*

The `transaction-type` element declares that a session bean either manages its own transactions, or that its transactions are managed by the container. This element can have one of two values: `Bean` or `Container`. A bean that manages its own transactions will not have `container-transaction` declarations in the `assembly-descriptor` section of the deployment descriptor.

Specifying Primary Keys

An entity bean does not always have to use a custom key class as a primary key. If there's a single field in the bean that can serve naturally as a unique identifier, you can use that field as the primary key without having to create a custom key. In the Cabin bean, for example, the primary key type was the `CabinPK`, which mapped to the bean class field `id` as shown here (the CabinBean is using bean-managed persistence to better illustrate):

```
public class CabinBean implements javax.ejb.EntityBean {

    public int id;
    public String name;
    public int deckLevel;
    public int ship;
    public int bedCount;

    public CabinPK ejbCreate(int id) {
        this.id = id;
        return new CabinPk(id);
    }
    ...
}
```

Instead of using the custom `CabinPK` class, we could have used the appropriate primitive wrapper, `java.lang.Integer`, and defined the CabinBean as:

```
public class CabinBean implements javax.ejb.EntityBean {

    public int id;
    public String name;
    public int deckLevel;
```

```
       public int ship;
       public int bedCount;

       public Integer ejbCreate(int id){
           this.id = id;
           return new Integer(id);
       }
       ...
   }
```

This simplifies things a lot. Instead of taking the time to define a custom primary key like CabinPK, we simply use the appropriate wrapper. To do this, we need to add a primkey-field element to the Cabin bean's deployment descriptor, so that it knows which field to use as the primary key. We also need to change the prim-key-class element to state that the Integer class is being used to represent the primary key. The following code shows how the Cabin bean's deployment descriptor would need to change to use Integer as the primary key field:

```
<entity>
    <description>
          This Cabin enterprise bean entity represents a cabin on
          a cruise ship.
    </description>
    <ejb-name>CabinBean</ejb-name>
    <home>com.titan.cabin.CabinHome</home>
    <remote>com.titan.cabin.Cabin</remote>
    <ejb-class>com.titan.cabin.CabinBean</ejb-class>
    <persistence-type>Bean</persistence-type>
    <prim-key-class>java.lang.Integer</prim-key-class>
    <primkey-field>id</primkey-field>
    <reentrant>False</reentrant>

    <cmp-field><field-name>id</field-name></cmp-field>
    <cmp-field><field-name>name</field-name></cmp-field>
    <cmp-field><field-name>deckLevel</field-name></cmp-field>
    <cmp-field><field-name>ship</field-name></cmp-field>
    <cmp-field><field-name>bedCount</field-name></cmp-field>
</entity>
```

Simple primary key fields are not limited to the primitive wrapper classes (Byte Boolean, Integer, etc.); any container-managed field can be used as a primary key as long as it's serializable. String types are probably the most common, but other types, such as java.lang.StringBuffer, java.util.Date, or even java.util.Hashtable are also valid. Custom types can also be primkey-fields providing that they are serializable. Of course, common sense should be used when choosing a primary key: because it is used as an index to the data in the database, it should be lightweight. Here's code for a bean that uses a Date as its primary key:

```
// bean class that uses Date as a primary key
public class HypotheticalBean implements javax.ejb.EntityBean {
```

```
    public Date creationDate;
    ...
    public Date ejbCreate() {
      creationDate = new Date();
      return creationDate;
    }
...
}
```

And here's the corresponding section of the deployment descriptor:

```
// primkey-field declaration for the Hypothetical bean
...
<entity>
    <ejb-name>HypotheticalBean</ejb-name>
    ...
    <prim-key-class>java.util.Date</prim-key-class>
    <primkey-field>creationDate</primkey-field>
    <reentrant>False</reentrant>

    <cmp-field><field-name>creationDate</field-name></cmp-field>
    ...
</entity>
```

Throughout the book we use custom compound primary keys, like ShipPK and CabinPK, instead of using simple primary keys. This may seem strange because these custom primary keys only wrap a single field, usually an integer, which could have been represented by an Integer and used as the primkey-field

The reason we use custom primary keys is simple: encapsulation. If the primary key fields of the beans change over time, using a custom key hides the changes from client applications that use the key. If, for example, the CabinBean changed to use both a String and a long primitive as the primary key fields instead of a single integer field (id), the Cabin bean's custom primary key class (CabinPK) would hide this change from the client application. If, however, we had used a primkey-field of java.lang.Integer, any client applications that use the findByPrimaryKey() method (and other similar operations involving the key) would have to be modified.

Deferring primary key definition

With container-managed persistence, it's also possible for the bean developer to defer defining the primary key, leaving key definition to the bean deployer. This feature might be needed if, for example, the primary key is generated by the database and is not a container-managed field in the bean class. Containers that have a tight integration with database or legacy systems that automatically generate primary keys might use this approach. It's also an attractive approach for vendors that sell shrink-wrapped beans because it makes the bean more portable. The following code shows how an entity bean using container-managed persistence defers the definition of the primary key to the deployer:

```
// bean class for bean that uses a deferred primary key
public class HypotheticalBean implements javax.ejb.EntityBean {
    ...
    public java.lang.Object ejbCreate(){
        ...
        return null;
    }
    ...
}


// home interface for bean with deferred primary key
public interface HypotheticalHome extends javax.ejb.EJBHome {

    public Hypothetical create() throws ...;

    public Hypothetical findByPrimaryKey(java.lang.Object key) throws ...;
}
```

Here's the relevant portion of the deployment descriptor:

```
// primkey-field declaration for the Hypothetical bean
...
<entity>
    <ejb-name>HypotheticalBean</ejb-name>
    ...
    <persistence-type>Container</persistence-type>
    <prim-key-class>java.lang.Object</prim-key-class>
    <reentrant>False</reentrant>

    <cmp-field><field-name>creationDate</field-name></cmp-field>
    ...
</entity>
```

Because the primary key is of type java.lang.Object, the client application's interaction with the bean's key is limited to the Object type and its methods.

Environment Entries

A deployment descriptor can define environment entries, which are values similar to properties that the bean can read when it is running. The bean can use environment entries to customize its behavior, find out about how it is deployed, etc.

The env-entry element is used to define environment entries. This element contains a description element (optional), env-entry-name (required), env-entry-type (required), and env-entry-value (optional). Here is a typical env-entry declaration:

```
<env-entry>
  <env-entry-name>minCheckNumber</env-entry-name>
  <env-entry-type>java.lang.Integer</env-entry-type>
  <env-entry-value>2000</env-entry-value>
</env-entry>
```

The env-entry-name is relative to the "java:comp/env" context. For example, the minCheckNumber entry can be accessed using the path "java:comp/env/minCheckNumber" in a JNDI ENC lookup:

```
InitialContext jndiContext = new InitialContext();
Integer miniumValue = (Integer)
    jndiContext.lookup("java:comp/env/minCheckNumber");
```

The env-entry-type can be of type String, or one of several primitive wrapper types including Integer, Long, Double, Float, Byte, Boolean, and Short.

The env-entry-value is optional. The value can be specified by the bean developer or deferred to the application assembler or deployer.

The subcontext "java:comp/env/ejb10-properties" can be used to make an entry available via the EJBContext.getEnvironment() method. This feature has been deprecated, but it may help you deploy EJB 1.0 beans within a EJB 1.1 server. The ejb-entry-type must always be java.lang.String for entries in this subcontext. Here's an example:

```
<env-entry>
  <description>This property is available through
      EJBContext.getEnvironment()</description>
  <env-entry-name>ejb10-properties/minCheckNumber</env-entry-name>
  <env-entry-type>java.lang.String</env-entry-name>
  <env-entry-value>20000</env-entry-value>
</env-entry>
```

References to Other Beans

The env-ref element is used to define references to other beans within the JNDI ENC. This makes it much easier for beans to reference other beans; they can use JNDI to look up a reference to the home interface for any beans that they are interested in.

The env-ref element contains description (optional), ejb-ref-name (required), ejb-ref-type (required), remote (required), home (required), and ejb-link (optional) elements. Here is a typical env-ref declaration:

```
<ejb-ref>
  <ejb-ref-name>ejb/CabinHome</ejb-ref-name>
```

```
        <ejb-ref-type>Entity</ejb-ref-type>
        <home>com.titan.cabin.CabinHome</home>
        <remote>com.titan.cabin.Cabin</remote>
    </ejb-ref>
```

The `ejb-ref-name` is relative to the `"java:comp/env"` context. It is recommended, but not required, that the name be placed under a subcontext of `ejb/`. Following this convention, the path used to access the Cabin bean's home would be `"java:comp/env/ejb/CabinHome"`. The following code shows how a client bean would use this context to look up a reference to the Cabin bean:

```
InitialContext jndiContext = new InititalContext();
Object ref = jndiContext.lookup("java:comp/env/ejb/CabinHome");
CabinHome home = (CabinHome)
        PortableRemoteObject.narrow(ref, CabinHome.class);
```

The `ejb-ref-type` can have one of two values: `Entity` or `Session`, according to whether the bean is an entity or a session bean.

The `home` element specifies the fully qualified class name of the bean's home interface; the `remote` element specifies the fully qualified class name of the bean's remote interface.

If the bean referenced by the `ejb-ref` element is deployed in the same deployment descriptor (it is defined under the same `ejb-jar` element), the `ejb-ref` element can be linked to the bean's declaration using the `ejb-link` element. If, for example, the TravelAgent bean uses references to the ProcessPayment and Customer beans and they are all declared in the same deployment descriptor, then the `ejb-ref` elements for the TravelAgent bean can use an `ejb-link` element to map its `ejb-ref` elements to the ProcessPayment and Customer beans. The `ejb-link` value must match one of the `ejb-name` values declared in the same deployment descriptor. Here's a portion of a deployment descriptor that uses the `ejb-link` element:

```
<ejb-jar>
<enterprise-beans>
    <session>
        <ejb-name>TravelAgentBean</ejb-name>
        <remote>com.titan.travelagent.TravelAgent</remote>
        ...
        <ejb-ref>
            <ejb-ref-name>ejb/ProcessPaymentHome</ejb-ref-name>
            <ejb-ref-type>Session</ejb-ref-type>
            <home>com.titan.processpayment.ProcessPaymentHome</home>
            <remote>com.titan.processpayment.ProcessPayment</remote>
            <ejb-link>ProcessPaymentBean</ejb-link>
        </ejb-ref>
        <ejb-ref>
            <ejb-ref-name>ejb/CustomerHome</ejb-ref-name>
```

```
            <ejb-ref-type>Entity</ejb-ref-type>
            <home>com.titan.customer.CustomerHome</home>
            <remote>com.titan.customer.Customer</remote>
            <ejb-link>CustomerBean</ejb-link>
        </ejb-ref>
    </session>
    <entity>
        <ejb-name>CustomerBean</ejb-name>
        <remote>com.titan.customer.Customer</remote>
        ...
    </entity>
    <session>
        <ejb-name>ProcessPaymentBean</ejb-name>
        <remote>com.titan.processpayment.ProcessPayment</remote>
        ...
    </session>
    ...
  </enterprise-beans>
  ...
</ejb-jar>
```

References to External Resources

Beans also use the JNDI ENC to look up external resources, like database connections, that they need to access. The mechanism for doing this is similar to the mechanism used for referencing other beans and environment entries: the external resources are mapped into a name within the JNDI ENC name space. For external resources, the mapping is performed by the resource-ref element.

The resource-ref element contains description (optional), res-ref-name (required), res-type (required), and res-auth (required) elements. Here is a resource-ref declaration used for a DataSource connection factory:

```
<resource-ref>
    <description>DataSource for the Titan database</description>
    <res-ref-name>jdbc/titanDB</res-ref-name>
    <res-type>javax.sql.DataSource</res-type>
    <res-auth>Container</res-auth>
</resource-ref>
```

The res-ref-name is relative to the "java:comp/env" context. Although it is not a requirement, it's a good idea to place connection factories under a subcontext that describes the resource type. For example:

• jdbc/ for a JDBC DataSource factory

• jms/ for a JMS QueueConnectionFactory or a TopicConnectionFactory factory

- mail/ for a JavaMail Session factory
- url/ for a javax.net.URL factory

Here is how a bean would use JNDI to look up a resource—in this case, a DataSource:

```
InitialContext jndiContext = new InitialContext();
DataSource source = (DataSource)
    jndiContext.lookup("java:comp/env/jdbc/titanDB");
```

The res-type is used to declare the fully qualified class name of the connection factory. In this example, the res-type is javax.sql.DataSource.

The res-auth tells the server who is responsible for authentication. It can have one of two values: Container or Application. If Container is specified, authentication (sign-on or login) to use the resource will be performed automatically by the container as specified at deployment time. If Application is specified, the bean itself must perform the necessary authentication before using the resource. The following code shows how a bean might sign on to a connection factory when Application is specified for res-auth:

```
InitialContext jndiContext = new InitialContext();
DataSource source = (DataSource)
    jndiContext.lookup("java:comp/env/jdbc/titanDB");

String loginName = ejbContext.getCallerPrincipal().getName();
String password = ...; // get password from somewhere

// use login name and password to obtain a database connection
java.sql.Connection con = source.getConnection(loginName, password);
```

Security Roles

The security-role-ref element is used to define the security roles that are used by a bean and to map them into the security roles that are in effect for the runtime environment. It can contain three subelements: an optional description, a role-name (required), and an optional role-link.

Here's how security roles are defined. When a role name is used in the EJBContext.isCallerInRole(String roleName) method, the role name must be statically defined (it cannot be derived at runtime) and it must be declared in the deployment descriptor using the security-role-ref element:

```
<-- security-role-ref declaration for Account bean -->
<entity>
  <ejb-name>AccountBean</ejb-name>
  ...
  <security-role-ref>
```

```
  <description>
      The caller must be a member of this role in
      order to withdraw over $10,000
  </description>
  <role-name>Manager</role-name>
  <role-link>Administrator</role-link>
 </security-role-ref>
  ..
</entity>
```

The role-name defined in the deployment descriptor must match the role name used in the EJBContext.isCallerInRole() method. Here is how the role name is used in the bean's code:

```
// Account bean uses the isCallerInRole() method
public class AccountBean implements EntityBean {
    int id;
    double balance;
    EntityContext context;

    public void withdraw(Double withdraw)
    throws AccessDeniedException {

        if (withdraw.doubleValue() > 10000) {
            boolean isManager = context.isCallerInRole("Manager");
            if (!isManager) {
                // only Managers can withdraw more than 10k
                throw new AccessDeniedException();
            }
        }
        balance = balance - withdraw.doubleValue();

    }
    ...
}
```

The role-link element is optional; it can be used to map the role name used in the bean to a logical role defined in a security-role element in the assembly-descriptor section of the deployment descriptor. If no role-link is specified, the deployer must map the security-role-ref to an existing security role in the target environment.

Describing Bean Assembly

At this point, we've said just about all that can be said about the bean itself. We've come to the end of the enterprise-beans element, and are now ready to describe how the beans are assembled into an application. That is, we are ready to talk about the other major element inside the ejb-jar element: the assembly-descriptor element.

The assembly-descriptor element is optional, though it's difficult to imagine a bean being deployed successfully without an assembly-descriptor. When we say that the assembly-descriptor is optional, we really mean that a developer whose only role is to create enterprise beans (for example, someone who is developing beans for use by another party and who has no role in deploying the beans) can omit this part of the deployment descriptor. The descriptor is valid without it—but someone will almost certainly have to fill in the assembly information before the bean can be deployed.

The assembly descriptor serves three purposes. It describes the transactional attributes of the bean's methods; it describes the logical security roles that are used in the method permissions; and it specifies method permissions (i.e., which roles are allowed to call each of the methods). To this end, an assembly-descriptor can contain three kinds of elements, each of which is fairly complex in its own right. These are:

<container-transaction> *(zero or more)*

> This element declares which transactional attributes apply to which methods. It contains an optional description element, one or more method elements, and exactly one trans-attribute element. Entity beans must have container-transaction declarations for all remote and home interface methods. Session beans that manage their own transactions will not have container-transaction declarations. This element is discussed in more detail in the section "Specifying a Bean's Transactional Attributes."

<security-role> *(zero or more)*

> The security-role element defines the security roles that are used when accessing a bean. These security roles are used in the method-permission element. A security-role element contains an optional description and one role-name. This element and the method-permission element are described in more detail in the section "Specifying Security Roles and Method Permissions."

<method-permission> *(zero or more)*

> This element specifies which security roles are allowed to call one or more of a bean's methods. It contains an optional description, one or more role-name elements, and one or more method elements. It is discussed in more detail in the section "Specifying Security Roles and Method Permissions," along with the security-role element.

The container-transaction and method-permission elements both rely on the ability to identify particular methods. This can be a complicated affair, given features of the Java language like method overloading. The method element is used within these tags to identify methods; it is described at length in the section "Identifying Specific Methods."

Specifying a Bean's Transactional Attributes

The container-transaction elements are used to declare the transaction attributes for all the beans defined in the deployment descriptor. A container-transaction element maps many bean methods to a single transaction attribute, so each container-transaction specifies one transaction attribute and one or more bean methods.

The container-transaction element includes a single trans-attribute element, which can have one of six values: NotSupported, Supports, Required, RequiresNew, Mandatory, and Never. These are the transactional attributes that we discussed in Chapter 8. In addition to the trans-attribute, the container-transaction element includes one or more method elements.

The method element itself contains at least two subelements: an ejb-name element, which specifies the name of the bean, and a method-name element, which specifies a subset of the bean's methods. The value of the method-name can be a method name or an asterisk (*), which acts as wildcard for all the bean's methods. There's a lot more complexity to handle overloading and other special cases, but that's enough for now; we'll discuss the rest later.

Here's an example that shows how the container-transaction element is typically used. Let's look again at the Cabin bean, which we've used as an example throughout. Let's assume that we want to give the transactional attribute Mandatory to the create() method; all other methods use the Required attribute:

```
<container-transaction>
    <method>
        <ejb-name>CabinBean</ejb-name>
        <method-name>*</method-name>
    </method>
    <trans-attribute>Required</trans-attribute>
</container-transaction>
<container-transaction>
    <method>
        <ejb-name>CabinBean</ejb-name>
        <method-name>create</method-name>
    </method>
    <trans-attribute>Mandatory</trans-attribute>
</container-transaction>
```

In the first container-transaction, we have a single method element that uses the wildcard character (*) to refer to all of the Cabin bean's methods. We set the transactional attribute for these methods to Required. Then, we have a second container-transaction element that specifies a single method of the Cabin bean: create(). We set the transactional attribute for this method to Mandatory.

This setting overrides the wildcard setting; in container-transaction elements, specific method declarations always override more general declarations.

The following methods must be assigned transaction attributes for each bean declared in the deployment descriptor:

For entity beans:

- *All business methods* defined in the remote interface (and all superinterfaces)
- *Create* methods defined in the home interface
- *Find* methods defined in the home interface
- *Remove* methods defined in the `EJBHome` and `EJBObject` interface

For session beans:

- *All Business methods* defined in the remote interface (and all superinterfaces)

For session beans, only the business methods have transaction attributes; the create and remove methods in session beans do not have truncation attributes.

Specifying Security Roles and Method Permissions

Two elements are used to define logical security roles and to specify which roles can call particular bean methods. The `security-role` element can contain an optional `description`, plus a single `role-name` that provides the name. An `assembly-descriptor` can contain any number of `security-role` elements.

It's important to realize that the security role names defined here are not derived from a specific security realm. These security role names are logical; they are simply labels that can be mapped to real security roles in the target environment at deployment time. For example, the following `security-role` declarations define two roles—everyone and administrator:

```
<security-role>
  <description>
    This role represents everyone who is allowed read/write access
    to existing cabin beans.
  </description>
  <role-name>everyone</role-name>
</security-role>
<security-role>
  <description>
    This role represents an administrator or manager who is
    allowed to create new cabin beans.  This role may also be a member
    or the everyone role.
  </description>
  <role-name>administrator</role-name>
</security-role>
```

These role names might not exist in the environment in which the beans will be deployed. There's nothing inherent about everyone that gives it fewer (or greater) privileges than an administrator. It's up to the deployer to map one or more roles from the target environment to the logical roles in the deployment descriptor. So for example, the deployer may find that the target environment has two roles, DBA (database administrator) and CSR (customer service representative), that map to the administrator and everyone roles defined in the security-role element.

Assigning roles to methods

Security roles in themselves wouldn't be worth much if you couldn't specify what the roles were allowed to do. That's where the method-permission element comes in. This element maps the security-roles to methods in the remote and home interfaces of the bean. A method-permission is a very flexible declaration that allows a many-to-many relationship between methods and roles. A method-permission contains an optional description, one or more method elements, and one or more role-name elements. The names specified in the role-name elements correspond to the roles that appear in the security-role elements. Here's one way to set method permissions for the Cabin bean:

```
<method-permission>
      <role-name>administrator</role-name>
      <method>
            <ejb-name>CabinBean</ejb-name>
            <method-name>*</method-name>
      </method>
</method-permission>
<method-permission>
      <role-name>everyone</role-name>
      <method>
            <ejb-name>CabinBean</ejb-name>
            <method-name>getDeckLevel</method-name>
      </method>
</method-permission>
```

In this example, the administrator role has access to all methods in the Cabin bean. The everyone role only has access to the getDeckLevel() method—it cannot access any of the other methods of the Cabin bean. Note that the specific method permissions are combined to form a union. The getDeckLevel() method, for example, is accessible by both the administrator and everyone roles, which is the union of the permissions declared in the descriptor. Once again, it's important to note that we still don't know what administrator and everyone mean. That's defined by the person deploying the bean, who must map these logical security roles to real security roles defined in the target environment.

All the methods defined in the remote or home interface and all superinterfaces, including the methods defined in the EJBObject and EJBHome interfaces, can be assigned security roles in the method-permission elements. Any method that is excluded will not be accessible by any security role.

Identifying Specific Methods

The method element is used by the method-permission and container-transaction elements to specify a specific group of methods in a particular bean. The method element always contains an ejb-name element that specifies the bean's name and a method-name element that specifies the method. It may also include a description, method-params elements that specify method parameters used to resolve overloaded methods, and a method-intf element that specifies whether the method belongs to the bean's home or remote interface. This last element takes care of the possibility that the same method name might be used in both interfaces.

Wildcard declarations

The method name in a method element can be a simple wildcard (*). A wildcard applies to all methods of the bean's home and remote interfaces. For example:

```
<method>
    <ejb-name>CabinBean</ejb-name>
    <method-name>*</method-name>
</method>
```

Although it's tempting to combine the wildcard with other characters, don't. The value get*, for example, is illegal. The asterisk (*) character can only be used by itself.

Named method declarations

Named declarations apply to all methods defined in the bean's remote and home interfaces that have the specified name. For example:

```
<method>
    <ejb-name>CabinBean</ejb-name>
    <method-name>create</method-name>
</method>
<method>
    <ejb-name>CabinBean</ejb-name>
    <method-name>getDeckLevel</method-name>
</method>
```

These declarations apply to all methods with the given name in both interfaces. They don't distinguish between overloaded methods. For example, if the home interface for the Cabin bean is modified so that it has three overloaded create() methods as shown here, the previous method declaration would apply to all three methods:

```
public interface CabinHome javax.ejb.EJBHome {
    public Cabin create()
        throws CreateException, RemoteException;
    public Cabin create(int id)
        throws CreateException, RemoteException;
    public Cabin create(int id, Ship ship, double [][] matrix)
        throws CreateException, RemoteException;
    ...
}
```

Specific method declarations

Specific method declarations use the method-params element to pinpoint a specific method by listing its parameters. This allows you to differentiate between overloaded methods. The method-params element contains zero or more method-param elements which correspond, in order, to each parameter type (including multidimensional arrays) declared in the method. To specify a method with no arguments, use a method-params element with no method-param elements nested within it.

For an example, let's look again at our Cabin bean, to which we've added some overloaded create() methods in the home interface. Here are three method elements, each of which specifies unambiguously one of the create() methods by listing its parameters:

```
<method>
    <description>
        Method: public Cabin create();
    </description>
    <ejb-name>CabinBean</ejb-name>
    <method-name>create</method-name>
    <method-params>
    </method-params>
</method>
<method>
    <description>
        Method: public Cabin create(int id);
    </description>
    <ejb-name>CabinBean</ejb-name>
    <method-name>create</method-name>
    <method-params>
```

```
            <method-param>int</method-param>
        </method-params>
    </method>
    <method>
        <description>
            Method: public Cabin create(int id, Ship ship, double [][] matrix);
        </description>
        <ejb-name>CabinBean</ejb-name>
        <method-name>create</method-name>
        <method-params>
            <method-param>int</method-param>
            <method-param>com.titan.ship.Ship</method-param>
            <method-param>double [][]</method-param>
        </method-params>
    </method>
```

Remote/home differentiation

There's one problem left. The same method name can be used in both the home
and remote interfaces. To resolve this ambiguity, you can add the method-intf
element to a method declaration as a modifier. Only two values are allowed for a
method-intf element: Remote and Home.

In reality, it's unlikely that a good developer would use the same method names in
both home and remote interfaces; that would lead to unnecessarily confusing
code. Realistically, it's more likely that you'll need the method-intf element in a
wildcarded declaration. For example, the following declaration specifies all of the
methods in the remote interface of the Cabin bean:

```
<method>
    <ejb-name>CabinBean</ejb-name>
    <method-name>*</method-name>
    <method-intf>Remote</method-intf>
</method>
```

All these styles of method declarations can be used in any combination within any
element that uses the method element. The method-permission elements are
combined to form a union of role-to-method permissions. For example, in the following listing, the first method-permission element declares that the administrator has access to the Cabin bean's home methods (create and find methods).
The second method-permission specifies that the everyone role has access to
the findByPrimaryKey() method. This means that both roles (everyone and
administrator) have access to the findByPrimaryKey() method.

```
<method-permission>
    <role-name>administrator</role-name>
    <method>
```

```
                <ejb-name>CabinBean</ejb-name>
                <method-name>*</method-name>
                <method-intf>Home</method_intf>
            </method>
        </method-permission>
    <method-permission>
            <role-name>everyone</role-name>
            <method>
                <ejb-name>CabinBean</ejb-name>
                <method-name>findByPrimaryKey</method-name>
            </method>
    </method-permission>
```

The ejb-jar File

The JAR file format is a platform-independent format for compressing, packaging, and delivering several files together. Based on ZIP file format and the ZLIB compression standards, the JAR (Java archive) packages and tool were originally developed to make downloads of Java applets more efficient. As a packaging mechanism, however, the JAR file format is a very convenient way to "shrink-wrap" components and other software for delivery to third parties. The original JavaBeans component architecture depends on JAR files for packaging, as does Enterprise JavaBeans. The goal in using the JAR file format in EJB is to package all the classes and interfaces associated with one or more beans, including the deployment descriptor, into one file.

The JAR file is created using a vendor-specific tool, or using the *jar* utility that is part of the Java 2, Standard Edition development kit. An ejb-jar file contains:

- The XML deployment descriptor
- The bean classes
- The remote and home interfaces
- The primary key class
- Dependent classes and interfaces

The XML deployment descriptor must be located in the path *META-INF/ejb-jar.xml*, and must contain all the deployment information for all the beans in the ejb-jar file. For each bean declared in the XML deployment descriptor, the ejb-jar file must contain its bean class, remote and home interfaces, and dependent classes and interfaces. Dependent classes and interfaces are usually things like application-specific exceptions, business interfaces, and other super types, and dependent objects that are used by the bean. In the ejb-jar file for the TravelAgent bean, for example, we would include the IncompleteConversationalState application exception and the Ticket and CreditCard classes, as well as the remote and home interfaces to other beans referenced by the TravelAgent bean, like the Customer and ProcessPayment bean.*

The *jar* utility can be used from the command line to package a bean in a JAR file. Here is an example of how the jar utility was used to package the Cabin bean in Chapter 4:

```
\dev % jar cf cabin.jar com/titan/cabin/*.class META-INF/ejb-jar.xml

F:\..\dev>jar cf cabin.jar com\titan\cabin\*.class META-INF\ejb-jar.xml
```

You might have to create the *META-INF* directory first, and copy *ejb-jar.xml* into that directory. The c option tells the *jar* utility to create a new JAR file that contains the files indicated in subsequent parameters. It also tells the *jar* utility to stream the resulting JAR file to standard output. The f option tells *jar* to redirect the standard output to a new file named in the second parameter (*cabin.jar*). It's important to get the order of the option letters and the command-line parameters to match. You can learn more about the *jar* utility and the java.util.zip package in *Java™ in a Nutshell* by David Flanagan (O'Reilly), or *Learning Java™*, by Pat Niemeyer and Jonathan Knudsen (formerly *Exploring Java™*, also published by O'Reilly).

The *jar* utility creates the file *cabin.jar* in the *dev* directory. If you're interested in looking at the contents of the JAR file, you can use any standard ZIP application (WinZip, PKZIP, etc.), or you can use the command *jar tvf cabin.jar*.

The client-jar File

EJB 1.1 also allows for a client-jar file, which includes only the interfaces and classes need by a client application to access a bean. This would include the remote and home interfaces, primary key, and any dependent types that the client is exposed to, such as application exceptions. The specification does not say how this is delivered to the client, what exactly it contains, or how it is packaged with the ejb-jar file. In other words, the client-jar file is a fairly vendor-specific concept in EJB.

---

* The EJB 1.1 specification also allows remote and home interfaces of referenced beans to be named in the manifest's Class-Path attribute, instead of including them in the JAR file. Use of the Class-Path entry in the JAR's manifest is addressed in more detail in the Java 2, Standard Edition specification.

11

Java 2, Enterprise Edition

The specification for the Java 2, Enterprise Edition (J2EE) defines a platform for developing web-enabled applications that includes Enterprise JavaBeans, Servlets, and Java Server Pages (JSP). J2EE products are application servers that provide a complete implementation of the EJB, Servlet, and JSP technologies. In addition, the J2EE outlines how these technologies work together to provide a complete solution. To understand what J2EE is, it's important that we introduce Servlets and JSP and explain the synergy between these technologies and Enterprise JavaBeans.

At risk of spoiling the story, J2EE provides two kinds of "glue" to make it easier for components to interact. We've already seen both types of glue. The JNDI Enterprise Naming Context (ENC) is used to standardize the way components look up resources that they need. We've seen the ENC in the context of enterprise beans; in this chapter, we'll look briefly at how servlets, JSPs, and even some clients can use the ENC to find resources. Second, the idea of deployment descriptors—in particular, the use of XML to define a language for deployment descriptors—has been extended to servlets and JSP. Java servlets and server pages can be packaged with deployment descriptors that define their relationship to their environment. Deployment descriptors are also used to define entire assemblies of many components into applications.

Servlets

The Servlet 2.2 specification defines a server-side component model that can be implemented by web server vendors. Servlets provide a simple but powerful API for generating web pages dynamically. (Although servlets can be used for many different request-response protocols, they are predominantly used to process HTTP requests for web pages.)

Servlets are developed in the same fashion as enterprise beans; they are Java classes that extend a base component class and have a deployment descriptor. Once a servlet is developed and packaged in a JAR file, it can be deployed in a web server. When a servlet is deployed, it is assigned to handle requests for a specific web page or assist other servlets in handling page requests. The following servlet, for example, might be assigned to handle any request for the *helloworld.html* page on a web server:

```
import javax.servlet.*;
import javax.servlet.http.*;

public class HelloWorld extends HttpServlet {

    protected void doGet(HttpServletRequest req, HttpServletResponse response)
        throws ServletException,java.io.IOException {

        try {
        ServletOutputStream writer = response.getWriter();
        writer.println("<HTML><BODY>");
        writer.println("<h1>Hello World!!</h1>");
        writer.println("</BODY></HTML>");
    } catch(Exception e) {
    // handle exception
    }
    ...
    }
```

When a browser sends a request for the page to the web server, the server delegates the request to the appropriate servlet instance by invoking the servlet's doGet() method.* The servlet is provided information about the request in the HttpServletRequest object, and can use the HttpServletResponse object to reply to the request. This simple servlet sends a short HTML document including the text "Hello World" back to the browser, which displays it. Figure 11-1 illustrates how a request is sent by a browser and serviced by a servlet running in a web server.

Servlets are similar to session beans because they both perform a service and can directly access backend resources like a database through JDBC, but they do not represent persistent data. Servlets do not, however, have support for transactions and are *not* composed of business methods. Servlets respond to very specific requests, usually HTTP requests, and respond by writing to an output stream.

---

* HttpServlets also have a doPost() method which handles requests for forms.

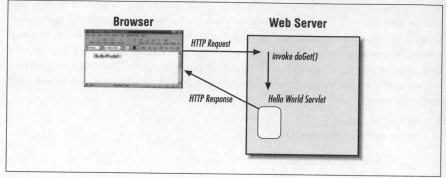

Figure 11-1. Servlet servicing an HTTP request

The Servlet specification is extensive and robust but also simple and elegant. It's a powerful server-side component model. You can learn more about servlets by reading *Java™ Servlet Programming*, by Jason Hunter and William Crawford (O'Reilly).

Java Server Pages

Java Server Pages (JSP) is an extension of the servlet component model that simplifies the process of generating HTML dynamically. JSP essentially allows you to incorporate Java directly into an HTML page as a scripting language. In J2EE, the Java code in a JSP page can access the JNDI ENC, just like the code in a servlet. In fact, JSP pages (text documents) are translated and compiled into Java servlets, which are then run in a web server just like any other servlet—some servers do the compilation automatically at runtime. JSP can also be used to generate XML documents dynamically.

Web Components and EJB

Together Servlets and JSP provide a powerful platform for generating web pages dynamically. Servlets and JSP, which are collectively called *web components*, can access resources like JDBC and enterprise beans. Because web components can access databases using JDBC, they can provide a powerful platform for e-commerce by allowing an enterprise to expose its business systems to the web through an HTML interface. HTML has several advantages over more conventional client applications, in Java or any other language. The most important advantages have to do with distribution and firewalls. Conventional clients need to be distributed and installed on client machines, which is their biggest limitation: they require additional work for deployment and maintenance. Applets, which are dynamically downloaded, can be used to eliminate the headache of installation, but applets have other limitations like sandbox restrictions and heavyweight downloads. In contrast, HTML is extremely lightweight, doesn't require prior installation, and doesn't suffer from security restrictions. In addition, HTML interfaces can be modified and enhanced at their source without having to update the clients.

Firewalls present another signification problem in e-commerce. HTTP, the protocol over which web pages are requested and delivered, can pass through most firewalls without a problem, but other protocols like IIOP or JRMP cannot. This has proven to be a significant barrier to the success of distributed object systems that must support access from anonymous clients. This means that distributed object applications generally cannot be created for a client base that may have arbitrary firewall configurations. HTTP does not have this limitation, since practically all firewalls allow HTTP to pass unhindered.

The problems with distribution and firewalls have lead the EJB industry to adopt, in large part, an architecture based on the collaborative use of web components (Servlets/JSP) and Enterprise JavaBeans. While web components provide the presentation logic for generating web pages, Enterprise JavaBeans provides a robust transactional middle tier for business logic. Web components access enterprise beans using the same API used by application clients. Each technology is doing what it does best: Servlets and JSP are excellent components for generating dynamic HTML, while Enterprise JavaBeans is an excellent platform for transactional business logic. Figure 11-2 illustrates how this architecture works.

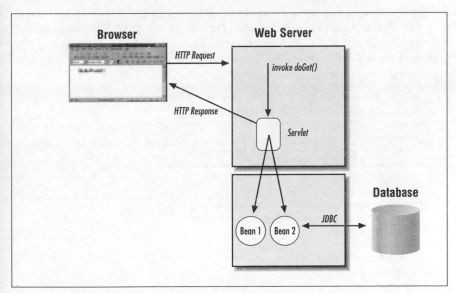

Figure 11-2. Using Servlets/JSP and EJB together

This web component–EJB architecture is so widely accepted that it begs the question, "Should there be a united platform?" This is the question that the J2EE specification is designed to answer. The J2EE specification defines a single application server platform that focuses on the interaction between these Servlets, JSP, and EJB. J2EE is important because it provides a specification for the interaction of web components with enterprise beans, making solutions more portable across vendors that support both component models.

J2EE Fills in the Gaps

The J2EE specification attempts to fill the gaps between the web components and Enterprise JavaBeans by defining how these technologies come together to form a complete platform.

One of the ways in which J2EE adds value is by creating a consistent programming model across web components and enterprise beans through the use of the JNDI ENC and XML deployment descriptors. A servlet in J2EE can access JDBC DataSource objects, environment entries, and references to enterprise beans through a JNDI ENC in exactly the same way that enterprise beans use the JNDI ENC. To support the JNDI ENC, web components have their own XML deployment descriptor that declares elements for the JNDI ENC (ejb-ref, resource-ref, env-entry) as well security roles and other elements specific to web components. In J2EE, web components (Servlets and JSP pages) along with their XML deployment descriptors, are packaged and deployed in JAR files with the extension .war, which stands for web archive. The use of the JNDI ENC, deployment descriptors, and JAR files in web components makes them consistent with the EJB programming model and unifies the entire J2EE platform. Here is a simple deployment descriptor for a web component:

```
<!DOCTYPE web-app PUBLIC "-//Sun Microsystems, Inc.//DTD Web Application 2.2//EN"
"http://java.sun.com/j2ee/dtds/web-app_1_2.dtd">
<web-app>
  <servlet>
    <servlet-name> HelloWorld </servlet-name>
    <servlet-class> HelloWorld.class </servlet-class>
  </servlet>
  <servlet-mapping>
    <servlet-name> HelloWorld </servlet-name>
    <url-pattern> /HelloWorld.jsp </url-pattern>
  </servlet-mapping>
  <session-config>
    <session-timeout>1</session-timeout>
  </session-config>
  <ejb-ref>
      <ejb-ref-name>ejb/ShipBean</ejb-ref-name>
      <ejb-ref-type>Entity</ejb-ref-type>
```

```
        <home>com.titan.ship.ShipBean</home>
        <remote>com.titan.ship.Ship</remote>
    </ejb-ref>
</web-app>
```

Use of the JNDI ENC makes it much simpler for web components to access Enterprise JavaBeans. The web component developer doesn't need to be concerned with the network location of beans; the server will map the ejb-ref elements listed in the deployment descriptor to the beans at deployment time. The JNDI ENC also supports access to a javax.jta.UserTransaction object, as is the case in EJB. The UserTransaction object allows the web component to manage transactions explicitly. The transaction context must be propagated to any enterprise beans accessed within the scope of the transaction (according to the transaction attribute of the bean method). A *.war* file can contain several servlets and JSP documents, which share an XML deployment descriptor.

J2EE also defines an *.ear* (Enterprise archive) file, which is a JAR file for packaging Enterprise JavaBean JAR files and web component JAR files (*.war* files) together into one complete deployment called a J2EE Application. A J2EE Application has its own XML deployment descriptor that points to the EJB and web component JAR files (called modules) as well as other elements like icons, descriptions, and the like. When a J2EE Application is created, interdependencies like ejb-ref elements can be resolved and security roles can be edited to provide a unified view of the entire web application. Here is a simple application deployment descriptor:

```
<!DOCTYPE application PUBLIC "-//Sun Microsystems, Inc.//DTDJ2EE Application 1.2//
EN" "http://java.sun.com/j2ee/dtds/application_1_2.dtd">

<application>
    <display-name>MyApplication</display-name>
    <module>
      <ejb>
         shipbean.jar
      </ejb>
    </module>
    <module>
      <web>
         <web-uri>
           helloworld.war
         </web-uri>
      </web>
    </module>
    <security-role>
       <role-name>Admistrator</role-name>
    </security-role>
</application>
```

The J2EE Enterprise Archive (*.ear*) file would contain the EJB JAR files and the web component *.war* files. Figure 11-3 illustrates the file structure inside a J2EE archive file.

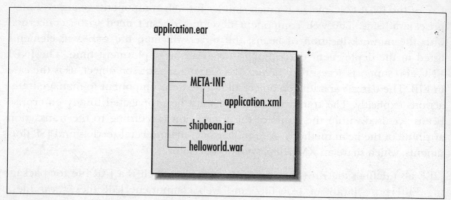

Figure 11-3. Contents of a J2EE EAR file

J2EE Application Client Components

In addition to integrating web and enterprise bean components, J2EE introduces a completely new component model: the application client component. An application client component is a Java application that resides on a client machine and accesses enterprise bean components on the J2EE server. Client components also have access to a JNDI ENC that operates the same way as the JNDI ENC for web and enterprise bean components. The client component also includes an XML deployment descriptor that declares the env-entry, ejb-ref, and resource-ref elements of the JNDI ENC in addition to a description, display-name, and icon that can be used to represent the client component in a deployment tool.

A client component is simply a Java program that uses the JNDI ENC to access environment properties, enterprise beans, and resources (JDBC, JavaMail, etc.) made available by the J2EE server. Client components reside on the client machine, not the J2EE server. Here is an extremely simple component:

```
public class MyJ2eeClient {

    public static void main(String [] args) {

        InitialContext jndiCntx = new InitialContext();

        Object ref = jndiCntx.lookup("java:comp/env/ejb/ShipBean");
        ShipHome home = (ShipHome)
            PortableRemoteObject.narrow(ref,ShipHome.class);
```

```
        Ship ship = home.findByPrimaryKey(new ShipPK(1));
        String name = ship.getName();
        System.out.println(name);
    }
}
```

MyJ2eeClient illustrates how a client component is written. Notice that the client component did not need to use a network-specific JNDI InitialContext. In other words, we did not have to specify the service provider in order to connect to the J2EE server. This is the real power of the J2EE Application client component: location transparency. The client component does not need to know the exact location of the Ship bean or choose a specific JNDI service provider; the JNDI ENC takes this care of locating the bean.

When application components are developed, an XML deployment descriptor is created that specifies the JNDI ENC entries. At deployment time, a vendor-specific J2EE tool generates the class files needed to deploy the component on client machines. The following code shows the deployment descriptor used by the MyJ2eeClient client component:

```
<!DOCTYPE application-client PUBLIC "-//Sun Microsystems,
Inc.//DTD J2EE Application Client 1.2//EN" "http://
java.sun.com/j2ee/dtds/application-client_1_2.dtd">

<application-client>
  <display-name>MyClient</display-name>
  <ejb-ref>
      <ejb-ref-name>ejb/ShipBean</ejb-ref-name>
      <ejb-ref-type>Entity</ejb-ref-type>
      <home>com.titan.ship.ShipHome</home>
      <remote>com.titan.ship.Ship</remote>
  </ejb-ref>
</application-client>
```

A client component is packaged into a JAR file with its XML deployment descriptor and can be included in a J2EE Application. The following application deployment descriptor shows how the client component is declared:

```
<!DOCTYPE application PUBLIC "-//Sun Microsystems, Inc.//DTDJ2EE
Application 1.2//EN" "http://java.sun.com/j2ee/dtds/application_1_2.dtd">

<application>
    <display-name>MyApplication</display-name>
    <module>
      <ejb>
          shipbean.jar
      </ejb>
    </module>
```

```
<module>
  <web>
    <web-uri>
      helloworld.war
    </web-uri>
  </web>
</module>
<module>
  <java>
    myclient.jar
  </java>
</module>
<security-role>
  <role-name>Admistrator</role-name>
</security-role>
</application>
```

Once a client component is included in the J2EE Application deployment descriptor, it can be packaged in the EAR file with the other components, as Figure 11-4 illustrates.

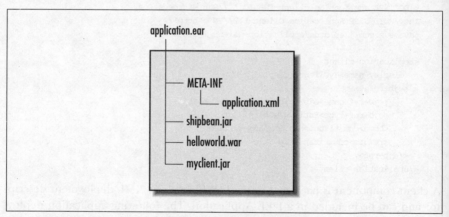

Figure 11-4. Contents of a J2EE EAR file with Application component

J2EE's application client component specification doesn't cover authentication, but it does require that client components authenticate (log in) before accessing any beans. This omission makes it difficult to develop truly portable client components because different vendors will require different authentication mechanisms. In a future version of the J2EE specification, client components may be required to use the Java Authentication and Authorization Service (JAAS), which would provide a consistent authorization mechanism across different implementations.

Guaranteed Services

The J2EE specification requires application servers to support a specific set of protocols and Java enterprise extensions. This ensures a consistent platform for deploying J2EE applications. J2EE application servers must provide the following "standard" services:

Enterprise JavaBeans 1.1

J2EE products must support the complete specification.

Servlets 2.2

J2EE products must support the complete specification.

Java Sever Pages 1.1

J2EE products must support the complete specification.

HTTP and HTTPS

Web components in a J2EE server service both HTTP and HTTPS requests. The Servlets specification itself only requires support for HTTP. The J2EE product must be capable of advertising HTTP 1.0 and HTTPS (HTTP 1.0 over SSL 3.0) on ports 80 and 443 respectively.

Java RMI-IIOP 1.0

As was the case with EJB 1.1, only the semantics of Java RMI-IIOP are required; the underlying protocol need not be IIOP. Therefore, components must use return and parameter types that are compatible with IIOP, and must use the PortableRemoteObject.narrow() method.

JavaIDL

Web components and enterprise beans must be able to access CORBA services hosted outside the J2EE environment using JavaIDL, a standard part of the Java 2 platform.

JDBC 2.0

J2EE requires support for the JDBC 2.0 Standard Extension, but not the JDBC 2.0 Optional Package.

JNDI 1.2

Web and enterprise bean components must have access to the JNDI ENC, which make available EJBHome objects, JTA UserTransaction objects, JDBC DataSource objects, and optionally Java Messaging Service connection factory objects.

JavaMail 1.1 and JAF 1.0

A J2EE products must provide access to the JavaMail API for sending basic Internet mail messages (the protocol is not specified) from web and enterprise bean components. J2EE products are not required to support message store protocols, which means you must be able to send mail but not necessarily to read mail. JAF is the Java Activation Framework, which is need to support different MIME types and is required for support of JavaMail functionality.

Java Transaction API 1.0

Web and enterprise bean components must have access to JTA UserTransaction objects via the JNDI ENC under the "java:comp/UserTransaction" context. The UserTransaction interface is used for explicit transaction control.

Java Messaging Service 1.0

J2EE products must support the JMS API definitions (base classes and interfaces), but are not required to provide a JMS implementation. This means that JMS is an optional service in J2EE. If a JMS implementation is supported, the connection factories can be made available through the JNDI ENC.

Connectivity and Interoperability

The J2EE specification currently specifies two mechanisms that can be used to connect non-J2EE systems with a J2EE system: client access to web component services and connectivity with external CORBA services via JavaIDL. Client connectivity with web components is via HTTP/HTTPS. In other words, any client that can make HTTP requests can access J2EE servlets and JSP pages, regardless of how the client is implemented. The requirement that web and enterprise bean components support JavaIDL ensures access to external CORBA services, CORBA objects hosted on ORBs outside the J2EE application server.

While these mechanisms support connectivity (the ability to connect things together), interoperability (the ability for services to collaborate) between J2EE servers or other kinds of servers is not yet supported. In fact, J2EE doesn't even require that J2EE servers of the same brand be interoperable. Security and transactional propagation between web components and enterprise beans are loosely specified in the J2EE specification; this area of the specification needs to be improved.

To have real interoperability, web and enterprise bean components must be able to exchange information about the context in which they operate when they request services for other J2EE processes. Just as EJB propagates security and transaction context from one bean to the next, interoperable services must share the same kind of contextual information. Although HTTP and JavaIDL provide for connectivity with external clients and services, they do not provide interoperability. HTTP, for example, doesn't support interoperability for security and transactions. CORBA interoperability is really nonexistent, since mechanisms for propagating security and transactional context between a J2EE server and CORBA services are not specified.

Fitting the Pieces Together

To illustrate how a J2EE platform would be used, imagine using a J2EE server in Titan's reservation system. To build this system, we would use the TravelAgent, Cabin, ProcessPayment, Customer, and other beans we defined in this book, along with web components that would provide a HTML interface.

The web components would access the enterprise beans in the same way that any Java client would, by using the beans' remote and home interfaces. The web components would generate HTML to represent the reservation system.

Figure 11-5 shows a web page generated by a servlet or JSP page for the Titan reservation system. This web page was generated by web components on the J2EE server. The person using the reservation system would have been guided through a login page, a customer selection page, and cruise selection page, and would be about to choose an available cabin for the customer.

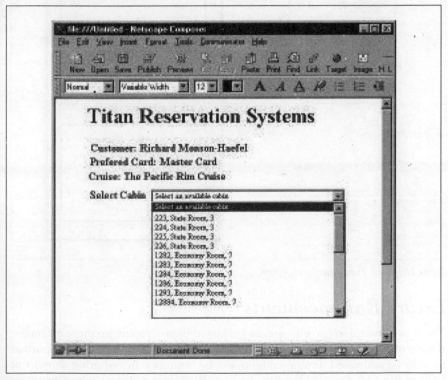

Figure 11-5. HTML interface to the Titan reservation system

The list of available cabins was obtained from the TravelAgent bean, whose
listAvailableCabins() method was invoked by the servlet that generated the
web page. The list of cabins was used to create a HTML list box in a web page that
was loaded into the user's browser. When the user chooses a cabin and submits the
selection, an HTTP request is sent to the J2EE server. The J2EE server receives the
request and delegates it to the ReservationServlet, which invokes the
TravelAgent.bookPassage() method to do the actual reservation. The Ticket
information returned by the bookPassage() method is then used to create
another web page that is sent back to the user's browser. Figure 11-6 shows how
the different components work together to process this request.

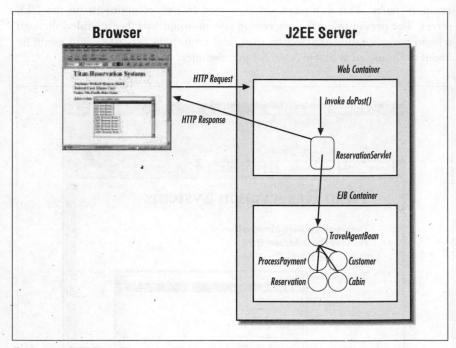

Figure 11-6. J2EE Titan Reservation System

Future Enhancements

There are several areas that are targeted for improvement in the next major
release of the J2EE specification. Interoperability is perhaps the most important
issue to be addressed. Interoperability will be improved by requiring support of
IIOP as the RMI protocol for EJB, because IIOP does a decent job of handling
transaction propagation between servers. Security, however, will offer its own chal-

lenges as the specification authors tackle problems concerned with negotiating security policies between environments.

The use of the Java Authorization and Authentication Service (JAAS) may be specified for client components, which would make them more portable. A J2EE SPI may be defined, which will offer vendors some level of pluggable services. This will make it easier to use one vendor's servlet container with another vendor's EJB container. The J2EE SPI will surely include a connector specification that allows legacy systems to be plugged into a J2EE platform, so that connections to resources like ERP (SAP, PeopleSoft, etc.) systems can be managed and accessed in the same fashion as JDBC, JavaMail, and JMS.

A

The Enterprise
JavaBeans API

This appendix is a quick reference guide to the Enterprise JavaBeans API. It is broken down into sections. First, we look at the classes in the `javax.ejb` package, followed by the classes in the `javax.ejb.deployment` package (EJB 1.0 only). Within each package, the classes are organized alphabetically.

Package: javax.ejb

This package contains the heart of the EJB API. It consists mostly of interfaces, many of which are implemented by your EJB vendor. These interfaces essentially define the services provided by the bean's container, the services that must be implemented by the bean itself, and the client interface to an enterprise bean. The package also contains a number of exceptions that are thrown by enterprise beans.

CreateException

This standard application exception must be thrown by all create methods defined in the home interface to indicate that the bean could not be created.

```
public class javax.ejb.CreateException extends java.lang.Exception
{
    public CreateException();
    public CreateException(String message);
}
```

DuplicateKeyException

This standard application exception is thrown by the create methods of the home
interface of entity beans, and it indicates that a bean already exists with the same
primary key.

```
public class javax.ejb.DuplicateKeyException
    extends javax.ejb.CreateException
{
    public DuplicateKeyException();
    public DuplicateKeyException(String message);
}
```

EJBContext

This is the base class for both EntityContext and SessionContext. EJBContext is the bean class's interface to the container system. It provides information
about the security identity and transaction status. It also provides access to environment variables and the bean's EJB home.

```
public interface javax.ejb.EJBContext
{
    public abstract Principal getCallerPrincipal(); // new in 1.1
    public abstract EJBHome getEJBHome();
    public abstract boolean getRollbackOnly();
    public abstract UserTransaction getUserTransaction();

    public abstract Properties getEnvironment(); // deprecated in 1.1
    public abstract Identity getCallerIdentity(); // deprecated in 1.1
    public abstract boolean isCallerInRole(Identity role); // deprecated in 1.1
    public abstract boolean isCallerInRole(String roleName); // new in 1.1
    public abstract void setRollbackOnly();
}
```

EJBException (1.1)

This RuntimeException is thrown by the bean class from its business methods
and callback methods to indicate that an unexpected exception has occurred. The
exception causes a transaction to be rolled back and the bean instance to be
destroyed.

```
public class javax.ejb.EJBException
    extends java.lang.RuntimeException
{
    public EJBException();
    public EJBException(String message);
    public EJBException(Exception exception);
```

```
        public Exception getCausedByException();
}
```

EJBHome

This interface must be extended by the bean's home interface, a developer-provided class that defines the life-cycle methods of the bean. The bean's create and find methods are defined in the home interface. This interface is implemented by the bean's EJB home.

```
public interface javax.ejb.EJBHome extends java.rmi.Remote
{
        public abstract HomeHandle getHomeHandle(); // new in 1.1
        public abstract EJBMetaData getEJBMetaData();
        public abstract void remove(Handle handle);
        public abstract void remove(Object primaryKey);
}
```

EJBMetaData

This interface is implemented by the container vendor to provide a serializable class that contains information about the bean.

```
public interface javax.ejb.EJBMetaData
{
        public abstract EJBHome getEJBHome();
        public abstract Class getHomeInterfaceClass();
        public abstract Class getPrimaryKeyClass();
        public abstract Class getRemoteInterfaceClass();
        public abstract boolean isSession();
        public abstract boolean isStatelessSession(); // new in 1.1
}
```

EJBObject

This interface defines the base functionality for access to enterprise beans; it is implemented by the EJB object. The developer must provide a remote interface for the bean that defines the business methods of the bean; the remote interface must extend the EJBObject interface.

```
public interface javax.ejb.EJBObject extends java.rmi.Remote
{
        public abstract EJBHome getEJBHome();
        public abstract Handle getHandle();
        public abstract Object getPrimaryKey();
        public abstract boolean isIdentical(EJBObject obj);
        public abstract void remove();
}
```

EnterpriseBean

This interface is extended by both the `EntityBean` and `SessionBean` interfaces. It serves as a common typing mechanism.

```
public interface javax.ejb.EnterpriseBean extends java.io.Serializable {}
```

EntityBean

This interface must be implemented by the entity bean class. It provides a set of callback notification methods that alert the bean instance that it is about to experience or just has experienced some change in its life cycle.

```
public interface javax.ejb.EntityBean extends javax.ejb.EnterpriseBean
{
    public abstract void ejbActivate();
    public abstract void ejbLoad();
    public abstract void ejbPassivate();
    public abstract void ejbRemove();
    public abstract void ejbStore();
    public abstract void setEntityContext(EntityContext ctx);
    public abstract void unsetEntityContext();
}
```

EntityContext

This interface is a specialization of the `EJBContext` that provides methods for obtaining an `EntityBean`'s EJB object reference and primary key. The `Entity-Context` provides the bean instance with an interface to the container.

```
public interface javax.ejb.EntityContext extends javax.ejb.EJBContext
{
    public abstract EJBObject getEJBObject();
    public abstract Object getPrimaryKey();
}
```

FinderException

This standard application exception is thrown by find methods defined in the home interface to indicate that a failure occurred during the execution of the find method.

```
public class javax.ejb.FinderException extends java.lang.Exception
{
    public FinderException();
    public FinderException(String message);
}
```

Handle

This interface provides the client with a serializable object that can be used to obtain a remote reference to a specific bean.

```
public interface javax.ejb.Handle
extends java.io.Serializable
{
    public abstract EJBObject getEJBObject();
}
```

HomeHandle (1.1)

This interface provides the client with a serializable object that can be used to obtain a remote reference to a bean's home.

```
public interface javax.ejb.HomeHandle
extends java.io.Serializable
{
    public abstract EJBHome getEJBHome();
}
```

NoSuchEntityException (1.1)

This EJBException is typically thrown by the bean class's ejbLoad() and ejbStore() methods to indicate that the entity's data does not exist. For example, this exception will be thrown if an entity bean with bean-managed persistence attempts to read its state (ejbLoad()) from a record that has been deleted from the database.

```
public class javax.ejb.NoSuchEntityException
    extends javax.ejb.EJBException
{
    public NoSuchEntityException();
    public NoSuchEntityException(String message);
    public NoSuchEntityException(Exception exception);

}
```

ObjectNotFoundException

This standard application exception is thrown by the home interface's find methods that return only one EJB object. It indicates that no bean matching the specified criteria could be found.

```
public class javax.ejb.ObjectNotFoundException
    extends javax.ejb.FinderException
{
```

```
    public ObjectNotFoundException();
    public ObjectNotFoundException(String message);
}
```

RemoveException

This standard application exception is thrown by remove methods to indicate that the failure occurred while removing the bean.

```
public class javax.ejb.RemoveException extends java.lang.Exception
{
    public RemoveException();
    public RemoveException(String message);
}
```

SessionBean

This interface must be implemented by the session bean class. It provides a set of callback notification methods that alert the bean instance that it has experienced, or is about to experience, some change in its life cycle.

```
public interface javax.ejb.SessionBean extends javax.ejb.EnterpriseBean
{
    public abstract void ejbActivate();
    public abstract void ejbPassivate();
    public abstract void ejbRemove();
    public abstract void setSessionContext(SessionContext ctx);
}
```

SessionContext

This interface is a specialization of the EJBContext that provides methods for obtaining the SessionBean's EJB object reference. SessionContext provides the bean instance with an interface to the container.

```
public interface javax.ejb.SessionContext extends javax.ejb.EJBContext
{
    public abstract EJBObject getEJBObject();
}
```

SessionSynchronization

This interface provides a stateful bean instance with additional callback notifications. These callback methods notify the bean of its current state with respect to a transaction.

```
public interface javax.ejb.SessionSynchronization
{
```

```
        public abstract void afterBegin();
        public abstract void afterCompletion(boolean committed);
        public abstract void beforeCompletion();
}
```

Package: javax.ejb.deployment (EJB 1.0 Only)

The javax.ejb.deployment package contains a number of classes used to deploy enterprise beans in a container. These classes provide mechanisms to tell the container about the bean's properties, define new properties at runtime, and define the relationship between the bean and its container.

This package has disappeared entirely from EJB 1.1, including all of its classes.

AccessControlEntry

A serialized object of this class is used to specify the security identities that are allowed to access the bean's methods. It may specify default access for the entire bean or access specific to one method.

```
    public class javax.ejb.deployment.AccessControlEntry
        extends java.lang.Object
        implements java.io.Serializable
    {
        public AccessControlEntry();
        public AccessControlEntry(Method method);
        public AccessControlEntry(Method method, Identity identities[]);
        public Identity[] getAllowedIdentities();
        public Identity getAllowedIdentities(int index);
        public Method getMethod();
        public void setAllowedIdentities(Identity values[]);
        public void setAllowedIdentities(int index, Identity value);
        public void setMethod(Method value);
    }
```

ControlDescriptor

A serialized object of this class is used to specify transactional and runAs attributes associated with the bean's methods. It may specify default attributes for the entire bean or attributes specific to one method.

```
    public class javax.ejb.deployment.ControlDescriptor
        extends java.lang.Object
        implements java.io.Serializable
    {
        public final static int CLIENT_IDENTITY;
```

```
    public final static int SPECIFIED_IDENTITY;
    public final static int SYSTEM_IDENTITY;
    public final static int TRANSACTION_READ_COMMITTED;
    public final static int TRANSACTION_READ_UNCOMMITTED;
    public final static int TRANSACTION_REPEATABLE_READ;
    public final static int TRANSACTION_SERIALIZABLE;
    public final static int TX_BEAN_MANAGED;
    public final static int TX_MANDATORY;
    public final static int TX_NOT_SUPPORTED;
    public final static int TX_REQUIRED;
    public final static int TX_REQUIRES_NEW;
    public final static int TX_SUPPORTS;

    public ControlDescriptor();
    public ControlDescriptor(Method method);
    public int getIsolationLevel();
    public Method getMethod();
    public Identity getRunAsIdentity();
    public int getRunAsMode();
    public int getTransactionAttribute();
    public void setIsolationLevel(int value);
    public void setMethod(Method value);
    public void setRunAsIdentity(Identity value);
    public void setRunAsMode(int value);
    public void setTransactionAttribute(int value);
}
```

DeploymentDescriptor

A serialized object of this class is used to describe the bean to the container at
deployment time. This object contains all the AccessControlEntry and ControlDescriptor objects for the bean. In addition, it contains descriptions of the
remote interface, the home interface, and the bean class names, as well as the
name binding and version number of the bean. This class serves as the base class
for the EntityDescriptor and the SessionDescriptor classes, which are used
by EntityBean and SessionBean types, respectively.

```
    public class javax.ejb.deployment.DeploymentDescriptor
        extends java.lang.Object
        implements java.io.Serializable
    {
        protected int versionNumber;
        public DeploymentDescriptor();
        public AccessControlEntry[] getAccessControlEntries();
        public AccessControlEntry getAccessControlEntries(int index);
        public Name getBeanHomeName();
        public ControlDescriptor[] getControlDescriptors();
        public ControlDescriptor getControlDescriptors(int index);
```

```
        public String getEnterpriseBeanClassName();
        public Properties getEnvironmentProperties();
        public String getHomeInterfaceClassName();
        public boolean getReentrant();
        public String getRemoteInterfaceClassName();
        public boolean isReentrant();
        public void setAccessControlEntries(AccessControlEntry values[]);
        public void setAccessControlEntries(int i, AccessControlEntry v);
        public void setBeanHomeName(Name value);
        public void setControlDescriptors(ControlDescriptor value[]);
        public void setControlDescriptors(int index, ControlDescriptor value);
        public void setEnterpriseBeanClassName(String value);
        public void setEnvironmentProperties(Properties value);
        public void setHomeInterfaceClassName(String value);
        public void setReentrant(boolean value);
        public void setRemoteInterfaceClassName(String value);
}
```

EntityDescriptor

This class extends the DeploymentDescriptor class, providing methods specific
to EntityBeans. Container-managed fields and the primary key class for the bean
can be set, in addition to all the values set using the DeploymentDescriptor
class.

```
public class javax.ejb.deployment.EntityDescriptor
    extends javax.ejb.deployment.DeploymentDescriptor
{
    public EntityDescriptor();
    public Field[] getContainerManagedFields();
    public Field getContainerManagedFields(int index);
    public String getPrimaryKeyClassName();
    public void setContainerManagedFields(Field values[]);
    public void setContainerManagedFields(int index, Field value);
    public void setPrimaryKeyClassName(String value);
}
```

SessionDescriptor

This class extends the DeploymentDescriptor class, providing methods specific
to SessionBeans. The session timeout and state management type can be set, in
addition to all the values set using the DeploymentDescriptor class.

```
public class javax.ejb.deployment.SessionDescriptor
    extends javax.ejb.deployment.DeploymentDescriptor
{
    public final static int STATEFUL_SESSION;
    public final static int STATELESS_SESSION;
```

```
        public SessionDescriptor();
        public int getSessionTimeout();
        public int getStateManagementType();
        public void setSessionTimeout(int value);
        public void setStateManagementType(int value);
}
```

B

State and Sequence Diagrams

The appendix contains state and sequence diagrams for all the bean types discussed in this book: container-managed and bean-managed entity beans, and stateless and stateful session beans. Although standard UML is used in these diagrams, some extensions were required to model EJB runtime characteristics. In the state diagrams, for example, actions of the client and container are shown in the standard format; callback methods and class instantiation operations are shown as part of the transition event. The separation of client and container requires this simple extension.

In the sequence diagrams, container-provided classes such as the container itself, EJB object, and EJB home are shown as separate classes but are also boxed together. Messages sent from classes in the container system box are considered to be sent from the container system as a whole, not necessarily the specific container-provided class. This generalization is necessary because the container's interaction with the bean is characterized by these classes but will be different from one vendor's implementation to the next. The exact source of the message is immaterial, as long as you realize that the container system sent it.

Entity Beans

Life Cycle State Diagram of the Entity Bean

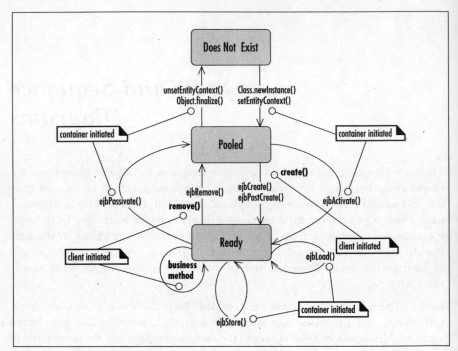

Figure B-1. Life cycle state diagram of the entity bean

Sequence Diagrams for Container-Managed Persistence

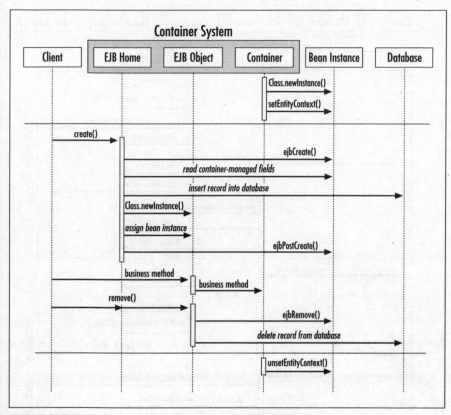

Figure B-2. Creation and removal in container-managed persistence

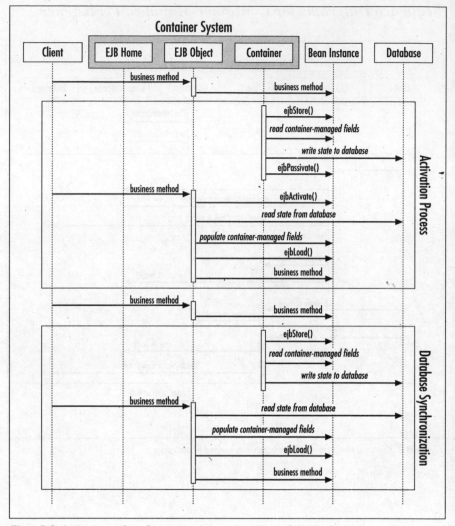

Figure B-3. Activation and synchronization in container-managed persistence

Sequence Diagrams for Bean-Managed Persistence

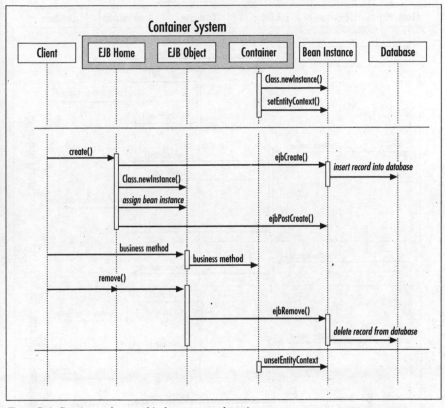

Figure B-4. Creation and removal in bean-managed persistence

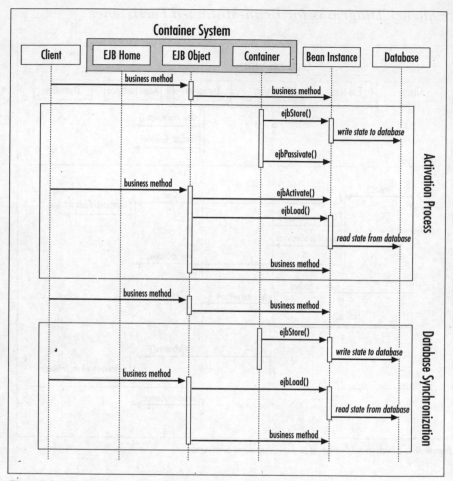

Figure B-5. Activation and synchronization in bean-managed persistence

Table B-1 and Table B-2 summarize the operations that an entity bean is allowed to perform in various stages of its life cycle.

Table B-1. Allowed Operations for Entity Beans in EJB 1.1

Method	Allowed Operations

setEntityContext()
unsetEntityContext()
	EntityContext methods:
	    getEJBHome()
	
	JNDI ENC contexts:
	    Properties java:comp/env

ejbCreate()
ejbFind()
	EntityContext methods:
	    getEJBHome()
	    getCallerPrincipal()
	    isCallerInRole()
	    getRollbackOnly()
	    setRollbackOnly()
	
	JNDI ENC contexts:
	    Properties java:comp/env
	    Resource Managers java:comp/env/jdbc
	    EJB references java:comp/env/ejb

ejbPostCreate()
ejbLoad()
ejbStore()
ejbRemove()
business methods
	EntityContext methods:
	    getEJBHome()
	    getCallerPrincipal()
	    isCallerInRole() getRollbackOnly()
	    setRollbackOnly()
	    getEJObject()
	    getPrimaryKey()
	
	JNDI ENC contexts:
	    Properties java:comp/env
	    Resource Managers java:comp/env/jdbc
	    EJB references java:comp/env/ejb

ejbActivate()
ejbPassivate()
	EntityContext methods:
	    getEJBHome()
	    getEJBObject()
	    getPrimaryKey()
	
	JNDI ENC contexts:
	    Properties java:comp/env

Note that entity beans in EJB 1.1 can never access the EJBContext.getUser-Transaction() method, because entity beans are not allowed to manage their own transactions. Only session beans can access this method.

Table B-2. Allowed Operations for Entity Beans in EJB 1.0

	Allowed Operations	
Method	**Container-Managed Transactions**	**Bean-Managed Transactions**

setEntityContext()
unsetEntityContext()
	EntityContext methods:
	  getEnvironment()
	  getEJBHome()
		EntityContext methods:
		  getEnvironment()
		  getEJBHome()

ejbCreate()
ejbFind()
	EntityContext methods:
	  getEnvironment()
	  getEJBHome()
	  getCallerIdentity()
	  isCallerInRole()
	  getRollbackOnly()
	  setRollbackOnly()
		EntityContext methods:
		  getEnvironment()
		  getEJBHome()
		  getCallerIdentity()
		  isCallerInRole()
		  getUserTransaction()

ejbPostCreate()
ejbLoad()
ejbStore()
ejbRemove()
business methods
	EntityContext methods:
	  getEnvironment()
	  getEJBHome()
	  getCallerPrincipal()
	  getRollbackOnly()
	  isCallerInRole()
	  setRollbackOnly()
	  getEJBObject()
	  getPrimaryKey()
		EntityContext methods:
		  getEnvironment()
		  getEJBHome()
		  getCallerPrincipal()
		  isCallerInRole()
		  getEJBObject()
		  getPrimaryKey()
		  getUserTransaction()

ejbActivate()
ejbPassivate()
	EntityContext methods:
	  getEnvironment()
	  getEJBHome()
	  getEJBObject()
	  getPrimaryKey()
		EntityContext methods:
		  getEnvironment()
		  getEJBHome()
		  getEJBObject()
		  getPrimaryKey()

Session Beans

Stateless Session Beans

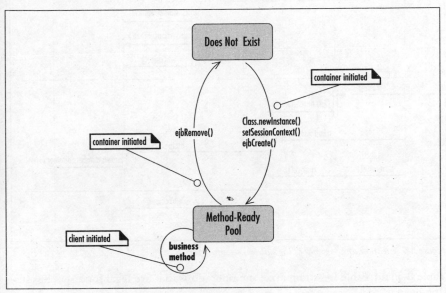

Figure B-6. Life cycle state diagram of the stateless session bean

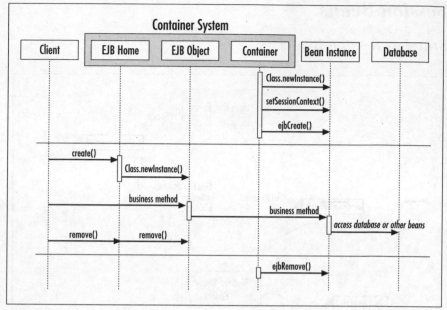

Figure B-7. Creation and removal of the stateless session bean

Table B-3 and Table B-4 summarize the operations that are legal for a stateless session bean.

Table B-3. Allowed Operations for Stateless Session Beans in EJB 1.1

Method	Allowed Operations	
	Container-Managed Transactions	**Bean-Managed Transactions**

setSessionContext()	EntityContext methods:
	    getEJBHome()
	
	JNDI ENC contexts:
	    Properties java:comp/
	    env
		EntityContext methods:
		    getEJBHome()
		
		JNDI ENC contexts:
		    Properties java:comp/env

ejbCreate()
ejbRemove()
	EntityContext methods:
	    getEJBHome()
	    getEJBObject()
	
	JNDI ENC contexts:
	    Properties java:comp/
	    env
		EntityContext methods:
		    getEJBHome()
		    getEJBObject()
		    getUserTransaction()
		
		JNDI ENC contexts:
		    Properties java:comp/env

Table B-3. Allowed Operations for Stateless Session Beans in EJB 1.1 (continued)

	Allowed Operations	
Method	**Container-Managed Transactions**	**Bean-Managed Transactions**

business methods	EntityContext methods:
	  getEJHome()
	  getCallerPrincipal()
	  isCallerInRole()
	  getRollbackOnly()
	  setRollbackOnly()
	  getEJObject()
	
	JNDI ENC contexts:
	  Properties java:comp/env
	  Resource Managers java:comp/env/jdbc
	  EJB references java:comp/env/ejb
		EntityContext methods:
		  getEJHome()
		  getCallerPrincipal()
		  isCallerInRole()
		  getEJObject()
		  getUserTransaction()
		
		JNDI ENC contexts:
		  Properties java:comp/env
		  Resource Managers java:comp/env/jdbc
		  EJB references java:comp/env/ejb

ejbActivate() ejbPassivate()	Not Supported (stateless beans do not use these methods)	Not Supported (stateless beans do not use these methods)

Table B-4. Allowed Operations for Stateless Session Beans in EJB 1.0

	Allowed Operations	
Method	**Container-Managed Transactions**	**Bean-Managed Transactions**

setSessionContext()	EntityContext methods:
	  getEnvironment()
	  getEJBHome()
		EntityContext methods:
		  getEnvironment()
		  getEJBHome()

ejbCreate()
ejbRemove()
	EntityContext methods:
	  getEnvironment()
	  getEJBHome()
	  getEJBObject()
		EntityContext methods:
		  getEnvironment()
		  getEJBHome()
		  getEJBObject()
		  getUserTransaction()

business methods	EntityContext methods:
	  getEnvironment()
	  getEJHome()
	  getCallerPrincipal()
	  isCallerInRole()
	  getRollbackOnly()
	  setRollbackOnly()
	  getEJObject()
		EntityContext methods:
		  getEnvironment()
		  getEJHome()
		  getCallerPrincipal()
		  isCallerInRole()
		  getEJObject()
		  getUserTransaction()

ejbActivate() ejbPassivate()	Not Supported (stateless beans do not use these methods)	Not Supported (stateless beans do not use these methods)

Stateful Session Beans

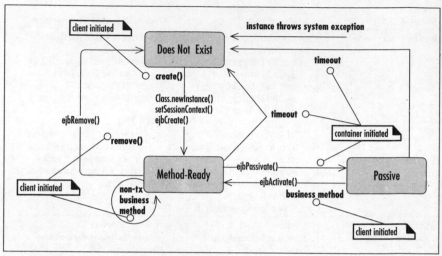

Figure B-8. EJB 1.1 stateful session bean life cycle

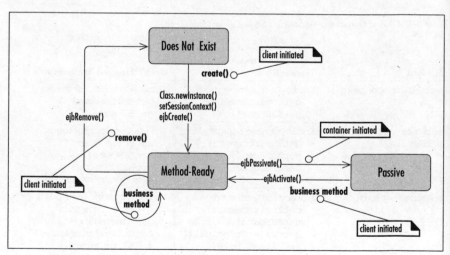

Figure B-9. EJB 1.0 life cycle state diagram of the stateful session bean life cycle

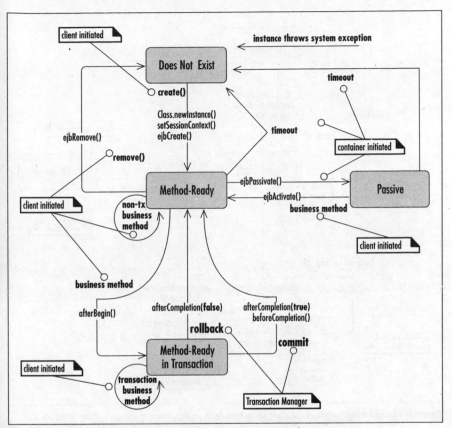

Figure B-10. EJB 1.1 life cycle of a stateful session bean with session synchronization interface

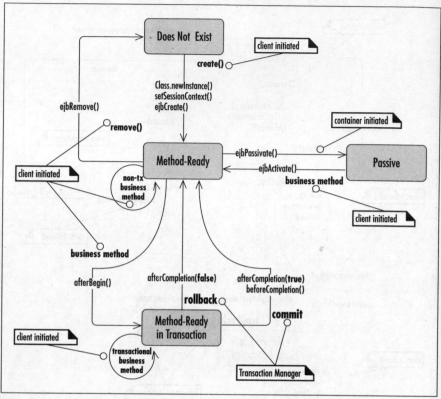

Figure B-11. EJB 1.0 life cycle of the stateful session bean with session synchronization interface

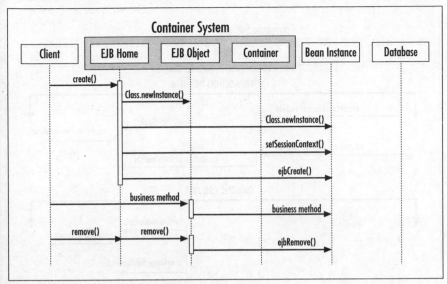

Figure B-12. Creation and removal of stateful session beans

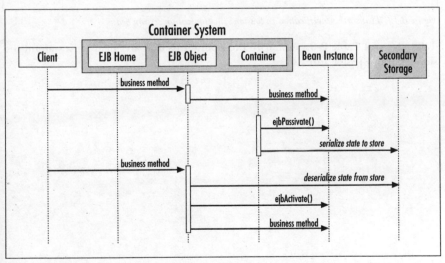

Figure B-13. Activation process in stateful session beans

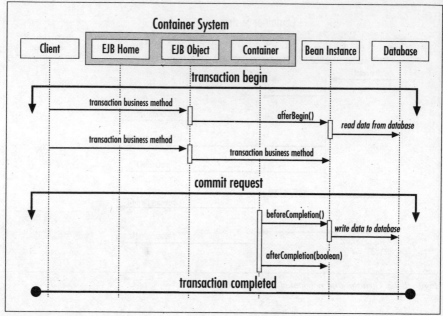

Figure B-14. Transaction notification in SessionSynchronization session beans

Table B-5 and Table B-6 summarize the operations that are legal for a stateful session bean in EJB 1.1 and 1.0.

Table B-5. Allowed Operations for Stateful Session Beans in EJB 1.1

| Method | Allowed Operations | |
	Container-Managed Transactions	Bean-Managed Transactions

setSessionContext()	EntityContext methods:
	  getEJBHome()
	
	JNDI ENC contexts:
	  Properties java:comp/
	  env
		EntityContext methods:
		  getEJBHome()
		
		JNDI ENC contexts:
		  Properties java:comp/
		  env

ejbCreate()
ejbRemove()
ejbActivate()
ejbPassivate()
	EntityContext methods:
	  getEJBHome()
	  getCallerPrincipal()
	  isCallerInRole()
	  getEJBObject()
	
	JNDI ENC contexts:
	  Properties java:comp/
	  env
	  Resource Managers
	  java:comp/env/jdbc
	  EJB references
	  java:comp/env/ejb
		EntityContext methods:
		  getEJBHome()
		  getCallerPrincipal()
		  isCallerInRole()
		  getEJBObject()
		  getUserTransaction()
		
		JNDI ENC contexts:
		  Properties java:comp/
		  env
		  Resource Managers
		  java:comp/env/jdbc
		  EJB references
		  java:comp/env/ejb

business methods	EntityContext methods:
	  getEJHome()
	  getCallerPrincipal()
	  isCallerInRole()
	  getRollbackOnly()
	  setRollbackOnly()
	  getEJObject()
	
	JNDI ENC contexts:
	  Properties java:comp/
	  env
	  Resource Managers
	  java:comp/env/jdbc
	  EJB references
	  java:comp/env/ejb
		EntityContext methods:
		  getEJHome()
		  getCallerPrincipal()
		  isCallerInRole()
		  getEJObject()
		  getUserTransaction()
		
		JNDI ENC contexts:
		  Properties java:comp/
		  env
		  Resource Managers
		  java:comp/env/jdbc
		  EJB references
		  java:comp/env/ejb

Table B-5. Allowed Operations for Stateful Session Beans in EJB 1.1 (continued)

| | Allowed Operations | |
Method	Container-Managed Transactions	Bean-Managed Transactions

afterBegin()
beforeCompetion()
	EntityContext methods:
	  getEJHome()
	  getCallerPrincipal()
	  isCallerInRole()
	  getRollbackOnly()
	  setRollbackOnly()
	  getEJObject()
	
	JNDI ENC contexts:
	  Properties java:comp/
	  env
	  Resource Managers
	  java:comp/env/jdbc
	  EJB references
	  java:comp/env/ejb
		Not Supported
		(bean-managed transaction beans can not implement the SessionSynchronization interface)

afterCompletion()	EntityContext methods:
	  getEJBHome()
	  getCallerPrincipal()
	  isCallerInRole()
	  getEJBObject()
	
	JNDI ENC contexts:
	  Properties java:comp/
	  env
		Not Supported
		(bean-managed transaction beans can not implement the SessionSynchronization interface)

Table B-6. Allowed Operations for Stateful Session Beans in EJB 1.0

| | Allowed Operations | |
Method	Container-Managed Transactions	Bean-Managed Transactions

setSessionContext()	EntityContext methods:
	  getEnvironment()
	  getEJBHome()
		EntityContext methods:
		  getEnvironment()
		  getEJBHome()

ejbCreate()
ejbRemove()
ejbActivate()
ejbPassivate()
	EntityContext methods:
	  getEnvironment()
	  getEJBHome()
	  getCallerPrincipal()
	  isCallerInRole()
	  getEJBObject()
		EntityContext methods:
		  getEnvironment()
		  getEJBHome()
		  getCallerPrincipal()
		  isCallerInRole()
		  getEJBObject()
		  getUserTransaction()

Table B-6. Allowed Operations for Stateful Session Beans in EJB 1.0 (continued)

Method	Allowed Operations Container-Managed Transactions	Bean-Managed Transactions

business methods	EntityContext methods:
	  getEnvironment()
	  getEJHome()
	  getCallerPrincipal()
	  isCallerInRole()
	  getRollbackOnly()
	  setRollbackOnly()
	  getEJObject()
		EntityContext methods:
		  getEnvironment()
		  getEJHome()
		  getCallerPrincipal()
		  isCallerInRole()
		  getEJObject()
		  getUserTransaction()

afterBegin()
beforeCompetion()
	EntityContext methods:
	  getEnvironment()
	  getEJHome()
	  getCallerPrincipal()
	  isCallerInRole()
	  getRollbackOnly()
	  setRollbackOnly()
	  getEJObject()
		Not Supported
		(bean-managed transaction beans can not implement the SessionSynchronization interface)

afterCompletion()	EntityContext methods:
	  getEnvironment()
	  getEJBHome()
	  getCallerPrincipal()
	  isCallerInRole()
	  getEJBObject()
		Not Supported
		(bean-managed transaction beans can not implement the SessionSynchronization interface)

EJB 1.1: Interactions Between Exceptions and Transactions

Table B-7 summarizes what happens to a transaction if an exception is thrown while the transaction is in process.

Table B-7. Exceptions and Transactions

Transaction Scope	Transactional Type Attributes	Exception Thrown	Container's Action	Client's View
Client Initiated Transaction Transaction is started by the client (application or bean) and is propagated to the bean method.	transaction-type = Container transaction-attribute = Required | Mandatory | Supports |	Application Exception	If the bean invoked `EJBContext.setRollbackOnly()`, then mark the client's transaction for rollback. Rethrow Application Exception.	Receives the Application Exception. The client's transaction may or may not have been marked for rolled back.
		System Exception	Mark the client's transaction for roll back. Log the error. Discard the instance. Rethrow `TransactionRollbackException`.	Receives the `TransactionRollbackException` The client's transaction has been rolled back.
Container Initiated Transaction The transaction started when the bean's method was invoked and will end when method completes.	transaction-type = Container transaction-attribute = Required | Requires New	Application Exception	If bean called `EJBContext.setRollbackOnly()`, then roll back the transaction and rethrow the Application Exception. If bean didn't explicitly rollback the transaction, then attempt to commit the transaction and rethrow the Application Exception.	Receives the Application Exception. The bean's transaction may or may not have been rolled back. The client's transaction is not affected.
		System Exception	Roll back the transaction. Log the error. Discard the instance. Rethrow `RemoteException`.	Receives the `RemoteException`. The bean's transaction was rolled back. The client's transaction is not affected.

Table B-7. Exceptions and Transactions (continued)

Transaction Scope	Transactional Type Attributes	Exception Thrown	Container's Action	Client's View
Bean is not part of a transaction. The bean was invoked but does not propagate the client's transaction and does not start its own transaction.	transaction-type = Container transaction-attribute = Never | Not Supported | Supports |	Application Exception	Rethrow Application Exception	Receives the Application Exception. The client's transaction is not affected.
		System Exception	Log the error. Discard the instance. Rethrow RemoteException.	Receives the RemoteException. The client's transaction is not affected.
Bean Managed Transaction. The stateful or stateless session bean use the EJBContext to explicitly manage its own transaction.	transaction-type = bean transaction-attribute = Bean-Managed Transaction beans do not use transaction attributes.	Application Exception	Rethrow the Application Exception.	Receive the Application Exception. The client's transaction is not affected.
		System Exception	Roll back the transaction. Log the error. Discard the instance. Rethrow RemoteException.	Receives the RemoteException. The client's transaction is not affected.

C

EJB Vendors

This appendix lists vendors of EJB servers. It includes all the vendors of which we're aware as of publication. However, with the number of vendors that already provide servers, and the number that are introducing new products daily, the list is obviously incomplete. Furthermore, we have made no attempt to distinguish EJB 1.1 servers from 1.0 servers; most (if not all) of the 1.0 vendors should be migrating to 1.1 over the next year. We will try to maintain a more up-to-date list on the book's web site, *http://www.oreilly.com/catalog/entjbeans2.*

Commercial Products

Table C-1. Commercial EJB Servers

Company Name	Company URL	EJB Server Name
BEA Systems	*www.beasys.com*	BEA WebLogic Server BEA WebLogic Enterprise
Bluestone Software	*www.bluestone.com*	Sapphire/Web
BROKAT Infosystems	*www.brokat.com*	BROKAT Twister
Fujitsu Software	*www.fsc.fujitsu.com*	Interstage
Gemstone Systems	*www.gemstone.com*	GemStone/J
Haht Software	*www.haht.com*	HAHTsite Application Server
IBM	*www.software.ibm.com*	WebSphere Application Server
Information Builders	*www.ibi.com*	Parlay Application Server
Inprise	*www.inprise.com*	Inprise Application Server
Iona Technologies	*www.iona.com*	Orbix Enterprise
Netscape Communications	*www.netscape.com*	Netscape Application Server
Novera Software	*www.novera.com*	jBusiness
ObjectSpace	*www.objectspace.com*	Voyager

Table C-1. Commercial EJB Servers (continued)

Company Name	Company URL	EJB Server Name
Oracle	www.oracle.com	Oracle Application Server Oracle8i
Progress	www.progress.com	Aptivity
Persistence Software	www.persistence.com	PowerTier for EJB
Secant Technologies	www.secant.com	Secant Extreme Enterprise Server
SIEMENS	www.siemens.com	Siemens Enterprise Application Server
Silverstream	www.silverstream.com	SilverStream Application Server
Sun Microsystems	www.netdynamics.com java.sun.com/j2ee	NetDynamics Application Server J2EE Reference Implementation
Sun-Netscape Alliance	www.iplanet.com	NetDynamics Application Server Netscape Application Server
Sybase	www.sybase.com	Sybase Enterprise Application Server
Allaire	www.allaire.com	Valto
Visient	www.visient.com	Arabica
Unify	www.unify.com	eWave

Open Source Projects

Several Open Source EJB servers have become available since the first edition of this book. The author of this book, Richard Monson-Haefel, is the lead architect of ExOffice's OpenEJB server.

Table C-2. Open Source EJB Servers

Sponsor Name	Company URL	EJB Server Name
ExOffice	www.exolab.org	OpenEJB
Telkel, Inc.	www.ejboss.org	EJBoss
Bull	www.bullsoft.com/ejb/	JOnAS
Lutris	www.enhydra.com	Enhydra (EJB server based on JOnAS)

D

New Features in
EJB 1.1

In December 1999, Sun Microsystems released the final specification of Enterprise JavaBeans 1.1. Enterprise JavaBeans 1.1 is, in many ways, a point release with corrections and clarifications over EJB 1.0 that allows vendors and bean developers to create more portable beans. This appendix summarizes the most important and visible modifications to the specification made in EJB 1.1.

The biggest changes between EJB 1.0 and EJB 1.1 include mandating entity bean support, the adoption of XML deployment descriptors, the creation of a default JNDI context, and changes to security.

Entity Beans

EJB 1.1 mandates support for the entity bean type. In EJB 1.0, entity bean support is optional, which means vendors can support them in whole, in part, or not at all. Most EJB server vendors chose to support entity beans in some way; for these vendors, the transition to full support shouldn't be difficult. For most EJB developers, the required support for entity beans is welcomed because it provides a more stable platform for portable beans.

The entity bean type itself has undergone some changes. The bean-managed transaction option has been removed from entity beans. This option is difficult to use because it requires explicit transactional control by the developer. Removing it from entity beans simplifies the EJB architecture. Stateful session beans, however, still retain the option of managing their own transactions.

Another welcome change is the expansion of valid return types from the find methods for entity beans. In EJB 1.0, find methods can return a single entity or a collection of entities. Find methods that return a single entity return the entity's remote interface type; entities that return a collection use `java.util.Enumer-`

ation. In EJB 1.1, a new return type has been added, java.util.Collection. This addition provides both the vendors and developers with more flexibility in how the find methods are implemented and used.

A seemingly minor change to the return value of ejbCreate() may turn out to be a headache when upgrading systems from EJB 1.0 to the EJB 1.1 specification. Because the ejbCreate() method works differently in bean-managed and container-managed beans, EJB 1.0 specified different return values: bean-managed entities return the unique identity of the bean, the primary key; container-managed entities return void. The following code shows the different method signatures used for container-managed and bean-managed ejbCreate() methods in EJB 1.0:

```
// container-managed entity, EJB 1.0
    public class AccountCMP implements javax.ejb.EntityBean {
    public int id;
    public double balance;

    public void ejbCreate(int myID) {
        id = myID;
    }
    // more bean code follows
}

// bean-managed entity, EJB 1.0
    public class AccountBMP implements javax.ejb.EntityBean {
    public int id;
    public double balance;

    public AccountPK ejbCreate(int myID) {
        id = myID;
        // do a database insert using JDBC
        AccountPK pk = new AccountPK(myID);
        return pk;
    }
    // more bean code follows
}
```

The EJB 1.1 specification changes this so that both bean-managed and container-managed entities have to return the primary key type from the ejbCreate() methods. However, container-managed beans are required to return null instead of a primary key object. This seemingly bizarre change was made to accommodate EJB vendors who want to support container-managed beans by extending them with generated bean-managed classes. The generated subclasses override the ejbCreate() methods to manually insert a record into the database. In EJB 1.0, the ejbCreate() methods in bean-managed and container-managed entities have different return values, so extending the class and overriding the ejbCreate()

methods doesn't work. By specifying that the `ejbCreate()` methods must always return the primary key class, container-managed beans can be extended to create bean-managed beans. Unfortunately, this change breaks forward compatibility with EJB 1.0 container-managed beans, forcing bean developers to make changes to their existing code if they want to transition to the EJB 1.1 specification.

The EJB 1.1 specification also contains some other changes regarding the primary key class. For bean-managed persistence, EJB 1.1 states that the primary key class can be any valid Java RMI-IIOP type—a clear indication that IIOP will be the standard distributed object protocol for EJB in a future version of the specification. In addition, the new specification requires the primary key class to implement the `Object.equals()` and `Object.hashCode()` methods to ensure that these methods evaluate properly when comparing keys and storing them in a `java.util.Hashtable`. The most significant change regarding primary keys is the option to defer their definition until deployment time. In other words, the primary key for an entity bean doesn't have to be defined by the developer, but can be left to the deployer. This is a significant departure from the previous specification, which required the bean developer to define the primary keys. By deferring the definition until deployment, persistence mapping becomes more flexible, allowing beans to become more portable. Although this is a convenient option, it's likely that most bean developers will continue to specify the primary class when they develop the bean.

Finally, a change in the EJB 1.1 specification allows entity bean references to be container-managed fields. In container-managed persistence, the container manages persistence automatically, so it must be told at deployment time which fields are persistent and how to map them to the database. In EJB 1.0, container-managed fields are limited to primitives and `java.io.Serializable` types. Limiting the container-managed fields to these simple types makes it more difficult to maintain persistent relationships to other entity beans; entity beans are always referenced using their `java.rmi.Remote` interface type, which is neither a primitive nor `Serializable`. EJB 1.1 specifies that container-managed fields can include references to other entity beans, which makes it much easier for the bean developer to model associations and aggregations of beans. How the container persists the relationships is not specified, but it's likely that options for converting the reference to a primary key will be provided at deployment time.

Session Beans

Session beans didn't change much from EJB 1.0 to EJB 1.1 because their behavior and functionality was well defined in the original specification. Several clarifications have been added to eliminate inconsistencies between vendors and provide a more predictable bean life cycle for developers. For example, the 1.1 specification requires that the SessionContext be preserved through passivation in nontransitive fields, and clarifies what resources can be accessed in which methods. These clarifications tighten up the specification and make it easier for both vendors and developers.

XML Deployment Descriptors

In EJB 1.0, the deployment descriptor information is stored in a serializable class defined in the javax.ejb.deployment package. While at first this appeared to be an excellent approach, it has limitations. It isn't clear which deployment information should be set by the bean developer and which by the deployer. In addition, the serializable classes are not very extensible and limit your ability to describe the bean's attributes.

To solve these problems, EJB 1.1 replaces the serializable deployment descriptor with an XML-based deployment descriptor. The XML deployment descriptor is defined by an XML DTD (Document Type Definition) that describes the structure that the XML deployment descriptors must have to be considered valid. The XML format is superior to the previous serializable object approach in many ways. First, it's more informative, allowing description tags to be associated with major elements so that the author can describe, in plain language, the purpose and expected behavior of attributes. Second, XML deployment descriptors can be viewed and edited using any text editor; the serializable deployment descriptor used in EJB 1.0 must be manipulated in a Java program (unless you're fluent in byte code!). Third, XML is more extensible and less fragile. In EJB 1.0, there are still problems with inconsistent versions of the deployment descriptor. As the specification evolves, the serializable deployment descriptor package would need to change, which introduces compatibility problems. With XML, new tags can be added without impacting existing deployment descriptor parsers. This makes deployment descriptors in EJB 1.1 more robust. Finally, XML is an industry standard, which means that deployment descriptors will enjoy universal support.

EJB 1.1 deployment descriptors also add some new declarative attributes and eliminate some old ones (like isolation levels!). Security, transactions, and environment properties change in EJB 1.1, necessitating changes in the type of information stored in the deployment descriptor. New features like bean and resource factory references were added, and the scope of the deployment descriptor was broadened to cover several beans for assembly. The division of labor for creating the deployment descriptor is better defined in EJB 1.1 as well. EJB 1.1 added new roles defining the development, assembly, deployment, and administration of beans. Contributions made by these roles to the deployment descriptor are well defined in EJB 1.1.

The Default JNDI Context

Environment variables have undergone a fairly radical change. Environment properties in EJB 1.0 are a powerful mechanism for modifying the behavior of a component without changing the component's code. In EJB 1.0, the environment properties are accessible to the bean through the EJBContext.getEnvironment() method, are set by the bean developer, and can be modified by the deployer. In EJB 1.0, the environment variables might, for example, be used to set a maximum withdraw amount for an account bean, as in the following code:

```
// EJB 1.0
public class AccountBean implements javax.ejb.EntityBean {

    public EntityContext context;

    public void withdraw(double amount) throws MaximumLimitException {
        try {
            Properties environment = context.getEnvironment();
            String value = environment.getProperty("withdraw_limit");
            Double limit = new Double(value);
            if ( amount > limit.doubleValue()) {
                throw new MaximumLimitException();
            else {
                // continue processing
            }
        }
    }
}
```

EJB 1.1 changes the environment properties from the java.util.Properties class, used in EJB 1.0, to a set of JNDI entries that exist in a name space called the *environment naming context*. All deployed beans in EJB 1.1 have an environment naming context (default JNDI context) that can be accessed using the JNDI API. This default JNDI context provides a set of immutable JNDI entries specific to each type of bean. The default JNDI context provides the bean with access to environment variables which can be of type String or one of several primitive wrappers including Double, Float, Integer, or Boolean. The entries are defined in the XML deployment descriptor using special tags specific to the environment naming context. Here is an example of how the default JNDI context is used at runtime by an EJB 1.1 bean:

```
// EJB 1.1
public class AccountBean implements javax.ejb.EntityBean {

    public EntityContext context;

    public void withdraw(double amount) throws MaximumLimitException {
```

```
try {
    InitialContext initCxt = InitialContext();
    Context defaultCxt = (Context)initCxt.lookup("java:comp/env");
    Double limit = (Double)
        defaultCxt.lookup("java:comp/env/withdraw_limit");
    if ( amount > limit.doubleValue()) {
        throw new MaximumLimitException();
    else {
        // continue processing
    }
    }
}
}
}
```

EJB 1.1–compliant servers are not required to support the EJB 1.0 environment properties, which are available through the EJBContext. The getEnvironment() method has been deprecated and will throw a runtime exception for EJB 1.1 servers that don't support backward compatibility.

Environment properties are only one of three sets of values that can be accessed through the default JNDI context. The default JNDI context is also used as a repository for linking to predefined resources and beans. When developing a bean, the bean developer can identify the types of resources and enterprise beans that will be referenced in the bean and bind them to the default JNDI context. This simplifies the process of looking up and obtaining bean references within beans, as well as locating and using resources like a JDBC database connection. The bean developer defines the types of beans and resources associated with the default JNDI entries in the XML deployment descriptor. The following code shows how a bean uses its default JNDI context to look up a bean and a JDBC DataSource:

```
// EJB 1.1
public class TellerBean implements javax.ejb.SessionBean {

    public void transfer(int sourceID, int targetID, double amount) {

        InitialContext initCtx = new InitialContext();

        // look up up the Account home
        AccountHome acctHome =
        (AccountHome)initCtx.lookup("java:comp/env/ejb/AccountHome");

        // transfer the money
        Account source = acctHome.findByPrimaryKey(
            new AccountKey(sourceID));
        Account target = acctHome.findByPrimaryKey(
            new AccountKey(targetID));
        source.withdraw(amount);
        target.deposit(amount);
```

```
    // Look up a the JDBC data source for recording transactions
    javax.sql.DataSource dataSource =
        (javax.sql.DataSource)initCtx.lookup("java:comp/env/jdbc/log");
    java.sql.Connection con = dataSource.getConnection();

    // continue processing: insert a log recording the transaction
    }
}
```

EJB 1.1 standardizes on the use of *resource connection factories* to access resources such as a JDBC connection. A resource factory provides access to resources in a manner that allows the container to manage the use of the resource. The use of the javax.sql.DataSource is a perfect example. It provides the bean with a JDBC connection that is managed transactionally and securely by the EJB container. In addition to JDBC, resource factories for the Java Messaging Service can also be used to obtain and manage access to an asynchronous message service.

The default JNDI context provides a powerful mechanism for obtaining pre-defined environment properties, bean references, and resource factories. It standardizes access to enterprise bean's environment through JNDI and lays the groundwork for future enhancements. As new facilities and services are made available to beans, they too can be accessed through the default JNDI context. A good example is the plan to provide a "connector" service that will allow beans to connect to legacy or "backend" systems using standard resource factories.

RMI over IIOP Narrowing

EJB 1.1 requires the use of Java RMI-IIOP reference and argument types when accessing enterprise beans from a client. EJB 1.1 servers are not required, however, to use IIOP as the distributed object protocol. They are only required to support the semantics and types used in Java RMI-IIOP.

Java RMI-IIOP requires that the remote references be explicitly narrowed when returned as supertypes from mechanisms like the JNDI context, Handle.getEJB-Object(), EJBContext.getEJBObject(), etc. Explicitly narrowing a remote reference is necessary because CORBA doesn't support casting. To support RMI over IIOP we would change the line that obtains a reference to the AccountHome so that it looks as follows:

```
// EJB 1.1 using RMI over IIOP
InitialContext initCtx = new InitialContext();
Object ref = initCtx.lookup("java:comp/env/ejb/AccountHome");
AccountHome acctHome = (AccountHome)
    javax.rmi.PortableRemoteObject.narrow(ref, AccountHome.class);
```

The javax.rmi.PortableRemoteObject class is part of the RMI-IIOP extension package.

Security

EJB specifies declarative attributes for security authorization. Once a user has been authenticated (logged in), access to enterprise beans can be monitored and controlled. The declarative authorization attributes allow the container to control which users can access which methods on specific bean types. In EJB 1.0, individual methods on a bean are associated with Identity objects that represent individual users or groups of users called roles. Only users that are associated with the correct Identity objects can access the bean's methods. Using this approach, bean methods can be mapped to a set of identities in the serializable deployment descriptor.

When a bean method is invoked at runtime, the container examines the Identity of the caller and compares it to the list of Identity objects associated with that method. If the caller's identity matches or is a member of one of the identities associated with the method, the method can be invoked. Although this authentication model works well—it allows fine-grained functional authentication without requiring any code in the bean itself—it also has some problems. In an operational environment that supports ACL-based security, all the identities and roles in an enterprise are part of the operational environment. To choose Identity objects to associate with bean methods, you must have access to the ACL repository of the environment that the bean will be deployed in. For this reason, it is normally assumed that the deployer in EJB 1.0 will map the bean's methods to the security domain. Unfortunately, the deployer may not have a good understanding of the purpose and function of the bean methods. This makes it difficult for the deployer to determine what identities and roles should be mapped to which methods—a problem that is compounded in beans that have numerous methods.

In recognition of the authentication problems in EJB 1.0, EJB 1.1 has changed authentication security significantly. In EJB 1.1, the authentication service remains implicit and fine-grained, but it's permission driven rather than method driven. In EJB 1.1, the bean provider and the application assembler (the same person in many cases) defines logical roles in the XML deployment descriptor. One or more roles can be associated with a list of methods they have permission (authorization) to access. The roles are logical and have only semantic meaning. They are not obtained from a specific operational environment; they simply describe the type of user who can access a set of methods. The bean developer can provide additional information about the logical roles by attaching description tags to roles with comments.

The bean deployer, who works in the operational environment, maps the logical roles defined by the bean developer and application assembler to real roles in the environment's security system. In this way, the bean developer and application assembler can define the type of roles that have access to methods without having to know anything about the operational environment in which the bean will be deployed. Similarly, the bean deployer can map roles in the operational environment to the logical roles in the deployment descriptor, based on semantic meaning of the logical roles and their attached descriptions, without having to understand the purpose or function of the methods involved. In fact, the deployer need not be concerned with the methods at all since she is only concerned with roles and the methods with which they are associated.

Looking Ahead to EJB 2.0

Enterprise JavaBeans 2.0 is likely to be the next release of the EJB specification, which we can expect to be finalized some time after the year 2000. It will include the definition of a connector interface that will allow legacy and ERP systems to be accessed by beans through resource factories. The Java Messaging Service will be integrated into the EJB architecture, which will probably require the creation of a new bean type or modification of the stateless session type. The definition of a standard object-to-relational mapping interface is possible, although this may not be included because of the difficulty in defining a standard. IIOP, the CORBA distributed object protocol, will be required for interoperability. Finally, a container interface or EJB Service-Provider Interface (SPI) will be defined that will allow containers and EJB servers to be more clearly delineated and therefore interchangeable.

Index

D

About the Author

Richard Monson-Haefel is one of the world's leading experts in Enterprise Java-Beans. He is the architect of OpenEJB (*www.exolab.org*), an open source EJB server, and has served as the EJB expert for jGuru.com, a portal for Java developers. Richard has consulted as an architect on Enterprise JavaBeans, CORBA, Java RMI, and other Java projects over the past few years. In addition to consulting, he has published many articles in national magazines, speaks at organizations and symposiums about EJB, and was a contributing author to the book *Special Edition: Using JavaBeans* (Ziff-Davis). Richard maintains a web site for the discussion of Enterprise JavaBeans and related distributed computing technologies at *www.EJBNow.com*.

Colophon

Our look is the result of reader comments, our own experimentation, and feedback from distribution channels. Distinctive covers complement our distinctive approach to technical topics, breathing personality and life into potentially dry subjects.

Melanie Wang was the production editor and proofreader for *Enterprise JavaBeans™, Second Edition*. Colleen Gorman was the copyeditor. Maureen Dempsey and Nicole Arigo performed quality control reviews. Emily Quill and Mary Sheehan provided production support. Ellen Troutman Zaig wrote the index.

Hanna Dyer designed the cover of this book, based on a series design by Edie Freedman. The image of the toy wooden train is from the Stock Options collection. It was manipulated in Adobe Photoshop by Michael Snow. The cover layout was produced by Emma Colby using QuarkXPress 3.3, the Bodoni Black font from URW Software, and BT Bodoni Bold Italic from Bitstream. The inside layout was designed by Nancy Priest.

Text was produced in FrameMaker 5.5.6 using a template implemented by Mike Sierra. The heading font is Bodoni BT; the text font is New Baskerville. The illustrations that appear in the book were created in Macromedia Freehand 8 and Adobe Photoshop 5 by Robert Romano and Rhon Porter.

Whenever possible, our books use RepKover™, a durable and flexible lay-flat binding. If the page count exceeds the maximum bulk possible for this type of binding, perfect binding is used.

Order Form / Price-List

QTY	ISBN	TITLE	AUTHOR	PRICE
__	8173661006	Access Database Design and Programming, 2ed, *448 Pages* **[January 2000]**	Roman	250.00*
__	8173660441	ASP in a Nutshell, *424 Pages*	Weissinger	210.00
__	8173661014	Building Internet Firewalls, *544 Pages* **[February 2000]**	Chapman	330.00*
__	8173661391	Building Linux Clusters (BOOK/CD-ROM), *452 Pages* **[March 2000]**	Spector	375.00*
__	817366045X	CGI Programming with Perl, 2/e, *456 Pages* **[April 2000]**	Gundavaram	300.00*
__	8173661022	Creating Documents with XML, *250 Pages* **[February 2000]**	Maden	220.00*
__	8173660468	Developing ASP Components, *500 Pages*	Powers	235.00*
__	8173660476	Developing Visual Basic Add-ins, *192 Pages*	Roman	135.00*
__	8173660484	Director in a Nutshell, *648 Pages*	Epstein	285.00*
__	8173660492	DNS and BIND, 3/e, *504 Pages*	Albitz	235.00*
__	8173660506	DNS on Windows NT, *352 Pages*	Albitz	185.00*
__	8173660263	Dynamic HTML: The Definitive Reference, *1,096 Pages*	Goodman	510.00
__	8173661030	Enterprise JavaBeans, *336 Pages*	Monson-Haefel	245.00*
__	8173660247	Essential System Administration, 2/e, *788 Pages*	Frisch	310.00
__	8173660255	Essential Windows NT System Administration, *488 Pages*	Frisch	220.00
__	8173660514	HTML: The Definitive Guide, 3/e, *616 Pages*	Musciano	325.00*
__	8173661049	Internet Application Protocols: The Definitive Guide (B/CD), *700 Pages* **[May 2000]**	Hall	450.00*
__	8173661057	Internet Core Protocols: The Def Guide (B/CD), *480 Pages* **[May 2000]**	Hall	375.00*
__	8173660158	Internet in a Nutshell, *456 Pages*	Quercia	215.00
__	8173660522	Java 2D Graphics, *376 Pages*	Knudsen	195.00*
__	8173660530	Java Enterprise in a Nutshell, *624 Pages*	Farley	275.00*
__	8173660549	Java Examples in a Nutshell, *416 Pages*	Flanagan	210.00
__	8173660557	Java Foundation Classes in a Nutshell, *752 Pages*	Flanagan	305.00*
__	8173660166	Java in a Nutshell, 2/e, *632 Pages*	Flanagan	260.00
__	8173661065	Java in a Nutshell, 3/e, *672 Pages* **[December 1999]**	Flanagan	325.00*
__	8173661073	Java Power Reference (BOOK/CD-ROM), *64 Pages* **[February 2000]**	Flanagan	240.00*
__	8173661081	Java Security, *474 Pages* **[February 2000]**	Oaks	305.00*
__	8173660565	Java Servlet Programming, *528 Pages*	Hunter	275.00*
__	817366109X	Java Swing, *1,252 Pages* **[February 2000]**	Eckstein	495.00*
__	8173660573	Java Threads, 2/e, *336 Pages*	Oaks	180.00*
__	8173661103	JavaScript Cookbook, *512 Pages* **[January 2000]**	Bradenbaugh	325.00*
__	8173661111	JavaScript Pocket Reference, *96 Pages*	Flanagan	65.00*
__	8173660581	JavaScript: The Definitive Guide, 3/e, *800 Pages*	Flanagan	385.00*
__	817366059X	Learning DCOM, *400 Pages*	Thai	220.00*
__	817366112X	Learning Perl, 2nd Edition, *302 Pages*	Schwartz	185.00*
__	8173660603	Learning Perl/Tk, *380 Pages* **[January 2000]**	Walsh	275.00*
__	8173661138	Learning Red Hat Linux (BOOK/CD-ROM), *400 Pages* **[January 2000]**	McCarty	350.00*
__	8173660611	Learning the vi Editor, 6/e, *352 Pages* **[January 2000]**	Lamb	205.00*
__	817366062X	lex & yacc, 2/e, 2/e, *392 Pages*	Levine	205.00*
__	8173660638	Lingo in a Nutshell, *640 Pages* **[March 2000]**	Epstein	375.00*
__	8173660646	Linux Device Drivers, *424 Pages*	Rubini	210.00*
__	8173660654	Linux in a Nutshell, 2/e, *624 Pages*	Siever	275.00*
__	8173661146	Lotus Notes Development in a Nutshell, *500 Pages* **[May 2000]**	Shefski	315.00*
__	8173660271	Managing IP Networks with Cisco Routers, *352 Pages*	Ballew	200.00
__	8173661154	Managing Microsoft Exchange Server, *704 Pages* **[March 2000]**	Robichaux	395.00*

QTY	ISBN	TITLE	AUTHOR	PRICE
__	8173661162	Mastering Algorithms with C, *560 Pages* **[January 2000]**	Loudon	340.00*
__	8173660174	MCSE: The Core Exams in a Nutshell, *424 Pages*	Moncur	210.00
__	8173660182	MCSE: The Electives in a Nutshell, *376 Pages*	Moncur	200.00
__	8173660921	Microsoft Exchange Server in a Nutshell, *400 Pages*	Tulloch	200.00*
__	8173660662	MySQL & mSQL, *504 Pages*	Yarger	275.00*
__	8173661170	Oracle Built-in Packages (BOOK/DISK), *956 Pages* **[January 2000]**	Feuerstein	475.00*
__	8173660670	Oracle DBA: The Essential Reference, *450 Pages*	Kreines	220.00*
__	8173660689	Oracle Distributed Systems, *500 Pages* **[January 2000]**	Dye	305.00*
__	8173661405	Oracle Essentials: Oracle8 and Oracle8i, *300 Pages* **[January 2000]**	Greenwald	175.00*
__	8173661189	Oracle PL/SQL Built-ins Pocket Reference, *78 Pages*	Feuerstein	60.00*
__	8173660697	Oracle PL/SQL Language Pocket Reference, *80 Pages*	Feuerstein	50.00*
__	8173660700	Oracle PL/SQL Programming, 2/e (BOOK/DISK), *1,032 Pages*	Feuerstein	360.00*
__	8173661197	Oracle PL/SQL Programming: Guide to Oracle8i, *250 Pages* **[January 2000]**	Feuerstein	175.00*
__	8173661200	Oracle SAP Administration, *208 Pages* **[January 2000]**	Burleson	150.00*
__	8173660298	Oracle Scripts (BOOK/CD-ROM), *208 Pages*	Lomansky	220.00
__	8173660719	Oracle Security, *448 Pages*	Theriault	220.00*
__	8173660727	Oracle SQLPlus: The Definitive Guide, *512 Pages*	Gennick	240.00*
__	8173661219	Oracle Web Applications: PL/SQL Developer's Intro, *264 Pages* **[Jan 2000]**	Odewahn	175.00*
__	817366028X	Oracle8 Design Tips, *136 Pages*	Ensor	120.00
__	8173661227	Perl 5 Pocket Reference, 2nd Edition, *72 Pages*	Vromans	60.00*
__	8173661235	Perl Cookbook, *794 Pages* **[December 1999]**	Christiansen	350.00*
__	8173660735	Perl in a Nutshell, *688 Pages* **[January 2000]**	Siever	345.00*
__	8173661243	Perl/Tk Pocket Reference, *104 Pages* **[February 2000]**	Lidie	65.00*
__	8173660743	Photoshop in a Nutshell, 2/e, *664 Pages* **[March 2000]**	O'Quinn	285.00*
__	8173661251	PNG: The Definitive Guide, *344 Pages* **[January 2000]**	Roelofs	195.00*
__	8173660301	Practical C Programming 3/e, *456 Pages*	Oualline	215.00
__	817366031X	Practical C++ Programming, *584 Pages*	Oualline	260.00
__	817366126X	Practical Internet Groupware, *384 Pages* **[January 2000]**	Udell	200.00*
__	8173660751	Practical UNIX & Internet Security, 2/e, *1,008 Pages*	Garfinkel	400.00*
__	817366076X	Programming Embedded Systems in C and C++, *200 Pages*	Barr	145.00*
__	8173661278	Programming Internet Email, *400 Pages* **[January 2000]**	Wood	225.00*
__	8173660328	Programming Perl 2/e, *672 Pages*	Wall	285.00
__	8173660778	Programming the Word Object Model, *480 Pages* **[February 2000]**	Sharer	240.00*
__	8173660190	QuarkXPress in a Nutshell, *552 Pages*	O'Quinn	240.00
__	8173661286	Running Linux, 3ed, *752 Pages* **[December 1999]**	Welsh	300.00*
__	8173660786	sed & awk, 2/e, *440 Pages*	Dougherty	235.00*
__	8173661294	sendmail Desktop Reference, *74 Pages*	Costales	60.00*
__	8173660794	sendmail, 2/e, *1,056 Pages*	Costales	415.00*
__	817366093X	Tcl/Tk in a Nutshell, *480 Pages* **[January 2000]**	Raines	240.00*
__	8173660336	TCP/IP Network Administration 2/e, *632 Pages*	Hunt	275.00
__	8173660816	Transact-SQL Programming (BOOK/CD-ROM), *856 Pages*	Kline	395.00*
__	8173660352	UML in a Nutshell, *336 Pages*	Alhir	210.00
__	8173661316	UNIX Backup and Recovery, *500 Pages* **[March 2000]**	Preston	235.00*
__	8173660200	UNIX in a Nutshell: System V, 2/e, *448 Pages*	Gilly	215.00
__	8173661324	UNIX in a Nutshell: System V, 3/e, *616 Pages* **[February 2000]**	Robbins	295.00*
__	8173660344	UNIX Power Tools 2/e (BOOK/CD-ROM), *1,120 Pages*	Peek	630.00

QTY	ISBN	TITLE	AUTHOR	PRICE
_ _	8173660948	Using & Managing PPP, *464 Pages*	Sun	240.00*
_ _	8173661332	Using Samba, *424 Pages* **[February 2000]**	Kelly	345.00*
_ _	8173660832	VB & VBA in a Nutshell: The Language, *656 Pages*	Lomax	285.00
_ _	8173661340	Virtual Private Networks, 2nd Edition, *228 Pages* **[February 2000]**	Scott	160.00*
_ _	8173660964	Visual Basic Controls in a Nutshell, *512 Pages*	Dictor	260.00*
_ _	8173660956	Web Design in a Nutshell, *592 Pages*	Niederst	275.00*
_ _	8173661359	Webmaster in a Nutshell, 2ed, *540 Pages* **[January 2000]**	Spainhour	250.00*
_ _	8173661308	The Whole Internet: The Next Generation, *576 Pages* **[January 2000]**	Conner/Krol	255.00*
_ _	8173661367	Win32 API Programming with Visual Basic, *450 Pages* **[February 2000]**	Roman	230.00*
_ _	8173660972	Win32 Multithreaded Programming, *728 Pages* **[December 1999]**	Cohen	430.00*
_ _	8173660220	Windows 95 in a Nutshell, *552 Pages*	Shulman	250.00
_ _	8173660875	Windows 98 Annoyances (BOOK/CD-ROM), *480 Pages* **[March 2000]**	Karp	360.00*
_ _	8173660212	Windows 98 in a Nutshell, *552 Pages* **[March 2000]**	O'Reilly	270.00*
_ _	8173660239	Windows NT in a Nutshell, *368 Pages*	Pearce	200.00
_ _	8173660883	Windows NT TCP/IP Network Administration, *512 Pages*	Hunt	250.00*
_ _	8173660891	Writing Excel Macros, *256 Pages* **[December 1999]**	Roman	175.00*
_ _	8173661375	XML Pocket Reference, *100 Pages* **[December 1999]**	Eckstein	65.00*
_ _	8173660905	XML: Principles, Tools, and Techniques, *264 Pages* **[March 2000]**	Connolly	180.00*
_ _	8173660360	Year 2000 in a Nutshell, *320 Pages*	Shakespeare	200.00
_ _	8173660913	Zero Administration for Windows, *400 Pages* **[March 2000]**	Zacker	215.00*

- **Dates and Prices of Forthcoming titles are tentative and subject to change without notice.**
- **All Prices are in Indian Rupees.**